D1823405

# Federalism and Internal Conflicts

Series Editors
Soeren Keil
School of Psychology, Politics and Sociology
Canterbury Christ Church University
Canterbury, UK

Eva Maria Belser
University of Freiburg
Freiburg, Switzerland

This series engages in the discussions on federalism as a tool of internal conflict resolution. Building on a growing body of literature on the use of federalism and territorial autonomy to solve ethnic, cultural, linguistic and identity conflicts, both in the West and in non-Western countries, this global series assesses to what extent different forms of federalism and territorial autonomy are being used as tools of conflict resolution and how successful these approaches are.

We welcome proposals on theoretical debates, single case studies and short comparative pieces covering topics such as:

- Federalism and peace-making in contemporary intra-state conflicts
- The link between federalism and democratization in countries facing intra-state conflict
- Secessionism, separatism, self-determination and power-sharing
- Inter-group violence and the potential of federalism to transform conflicts
- Successes and failures of federalism and other forms of territorial autonomy in post-conflict countries
- Federalism, decentralisation and resource conflicts
- Peace treaties, interim constitutions and permanent power sharing arrangements
- The role of international actors in the promotion of federalism (and other forms of territorial autonomy) as tools of internal conflict resolution
- Federalism and state-building
- Federalism, democracy and minority protection

For further information on the series and to submit a proposal for consideration, please get in touch with Ambra Finotello ambra.finotello@palgrave.com, or series editors Soeren Keil soeren.keil@canterbury.ac.uk and Eva Maria Belser evamaria.belser@unifr.ch

More information about this series at
http://www.palgrave.com/gp/series/15730

Alain-G. Gagnon • Arjun Tremblay
Editors

# Federalism and National Diversity in the 21st Century

palgrave
macmillan

*Editors*
Alain-G. Gagnon
Department of Political Science
Université du Québec à Montréal
Montréal, Canada

Arjun Tremblay
Department of Politics and
International Studies
University of Regina
Regina, Canada

Federalism and Internal Conflicts
ISBN 978-3-030-38421-0          ISBN 978-3-030-38419-7   (eBook)
https://doi.org/10.1007/978-3-030-38419-7

# Acknowledgements

This volume is the product of a two-day conference entitled *Federalism, National Diversity, and Democracy in the 21st Century: Challenges and Opportunities* hosted on 31 October and 1 November 2018 by the Canada Research Chair in Québec and Canada Studies (CRÉQC) in partnership with the Centre d'analyse politique: Constitution-Fédéralisme (CAP-CF) at the Université du Québec in Montréal (UQAM). The conference was funded by a Social Sciences and Humanities Research Council of Canada (SSHRC) Connection Grant and by the Programme de soutien à la recherche en matière d'affaires intergouvernementales et d'identité québécoise: volet Affaires intergouvernementales et volet Identité québécoise (Quebec Government). The completion of the volume was aided by a University of Regina Undergraduate Research Fellowship grant. Thanks also to Olivier De Champlain at UQAM for his continued support and professionalism.

Special thanks to Katelynn Kowalchuk and Brendan Anderson in their capacity as research assistants at the University of Regina; they have assisted us with dedication during the preparation of this volume. At Palgrave Macmillan, we would like to express our gratitude to Ambra Finotello and to Anne-Kathrin Birchley-Brun for their dedication and support.

# CONTENTS

# Notes on Contributors

**Pierre-Olivier Bonin** is a PhD candidate in the Department of Political Science at the University of Toronto. He specializes in Canadian politics and Quebec politics, with a focus on language politics and language policy. His dissertation draws comparisons between two official language minorities in two of the "founding provinces" of Canada: Francophones in Ontario and Anglophones in Quebec. His doctoral work relies primarily on survey methods and regression analysis; he also has experience with conducting semi-structured interviews and applying quantitative text analysis methods (e.g. dictionary-based sentiment analysis). His research has been funded by the Fonds de recherche du Québec société et culture.

**Isabelle Côté** is Associate Professor in the Department of Political Science at Memorial University of Newfoundland. She received her PhD in Political Science from the University of Toronto in 2014. She has published in journals such as *Democratization; Civil Wars; Ethnopolitics; Studies in Conflict and Terrorism; Ethnic and Racial Studies; PS: Political Science and Politics; Canadian Journal of Political Science* and *Journal of Southeast Asian Studies.* Most recently, she has co-edited a volume on 'Sons of the Soil' conflict (2019).

**Beza Dessalegn** is Assistant Professor of Law at Hawassa University, School of Law. He was a postdoctoral fellow at the University of the Western Cape, Department of Public Law and Jurisprudence. His research focuses on minority rights, federalism, human rights and constitutional law, electoral laws, political participation, subnational autonomy and local governments in Ethiopia. His recent publications include "Challenges of Ethnic Representation in Ethiopia and the Need for Reform" (*Mizan Law Review*, 2018) and "Experimenting with Non-Territorial Autonomy: Indigenous Councils in Ethiopia2 (*Journal on Ethnopolitics & Minority Issues in Europe*, 2019)

**Jean-François Dupré** is a Postdoctoral Fellow at the Institute of Sociology, Academia Sinica, Taiwan. His research focuses on cultural recognition, democratization, national identity, party politics and social movements from a comparative perspective. In addition to *Culture Politics and Linguistic Recognition in Taiwan: Ethnicity, National Identity and the Party System* (2017), he has published journal articles and book chapters on language, nationalism and identity in Taiwan, Hong Kong, Québec and Catalonia. His current research centres on the emerging Hong Kong nationalist movement.

**Yonatan T. Fessha, LLB, LLM, PhD** is a Marie Curie Fellow at Eurac Research Bolzano/Bozen (Italy) and Associate Professor of Law at the University of the Western Cape. His research explores constitutional law and human rights and focuses on examining the relevance of constitutional design in dealing with the challenges of divided societies. He has published widely on matters pertaining to but not limited to federalism, constitutional design, autonomy and politicised ethnicity. He is the author of *Ethnic diversity and federalism: Constitution making in South Africa and Ethiopia* (2010). He has contributed to a number of constitution building projects, including in Sudan, South Sudan and Yemen.

**Alain-G. Gagnon** is Professor in the Department of Political Science at the Université du Québec à Montréal and Founding Director of the Interdisciplinary Research Centre on Diversity and Democracy. Holder of the Canada Research Chair in Quebec and Canadian Studies (www.creqc.uqam.ca) since 2003, he is also Director of the Research Group on Plurinational Societies. He is the laureate of the 2016 Governor General's International Award for Canadian Studies and received the Insigne de la Pléiade in 2018. He is the author of more than 500 works in political sociology, federal studies and Canadian politics. His research has been translated into twenty languages.

**Augustin Habra** holds masters' degrees in Politics and History from the Université catholique de Louvain. His graduate work examined current and former bipolar states around the world from a comparative perspective and provincialism as a territorial and institutional alternative for Belgian federalism. He is currently working as a project manager at perspective.brussels, a regional center of expertise and initiator of the regional development strategy in Brussels.

**Susan J. Henders** is Associate Professor in the Department of Politics at York University and Faculty Associate at the York Centre for Asian Research. She studies the domestic and international politics of territorial autonomy arrangements in culturally regionalized states. Her chapter examining the gendered effects of Hong Kong's autonomy appears in *Gendering Nationalism* (2018) and her analysis of post-WWI internationalized autonomy arrangements was published in *International Approaches to Governing Ethnic Diversity* (2015). Her forthcoming research explores the political significance of Hong Kong's "foreign" residents, focusing on Canadians. Her monograph, *Territoriality, Asymmetry, Autonomy* (2010) examines the special status of Catalonia, Corsica, Hong Kong and Tibet.

**James Kennedy** is Senior Lecturer in Sociology at the University of Edinburgh. His *Liberal Nationalisms: Empire, State and Civil Society in Scotland and Quebec* (2013) was awarded the Canadian Sociology Association's John Porter Award. His recent publications include: "The Emergence of Conjoined Nationalism and Regionalism in the British Isles" in X.-M. Núñez Seixas and H.J. Storm (eds.) *Regionalism and Modern Europe* (2019) and "Liberal Nationalisms Revisited" (*Canadian Review of Sociology* 2016). He is currently Director of the Centre of Canadian Studies at the University of Edinburgh and President of the British Association for Canadian Studies.

**John Kincaid** is the Robert B. and Helen S. Meyner Professor of Government and Public Service and Director of the Meyner Center for the Study of State and Local Government at Lafayette College, Easton, PA. He is former executive director of the U.S. Advisory Commission on Intergovernmental Relations and editor of *Publius: The Journal of Federalism*. He has published many articles on federalism and intergovernmental relations, edited *Federalism* (4 vols., 2011), and co-edited *Courts in Federal Systems: Federalists or Unitarists?* (2017), *Intergovernmental Relations in Federal Systems: Comparative Structures and Dynamics* (2015), *Political Parties and Civil Society in Federal Countries* (2015), and the *Routledge Handbook of Regionalism and Federalism* (2013).

**Christoph Niessen** is a PhD Candidate at the Université de Namur and Université catholique de Louvain, as well as Research Fellow at the Fund for Research in the Humanities (F.R.S.-FNRS). His doctoral research examines the evolution of self-government demands and statutes in territorial communities in Belgium, Spain and the United Kingdom. His research also examines citizen deliberation and its reception by traditional decision-making actors. He is the co-author of "Intercameral Relations in a Bicameral Elected and Sortition Legislature" (with Pierre-Étienne Vandamme, Vincent Jacquet, John Pitseys, and Min Reuchamps, *Politics and Society*, 2018) and the author of "When citizen deliberation enters real politics: how politicians and stakeholders envision the place of a deliberative mini-public in political decision-making" (*Policy Sciences*, 2019).

**Tejas Pandya** is a graduate of the Political Science and Outstanding Scholar programs at the University of Windsor. He is the co-author (with Emmanuelle Richez and Rebecca Major) of "Revitalizing and Promoting Indigenous Languages through Rights Recognition, Self-Government, and Effective Consultations", a brief submitted to the House of Commons Standing Committee on Canadian Heritage regarding *Bill C-91: An Act respecting Indigenous Languages*.

**Lucía Payero-López** is Lecturer in Philosophy of Law at the University of Granada. Previously, she was a Research Associate in the European Research Council Project 'Federalism: Dividing Political Power among People(s)' (Durham Law School) and in the Department of Philosophy of Law at the University of Oviedo. Her reserach interests lie in the fields of Legal Philosophy, Political Theory and Constitutional Theory. She has published a number of articles on national self-determination, secession, and federalism. Her publications include "the 'citizen participation process' in Catalonia: past, present and future" (*Liverpool Law Review*, 2015) and "Justicia de transición en España: claves para aprobar una asignatura pendiente" (*Revista de Paz y Conflictos*, 2016).

**Mira Raatikainen** is a masters' student at the Norman Paterson School of International Affairs at Carleton University. Her graduate work focuses on the intersection between conflict analysis, conflict resolution, migration, and citizenship. She is the recipient of the Joubin-Selig Scholarship in International Affairs at Carleton. She was also the recipient of numerous prizes as an undergraduate student at the Memorial University of Newfoundland, including the Heaslip Scholarship and the Memorial University Medal for Academic Excellence for Political Science.

**Min Reuchamps** is Professor of Political Science at the Université catholique de Louvain. He is a graduate of the Université de Liège and Boston University. His research focuses on federalism and multi-level governance, democracy and its different dimensions, relations between language(s) and politics and in particular the role of metaphors, as well as participatory and deliberative methods. He recently co-authored *The Legitimacy of Citizen-Led Deliberative Democracy: The G1000 in Belgium* (with Didier Caluwaerts, 2018), co-edited *Constitutional Deliberative Democracy in Europe* (with Jane Suiter, 2017) and edited *Minority nations in multinational federations: A comparative study of Quebec and Wallonia* (2016).

**Emmanuelle Richez** is Associate Professor of Political Science at the University of Windsor. Her research examines law and politics in Canada and other advanced liberal democracies, with a particular focus on ethno-cultural minority and Indigenous rights. She co-authored "Revitalizing and Promoting Indigenous Languages through Rights Recognition, Self-Government, and Effective Consultations" (with Rebecca Major and Tejas Pandya), a brief submitted to the House of Commons Standing Committee on Canadian Heritage regarding *Bill C-91: An Act respecting Indigenous Languages*. Her most recent publication is "Dynamics of Digital Constituent Outreach and Engagement in Linguistically Divided Societies: A Quantitative Look at the Canadian Case" (*International Journal of Medial and Cultural Politics*, 2019). She is currently a member of the Expert Panel on Official Language Rights of the Court Challenges Program of Canada.

**Dejan Stjepanović** is Lecturer in Politics at the University of Dundee. Previously, he was Postdoctoral Researcher at the Université catholique de Louvain. He has taught at the University of Edinburgh, University College Dublin, the University of Chichester, the University of Brighton and has worked for several international NGOs. His research focuses on territorial politics, nationalism and citizenship. His most recent books include *Multiethnic Regionalisms in Southeastern Europe* (2017) and *Migrating Borders: Territorial Rescaling and Citizenship Realignment in Europe* (co-edited with Jean-Thomas Arrighi, 2019).

**Arjun Tremblay** is Assistant Professor in the Department of Politics and International Studies at the University of Regina. He specializes in the field of comparative politics. He obtained his PhD in Political Science from the University of Toronto in 2017 and was a postdoctoral fellow (2017–2018) at the Canada Research Chair in Québec and Canadian Studies (CREQC) at the Université du Québec à Montréal. He is the author of *Diversity in Decline? The Rise of the Political Right and the Fate of Multiculturalism* (2019). He is co-author of "Federalism and Diversity: A New Research Agenda" (with Alain-G. Gagnon, in *A Research Agenda for Federalism Studies*, 2019). His research explores the near and longer-term prospects of diversity-oriented policies and institutions (such as multiculturalism and multinational federalism) from a comparative perspective.

**Catherine Xhardez** is a Postdoctoral Fellow in the Department of Political Science at Concordia University. She is also a research fellow at CRIDAQ (*Centre de recherche interdisciplinaire sur la diversité et la démocratie*) and Concordia's Centre for the Study of Immigration and Politics (CSPI). She holds a dual PhD in Political Science from Sciences Po Paris and Université Saint-Louis – Bruxelles. Her research focuses on the immigration-federalism nexus and explores the dynamics of immigration and immigrant integration policymaking at the subnational level in federal states. Her most recent publication is "From different paths to a similar road? Understanding the convergence of subnational immigrant integration policies in Belgium" (*Regional Studies*, 2019).

# List of Figures

# LIST OF TABLES

XX    LIST OF TABLES

## CHAPTER 1

# Introduction: Puzzles of Multinational Federalism

*Alain-G. Gagnon and Arjun Tremblay*

## INTRODUCTION

Scholars continue to envision a world in which different national and ethnic groups can co-exist under the ambit of democratic institutions that combine shared rule with self-rule. However, the development and entrenchment of multinational and multiethnic federalism continues to lag behind. Despite this striking contrast, there has been very little discussion on the obstacles to and opportunities for the development and entrenchment of a sustainable, representative and deeply democratic multinational federalism. Authors mobilized for this project bring these issues to the fore. Our hope is that this volume can play an important role in helping to fulfill, at the outset of the twenty-first century, the federal

A.-G. Gagnon (✉)
Department of Political Science, Université du Québec à Montréal, Montreal, QC, Canada
e-mail: gagnon.alain@uqam.ca

A. Tremblay
Department of Politics and International Studies, University of Regina, Regina, SK, Canada
e-mail: Arjun.tremblay@uregina.ca

A.-G. Gagnon, A. Tremblay (eds.), *Federalism and National Diversity in the 21st Century*, Federalism and Internal Conflicts, https://doi.org/10.1007/978-3-030-38419-7_1

1

promise of multinational democracies built on the dual principles of unity and diversity.

We are presented with a striking puzzle when we contrast recent developments in federal theory with the institutional status quo in multinational polities. On the one hand, there is ever-growing scholarly agreement on the value of institutionalizing multinational federalism, a framework for a division of powers that reflects, respects and accommodates territorially concentrated diversity and that is meant to empower minority nations and large ethnic groups. This ever-growing agreement has been buttressed by the emergence of the paradigm of 'liberal nationalism', according to which 'it is a legitimate function of the state to protect and promote the national cultures and languages of the nations within its borders' (Kymlicka 2001, p. 39).

On the other hand, there has also been a glaring absence of institutional and substantive transitions to multinational federalism in deeply diverse multinational and multiethnic polities. As Leonce Röth and André Kaiser (2019, p. 557) put it: 'Concessions via autonomy or asymmetric decentralization have been a familiar, albeit rarely implemented, mechanism of statecraft to accommodate the demands of territorially based ethnic groups for at least the past two centuries.' In fact, the recent referenda on independence in Scotland (in 2014) and Catalonia (in 2017) can be taken as indications that the UK and Spanish governments, respectively, failed to respond to proponents of multinational federalism much as the Canadian government did in the lead-up to the Quebec referenda in 1980 and 1995 (see Gagnon 2010, p. 5).

In brief, the emerging normative consensus on multinational federalism and demands for national recognition have yet to translate into the development and entrenchment of a sustainable, representative and substantively democratic multinational federalism in and across deeply diverse states. In light of these contrasting trends, this volume asks the following questions: Why is this happening? What are the main 'roadblocks' to the institutionalization of multinational federalism? Can we imagine 'roadmaps' that can help policymakers and state managers achieve multinational federalism in the twenty-first century?

The chapters in this volume contribute, albeit in different ways and to different degrees, to developing answers to these questions—which are summarized in the volume's conclusion. The volume's chapters also intersect with other concerns in the scholarly discussion on federalism and national diversity and, in so doing, explore other puzzles of multinational federalism. Some chapters identify the factors that have led multinational federations to fail despite democratic consolidation and legacies of subnational accommodation, while others set out to understand why some types of multinational federations have succeeded despite multinational federalism's seemingly 'abysmal track record' (McGarry and O'Leary 2015, p. 43). Other chapters focus on cases that show no signs of moving towards multinational federalism despite indications of increasing national polarization (the U.S. for example) and previous optimistic accounts (in the 2000s for the China-Hong Kong case). Several chapters explore cases that, despite their seeming openness to the accommodation of national diversity, obviate or neglect minority groups that can and should be considered under the ambit of multinational federalism.

Overall, this volume's chapters address an array of puzzles of multinational federalism. They aid in identifying, understanding and explaining both the main challenges to and the opportunities for truly fulfilling, at the outset of the twenty-first century, the federal promise of multinational democracies built on the dual principles of unity and diversity. This endeavour is both important and timely, for despite the mainstreaming of an anti-diversity public discourse, national minorities as well as other collective identities continue to demand greater institutional recognition in democracies, in democratising states and in 'federalizing' polities.

## CONTEXT AND BACKGROUND

This volume situates itself against the backdrop of renewed interest in the study of federalism, driven in recent years by a critique of the American tradition of federalism. This critique is based first and foremost on the acknowledgement that many modern democracies, emerging democracies and democratising polities comprise multiple demoi/peoples or, in other words, are multinational and multiethnic in composition. In turn, a growing number of social scientists and philosophers (e.g. Tillin 2007; Smith 2007; Seymour and Laforest 2011; Stepan et al. 2011; Seymour and Gagnon 2012; Burgess 2013; Gagnon 2010; Gagnon and Schwartz 2015; Keil 2016; Requejo 2016) now advocate the design and implementation of multinational federalism—albeit with some disagreement over specific institutional arrangements as a way of both 'holding-together' (Stepan 1999) deeply diverse societies and recognizing and empowering the polity's constituent nations and ethnic groups.

A multinational or multiethnic polity (e.g. Canada, South Africa, Belgium, the United Kingdom, Ethiopia, Spain) comprises a national majority as well as one or several minority nations/national minorities/ territorially concentrated ethnic groups. Public institutions in multinational or multiethnic polities (we use the terms interchangeably in this volume) tend to reflect the culture, language, customs, traditions and religion of the national majority. Consequently, many minority nations/ national minorities/territorially concentrated ethnic groups have made and continue to make demands for the recognition of group-differentiated rights (i.e. demands for linguistic, religious autonomy) that, in a federal setting, would require the design and implementation of an asymmetrical federal arrangement. However, the American tradition of federalism views all constituent units of a federation as equal and therefore advocates a federalism that is "constitutionally symmetrical" (Stepan 1999, p. 21). At a more fundamental level, the American tradition of federalism embraces a territorial logic that fails to recognize the co-existence of different 'peoples' within the same state (Seymour and Gagnon 2012).

Studies that examine deeply diverse democracies (e.g. Codagnone and Filippov 2000; McGarry and O'Leary 2005; De Schutter 2011; Gagnon and Tremblay 2019) agree that the American tradition of federalism is antiquated and that democracies marked by deep national and ethnic diversity must embrace a type of federalism with institutions that reflect, respect, accommodate, enrich and protect this diversity. To be clear, akin to an American-inspired model of federalism, a multinational federation would also constitutionally enshrine a division of powers between different levels of government, yet it would also differ in significant ways. Examples of its unique institutional features could include: the formal recognition of the distinct status of national minorities, the inclusion of national minorities in foreign policymaking and asymmetrical federal arrangements (McGarry and O'Leary 2005). Perhaps what is less clear is how multinational federalism might differ from other diversity-oriented federal models, such as 'multicultural federalism' (Tremblay 2005).

Despite the developing consensus on the desirability of multinational federalism, there are also a number of critical concerns about the near and longer-term prospects of multinational federal arrangements. For one, studies of federalism show that very few multinational democracies have in fact formally institutionalized multinational federalism (Kymlicka 1998; Habtu 2005; Gagnon and Iacovino 2007; Gagnon et al. 2017) and that, where this project has been undertaken, multinational federal institutions have a symbolic/'inconsequential' effect (Caron and Laforest 2009). Recent studies of federalism also show that national/central/federal governments tend to be driven by 'unitarist' or centralizing imperatives and, consequently, that they rarely accept that sub-national governments are their equal partners (Requejo 2004; Bohman 2007; Lajoie 2009). And emerging trends in the study of federalism illustrate that transitions to multinational federalism have, in many cases, failed (McGarry 2004; Kavalski and Żółkoś 2008; Basta et al. 2015). They also show that multinational federalism is rooted in a 'multinationalism' that may be neglecting Indigenous Peoples, the distinct cultures of minorities borne out of individual and familial immigration as well as those of collective identities, including those founded on lifestyles, gender and sexual orientation (Karmis 2008, 2009; Smith 2010; Woods 2012; Dubois and Saunders 2013).

This volume therefore situates itself at the cross-roads of the developing consensus on the desirability of multinational federalism, continued demands for national recognition (evidenced in part by recent referenda in Scotland and Catalonia) and the absence of institutional and substantive transitions to multinational federalism, as well as growing critical concerns about the near and longer-term prospects of multinational federal arrangements. The volume's overall goal is to contribute in identifying the challenges to (i.e. 'roadblocks') and opportunities for (i.e. 'roadmaps') fulfilling the promise of multinational federalism; that is of democracies built on the dual principles of unity and diversity. Along the way the volume intersects with longstanding and developing concerns in the study of deeply diverse federal polities.

## Chapter Overview

The volume consists of 11 chapters divided in three parts as well as an editors' conclusion that addresses its main research questions. In examining a range of cases (e.g. Spain, Canada, Belgium, Nigeria), the three chapters in Part I (Multinational Federations at Risk and in Retreat) bring to light factors that may prevent the long-term success/persistence of a multinational federation, such as the implementation of a simple member plurality electoral system, the uneven distribution of economic resources across the multinational federation's constituent units and ensuring that federalism is both institutionalized but forgetting to 'practice' federalism. Cases analysed in Part I also provide evidence that the institutional protection of autonomy can be both beneficial and detrimental to sustainable multinational federalism.

In 'Diverse Democracies and the Practice of Federalism,' James Kennedy draws a distinction between the institutions of federalism and the informal practices of federalism within the context of multinational democracies. Building on this distinction, the chapter argues that informal practices of federalism may be just as important, if not more important, than the formal institutions of federalism in reconciling unity and diversity in multinational settings. The argument is developed through a comparison of the workings of four multinational democracies: interwar Czechoslovakia, post-Quiet Revolution Québec, post-Franco Spain, and post-devolution United Kingdom. In the chapter's conclusion, Kennedy applies the argument to understanding the possible implications, in India, of the Modi government's decision to impose direct rule on Jammu and Kashmir.

In 'When Have Dyadic Federations Succeeded and When Have They Failed? A Comparative Analysis of Bipolar Federalism around the World', Christoph Niessen, Min Reuchamps, Dejan Stjepanović and Augustin Habra highlight the conditions under which *dyadic federations*—a genus of the multinational federation family that comprises federations where two communities or national groups dominate control of sociopolitical institutions—have 'succeeded' (i.e. survived) and have 'failed' (i.e. broken apart). These conditions are identified through a fuzzy-set Qualitative Comparative Analysis of all dyadic federations, past and present. In brief, the results of the comparative analysis suggests that a dyadic federation is most likely to 'succeed' if geographical factors such as the territorial dispersion of the dominant groups play in its favour and in the presence of institutional arrangements such as a proportional electoral system or a national party system. The comparison also shows that a dyadic federation is more likely to succeed the longer it endures, meaning that, under certain conditions, these types of federations might actually 'consolidate.' By contrast, the comparison also suggests that a dyadic federation is more likely to 'fail' (i.e. break-up) in the absence of stabilizing institutional factors like executive inclusiveness and a national party system, especially when economic resource are unequally distributed among groups and when the latter are clearly separable along territorial lines.

In 'Assessing the Spanish State's Response to Catalan Independence: The Application of Federal Coercion', Lucía Payero-López explores recent developments in Spain, a multinational unitary democracy with quasi-federal features currently experiencing a constitutional and democratic crisis. The chapter provides detailed accounts of the lead-up to and of the response by the Spanish central government to the Catalan declaration of independence on 1 October 2017. It shows that the Spanish central government's response to the declaration has entailed the application of *federal coercion*, an ostensibly exceptional mechanism established in Article 155 of the 1978 Constitution of Spain. The chapter argues that the actual application of Article 155 has been 'excessive' and that measures adopted under the aegis of Article 155 can be seen as unconstitutional. The chapter concludes that the application of Article 155 is in actuality indicative of an ongoing trend towards the 'recentralization' of authority in Spain and at that despite the existence of the Statutes of Autonomy.

The three chapters in Part II (The Stalled Emergence of Multinational Federalism) explore two cases—the United States and Hong Kong—that are often overlooked in comparative studies of multinational federations but that can reveal a lot about the relationship between diversity and federalism. These chapters argue, albeit in different ways, that overcoming obstacles to the development of meaningfully democratic and internally inclusive minority autonomy arrangements, such as multinational federalism, may depend on an acute understanding of a polity's history and institutional legacies.

In 'Origins and Consequences of American Multicultural Federalism: Constitutional Patriotism, Territorial Neutrality, and National Polarisation', John Kincaid explores the key counter-example in the study of multinational federalism and explains why it is that the United States became a *multicultural federation*. In brief, the chapter argues that, in deciding not to impose culturally homogenizing policies on a heterogeneous society, the founders opted to foster national unity around the Constitution, thus allowing expressions of cultural preferences to differ across constituent territories. Consequently, American multicultural federalism has proven to be a 'double-edged sword.' Kincaid argues that, on one edge, federal tolerance of territorial and non-territorial expressions of diverse cultural preferences has fostered national unity. He also argues that, on the other edge, some of the most ardent expressions of such preferences, especially those pivoting on racism, have provoked moral approbation that has generated calls for federal intervention that, in turn, have triggered national polarization. Overall, Kincaid's chapter helps to conceptually distinguish multinational from multicultural federalism and to highlight the factors that led one polity to veer towards the latter rather than the former.

The examination of exceptional cases continues in the following two chapters, both of which apply an institutional explanatory framework to understanding the flagging autonomy of the Hong Kong Special Administrative Region. In '"Nested Newness" and the Quality of Self-Government: The Case of the Hong Kong Special Administrative Region', Susan J. Henders employs an analytical framework, drawn from feminist institutional theories, to assess the quality of minority accommodation, understanding it as shaped by continuities and changes in the multi-levelled structural, institutional, relational and other contexts of such arrangements. The framework is used to examine the emergence and out-comes to date of the post-1997 quasi-federal autonomy arrangement for Hong Kong, where many residents claim a distinctive collective identity and values vis-à-vis the wider People's Republic of China. Henders argues that the Hong Kong autonomy arrangement underscores the need for analyses of multinational accommodation that go beyond political institu-tions and policies and state architectures, to also assess how these are shaped by their nestedness in contexts, histories and relations. For Henders, the very explicit and institutionalized nature of the political economy of Hong Kong's autonomy arrangement is a reminder of the need to situate particular instances of multinational accommodation and the political contestation surrounding them, within evolving structures of world order, to understand current and potential future possibilities for meaningful and inclusive minority self-government.

In 'Federalism, Democracy and National Diversity in 21st Century China: Reinterpreting Hong Kong's Autonomy, Subverting its Democracy', Jean-François Dupré investigates the politics of federalism, democracy and national diversity in China, tracing the process through which the central and local governments have furthered *national integration* and *authori-tarianisation* in Hong Kong. Dupré argues that these joint processes were enabled not by a sudden and drastic institutional takeover by China, but by an incremental process of institutional conversion in which institutions governing Hong Kong's autonomy and democratisation were brought to serve objectives that seem contrary to their stated purposes. Beijing and the local establishment carried out this institutional conversion process in part by reframing and reinterpreting institutions and their purposes, and by tak-ing advantage of power asymmetries entrenched in institutions. This was itself enabled by a weakly defined constitutional order, the lack of a tradi-tion of multi-level governance, and an institutional setting that was designed to facilitate elite co-option by the establishment. On a more theoretical note, this chapter draws attention to the social constructedness of autonomy and points to the importance of observing 'multi-level governance' in practice. Dupré concludes his chapter by briefly discussing the implications of his argument in light of the wide-spread protests in Hong Kong and by providing preliminary speculation about the possibility of institutional conversion giving way to institutional displacement.

The five chapters in Part III (Recognizing and Accommodating National and Other Diversities: Success or Failure?) explore the intersection between national diversity and non-territorial collective identities in multinational federations. More precisely, they examine the ways in which national minorities and federal institutions have responded, for better and worse, to the dynamics of internal migration and immigration and to demands by receding national majorities and by Indigenous Peoples for greater recognition. In so doing, they point to local governments and political elites as both facilitators and opponents of accommodation in multinational federations. These chapters also offer a critical assessment of the study of multinational federalism—which may even be its own worst enemy—and open up new comparative and conceptual horizons in the discussion on the protection and empowerment of national minorities/ minority nations/territorially concentrated ethnic groups and other collective identities in federal states.

In 'Internal Migration in Asian Multinational Countries: Attitudes, Challenges and Institutions', Isabelle Côté and Mira Raatikainen discuss the regulation of population movements in multinational settings. While regulation has historically been the domain of the state, provinces and other sub-national units have recently started to ask for a larger say over both international and *internal* migration. In exploring the dynamics of internal migration in multinational federations in Asia, Côté and Raatikainen ask three questions: (1) What factors shape local attitudes towards internal migrants? (2) How do sub-national and national actors recognize and accommodate the challenges of national diversity resulting from increased levels of population mobility? (3) Does federalism matter in cases of sub-national migration governance? The chapter provides an examination of the economic/utilitarian motives and nativist discourses used to curtail flows of inter-provincial migrants in India and Malaysia; it also includes a brief comparison with the dynamics of internal migration in China. Overall, Côté and Raatikainen illustrate that local resentment towards incoming domestic migrants is fueled by a myriad of factors, from language and ethnicity to labour market considerations and a fear of loss of amenities. They argue that opposition to internal migration is not unique to a unitary or federal political systems. However, they also establish that federal states and other decentralized systems actually facilitate the creation and implementation of sub-national barriers to internal mobility.

In 'Immigration Federalism, Multinational States, and Subnational Communities: Comparing Flanders and Quebec', Catherine Xhardez discusses the dynamics of international migration in multinational federations. More specifically, she explores parliamentary debates (between 1999 and 2014) in two sub-national communities in multinational federal states. She does so with an eye to highlighting arguments in favour and against 'immigration federalism,' which is to say the 'involvement of different levels of government in immigration-related activities.' In so doing, Xhardez' chapter addresses three main questions: (1) Has the issue of immigration federalism been handled in similar or different ways in Flanders and Quebec? (2) Within each of these sub-national communities (SNCs), what are the points of tension and convergence in debates over immigration federalism? (3) What are the key similarities and differences in approaches to immigration federalism in the two SNCs? In brief, her comparison shows that Flemish and Québécois political elites have deployed different approaches to using immigrant integration regulation both as a way of strengthening their respective claims for recognizing cultural and linguistic diversity along national lines as well as for influencing the balance of power between sub-national and national jurisdictions.

In 'Relative Deprivation and Perceived Discrimination among Quebec's English-Speaking Minority Communities: "Second-Class Citizens" in a Multi-National Context?', Pierre-Olivier Bonin investigates the perceptions of disenfranchisement in English-speaking communities living in Quebec. The chapter draws upon original data from an online survey conducted in 2017 and tests two hypotheses: (1) The Relative Deprivation Hypothesis and (2) The Perceived Discrimination Hypothesis. The evidence presented in the chapter suggests that there exists a state of 'relative deprivation' in English-speaking minority communities in Quebec and that a strong majority of Anglo-Quebecers believe that their group faces discrimination often if not most of the time. Contrary to theoretical expectations, however, these two factors predict a lower likelihood of Anglo-Quebecer organizational engagement and volunteerism. In light of these findings, the chapter discusses implications for the accommodation of minorities (in this case a 'receding' majority) within multinational federal settings that perceive discrimination but fail to mobilize around their concerns.

Yonatan T. Fessha and Beza Dessalegn continue to enrich the discussion on internal migration in 'Internal Migration, Ethnic Federalism, and Differentiated Citizenship in an African Federation: the Case of Ethiopia'. Their chapter brings to light a 'tension' between internal migration and the self-rule rights of ethnic communities in Ethiopia. Making ethnicity the basis for the political and administrative organization of the Ethiopian federation has set the stage for the emergence of tacit (what they refer to as 'traces of') group-differentiated rights that, the authors argue, are coming into conflict with the protection of the individual rights of internal migrants. This leads Fessha and Dessalegn to argue that differentiated citizenship is necessary but insufficient to deal with the increasingly complex dynamics of ethnic diversity within the context of multiethnic (and multinational) federations. They conclude their chapter by arguing that the enshrinement of rights in multinational and multiethnic settings must be done in such a way as to ensure that the protection and empowerment of ethnic communities does not unreasonably restrict the rights of individuals who do not belong to the empowered group.

In 'Ensuring a Future for Indigenous Languages in Canada: Can 'Consequentialist' Multinational Federalism Provide an Answer?', Emmanuelle Richez and Tejas Pandya highlight the precarious position in which Indigenous language minorities continue to find themselves in Canada and ask whether 'consequentialist' multinational federalism can help to ensure a future for Indigenous languages in Canada. In so doing, they highlight potential 'symbolic', 'hybrid' and 'consequentialist' solutions to Indigenous language revitalization in Canada. The chapter concludes that a 'consequential' multinational approach to federalism in the area of Indigenous languages can only be achieved if three conditions are met: (1) treaty scope expansion; (2) treaty negotiation that emphasizes a nation-to-nation relationship between Indigenous Peoples and the Crown; (3) the empowerment of indigenous self-government (given that linguistic expertise and knowledge is highly localized and based primarily in Indigenous communities).

Building on the preceding chapters, the volume's conclusion sets out to highlight the main challenges (i.e. 'roadblocks') to and the potential opportunities for (i.e. 'roadmaps') fully realizing the federal promise in deeply diverse multinational states in the twenty-first century. Before doing so, however, the conclusion shows how the volume's chapters help us to imagine what a transition to substantive multinational federalism would look like. In particular, the chapters bring to light several key indicators of substantive multinational federalism—such as the need for multinational federal institutions to be undergirded by multinational federal practices, the adoption of a principle of territorial *partiality*, and a pluralist understanding of multinational federalism—that go above and beyond the generally agreed upon procedural indicator of an asymmetrical political arrangement. The conclusion then provides answers to the volume's main puzzle. More precisely, the conclusion demonstrates that the volume's chapters bring to light several main challenges or 'roadblocks' to achieving the federal promise in deeply diverse multinational states. Finally, the conclusion also introduces preliminary 'roadmaps' for realizing the promise of multinational federalism in deeply diverse settings. In brief, we conclude that there is no single institutional path to overcoming the challenges to achieving a true multinational federalism in the twenty-first century. Instead, the way forward likely depends on the mutual good will of majority and minority political actors, on decision making guided by three principles (moderation, dignity and hospitality) and on a receptiveness to the design and implementation of other emancipatory institutional initiatives.

In addition to addressing this volume's driving puzzle, the chapters in this volume make three contributions to the ongoing study of federalism in deeply diverse polities. First, this volume's chapters on the plight of Indigenous Peoples and other minorities in multinational federations show that the appearance of institutional stability can hide deep flaws in federal arrangements; consequently, significant institutional and conceptual steps must be taken to arrive at a more complete understanding of federal success, one that accounts for the empowerment of multiple diversities. These chapters also challenge the conclusion (see Moreno and Colino 2010) that federal success requires the recognition and accommodation of diversity and that it is evidenced by institutional stability and by the avoidance of conflict.

Second, and following from the previous point, the chapters bring a much-needed complexity to the issue of minority national recognition and accommodation by situating multinational states squarely within the 'age of migration' (Castles et al. 2013). In so doing, the volume also opens up onto a shared avenue of inquiry with an emerging empirical and theoretical research programme on the fate of multiculturalism and multicultural policies; our hope is that the volume will be a significant step forward in the cross-pollination between research on multinationalism, multiculturalism and the recognition and accommodation of both minority nations and polyethnic/immigrant minorities.

Finally, this volume builds on recent debates on 'new institutional realities' (Gagnon and Burgess 2018) in multinational federations by providing important theoretical, empirical, conceptual and critical contributions to the developing institutionalist turn in the study of multinational federalism. This turn has seen scholars employ historical institutionalist frameworks to explain resistance to federalism (Breen 2018) and to multinational federalism (Lecours 2018) in multinational settings and the increased tensions between national minorities and the national majority in multinational federations (Basta 2018). Several chapters in the volume also employ variants of the new institutionalism to explain patterns of change and continuity in the accommodation of national minorities. Some chapters draw conceptual and explanatory links with emerging theories of subtle institutional change (see Mahoney and Thelen 2010), and finally, in a novel application of feminist institutionalism, one chapter discusses the 'nested newness' of decentralization agreements as well as their unintended consequences.

## REFERENCES

Basta, Karlo. 2018. The State between Minority and Majority Nationalism: Decentralization, Symbolic Recognition, and Secessionist Crises in Spain and Canada. *Publius* 48 (1): 51–75.

Basta, Karlo, John McGarry, and Richard Simeon, eds. 2015. *Territorial Pluralism: Managing Difference in Multinational States*. Vancouver: University of British Columbia Press.

Bohman, James. 2007. *Democracy across Borders: From Démos to Démoi*. Cambridge, MA and London: MIT.

Breen, Michael G. 2018. *The Road to Federalism in Nepal, Myanmar and Sri Lanka: Finding the Middle Ground*. London and New York: Routledge.

Burgess, Michael. 2013. *In Search of the Federal Spirit: New Comparative Empirical and Theoretical Perspectives*. Oxford: Oxford University Press.

Caron, Jean-François, and Guy Laforest. 2009. Canada and Multinational Federalism: From the Spirit of 1982 to Stephen Harper's Open Federalism. *Nationalism and Ethnic Politics* 15 (1): 27–55.

Castles, Stephen, Mark J. Miller, and Hein de Haas. 2013. *The Age of Migration*. London: Palgrave Macmillan.

Codagnone, Cristiano, and Vassily Filippov. 2000. Equity, Exit and National Identity in a Multinational Federation: The 'Multicultural Constitutional Patriotism' Project in Russia. *Journal of Ethnic and Migration Studies* 26 (2): 263–288.

De Schutter, Helder. 2011. Federalism as Fairness. *The Journal of Political Philosophy* 19 (2): 167–189.

Dubois, Janique, and Kelly Saunders. 2013. "Just Do It!": Carving Out a Space for the Métis in Canadian Federalism. *Canadian Journal of Political Science* 46 (1): 187–214.

Gagnon, Alain-G. 2010. *The Case for Multinational Federalism: Beyond the All-Encompassing Nation*. London and New York: Routledge.

Gagnon, Alain-G., and Michael Burgess, eds. 2018. *Revisiting Unity and Diversity in Federal Countries: Changing Concepts, Reform Proposals and New Institutional Realities*. Boston and Leiden: Brill Nijhoff.

Gagnon, Alain-G., and Raffaele Iacovino. 2007. *Federalism, Citizenship, and Québec: Debating Multinationalism*. Toronto: University of Toronto Press.

Gagnon, Alain-G., and Alex Schwartz. 2015. Canadian Federalism Since Patriation: Advancing a Federalism of Empowerment. In *Patriation and Its Consequences*, ed. Lois Harder and Steve Patten, 244–266. Vancouver and Toronto: University of British Columbia Press.

Gagnon, Alain-G., and Arjun Tremblay. 2019. Federalism and Diversity: Towards a New Research Agenda. In *A Research Agenda for Federalism Studies*, ed. John Kincaid, 129–139. Cheltenham: Edward Elgar.

Gagnon, Alain-G., Soeren Keil, and Sean Mueller, eds. 2017. *Understanding Federalism and Federation*. Abingdon: Ashgate.

Habtu, Alem. 2005. Multiethnic Federalism in Ethiopia: A Study of the Secession Clause in the Constitution. *Publius* 35 (2): 313–335.

Karmis, Dimitrios. 2008. Pluralism and National Identity(ies) in Contemporary Québec: Conceptual Clarifications, Typology, and Discourse Analysis. In *Québec: State and Society*, ed. Alain-G. Gagnon, 3rd ed., 69–96. Toronto and Buffalo: University of Toronto Press.

———. 2009. The Multiple Voices of the Federal Tradition and the Turmoil of Canadian Federalism. In *Contemporary Canadian Federalism: Foundations, Traditions, Institutions*, ed. Alain-G. Gagnon, 53–75. Toronto and Buffalo: University of Toronto Press.

Kavalski, Emilian, and Magdalena Żółkoś. 2008. *Defunct Federalisms: Critical Perspectives on Federal Failure*. Surrey: Ashgate Publishing Group.

Keil, Soeren. 2016. *Multinational Federalism in Bosnia and Herzegovina*. London and New York: Routledge.

Kymlicka, Will. 1998. Multinational Federalism in Canada: Rethinking the Partnership. In *Beyond the Impasse: Towards Reconciliation*, ed. Roger Gibbins and Guy Laforest, 15–50. Montréal: Institute for Research on Public Policy.

———. 2001. *Politics in the Vernacular: Nationalism, Multiculturalism, and Citizenship*. Oxford: Oxford University Press.

Lajoie, Andrée. 2009. Federalism in Canada: Provinces and Minorities – Same Fight. In *Contemporary Canadian Federalism: Foundations, Traditions, Institutions*, ed. Alain-G. Gagnon, 163–186. Toronto and Buffalo: University of Toronto Press.

Lecours, André. 2018. The Political Consequences of Independence Referenda in Liberal Democracies: Québec, Scotland, and Catalonia. *Polity* 50 (2): 243–274.

Mahoney, James, and Kathleen Kathleen Thelen. 2010. *Explaining Institutional Change: Ambiguity, Agency, and Power*. Cambridge: Cambridge University Press.

McGarry, John. 2004. Can Federalism Help to Manage Ethnic and National Diversity? *Forum of Federations* 4 (1): 15–17.

McGarry, John, and Brendan O'Leary. 2005. Federation as a Method of Ethnic Conflict Regulation. In *From Power Sharing to Democracy: Post-Conflict Institutions in Ethnically Divided Societies*, ed. Sid Noel, 263–296. Montréal and Kingston: McGill-Queen's University Press.

———. 2015. Territorial Pluralism: Taxonomizing Its Forms, Virtues, and Flaws. In *Territorial Pluralism: Managing Difference in Multinational States*, ed. Richard Simeon, Karlo Basta, and John McGarry, 13–53. Vancouver: University of British Columbia Press.

Moreno, Luis, and Cesar Colino, eds. 2010. *Diversity and Unity in Federal Countries*. Montréal and Kingston: McGill-Queen's University Press.

Requejo, Ferran. 2004. Value Pluralism and Multinational Federalism. *Australian Journal of Political Theory* 50 (1): 23–40.

———. 2016. *Multinational Federalism and Value Pluralism: The Spanish case*. London and New York: Routledge.

Röth, Leonce, and André Kaiser. 2019. Why Accommodate Minorities Asymmetrically? A Theory of Ideological Authority Insulation. *European Journal of Political Research* 58 (2): 557–581.

Seymour, Michel, and Alain-G. Gagnon. 2012. Introduction: Multinational Federalism: Questions and Queries. In *Multinational Federalism. Problems and Prospects*, ed. Michel Seymour and Alain-G. Gagnon, 1–19. Houndmills, Basingstoke and Hampshire, NY: Palgrave Macmillan.

Seymour, Michel, and Guy Laforest, eds. 2011. *Le fédéralisme multinational: un modèle viable*. Brusells: P.I.E. Peter Lang.

Smith, Lahra. 2007. Voting for an Ethnic Identity: Procedural and Institutional Responses to Ethnic Conflict in Ethiopia. *The Journal of Modern African Studies* 45 (4): 565–594.

Smith, Miriam. 2010. Federalism and LGBT Rights in the US and Canada: A Comparative Policy Analysis. In *Federalism, Feminism and Multilevel*

*Governance*, ed. Melissa Haussman, Marian Sawer, and Jill Vickers, 97–109. Surrey: Ashgate Publishing Ltd.

Stepan, Alfred C. 1999. Federalism and Democracy: Beyond the U.S. Model. *Journal of Democracy* 10: 19–33.

Stepan, Alfred C., Juan J. Linz, and Yogendra Yadav, eds. 2011. *Crafting State-Nations: India and Other Multinational Democracies*. Baltimore: Johns Hopkins University Press.

Tillin, Louise. 2007. United in Diversity? Asymmetry in Indian Federalism. *Publius* 37 (1): 45–67.

Tremblay, Reeta Chowdhari. 2005. Afghanistan: Multicultural Federalism as a Means to Achieve Democracy, Representation and Stability. In *From Power Sharing to Democracy: Post-Conflict Institutions in Ethnically Divided Societies*, ed. Sid Noel, 198–214. Montréal and Kingston: McGill-Queen's University Press.

Woods, Eric Taylor. 2012. Beyond Multination Federalism: Reflections on Nations and Nationalism in Canada. *Ethnicities* 12 (3): 270–292.

# PART I

# Multinational Federations at Risk and in Retreat

## CHAPTER 2

# Diverse Democracies and the Practice of Federalism

*James Kennedy*

## INTRODUCTION

This chapter argues descriptively that while informal practices of federalism exist outside the framework of formal federations, normatively federations require practices of federalism both to safeguard territorial accommodation and to effectively reconcile unity and diversity. The chapter considers this relationship in four instances: interwar Czechoslovakia, post-Quiet Revolution Canada, post-Franco Spain and post-devolution United Kingdom. These are multinational states that, with the exception of Canada, are not conventionally considered as federations; yet in each the practices of federalism were and remain key to the management of diversity and stability. While there is a particular focus on the familiar sub-state nations of Québec, Catalonia and Scotland within their respective states, the attempt here is to place them, and contemporary developments in Spain and the UK, within an historical context, and in this regard Czechoslovakia offers additional comparative leverage. Each of the cases underline the importance of shared norms and understandings contained

J. Kennedy (✉)
University of Edinburgh, Edinburgh, UK
e-mail: j.kennedy@ed.ac.uk

© The Author(s) 2020
A.-G. Gagnon, A. Tremblay (eds.), *Federalism and National Diversity in the 21st Century*, Federalism and Internal Conflicts,
https://doi.org/10.1007/978-3-030-38419-7_2

in the practices of federalism. The concluding section reflects on the theoretical and substantive lessons learned from engagement with these historical and contemporary cases.

## THEORETICAL FOUNDATIONS

The political philosopher John Stuart Mill (1991 [1861]: 444–445) argued that 'a people may have the desire, and the capacity, for a closer union than one merely federal, while yet their local peculiarities and antecedents render considerable diversities desirable in the details of their government.' Mill was grappling with the ways in which unity and diversity might be reconciled within a single state, and in doing so he reflected upon the union between Scotland and England and the way in which 'a totally different system of law, and very different administrative institutions, may exist in two portions of a country without being any obstacle to legislative union.' This, of course, required a very considerable capacity for the tolerance of territorial diversity.

Implicitly, it might be said that Mill was making a distinction between formal institutionalised 'federations', with their clear institutional separation of powers and nicely summarised in Elazar's (1987) oft quoted phrase that federations combine both 'self-rule and shared rule,' and the more informal 'practices of federalism,' in which diverse, territorially concentrated groups (national, linguistic, religious, etc.) are recognised in a variety of ways that are not necessarily institutional. This chapter explores the relationship between formal institutional federations and the informal practices of federalism. This is to distinguish between 'federation' and 'federalism' (King 1982). *Federation* refers to institutional makeup, as in Riker's (1964) classic study, which is marked by the division between the government of a federation and the governments of member units that share governance over the same territory and people. While *federalism* is more sociological, and as Livingston (1952) suggests, is concerned with articulating and protecting the federal qualities of a particular society, in which diversity is grouped territorially. This is succinctly caught by François Rocher's (2009) distinction between 'federation as a principle of organization' and 'federalism as a normative model.'

Richard Simeon (2009, 241) offers the following as examples of informal processes and practices that can give rise to adaption and change within federations: 'interpretations of the constitution by the courts, changes in party systems and alliances, changing fiscal arrangements, and intergovernmental accords, agreements, and concordat'. The practices that are the focus here are more informal still and more general; that is, they evidence an overarching philosophy that seeks to reconcile unity and diversity and one that corresponds, in part, to Máiz et al.'s (2010) call for a philosophy of 'plurinational federalism', which governs the interaction between politicians.

It shares much with Michael Burgess' (2012) evocative use of the idea of the 'federal spirit' as a 'distinct set of political values and principles.' Burgess suggests that in abstract theoretical terms, the federal spirit can be understood as

> essentially a moral undertaking or enterprise in that it is based upon the faith and trust that is bound up in the commitment of a promise or a voluntary agreement, itself rooted in the recognition and equality of partnership. The moral basis of such an association or union arises from the presumed integrity and mutual respect of the participating entities. (Burgess 2012: 7–8)

Of course, in reality, federations originate through a multitude of circumstances. And theorists of federalism recognise this in how they conceive the federal spirit. These vary considerably in each of the hugely influential conceptions of federalism (those by Kenneth Wheare, William Livingston, William Riker, Carl Friedrich, and Daniel Elazar), which Burgess (2012) reviews. Each offers a somewhat different emphasis.

Burgess usefully discerns four broad recurrent 'properties', which he calls *self-restraint* through an awareness of respective federal and state interests; *damage limitation* not to imperil the federation in the exercise of power; *moral imperative* to observe unwritten constitutional norms; and *political empathy* in relations between levels of government. Taken together they are concerned with identifying the unwritten norms that should govern relations between the political units within a federation based on mutual respect (Burgess 2012: 20–21). I share Rocher's (2009: 97) warning that 'to canonize these fuzzy concepts would be to risk the substitution of a hermeneutic approach with the ideological justification, explicit or implicit, of certain political options.' Rocher (2009: 98–99) instead offers an approach that conceives federalism as a normative commitment to both autonomy and interdependence.

I want to extend this a little and suggest that what must underpin that commitment is what John Hall (2013: 22) has referred to as 'civility' which is 'based on recognition of difference and diversity' as itself underwritten by 'the agreement to tolerate, albeit within clear limits, so that it becomes possible to live in peace'. Those limits are grounded in liberalism and respect for individual autonomy. Civility might be extended to the realm of federations and respect for state autonomy, and the diversity often embodied in these entities. My own conception, therefore, shares much in common with Burgess, and his careful dissection of the properties that the 'federal spirit' might embody, but I wish to place it within a broader context and position it alongside the need for a civil politics, as outlined by Hall. I argue that the practices of federalism must be grounded in the *tolerance of territorial diversity*, most especially when territories are understood in national or ethnic terms.

## BUILDING FEDERALISM AND FEDERATION: INTERWAR CZECHOSLOVAKIA

Interwar multiethnic Czechoslovakia was something of a liberal oasis in East Central Europe (ECE), under its presidents, Tomáš Masaryk (1918–1935) and Edvard Beneš (1935–1938). While across ECE post-Versailles states were turning rightist and authoritarian, Czechoslovakia remained a functioning constitutional liberal democracy until it was effectively dismembered and then absorbed within the expanding Nazi Empire. Through the interwar it acquired something of the trappings of a federation and its constituent territories became increasingly politically delimited (e.g. Slovakia and Ruthenia, previously subdivided into counties, became political entities). Yet it was the practices of federalism undertaken by its founding president Masaryk and his successor Beneš that secured its stability for so long.

Czechoslovakia was created with a declaration of independence in 1919, while the precise boundaries of the new state were formalised the following year. It brought together territories and ethnic groups that had been governed by both sides of the Habsburg Dual Monarchy: Austrian ruled Bohemia, Moravia and Silesia, and Hungarian ruled Slovakia and Ruthenia. Importantly, it also comprised a very significant German-speaking minority, largely concentrated in the Sudetenland to the west, south and north of the former Austrian ruled Czech lands, and which constituted between a fifth and a quarter of the total population. It was the accommodation of this minority that was to exercise considerable attention of the Czechoslovak government (King 2005: chapter 5).

The Versailles minority treaties regime to which Czechoslovakia was subject played an important role in the developing tensions with the German-speaking minority. Intended as a way of accommodating minorities within the new states across ECE, the Czechoslovak minority treaty was oriented to the accommodation of Germans, Jews and Ruthenians (only the latter was regarded as a national minority). It provided individual rights to members of these ethnocultural communities in the form of, for example, a right to minority language schooling. Like its counterparts elsewhere, there was resentment on the part of the Czechoslovak state that its domestic sovereignty was infringed by a system that did not apply to western states. Moreover, the once dominant German-speakers had experienced an 'ethnic reversal'; this once 'dominant majority' had suffered a reversal in its political status, and resented this decline (Riga and Kennedy 2009). Extreme nationalists manipulated the minority treaty for their own ends, and this was further exacerbated by geopolitics.

The German political parties had initially set themselves against the new state. That is, the interwar Czechoslovak state was founded as Czech, and that Czechness remained ethnic, rather than civic, and with an anti-German strain. However, this needs to be qualified, since Czechness could be acquired. Indeed, the expectation towards the end of the 1920s was that as German children acquired native Czech language proficiency through attendance at Czechoslovak schools, the state would regard them as Czechoslovak, and while Germanness would not be lost, Germans would be loyal to the new state. What changed were external events, namely the rise of the Nazis in Germany. The influence of Nazi propaganda through the 1930s meant that, increasingly, members of the German minority looked to Nazi Germany, and became less likely to accept their new state (King 2005: 154–169). It established what Rogers Brubaker (1996) has described as a 'triadic nexus', in which Germany was now understood as the homeland state for the German minority, within the nationalising Czechoslovak state, conditions which accounted for considerable instability. The Sudeten Homeland Front (SHF) emerged as the political carrier of this increasingly disaffected minority. Following the 1935 election it became the largest party in Czechoslovakia, and an internal threat to the very existence of a democratic state (Capoccia 2005: 71, 77–81).

Yet practices of federalism prevailed. The charismatic Masaryk had had particular success in including German parties in government coalitions through his personal powers of influence, and this continued. As Giovanni

Capoccia (2005: 90) writes, Masaryk and his successor, Beneš 'relied less on the formal powers granted to them by the parliamentary Czechoslovak constitution of 1920 than on the informal practices made possible by the political charisma of Masaryk himself, who during his 15-year presidential tenure acquired broad influence on national politics.'

Government in interwar Czechoslovakia was organised primarily by means of a coalition, a combination of largely five Czechoslovak parties, 'the Petka': the conservative National Democratic Party, the Catholic People's Party, the moderate socialist parties, the Social Democratic Party and the National Socialist Party, and the largest and most important party for much of the interwar, the Republican Party of Agrarians and Peasants. There were many smaller parties on the extremes, left and right, as well as ethnic parties representing Slovaks and Germans. Masaryk and Beneš' aim, however, was to integrate moderate ethnic formations within this wider coalition, especially German. The key to this strategy was to keep Socialists and Agrarians united, regardless of the changing party composition of the various coalition governments. The accommodation of the dominant Agrarian parties, both Czechoslovak and German, was therefore especially important, as was the incorporation of German Christian Democrat and Social Democrat parties in coalition governments. Indeed, a moderate coalition held firm during the crisis years of 1933 to 1938; its maintenance and its attempts to win back Sudeten German support, while marginalising the SHF through, for example, banning the use of foreign political symbols, ensured the political success of the democratic forces (Capoccia 2005: 73–74, 71–72, 77, 90–108).

It is possible to counterfactually surmise, as Capoccia (2005: 72) does, that Czechoslovakia could have withstood its internal challenges. The role of Nazi Germany sealed its fate. Following the Munich Agreement, it was dismembered in a series of steps: the German-speaking Sudetenland was incorporated within the Third Reich, Silesia was lost to Poland and Ruthenia to Hungary, the Slovak Republic was created and Bohemia and Moravia became a Protectorate of the Third Reich. However, its consequences were also apparent in the postwar reconstituted Czechoslovakia. Beneš (1942: 235–239), the liberal politician who had done so much to bring together Czechoslovakia's nationally and ethnically diverse populations together in government, now supported the transfer of the German minority from Czechoslovakia, or certainly those who did not wish to be part of a Czechoslovak state, convinced that its accommodation had proved impossible. The implication was that only a culturally homogenous state could provide the necessary stability upon which democracy might be rebuilt. This, of course, is the premise that lies at the heart of the most celebrated theory of nationalism, that of the Czech philosopher, Ernest Gellner. The analytic point being made here is that tolerance of difference itself is easier when there is shared identity (Hall 2010: 310–320, 151).

## FEDERALISM BEFORE AND FOLLOWING FEDERATION: CANADA

Canada's federation and its practices of federalism are much longer established. At their core was an attempt to reconcile the completing political desires of British and French settlers. It was a federal spirit that made the Canadian Confederation possible. The French Canadian politician and businessman George-Etienne Cartier was especially important in ensuring that a federation, the first under the British Crown, was the result of constitutional negotiations in the mid-nineteenth century. It was a means of protecting French Canadian culture and language against the more centralising interests of British Canadians (Burgess 2012: 17–19).

However, the practices of federalism predate the 1867 Confederation in the ways in which political elites from the territorially concentrated French and British origin populations found means to reach accommodation in their shared state, the Province of Canada. These practices, including government by grand coalition, the maintenance of self-governing communities, mutual veto and proportionality, have since been labelled consociationalism (Lijphart 1977). Indeed, the Union governments from 1842 lay claim to be the first consociational democracy, predating the more celebrated Swiss Confederation by some six years (Noel 1993: 46). It was, in part, this history that inspired Henri Bourassa and the Nationalistes' political project in the early twentieth century. At a moment in which French Canadian influence in Confederation appeared to be diminishing through significant non-francophone immigration, the accession of new non-francophone provinces (British Columbia, Alberta, Saskatchewan) and the diminishing status of French in existing provinces (schooling crises in Manitoba and Ontario), they offered a bi-national vision of Canada, in which its distinct British and French nations would be accommodated consociationally (Kennedy 2013: chapter 6).

The Canadian Confederation and its particular form of federation has been the subject of considerable debate and interpretation, which broadly corresponds to anglophone and francophone scholarship on the topic. Among francophone scholars it is an understanding of federal relations that draws on this pre-Confederation history that dominates, in which autonomy is emphasised. In contrast, anglophone scholarship is more concerned with functional matters, with utility and efficiency in enacting public policy. Its origins lie in the postwar Canadian welfare state and the simultaneous growth of both tiers of government (Rocher 2009: 112; cf. Gauvreau 2017: 283). Rocher (2009: 97–99) suggests that these contrasting interpretations are expressed best in the Quebec government's Royal Commission on Constitutional Problems, the Tremblay Report of 1956, and the federal government's earlier Rowell-Sirois Commission and its Report of the Royal Commission on Dominion-Provincial Relations in 1940. He argues that subsequent interventions are in effect derivative of the arguments set out in these reports.

These conceptions of federalism are partially reflected in the views of the principal exponents of rival currents in Canadian liberalism, Pierre Elliott Trudeau and Claude Ryan, both francophone Quebecers. Their liberalism was key to understanding how they thought federalism should be organised and practised. Michael Gauvreau's (2017) brilliant biography of Ryan offers considerable insight into the emergence of these competing schools of thought and their intellectual origins. Ryan, the Catholic intellectual and editor of *Le Devoir* (1964–1978), espoused a social liberalism and envisioned an asymmetric form of federalism in which French language and cultural rights would be guaranteed throughout Canada, yet Quebec would be recognised as the political and cultural homeland of the French Canadian people. He was also pragmatic, though, and suggested that competencies might be shared between the Canadian and Quebec governments. This was a clear reflection of his early mentors, the conservative Lionel Groulx and the liberal Olivar Asselin, through whom Ryan sought to keep faith with Quebec's Catholic tradition while still embracing a deep commitment to pluralism. This was a position, in broad terms, not dissimilar to the Nationalistes. In contrast, Trudeau's federalism was uncompromisingly rigid in its commitment to the symmetrical equality of provinces, with the central government accorded an elevated position. His advocacy of a highly individualised liberalism was similarly unyielding. He was dismissive of proposals to confer on Quebec a special status based on historical argument, and was unwilling to contemplate additional powers (Gauvreau 2017: 23–24, 290, 482–483, 499–502, 181–182). This latter position, and the practices of federalism that emanated from it, held sway in Trudeau's years in power (1968–1979, 1980–1984).

In the lead up to and during Quebec's Quiet Revolution these ideas came to the fore. During the 1950s Quebecers of varying political stripes came together in opposition to the societal dominance of Maurice Duplessis' *Union Nationale* governments in groups like *Cité Libre* or as critics within the Catholic Church. Fundamentally, and *contra* Behiels (1985), these were arguments *within* liberalism, and the product of a dynamic civil society. Contemporary federal relations in many ways date from this moment, the result of a more assertive Quebec claiming a distinct federal relationship. These arguments, of course, influenced subsequent political debate and developments, most especially the tension between symmetric and asymmetric forms of federalism, not least given the prominent roles their advocates were to play in subsequent Canadian and Quebec politics.

In this light, René Lévesque's sovereignty association offered a new asymmetrical though no longer federal relationship in which Québec would be politically independent but would remain economically integrated. The proposal was defeated in the 1980 referendum. While Ryan led the No campaign during that referendum campaign, it was Prime Minister Trudeau's ultimately empty call for 'renewed federalism' that caught the attention. Yet it was not renewal but repatriation that became Trudeau's immediate post-referendum goal. The British North America (BNA) Act, which had established Confederation through an act and then subsequent amendments of the British parliament was brought home and renamed the Constitution Act. This took place together with the creation of a Charter of Rights and Freedoms in 1982 without the consent of the Quebec government. Its failure to effectively accommodate Quebec's demands from both Liberal and Parti Québécois (PQ) governments shaped constitutional debate over the next decade and a half. The Meech Lake and Charlottetown Accords were the result, genuine attempts by Brian Mulroney's Progressive Conservative government to effectively bring Quebec into the constitution, most famously through the constitutional recognition of Quebec as a 'distinct society'. It was their failure, and the sense of rejection felt in Quebec, which led to the second sovereignty referendum in 1995, and the narrowest of results, 50.58% No and 49.42% Yes.

The shared dialogical experience forged in the Quiet Revolution did translate into an especially important practice of federalism when those participants achieved later prominence in Canadian and Quebec politics. While there were competing conceptions of Quebec's place within Canadian Confederation, this was overridden by a commitment to provincial democracy forged during those years. Counter-intuitively, this understanding that permitted two referenda on Quebec independence to be held might be considered a practice of federalism because it effectively recognised Quebec's distinct position in Confederation. That is, Canada does indeed constitute an asymmetric federation. Quebec enjoys many more powers and competencies than other provinces, not least in immigration and pensions, and yet the formal recognition of its national distinctiveness has been less forthcoming. The closest has been the passing of a parliamentary motion that recognises that 'the Québécois form a nation within a united Canada', which was passed by the Canadian House of Commons on 22 November 2006.

## Federation Without Federalism? Spain

Spain offers a very different sort of federation. Michael Keating (1999) has described it (and similar developments in the UK and Belgium) as being reflective of a 'new asymmetrical territorial politics'. Spain's successful transition to democracy was made possible by practices of federalism. That is, there was a determination by key politicians to ensure recognition of Spain's territorial diversity, most especially Catalonia and the Basque country, as being necessary to avoid another civil war (Elliott 2018: 227). This territorial recognition was constructed as part of an 'all Spain' set of reforms, and it was skilfully reinforced by ensuring that Spain-wide elections preceded those to the re-established sub-state authorities (Linz and Stepan 1992). These institutional reforms were also reflective of wider societal changes afoot, which had over the preceding years let to 'the return of civil society' (Pérez Díaz 1998). This return and the civility that it engendered made possible the compromises that ensured a peaceful transition.

The constitution, therefore, was something of a fudge. The use of 'nation' was reserved only for Spain, and studiously avoided in referring to the place and powers of Catalonia and the Basque Country in the post-Franco constitution. While article 2 refers to the 'the indissoluble unity of the Spanish nation,' it guaranteed 'the right of autonomy for the nationalities and regions that integrate it and the solidarity between them all;' 'autonomous communities' (ACs) was preferred in title VIII, thereby avoiding a distinction between regions and the historic nations, and instead the two were effectively elided (Elliott 2018: 228). The tension was in striking a balance between unity and diversity. However, this constitutional ambiguity was often identified as a strength rather than as a weakness. It allowed all parties to find some recognition of their position, or they could simply choose to ignore it.

As a result of these political developments, post-Franco Spain was identified by social scientists as a model of a multinational state. Its form of asymmetric federation was especially lauded. Yet as important were the informal practices that existed in the relationships between, for example, Spanish Prime Minister Filipe Gonzales and Catalan President Jordi Pujol, members of Spain's first democratic generation. Both shared a background of resistance to Franco. The wily Pujol, in particular, was adept at exploiting political impasses in Madrid to the Generalitat's gain. During his 23-year reign as president, Pujol and his *Convergència i Unió* (CiU) oversaw an increase in the Generalitat's competencies from 89 as laid down in the 1979 statute of autonomy, and more than any other AC, including the Basque Country, to 274. To achieve this, the CiU kept the political temperature down in Catalonia, giving support to Madrid governments; but it crucially ensured a significant, though incremental, increase in the powers of the Generalitat. At the same time, this considerable state-building went hand in hand with cultural Catalanization in which the Catalan language received Generalitat support through its promotion in schooling and in the establishment of a Catalan Corporation of Radio and Television (Elliott 2018: 233, 235, 237).

This relatively quiet state/nation building, the result of practices of federalism, contrasted with instances in which the legality of the Spanish and Catalan governments' actions (and those of the other ACs) were challenged at the Constitutional Tribunal in Madrid. J.H. Elliott calculates that between 1986 and 1988 the Catalan government complained that there had been 77 breaches of the stature of autonomy by Spanish authorities; the Spanish government made similar complaints. These objections could become politically charged, most spectacularly surrounding the *Estatut*, a revision of the statute of autonomy agreed between the Spanish Zapatero Socialist government and the Maragall Catalan government in 2005; a modified version was endorsed by a Catalan referendum in 2006. This was an attempt to secure Catalan autonomy within a 'genuinely federal' Spain. There is an obvious parallel with the Meech and Charlottetown proposals and the attempts to accommodate Quebec within the Canadian

Constitution. Spain's conservative *Partido Popular* (PP) objections were constitutional. It objected to the use of 'nation' to designate Catalonia, and it opposed the elevated status that Catalonia would enjoy compared to the other ACs (with the exception of the Basque Country and Navarre, which enjoyed privileges dating from 1878). Four years later, the Tribunal ruled that the *Estatut* should be modified. But importantly and symbolically the reference to 'nation' was struck down since it had no juridical standing. While the PP hailed a victory, Catalan nationalists were incensed and support for independence increased (Elliott 2018: 237–239, 240–241).

With the CiU under the leadership of Artur Mas in Catalonia, and Mariano Rajoy and the PP in Madrid, following elections in November 2010, intransigence was the result. Both sides were locked into their respective positions and practices of federalism were absent. That said, Mas, a somewhat reluctant leader of the independence movement, did offer a compromise proposal that Catalonia could acquire the same fiscal powers as the Basque Country and Navarre; however, this was rejected. The PP had effectively undertaken an anti-Catalan campaign since the *Estatut* had first been proposed, and did not change course (Elliott 2018: 240–243, 238–239).

Rajoy's refusal to negotiate with the Catalan government over new powers, a move which may have diffused the looming crisis between Madrid and Barcelona, instead escalated it. A non-binding referendum, or 'citizen participation process' on Catalan independence as it was renamed, was held on 9 November 2014, and while it secured 80% for independence, it did so on a 40% turnout. A rethink took place in the CiU, Mas stepped down, and he was replaced by a convinced independentist, Carles Puigdemont. There was effectively a vacuum at the centre with two general elections held in 2016; corruption scandals had beset both of Spain's main parties, the PP and the Socialists (Elliott 2018: 248–249). The upshot was that there was no effective response to Catalonia's demands. Instead, a second referendum was held on 1 October 2017. It, too, lacked legality, and while support for independence was now 92%, it was again a 40% turnout. Like the UK, only the central government can authorise a referendum. Rajoy had not only refused to countenance a referendum on Catalan independence, but also actively sought to disrupt it. The intervention of Spanish police and Guardia Civil to close polling stations, and to seize ballot boxes was at best clumsy and ill judged (Elliott 2018: 240, 250–255).

The same might also be said of the Catalan government's declaration of independence on 10 October. This remained a referendum that had failed to secure legality. The immediate suspension of the declaration and the suggestion that new elections could be called was an attempt to ignite negotiations with Madrid; the Spanish Socialists suggested that Catalonia might be accommodated through a revised Constitution on more federal lines. However, when no engagement was forthcoming, in a rather last ditch and purely symbolic gesture the Catalan parliament voted to endorse a unilateral declaration of independence. In an unprecedented move, the Spanish government invoked Article 155 and suspended the Catalan parliament (Elliott 2018: 256–258). However, the Spanish government's pursuit of elected Catalan government ministers, the arrest of 12, the charge of 9 with 'rebellion', and the effective forced exile of Puigdemont (the refusal of a German court to acquiesce with a Spanish arrest warrant and its charge of rebellion was notable) defies any notion of civility. A breakdown in the practice of federalism marked the controversies surrounding the 2017 referendum on independence and its aftermath. This breakdown, should it continue, can only provide the independence movement with further support.

There are also structural causes behind this breakdown in the practices of federalism, rooted in the very logic of Spain's asymmetric devolution. That is, its tendency to symmetrize, with more recent Autonomous Communities acquiring the same powers as the historic (and original) ACs, such as Catalonia, gives rise to demands that their asymmetric status be preserved. At the same time, the apparent loss of competencies devolved to the ACs has resulted in a reputed loss of a *raison d'être* by the central government, with calls for it to re-centralise. The result is that relationship between the central government and especially the original ACs has become highly politicised (Máiz et al. 2010; Aja and Colino 2014).

The formalization of mechanisms for intergovernmental relations has led to further politicization, and in these relations, the party political colour of the tiers of government matters. This is especially the case where the ruling party in the central government and the AC government differs (Aja and Colino 2014). In Catalonia, rule has alternated between CiU, now the Catalan European Democratic Party, and the Catalan Socialists (allied with the Spanish PSOE), though *Convergència* has supported both minority PP and PSOE governments in Madrid. This suggests that the practices of federalism are subject to the vagaries of party political advantage and strategy. Indeed, the Spanish PSOE government of Pedro

Sánchez, formed in January 2018, with the support of Catalan, Basque and Valencian nationalists, has broken with the practice of the previous government and has undertaken to enter dialogue with Catalan nationalists.

The commentator John Carlin (2019) discerns a dark undercurrent in contemporary Spanish politics, one that harks back to the pre-democratic era, and that is not reconciled to democratic politics. It may be that a republican impulse is at work here; an impulse that, like republicanism in France, views Spain as 'one and indivisible' and is thereby intolerant of any threats to this integrity of Spain. This is a political philosophy which demands conformity, the very opposite of liberalism's tolerance of diversity. The use of 'Catalonia,' however, has created much angst in the 'rest of Spain' and provided the PP and the extreme right Vox with an issue with which to mobilise. Its toxicity may also prove a stumbling bloc in relations between the parties on the left willing to seek compromise, the Socialists and Podermos. The latter supports the right of Catalans to hold a referendum.

## Federalism Without Federation: UK

The United Kingdom's acquisition of some of the trappings of federation is more recent still. Scotland achieved devolved sub-state government only in 1999, during a moment in which the UK effectively established a quasi-federal system through a series of measures that devolved powers not only to Scotland but also to Wales, to Northern Ireland as a result of a separate peace process, and to London (this was to be part of a wider devolution to English regions). Until then, Scotland's institutional distinctiveness had been recognised through a mixture of formal and informal practices. Throughout, Scotland's 'national status' was never in question. The practice of federalism not without moments of tension was evident, therefore, prior to Scotland's formal institutionalisation as a sub-state government.

Scotland, in other words, enjoyed very considerable autonomy following its union with England in 1707. Its institutional trinity of church, education and law (local government might also be included) continued to be the nexus through which domestic Scottish politics were undertaken through the eighteenth and much of the nineteenth centuries. Following nationalist agitation, in the guise of home rule campaigns, administrative devolution was initiated from the late nineteenth century, notably in the form of a Secretary (of State) for Scotland and a Scottish Office to administer UK domestic policy in Scotland. This administrative devolution ensured that the development of the postwar British welfare state had distinctly 'Scottish characteristics' (Kennedy 2013: chapter 2; cf. Paterson 1994).

The recognition of Scottish institutional distinctiveness and the provision of a degree of political voice within the British political system constituted practices of federalism. It was the failure to adhere to these established practices that led to the ultimately successful campaign for a Scottish Parliament. That is, Scottish institutions provided no check on Margaret Thatcher's radical Conservative agenda, epitomised by the introduction of a Poll Tax in Scotland one year ahead of the rest of the UK. Instead, it resulted in a determination to establish a parliament for Scotland.

With the establishment of a Scottish Parliament, together with a Welsh Assembly and a Northern Ireland Assembly, following the Good Friday Agreement (GFA), a quasi-federation has developed across the UK. However, a formal mechanism to adjudicate competing interests remains absent, although the British-Irish Council, established by the GFA, provides a forum for the devolved nations, the crown protectorates, and the UK and Irish governments. It is, therefore, the practices of federalism rather than formal institutions that are essential.

Two referenda offer key instances in which the presence and absence of practices of federalism are highlighted. Counter-intuitively, Prime Minister David Cameron's decision to permit the newly elected majority Scottish National Party (SNP) government to proceed with its manifesto commitment to hold a referendum on independence can be considered a practice of federalism. Since the UK Constitution is a 'reserved matter', the Scottish Government had to seek the UK government's agreement that the constitution should be devolved to ensure a legally binding referendum. This was recognition of the composite nature of the British state and its multinational character; it was perhaps also a calculation that the SNP was unlikely to win (polls at the time showed only 30% support for independence). Further, the British and Scottish governments agreed the terms for the referendum vote: the question, the date, the electorate (including lowering the voting age to 16) and the authority that would organise the ballot. This became known as the 'Edinburgh Agreement'. In the end, while the 'Yes' vote increased considerably through the campaign, it was ultimately defeated by 55% to 45% in the 2014 vote. By providing 'voice', Cameron may have prevented 'exit' (cf. Hall 2013: 68).

However, Cameron's calculation backfired for the next referendum on UK membership of the European Union (EU) in 2016. That referendum was lost, 51.9% to 48.1%. His replacement as Prime Minister, Theresa

May, was keen to emphasise her unionist credentials, resolute that she would proceed for all the United Kingdom in Brexit negotiations with the EU. Indeed, her first act as prime minister was to visit Scotland and its First Minister, Nicola Sturgeon. While May had supported Remain in the referendum, though not vociferously, she was keen to emphasise that her efforts would be directed at bringing together Remain and Leave supporters, and those parts of the country where their respective support was concentrated.

The referendum result revealed the extent of the divergence in political cultures among the nations and regions of the United Kingdom. While Scotland, Northern Ireland (NI) and London voted to remain, Wales and the English regions voted to leave. Indeed, Brexit was in many ways 'made in England'; antipathy to the EU has been consistently pronounced in England before and after devolution. In the Brexit referendum, a new, post-devolution, distinct English national identity drove support for Leave (Henderson et al. 2017). While Scotland voted overwhelmingly to Remain (62%), England voted by a clear majority to Leave (53.4%). Reconciling this divergence would be difficult. Yet, ultimately, an 'all British' approach, which might have reached beyond convinced Brexiteers was discarded in favour of a 'hard Brexit' that sought withdrawal from both the EU's single market and customs union, an approach which appealed most to Tory Brexiteers. These became the British government's redlines in its negotiations with the EU.

When May's decision to call an early general election and secure an enhanced mandate backfired, and the Tories lost their overall majority, the approach did not change. Instead, May turned to Northern Ireland's Democratic Unionist Party (DUP), the largest Protestant unionist party, crucially a Brexit supporting party and out of step with majority opinion in Northern Ireland. This effectively added a further complication. Northern Ireland possesses the UK's only land border with the EU; its fate was debated little during the referendum. May was adamant that there would be no return to a 'hard border'. Indeed, the EU had effectively facilitated the GFA by ensuring borderless movement between the UK and the Republic of Ireland. In the British Government's negotiated agreement with the EU, Northern Ireland's 'soft border' with the Republic was to be protected by a 'backstop' ensuring that even under circumstances in which the UK and EU failed to agree trade terms, NI would continue to be governed by EU trade rules (later extended to the rest of the UK). This was too much for the DUP, and was seized upon by the

Conservative 'European Research Group' of Conservative MPs in their opposition to the May deal. The subsequent failure of the House of Commons to pass the deal (on three separate occasions) paved the way for Boris Johnson's accession as prime minister.

Despite his 'awesome foursome' rhetoric, and his tour of the devolved nations on assuming office in July 2019, Johnson has done little to placate their governments' concerns. If anything, there is hardening of the line on Brexit. Notably, the former Remain supporting Secretary of State for Scotland, David Mundell, was replaced with Leave supporting Alister Jack, against the wishes of the Scottish Tory leader, Ruth Davidson, who later resigned. Another Leaver, Michael Gove has overall responsibility for the Brexit implications for the devolved nations. At the same time, support for Scottish independence has increased. Though like May before him, Johnson will not grant a second referendum, referred to as 'IndyRef2'.

## Reprise: The Practices of Federalism and Its Discontents

Much contemporary politics is characterised by the tensions between unity and diversity. Federations, or federated states, in which there is a clear division in jurisdiction by their very nature are especially susceptible to these threats. Institutions are certainly more resilient than practices; however, on their own they are no guarantee of the necessary compromises that reconcile unity and diversity. William H. Riker's (1964: xi, 5) classic study suggested that the definition of federalism is unproblematic since it is a 'precisely definable and easily recognizable constitutional artefact' demarked as it is by specific institutions: 'a government of the federation and a set of governments of the member units, in which both kinds of governments rule over the same territory and people and each kind has the authority to make some decisions independently of the other.' Yet Riker's definition allowed Canada, the United States, Yugoslavia and the Soviet Union to be classed as federal systems based on their possession of a set of institutions, and not on the actual practice of these states. Institutions are poor indicators of the practice of federalism. The institutional mechanics of federations are important, yet it is the more informal practices of federalism that provide the lubrication.

In each of the cases reviewed, practices of federalism were examined against the backdrop of liberal democracy, which Burgess viewed as vital to federalism's successful operation. The review has likewise hinted at the role of civil society in establishing a political culture conducive to the practices of federalism (Burgess 2012: chapter 8). The threats to the practices of federalism across the four cases have been distinct. The most profound was the geo-politically driven existential threat faced by interwar Czechoslovakia; yet remarkably, practices of federalism were innovated and prevailed. In Canada practices of federalism have been closely linked to debates surrounding the form of federation, symmetric or asymmetric, that would best accommodate Québec, while in Spain, it has been the absence of practices of federalism that have surrounded the failure to accommodate Catalonia. While practices of federalism ensured a peaceful referendum on Scottish independence in the UK, the constitutional crisis that followed the Brexit referendum was entirely self-inflicted, and has deepened fissures in the UK's territorial politics. The shifting balance of electoral politics played an important role in each of these political moments.

While the cases chosen are from within the developed North, they resonate with developments in the contemporary South. India is a case in point. In its short history, India has combined an ability to accommodate cultural and ethnic diversity and foster national coherence (Stepan et al. 2011); it is a composite state, which includes recognisably federal institutions. Since 2014, however, the Hindu nationalist, Bharatiya Janata Party (BJP) and its powerful Prime Minister, Narendra Modi, have effectively 'Modi-fied' Indian federalism since becoming a majority government. Curiously, despite its all India Hindu nationalism, the BJP had championed state autonomy and had been willing to make common cause with Sikh nationalists in Punjab and regionalists in Assam and Tamil Nadu. Yet with the exception of fiscal matters, particularly in relation to India's Goods and Services Tax which have remained largely untouched, there has been an increasing political and administrative centralisation. Most striking has been the failure to recognise the 'special regional autonomy' in the restive state of Jammu and Kashmir. No longer dependent on smaller state parties for support, the BJP has played to its base by calling for a ban on the slaughter of cows and the selling of beef in the Muslim majority state. It eschewed calls to reinstate full autonomy or engage with secessionists, and called off talks with neighbouring Pakistan on the region (Sharma and Swenden 2018: 54–55, 61–64).

In August 2019, however, following its landslide re-election, the Modi government went much further and broke with 70 years of practice and without consultation with state elites imposed direct rule on Jammu Kashmir and abolished its remaining autonomy. This was in direct contravention of Article 370 which detailed the terms on which it had entered India. The special status that Muslim majority Jammu and Kashmir enjoyed has long irritated Hindu nationalists. It also abolished the residency requirement for property ownership in the state, paving the way for a potential demographic shift in the state. This development is especially notable in a country with an established federal tradition in its governance of its diverse democracy. This majoritarian version of democracy contrasts with India's historic liberalism, and sets a worrying precedent for other parts of India, such as Nagaland, Uttar Pradesh and Bengal, which enjoy an asymmetric federal arrangement.

Ernest Gellner understood that democracy need not lead to softer political rule and liberty (Hall 2010: 151). Democracy does not guarantee liberalism, since many illiberal impulses may prove democratically popular. The distinction drawn here between institutional federation and practices of federalism might be similarly construed. The institutions of federalism are not a guarantee of the practices of federalism. Indeed, federalism has historically been posited as a response to what Tocqueville labelled the 'tyranny of the majority', an institutional arrangement that secures the diversity upon which liberalism embraces, albeit within clear limits. In multinational democracies this is especially important. Brendan O'Leary has argued that a dominant people, or in his terms, a *Staatsvolk*, has proved determinative to the stability of federations (O'Leary 2001; cf. McGarry and O'Leary 2009). The corollary, among states without a Staatsvolk in which there is a balance of national or ethnic groups, consociational arrangements are necessary. Masaryk's Czechoslovakia and Union era Canada are exemplars of states, which undertook such practices. However, the rise of a 'new majoritarianism' across states may challenge this premise, especially since it is based on the idea that 'A Staatsvolk can feel secure—and live with the concessions attached to pluri-national federation' (McGarry and O'Leary 2009: 15). The very insecurity of majority Castilians in Spain and the majority English in the UK must be part of an explanation for the reaction to the referendum in Catalonia and support for Brexit in the UK. Curiously, a survey of UK Conservative party members prioritised Brexit over the maintenance of the British union (BBC 2019). It is on liberalism, and tolerance, as Mill implied, that practices of federalism have depended. Its current fragility has implications for federations, in all their guises, regardless of how well its institutions are designed.

# References

Aja, Eliseo, and César Colino. 2014. Multilevel Structures, Coordination and Partisan Politics in Spanish Intergovernmental Relations. *Comparative European Politics* 12 (4–5): 444–467.

Behiels, Michael. 1985. *Prelude to Quebec's Quiet Revolution: Liberalism versus Neo-Nationalism, 1945–1960.* Montreal: McGill-Queen's University Press.

Beneš, Eduard. 1942. The Organization of Postwar Europe. *Foreign Affairs* 20 (2): 226–242.

British Broadcasting Corporation (BBC). 2019. Tory Tensions over Keeping the UK Intact. Accessed 29 January 2020. https://www.bbc.co.uk/news/uk-scotland-scotland-politics-48729801.

Brubaker, Rogers. 1996. *Nationalism Reframed: Nationhood and the National Question in the New Europe.* Cambridge: Cambridge University Press.

Burgess, Michael. 2012. *In Search of the Federal Spirit: New Theoretical and Empirical Perspectives on Comparative Federalism.* Oxford: Oxford University Press.

Capoccia, Giovanni. 2005. *Defending Democracy: Reactions to Extremism in Interwar Europe.* Baltimore: Johns Hopkins University Press.

Carlin, John. 2019. Ghosts of Civil War Haunt Spain in Its Catalonia Madness. *The Times* (London), February 16.

Elazar, Daniel J. 1987. *Exploring Federalism.* Tuscaloosa: University of Alabama Press.

Elliott, John H. 2018. *Scots and Catalans: Union and Disunion.* New Haven: Yale University Press.

Gauvreau, Michael. 2017. *The Hand of God: Claude Ryan and the Fate of Canadian Liberalism, 1925–1971.* Montreal: McGill-Queen's University Press.

Hall, John A. 2010. *Ernest Gellner: An Intellectual Biography.* London: Verso.

———. 2013. *The Importance of Being Civil: The Struggle for Political Decency.* Princeton: Princeton University Press.

Henderson, Ailsa, Charlie Jeffery, Dan Wincott, and Richard Wyn Jones. 2017. How Brexit Was Made in England. *British Journal of Politics and International Relations* 19 (4): 631–646.

Keating, Michael. 1999. Asymmetrical Government: Multinational States in an Integrating Europe. *Publius: The Journal of Federalism* 29 (1): 71–86.

Kennedy, James. 2013. *Liberal Nationalisms: Empire, State and Civil Society in Scotland and Quebec.* Montréal: McGill-Queen's University Press.

King, Preston. 1982. *Federalism and Federation.* London: Croom Helm.

King, Jeremy. 2005. *Budweisers into Czechs and Germans.* Princeton: Princeton University Press.

Lijphart, Arend. 1977. *Democracy in Plural Societies: A Comparative Exploration.* New Haven: Yale University Press.

Linz, Juan, and Alfred Stepan. 1992. Political Identities and Electoral Sequences: Spain, the Soviet Union and Yugoslavia. *Daedalus* 121 (2): 123–139.

Livingston, William S. 1952. A Note on the Nature of Federalism. *Political Science Quarterly* 67.

Máiz, Ramon, Francisco Caamanño, and Miguel Azpitarte. 2010. The Hidden Counterpoint of Spanish Federalism: Recentralization and Resymmetrization in Spain (1978–2008). *Regional and Federal Studies* 20 (1): 63–82.

McGarry, John, and Brendan O'Leary. 2009. Must Pluri-national Federations Fail? *Ethnopolitics* 8 (1): 5–25.

Mill, John S. 1991 [1861]. Considerations on Representative Government. In *On Liberty and Other Essays*, ed. John Gray. Oxford: Oxford University Press.

Noel, S.L.R. 1993. Canadian Responses to Ethnic Conflict: Consociationalism, Federalism and Control. In *The Politics of Ethnic Conflict Regulation*, ed. John McGarry and Brendan O'Leary. London: Routledge.

O'Leary, Brendan. 2001. An Iron Law of Nationalism and Federation? A (Neo-Diceyian) Theory of the Necessity of a Federal Staatsvolk, and of Consociational Rescue. *Nations and Nationalism* 7 (3): 273–296.

Paterson, Lindsay. 1994. *The Autonomy of Modern Scotland*. Edinburgh: Edinburgh University Press.

Pérez Díaz, Víctor. 1998. *The Return of Civil Society: The Emergence of Democratic Spain*. Cambridge, MA: Harvard University Press.

Riga, Liliana, and James Kennedy. 2009. Tolerant Majorities, Loyal Minorities and 'Ethnic Reversals': Constructing Minority Rights at Versailles 1919. *Nations and Nationalism* 15 (3): 461–482.

Riker, William H. 1964. *Federalism: Origin, Operation, Significance*. Boston: Little Brown.

Rocher, François. 2009. The Quebec-Canada Dynamic or the Negation of the Ideal of Federalism. In *Contemporary Canadian Federalism: Foundations, Traditions, Institutions*, ed. A.-G. Gagnon. Toronto: University of Toronto Press.

Sharma, Chanchal K., and Wilfried Swenden. 2018. Modi-fying Indian Federalism? Center–State Relations under Modi's Tenure as Prime Minister. *Indian Politics and Policy* 1 (1): 51–81.

Simeon, Richard. 2009. Constitutional Design and Change in Federal Systems: Issues and Questions. *Publius* 39 (2): 241–261.

Stepan, Alfred, Juan Linz, and Yogendra Yadav. 2011. *Crafting State-Nations: India and Other Multinational Democracies*. Baltimore: Johns Hopkins University Press.

## CHAPTER 3

# When Have Dyadic Federations Succeeded and When Have They Failed? A Comparative Analysis of Bipolar Federalism Around the World

*Christoph Niessen, Min Reuchamps, Dejan Stjepanović, and Augustin Habra*

## INTRODUCTION

The dynamics of dyadic federations have proven to be of particular interest to scholars of federalism. One of the first amongst them to pay close attention to this type of federation was Ivo Duchacek who, 30 years ago in a special issue of *Publius*, defined dyadic federations as 'societies and polities in which two distinct communities clearly dominate the political arena' (1988, 5). Since then, most of the scholarship on dyadic federations has pinpointed the tensions that these federations often embody. For

C. Niessen (✉)
Université catholique de Louvain, Louvain-la-Neuve, Belgium

Université de Namur, Namur, Belgium
e-mail: christoph.niessen@unamur.be

41

A.-G. Gagnon, A. Tremblay (eds.), *Federalism and National Diversity in the 21st Century*, Federalism and Internal Conflicts,
https://doi.org/10.1007/978-3-030-38419-7_3

example, Ronald Watts identifies these 'two-unit federations' as one of the 'pathologies of federalism' and argues that 'the experience of bipolar or dyadic federal systems is not encouraging' (2008, 184). At first blush, this scepticism would seem valid given the social and political dualism of dyadic federalism and the absence of relations with multiple constituent units, both of which are factors that can often lead to institutional deadlock and to societal confrontation (Schmitt 1991). However, while several dyadic federations have indeed broken up, there is also clear evidence that, as of today, many dyadic federations have survived and even attained some degree of political stability. Consequently, the success of dyadic federations presents us with a compelling puzzle as well as a comparative question in need of an answer: how is it that some dyadic federations have succeeded (i.e. survived), while others have failed (i.e. broken apart)?

To be sure, there is research on the political dynamics of both successful and failed dyadic federations, however, this research mostly entails single case studies or small-n comparisons (e.g. Milne 1988; Innes 1997; Singh 2008), and there has been only one comprehensive comparison of a large number of cases and political realities (Duchacek 1988). In light of the substantial number of both existing and defunct dyadic federations, as well as some major political changes that have taken place over the last 30 years (e.g. the breakup Czechoslovakia, the collapse of the former Yugoslavia and the independence of Bosnia-Herzegovina), there is a clear need to expand and to update the comparative discussion on the conditions leading to and/or facilitating the failures and successes of dyadic federations. The present chapter does so by mapping the institutional, geographic and economic realities for all democratic dyadic federations, past and present. In so doing, this chapter aims to identify in the presence or absence of which factors dyadic federal projects have succeeded and in which they have failed.

The chapter is divided into three sections. The first section clarifies the universe of cases under analysis, expands on what is meant by the 'success' and 'failure' of dyadic federations and briefly discusses six key factors that have been identified as being potentially responsible for these outcomes.

M. Reuchamps • A. Habra
Université catholique de Louvain, Louvain-la-Neuve, Belgium
e-mail: min.reuchamps@uclouvain.be

D. Stjepanović
University of Dundee, Dundee, UK
e-mail: d.stjepanovic@dundee.ac.uk

The second section presents the chapter's methodological framework, operationalises the six key factors and provides the rationale of a *fuzzy-set Qualitative Comparative Analysis* that we use to perform a systematic cross-case comparison in order to draw logical inferences about the factors and combination of factors that are most likely to contribute to the successes and failures of dyadic federations. The third section presents our findings in detail. In the chapter's concluding section, we put these findings into a broader perspective and set the stage for further studies on the prospects of federalism and power-sharing in deeply diverse democracies.[1]

## STUDYING THE SUCCESSES AND FAILURES OF DYADIC FEDERATIONS

Three questions must be addressed as a preliminary step in understanding the successes and failures of dyadic federations: (1) What cases can be considered as a dyadic federation and must therefore be included in this study? (2) What exactly is meant by the 'success' or 'failure' of a dyadic federation? (3) And what factors can we identify as potentially accounting for the success or failure of a dyadic federation?

### *Establishing the Universe of Cases*

The defining feature of a dyadic federation is its bipolarity—both when it comes to its society and its institutions. In societal terms, a dyadic federation's population is composed of two major communities that are distinctly characterised by linguistic, cultural, historic and/or religious differences.[2] To be clear, this does not mean that these two major communities must be the only ones on the state's territory, but they should be clearly politically dominant and must be substantively larger in population size than other groups. Along institutional lines, dyadic federations are

[1] This chapter originally emerged from the Master's thesis of Augustin Habra presented at the Université catholique de Louvain, Belgium. This much revised version has benefited from the insightful suggestions of Jérémy Dodeigne throughout the transformation to its current form. For their comments on earlier drafts, we would like to express our gratitude to Arjun Tremblay and Alain-G. Gagnon, as well as to the participants of the Conference on Federalism, Democracy and National Diversity in the Twenty-First Century held in Montréal, and notably Jan Erk for his subsequent suggestions. All remaining errors are our sole responsibility.
[2] These differences may be manifest or, at least, 'imagined' (Anderson 1983).

characterised by institutionalised self- and/or shared-rule prerogatives (whether that be in the legislative, executive or judicial branch of government, or a combination of them) corresponding to the two dominant communities' self-determination projects. Reflecting the literature's use of these characteristics in reference to dyadic federations and, to a lesser degree, 'bipolar', 'bicommunal' or 'two-unit' federations, we use these four terms interchangeably.[3]

Based on the foregoing definition, we employed three specific selection criteria in establishing a universe of cases of dyadic federations:

1. Each case had to have two dominant communities represented in the institutional and socio-political structure of the state.
2. Each case had to have some form of accommodative communitarian mechanisms (formal or informal) within shared political organisations. Some of the cases that we selected were/are constitutionally federal, while others were/are characterised by other forms of federal power-sharing.[4] When cases had two major communities but had no (effective) federal or power-sharing traits, they were not included in the study.[5]
3. The cases under examination needed to be democracies. While this criterion is exogenous to the concept of dyadic federation *per se*, it was included to assure the comparability of cases. In determining what constitutes a democracy, we employed the Freedom House (2018) data and only included countries that were considered at least 'partly free'.[6] Some cases (such as the Fiji Islands and Tanzania)

---

[3] Some conceived 'dyadic federations' exclusively as polities made of two communities and called federations with other smaller groups besides the two major ones 'bipolar' instead (Burgess 2006, 110–117). We use these terms interchangeably because both dyadic and bipolar federations share the major political stake that lies at the heart of this paper: the survival of their federal state despite a high potential for centrifugal pressures in their bipolar federal society.

[4] For example, Trinidad and Tobago is formally a unitary state, but we consider the creation of the semi-autonomous Tobago House of Assembly in 1980 as evidence of a federal accommodative mechanism.

[5] For example, the United Arab Republic of Egypt and Syria (1958–1971) was entirely dominated by Egypt. Similarly, the power-sharing mechanisms in the Federation of Ethiopia and Eritrea (1952–1962) were prevented from entering into force by Ethiopia.

[6] Examples of dyadic federations that were excluded because of their insufficient level of democratization are Burundi, Cameroun, the Federation of Pakistan, Rwanda and Yemen.

failed to meet this criterion in the past but have demonstrated democratic developments in recent years. These cases were thus included in the study once they could be considered 'partly free'.

In following these three selection criteria, we identified 15 cases as democratic dyadic federations. They are listed in Table 3.1, below.

### Defining the 'Success' and 'Failure' of a Dyadic Federal Project

The objective of this study is to identify in the presence or absence of which factors dyadic federal projects have succeeded and in which they have failed. By 'success', we mean the *survival* of a dyadic federation, that is, its continued existence comprising both major communities. By 'failure', we mean the *breaking apart* of a dyadic federation, that is, its demise as a result of either its dissolution or the secession of one of the two major communities. Amongst the cases listed above, five have 'failed' (Cyprus, Czechoslovakia, the Federation of Malaysia, Senegambia and Serbia and Montenegro) while 10 have 'survived'.

Two caveats need to be mentioned about this conceptualisation. First, one should note that between the survival and the breakup of a state, there may be multiple degrees of (in)stability. However, measuring such a fine-grained reality is unfortunately beyond the scope of the current analysis. Second, speaking about the survival and breakup of a state always entails some degree of normativity. Traditionally, state survival has positive connotations while the 'breakup' of a state has negative undertones. However, state survival can be very problematic in the presence of unresolvable ethnic tensions (even if it is the only possible solution), just as state breakup can actually attenuate tensions between communities. In this study, our objective is primarily empirical and we do not attach any desirability to either of the outcomes *a priori*. We do nevertheless engage in making normative assessments when drawing conclusions from our empirical findings on the prospect of federalism (or particular aspects of it) as an appropriate institutional arrangement for bipolar polities.

### Identifying the Factors Under Analysis

Existing research on dyadic federations in the form of single or small-n case studies provides a repository of factors that can potentially explain

**Table 3.1**  The 15 democratic dyadic federations included in the study

| Polity | Dominant socio-political groups | | Federal mechanisms | | Degree of democratisation (Freedom House) |
|---|---|---|---|---|---|
| | Largest group | 2nd largest group | Federal constitution | Power-sharing | |
| Belgium (1970–today) | Dutch-speakers | French-speakers | • | • | Free |
| Bosnia and Herzegovina (1995–today) | Bosniaks | Serbs | • | • | Partly free |
| Canada (1987–today) | English-speakers | French-speakers | • | • | Free |
| Cyprus (1960–1974) | Greek-Cypriots | Turk-Cypriots | | • | Free |
| Czechoslovakia (1990–1992) | Czechs | Slovaks | • | • | Free |
| Federation of Malaysia (1963–1965) | Malays | Singaporeans | • | • | Partly free[a] |
| Fiji Islands (2014–today) | Melanesians | Indo-Fijians | | • | Partly free |
| Guyana (1966–today) | Indo-Guyanese | Afro-Guyanese | | • | Free |
| Northern Ireland (1998–today) | Unionists | Republicans | | • | Free |
| Saint-Kitts and Nevis (1983–today) | Kittitians | Nevisians | • | • | Free |
| Senegambia (1982–1989) | Senegalese | Gambians | • | • | Partly free |
| Serbia and Montenegro (2003–2006) | Serbs | Montenegrins | • | • | Free |
| Suriname (1991–today) | Hindustanis | Creoles | | • | Free |
| Tanzania (1992–today) | Tanganyikans | Zanzibari | | • | Partly free |
| Trinidad and Tobago (1976–today) | Indo-Trinidadian | Afro-Trinidadian | | • | Free |

• = present

[a]Not covered by the Freedom House index but considered partly free by the authors

their survival or breakup.[7] Based on a comprehensive review of this research,[8] we have opted to include six factors in our comparative analysis:

1. The degree to which groups are territorially concentrated.
2. The degree of countrywide electoral proportionality.
3. The degree of nationalisation of the party system.
4. The degree of inclusiveness in the state executive.
5. The degree to which economic resources are equally distributed across groups.
6. The amount of time that the dyadic federation has held together.

*Territorial Concentration*

The first factor that we identified as potentially decisive for the survival of a dyadic federation is geographical in nature. In fact, one of the key concerns that needs to be resolved when dissolving a state or when dealing with the effects of secession is that of the borders between groups (Coakley 2012, 234–239). If an *intra*-state border between two communities is accepted by both of them, it may become an *inter*-state border following

---

[7] For single case studies on Belgium, cf. Beaufays (1988), Reuchamps and Onclin (2009), Deschouwer (2012), Reuchamps (2013). On Bosnia and Herzegovina, cf. Bieber (2002, 2003), Keil (2016), Hulsey and Stjepanović (2017). On Canada, cf. Leslie (1988), Watts (2000), Gagnon (2006). On Cyprus, cf. Bryant (2011), Trimikliniotis and Bozkurt (2012), Salih (2013), Bahcheli and Noel (2013), Özgür et al. (2019). On Czechoslovakia, cf. Innes (1997). On the Federation of Malaysia, cf. Josey (2013). On Fiji, cf. Fraenkel (2006), Fraenkel and Grofman (2006). On Guyana, cf. Hinds (2011). On Northern Ireland, cf. Ruane and Todd (1996), Taylor (2009). On Saint-Kitts and Nevis, cf. Premdas (1998), Midgett (2005). On Senegambia, cf. Hughes (1992) and Richmond (1993). On Serbia and Montenegro, cf. Fraser (2003), Kim (2006). On Suriname, cf. Hoefte (2013). On Tanzania, cf. Nassor and Jose (2014), Cameron (2019). On Trinidad and Tobago, cf. Premdas (2002). For low-n comparisons on Belgium and Canada, cf. Karmis and Gagnon (1996), Erk and Gagnon (2000), Fournier and Reuchamps (2009), Reuchamps (2011), Reuchamps (2015). On Belgium and Bosnia and Herzegovina, cf. Stroschein (2003). On Czechoslovakia and Serbia and Montenegro, cf. Macek-Mackova (2011). On Fiji, Guyana and Malaysia, cf. Milne (1988). On Guyana and Suriname, cf. Singh (2008). On Guyana, Suriname and Trinidad and Tobago, cf. Ryan (2002).

[8] This study also situates itself against the backdrop of a literature on state failure, which has largely been devoted to the comparative study of conflict and divided polities (Roeder and Rothchild 2005; Guelke 2012)—from an institutional (Hale 2004; Lijphart 2004) or a peace-building perspective (Lederach 1997; Oberschall 2007). Bipolar polities have hitherto received much less of such systematic attention.

dissolution or secession. Conversely, if the communities' populations are so intermingled that agreeing on a state border proves to be impossible, dissolution or secession may be impossible. Consequently, we expect 'territorial heterogeneity' to contribute to the survival of dyadic federations, while we expect 'territorial homogeneity' to contribute to its failure.

### Electoral Proportionality

The second factor that we identified relates to the voting system that is used for determining the representatives in the state legislature. Traditionally, the conflict literature is divided between consociationalists who argue in favour of a group-based representation (Lijphart 1977, 2004) and centripetalists who argue in favour of electoral incentives for cross-group vote pooling (Horowitz 1993; Reilly 2001). Both agree, however, that an electoral system should be as proportional as possible in order to prevent groups from feeling underrepresented (or others as overrepresented). Consequently, we expect a proportional electoral system to contribute to the survival of a dyadic federation, while we expect a nonproportional electoral system to contribute to its failure.

### Nationalisation of the Party System

The third factor that we identified is the degree to which political parties are nationalised or regionalised, that is, whether parties seek support on a statewide basis and across the dominant groups or whether they address only the electorate of a single region and community. This factor is closely related to the centripetal argument according to which parties that are institutionally obliged (or at least incentivised) to address a cross-community electorate will moderate their ethno-regional claims and, in so doing, contribute to greater statewide stability (Horowitz 1993; Reilly 2001). Consequently, one should expect a nationalised party system to contribute to the survival of a dyadic federation, while a regionalised party system can be expected to contribute to its failure.[9]

---

[9] To be clear, the degree of nationalization of a party system is influenced by the electoral system and, in a divided society, by the territorial overlap of voting constituencies and the residing area of different societal groups. Nevertheless, it is ultimately the party's decision on how it decides to seek support.

## Executive Inclusiveness

The fourth factor that we have identified relates to the representation of societal groups in the statewide executive. This factor is related to the consociational argument that all groups divided by politically salient cleavages should have guaranteed access to political power (Lijphart 1977, 2004; Reuchamps 2007). While advocates recognise the risk of institutionally reinforcing existing societal divides, they argue that executive power-sharing will still have a pacifying effect because all societal groups feel represented in the body that executes the state's major political decisions (Lijphart 1995). Consequently, we expect the inclusion of the dominant groups in the statewide executive to contribute to the survival of a dyadic federation, while we expect their absence or exclusion from the statewide executive to contribute to the opposite outcome.[10]

## Equally Distributed Economic Resources

The fifth factor that we have identified as potentially decisive for the survival of a dyadic federation is economic in nature: the equal distribution of economic resources across groups. While the share of common wealth is an important issue in all societies (divided as well as undivided), it can be expected to be of even more importance in a dyadic federation where economic advantages of one community are very highly likely to also mean economic disadvantages for the other community (Elazar 1988). More concretely, one can expect mutually reinforcing phenomena of greed—when the advantaged societal group does not want to share resources with the disadvantaged—and grievance—when the disadvantaged group feels deprived or dominated—to create instability (Gurr 1993, 2015). Consequently, we expect that an equal distribution of economic resources across groups will contribute to the survival of a dyadic federation, while we should expect an unequal distribution of economic resources across groups to contribute to its failure.[11]

---

[10] One should note that executive inclusiveness may be a formal constitutional requirement in some cases, while it may be a tacit historical, cultural or political arrangement in others (Reynolds and Reilly 1999; Roeder and Rothchild 2005).

[11] One should note that the distribution of economic resources involves both the *de facto* repartition of natural and economic wealth as well as the distribution of economic resources through the intermediary of national redistribution mechanisms (Gordon and Cullen 2012).

*Long Duration of the Dyadic Union*

The sixth factor that we have identified relates to the duration of the dyadic union, that is, the amount of time that the constituent units have shared the same state. Explaining the survival of a dyadic federation by the duration of its existence might seem tautological at first glance (Caluwaerts and Reuchamps 2015). However, there are good reasons to believe that the duration of a federal arrangement can actually greatly contribute to its survival. Put another way, the breakup of a dyadic federation may become increasingly less likely over time because political institutions become integrated, because economic relations between the communities become interdependent, or simply because populations have started to develop closer relations and/or shared beliefs. Consequently, we should expect failed dyadic federations to have been dyadic unions of short duration. By contrast, we should expect successful dyadic federations to be either of long duration, if they are consolidated, or of short duration, if they are at their start.

## MAPPING AND EXPLAINING CROSS-CASE DIVERSITY: A FUZZY-SET QUALITATIVE COMPARATIVE ANALYSIS

The present chapter has two main objectives—one descriptive and one analytical. At a descriptive level, its objective is to map the political, geographic and economic context of dyadic federations, both past and present. In so doing, the chapter updates existing accounts, prepares the analytical step and provides raw data for future research. At an analytical level, its objective is to bring to light the combinations of factors in the presence or absence of which dyadic federations have succeeded and failed. Based on this analysis, the chapter seeks to inform the broader literature on federalism, national diversity and democracy regarding the near and longer-term prospects of federal arrangements in bipolar polities. To achieve this, we use a *fuzzy-set Qualitative Comparative Analysis*. This method allows for systematically mapping and comparing the identified factors across all 15 dyadic federations. In this section, we discuss, first, how the six factors under examination have been translated into fuzzy-set conditions and how data has been collected for each of them, and second, the rationale upon which the analysis is built.

### Operationalisation of the Conditions and Data Collection

Qualitative Comparative Analysis (QCA) is based on Boolean logic. It systematically compares 'conditions' that are calibrated as 'crisp-sets' or 'fuzzy-sets' (Berg-Schlosser et al. 2009). Conditions are assessments of how much a phenomenon, in this case a factor, is present or absent in a given case (e.g. the degree to which electoral proportionality is present in Belgium). In set-theoretic terms, conditions assess how much a case belongs to a given set that is defined vis-à-vis a concept (e.g. the degree to which Belgium belongs to the set of electorally proportional countries) (Schneider and Wagemann 2012). While crisp-sets assess conditions dichotomously and only allow for differentiations in kind (presence (1) vs. absence (0) of a condition), fuzzy-sets are fine-grained assessments of conditions (calibrated as ratios from 0.00 to 1.00) and allow for differentiations in both kind (0.50 being the discriminating point) and degree (e.g. 0.60 < 0.80).

As summarised in Table 3.2, the six factors identified above have been translated into conditions and were calibrated as 4-point fuzzy-sets: 1.00 for the 'full presence' of the factor in a case, 0.67 when it was 'rather present,' 0.33 when it was 'rather *not* present' and 0.00 when it was 'fully absent.' An outcome condition accounting for whether a dyadic federation survived or broke up was calibrated as crisp-set: 1 when the federation survived, 0 when it broke up.

The assessment of a case's territorial concentration was made qualitatively by the authors. A case was considered 'fully separable' when the dominant communities lived in territorially homogenous areas that could be separated by a clear line. The case was considered 'rather separable' when there was some territorial heterogeneity between the communities but when a clear line could still be drawn. The case was considered 'rather not separable' when this line could not clearly be drawn. And, the case was considered 'fully not separable' when communities were highly dispersed territorially and no clear line could be drawn.

The assessment of a case's electoral proportionality was made using the *Gallagher Index* (Gallagher 2018).[12] More specifically, the cases' mean

---

[12] The Gallagher Index or 'least squares index' calculates the degree of electoral proportionality by taking the square root of the half of the sum of all parties' squared difference between their share of votes and share of seats for one election:

$$\text{Lsq} = \sqrt{\frac{1}{2} \sum_{i=1}^{n} \left( \%\text{Votes}_i - \%\text{Seats}_i \right)^2}.$$

**Table 3.2**  Operationalisation of the conditions as fuzzy-sets

| Label | Conditions | Fuzzy scale | Operationalisation |
|---|---|---|---|
| OUTC | Survival/Breakup of the dyadic federation | 2-point (crisp-set) | *Qualitative assessment:* Survival = 1, breakup = 0. |
| TER.CON | Territorial concentration | 4-point | *Qualitative assessment:* Fully separable = 1, rather separable = 0.67, rather not separable = 0.33, fully not separable = 0. |
| ELC.PROP | Electoral proportionality | 4-point | *Mean score on Gallagher Index:* Anchors: 0–4 = 0, 5–9 = 0.33, 10–14 = 0.67, 15–20 = 1. |
| NAT.P.SYS | Nationalised party system | 4-point | *Qualitative assessment:* Fully national = 1, rather national = 0.67, rather not national = 0.33, fully not national = 0. |
| EXE.INC | Executive inclusiveness | 4-point | *Qualitative assessment:* Perfect cabinet share = 1, significant share = 0.67, ineffective share = 0.33, no share = 0. |
| EQ.ECO.DIS | Equal economic distribution | 4-point | *Quantitative (GDP) and qualitative assessment:* Largely equal = 1, minor inequalities = 0.67, substantive inequalities = 0.33, major inequalities = 0. |
| LG.DUR | Long duration of the union | 4-point | *Quantitative assessment with observation-based anchors:* ≥30 years = 1, ≥20 years = 0.67, ≥10 years = 0.33, <10 years = 0. |

Gallagher score was taken for all lower house elections with available data.[13] During calibration, a Gallagher score of 0–4 was translated into 0.00, a score of 5–9 was translated into 0.33, a score of 10–14 was translated into 10–14 and a score of 15–20 was translated into 1.00.

[13] For Belgium, Canada, Guyana, Saint-Kitts and Nevis, Serbia and Montenegro, Suriname and Trinidad and Tobago, calculations were borrowed from Gallagher (2018). For Bosnia and Herzegovina, Czechoslovakia, Cyprus, Fiji, the Federation of Malaysia, Nigeria, Northern Ireland, Senegambia and Tanzania, calculations were made by the authors.

The assessment of a case's degree of party system nationalisation was made qualitatively by the authors. A case was considered 'fully national' when the party system was exclusively national. A case was considered 'rather national' when the system was predominantly national. A case was considered 'rather not national' when the system was predominantly regional. A case was considered 'fully not national' when the system was exclusively regional.

The assessment of a case's executive inclusiveness was also made qualitatively by the authors. A case was considered 'fully inclusive' in the presence of an (almost) perfect (or equal) sharing of the cabinet between the two dominant communities. A case was considered 'rather inclusive' when there was a significant sharing of the cabinet between communities. A case was considered 'rather not inclusive' when the sharing of the cabinet proved to be ineffective (e.g. in Fiji where the political party representing one community often refuses to sit in the cabinet with a political party representing the other community). A case was considered 'fully not inclusive' when there was no sharing whatsoever of the cabinet between communities.

The assessment of a case's economic distribution was made both quantitatively and qualitatively by the authors. When available, the GDP per capita of both dominant communities was compared. In the absence of data, secondary sources (cf. *supra*) were used to classify each polity. A case was considered 'largely equal' when both groups could be considered of generally equal wealth. A case was considered to be 'rather equal' when small wealth inequalities were observed. A case was considered 'rather not equal' when there was a non-negligible difference in wealth between communities. And, a case was considered to be 'fully not equal' when a clear wealth difference between communities was observed.

Finally, the assessment of the duration of a case's intactness was made quantitatively using observation-based anchors. When mapping the number of years that the case under examination remained intact (cf. the Appendix),[14] three gaps tended to appear and were thus used to set the qualitative anchors. Cases that remained intact for over 30 years were deemed to be of 'long duration'. Cases that remained intact for 20–29 years

---

[14]We considered the number of years during which the case qualified for our three selection criteria, even though some cases remained together even longer. We did so because centrifugal dynamics might only come up when power-sharing agreements are entrenched and when states are democratic. Our findings remain robust, however, even when considering longer periods.

were deemed to be of 'rather long duration'. Cases that remained intact for 10–19 years were deemed to be of 'rather short duration'. And cases that remained intact for less than 10 years were deemed to be of 'short duration'.

When applying this operationalisation and calibrating the collected data on all factors for the 15 dyadic federations under examination, we obtained the final data distribution displayed in Table 3.3, below.

### Rationale of the Fuzzy-Set Qualitative Comparative Analysis[15]

Qualitative Comparative Analysis (QCA) has an equifinal, asymmetrical and constellational view of causality. It is equifinal in that it understands outcomes as being (potentially) produced by multiple distinct factors. It is asymmetrical in that it understands factors that explain the presence of an outcome as not necessarily explaining its absence when they are negated. And it is constellational in that it explicitly looks for the occurrence of outcomes in the presence or absence of multiple conditions that are linked by a logical AND or OR.

Drawing on Boolean logic,[16] QCA systematically compares cases' condition scores and their outcome. The analysis is based on the so-called 'truth table' which comprises all combinations of present or absent conditions that are observed in the cases, together with the respective outcome. When conditions are operationalised as fuzzy-sets, cases have partial membership in truth table rows (equal to their lowest membership in one of the conditions) and eventually belong to the only row in which their membership is higher than 0.50. The truth table is both a descriptive and analytical tool. It is descriptive in that it allows us to map all existing constellations of conditions and the outcome with which they are associated. It is analytical in that it allows us to determine which (combination of) conditions appear to be necessary and/or sufficient for an outcome to occur, and how combinations of conditions can be minimised as to obtain the most parsimonious solution for explaining an outcome (cf. *infra*).

In an analysis of necessity, one determines the degree to which (a combination of) conditions are (is) consistently present when the outcome occurs. In crisp-set terms, for it to be necessary one always wants condition

---

[15] This section draws on Ragin and Rihoux (2009) and Schneider and Wagemann (2012).

[16] The Boolean operators used in this chapter are the logical AND ($*$), the logical OR ($+$), the logical negation ($\sim$) and the logical implication ($\rightarrow$).

**Table 3.3** Data distribution on the six conditions and the outcome for all 15 dyadic federations

| ID | Cases | TER.CON | ELC.PROP | NAT.P.SYS | EXE.INC | EQ.ECO.DIS | LG.DUR | OUTC |
|---|---|---|---|---|---|---|---|---|
| BEL | Belgium (1970–today) | 0.33 | 1.00 | 0.00 | 1.00 | 0.33 | 1.00 | 1 |
| BAH | Bosnia and Herzegovina (1995–today) | 0.33 | 0.67 | 0.00 | 0.67 | 0.33 | 0.67 | 1 |
| CAN | Canada (1987–today) | 0.67 | 0.33 | 0.33 | 0.67 | 0.67 | 1.00 | 1 |
| CYP | Cyprus (1960–1974) | 0.00 | 0.00 | 0.00 | 0.67 | 0.00 | 0.33 | 0 |
| CZE | Czechoslovakia (1990–1992) | 1.00 | 0.67 | 0.00 | 0.00 | 0.00 | 0.00 | 0 |
| MAL | Federation of Malaysia (1963–1965) | 1.00 | 0.00 | 0.00 | 0.00 | 0.33 | 0.00 | 0 |
| FIJ | Fiji Islands (2014–today) | 0.00 | 1.00 | 0.33 | 0.33 | 0.67 | 0.00 | 1 |
| GUY | Guyana (1966–today) | 0.00 | 1.00 | 0.33 | 0.00 | 0.33 | 1.00 | 1 |
| NIR | Northern Ireland (1998–today) | 0.00 | 1.00 | 0.33 | 0.67 | 0.33 | 0.67 | 1 |
| SKN | Saint-Kitts and Nevis (1983–today) | 0.00 | 0.00 | 0.67 | 0.00 | 0.33 | 1.00 | 1 |
| SGB | Senegambia (1982–1989) | 1.00 | 0.00 | 0.00 | 0.67 | 0.33 | 0.00 | 0 |
| SAM | Serbia and Montenegro (2003–2006) | 1.00 | 0.67 | 0.00 | 0.00 | 0.00 | 0.00 | 0 |
| SUR | Suriname (1991–today) | 0.00 | 1.00 | 0.33 | 0.00 | 0.67 | 0.67 | 1 |
| TZN | Tanzania (1992–today) | 1.00 | 1.00 | 0.00 | 0.67 | 1.00 | 0.67 | 1 |
| TAT | Trinidad and Tobago (1976–today) | 0.00 | 0.33 | 0.33 | 0.00 | 0.33 | 1.00 | 1 |

X to be present when outcome Y occurs. When using fuzzy-sets, one wants cases' membership in X to be higher than their membership in Y. The 'consistency' of necessity (i.e. the extent to which a condition is

necessary) is obtained by $\dfrac{\sum_{i=1}^{I} \min\left(X_i, Y_i\right)}{\sum_{i=1}^{I} Y_i}$. One also assesses how many

cases are 'covered' by a necessary condition (i.e. the share of cases for which the condition is necessary). The coverage of necessity is

obtained by $\dfrac{\sum_{i=1}^{I} \min\left(X_i, Y_i\right)}{\sum_{i=1}^{I} X_i}$.

In an analysis of sufficiency, one determines to what degree an outcome is always present when a (combination of) condition(s) is present. In crisp-set terms, for it to be sufficient one always wants outcome Y to occur when condition X is present. When using fuzzy-sets, one wants cases' membership in Y to be higher than their membership in X. The 'consistency' of sufficiency (i.e. the extent to which a condition is sufficient) is

obtained by $\dfrac{\sum_{i=1}^{I} \min\left(X_i, Y_i\right)}{\sum_{i=1}^{I} X_i}$. One also assesses how many cases are 'cov-

ered' by a sufficient condition (i.e. the share of cases for which the condi-

tion is sufficient). The coverage of sufficiency is obtained by $\dfrac{\sum_{i=1}^{I} \min\left(X_i, Y_i\right)}{\sum_{i=1}^{I} Y_i}$.

When it comes to finding the most parsimonious solution that explains (is sufficient for) an outcome, the so-called 'minimisation process' is involved. Based on the *Quine-McClusky algorithm*, 'similar conjunctions' are matched so that conditional specifications that logically lead to identical outcomes are excluded.[17] In addition, 'logically redundant prime implicants' (i.e. terms that are logically implied twice in a formula) are equally excluded.[18] This reduction potential is limited when the number of possible configurations (i.e. combinations of conditions) exceeds the actual number of observed configurations. Non-observed configurations (so-called *logical remainders*) reduce the number of occurring similar con-

[17] E.g., If A∗B∗C → D, and if A∗B∗~C → D, then A∗B → D and the formula can be reduced.
[18] E.g., If A∗B∗C + A∗B∗~C + ~A∗B∗C + ~A∗~B∗C → D, then A∗B + ~A∗C → D.

junctions and hence the possibilities of minimisation. Given that a *fcQCA* with six fuzzy-sets involves 64 possible configurations,[19] but that the present one only comprises 11 observed configurations (cf. *infra*), 'simplifying assumptions' about the outcome of non-observed cases will be made by combining observed data with theoretical reasoning. This allows for further and final minimisation. One should note that since *QCA* has an asymmetric view of causality, the occurrence and non-occurrence of the outcome have to be analysed separately.

## WHEN DYADIC FEDERATIONS HAVE SUCCEEDED AND WHEN THEY HAVE FAILED

The *fsQCA* analyses suggest that dyadic federations survived when the dominant communities were territorially dispersed and had, at the same time, either a proportional electoral system or a nationalised party system. In the absence of territorial dispersion, other institutional arrangements such as executive inclusiveness and an equal economic distribution appear to be important. In general, the analysis shows that dyadic federations that survive do so for many years. By contrast, our results suggest that a dyadic federal project is likely to fail in the absence of stabilising institutional factors like electoral proportionality and a national party system, especially when economic resources are unequally distributed between groups and when they are territorially clearly separable. The (short) duration of the union is important too. Table 3.4, below, displays the truth table upon which these results are based.[20]

### *When Have Dyadic Federations Succeeded?*

The analysis of necessary and sufficient conditions for the survival of dyadic federations (outcome = 1), summarised in Table 3.5, below, suggests that no condition is, on its own, truly necessary but that a few come close to or even reach sufficiency. Concerning necessity, one can see that most surviving dyadic federations are of long duration (nine out of ten)

---

[19] For *n* fuzzy-sets, the total number of possible configurations is $2^n$. In this case, $2^6 = 64$.

[20] An inclusiveness threshold of 0.67 has been chosen for a case to be included in the analysis. While this comes with some deviance in degree (depending on cases' membership scores in the conditions), no row comprised deviance in kind (all cases were member of the same outcome) and all cases could be included in the analysis.

**Table 3.4** Truth table for the *fsQCA* analysis

| TER.CON | ELC.PROP | NAT.P.SYS | EXE.INC | EQ.ECO.DIS | LG.DUR | OUTC | Incl. | | Cases |
|---|---|---|---|---|---|---|---|---|---|
| | | | | | | | Prs. | Abs. | |
| 0 | 1 | 0 | 1 | 0 | 1 | 1 | 1.000 | 0.000 | BEL, BAH, NOI |
| 0 | 1 | 0 | 0 | 1 | 1 | 1 | 1.000 | 0.000 | GUY, SUR |
| 1 | 0 | 0 | 1 | 1 | 1 | 1 | 1.000 | 0.000 | CAN |
| 0 | 1 | 1 | 0 | 0 | 0 | 1 | 1.000 | 0.000 | FIJ |
| 0 | 0 | 0 | 0 | 0 | 1 | 1 | 1.000 | 0.000 | SKN |
| 1 | 1 | 0 | 1 | 1 | 1 | 1 | 1.000 | 0.000 | TZN |
| 0 | 0 | 0 | 0 | 0 | 1 | 1 | 0.834 | 0.166 | TAT |
| 1 | 0 | 0 | 0 | 0 | 0 | 0 | 0.142 | 0.858 | MAL |
| 1 | 1 | 0 | 0 | 0 | 0 | 0 | 0.198 | 0.802 | CZS, SAM |
| 1 | 0 | 0 | 1 | 0 | 0 | 0 | 0.330 | 0.670 | SGB |
| 0 | 0 | 0 | 1 | 0 | 0 | 0 | 0.330 | 0.670 | CYP |

**Table 3.5**  Consistency and coverage scores for conditions' necessity and sufficiency for explaining the survival of dyadic federations (Outc. = 1)

| Analysis | Condition[a] | Consistency | Coverage | RoN | PRI |
|---|---|---|---|---|---|
| Necessity | LG.DUR | 0.768 | 0.959 | 0.955 | – |
| | ~TER.CON | 0.767 | 0.885 | 0.864 | – |
| Sufficiency | NAT.P.SYS | 1.000 | 0.265 | – | 1.000 |
| | LG.DUR | 0.959 | 0.768 | – | 0.959 |
| | EQ.ECO.DIS | 0.938 | 0.499 | – | 0.938 |
| | ELC.PROP | 0.845 | 0.733 | – | 0.845 |
| | EXE.INC | 0.750 | 0.401 | – | 0.750 |

[a]Only conditions whose consistency of necessity or sufficiency exceeds 0.75 are presented

and that they are composed of territorially non-concentrated groups (eight out of ten). Consequently, both seem to be important contextual conditions for preventing the breaking apart of a dyadic federation. One should note, however, that neither of these conditions is fully necessary because two dyadic federations survived despite having territorially concentrated groups (Canada and Tanzania), and one survived although it is only a recent democratic dyadic federal project (Fiji). For the former, we will see that other stabilising factors have been at work. For the latter, one should note that, despite democracy having only been achieved recently, the common state history of both groups dates back much longer. When looking at the sufficiency, one can see that the survival rate of dyadic federations is fairly high (not to say perfect) when they are of long duration (9/9), have an equal economic distribution between groups (4/4), have a nationalised party system (1/1) or a proportional electoral system (7/9).[21] This shows that these are important stabilising factors in bipolar federal settings. However, their importance comes in combination with other factors as the constellational analysis below suggests.

Three constellations can be identified when exploring the combination of conditions under which dyadic federations have survived, as we can see in Table 3.6, below.[22] Six out of the ten surviving dyadic federations had territorially non-concentrated groups and a proportional electoral system

[21] The consistency of sufficiency does not reach 1.000 because of some deviance in degree (remember that these are fuzzy-sets).

[22] The minimisation process of solution 1.A relied on six, that of 1.B on seven and that of 1.C on six simplifying assumptions. They were based on the directional expectation that conditions $(0,1,1,1,-) \rightarrow$ outcome(1).

**Table 3.6**  Minimised conjunctions explaining the survival of dyadic federations (Outc. = 1)

| Solution | 1 | | | 2 |
|---|---|---|---|---|
| Path | A | B | C | A |
| Territorial concentration | ⊗ | ⊗ | | ⊗ |
| Electoral proportionality | ● | | | |
| Nationalised party system | | ● | | |
| Executive inclusiveness | | | ● | |
| Equal economic distribution | | | ● | |
| Duration of the union | (●) | ● | ● | ● |
| Consistency | 1.000 | 1.000 | 1.000 | 0.948 |
| Raw coverage | 0.600 | 0.232 | 0.233 | 0.601 |
| Unique coverage | 0.369 | 0.067 | 0.101 | 0.601 |
| Covered cases | BEL, BAH, FIJ, GUY, NOI, SUR | SKN | CAN, TZN | BEL, BAH, GUY, NOI, SKN, SUR, TAT |
| Contradictory cases | – | – | – | CYP (in degree) |
| Solution consistency | 1.000 | | | 0.948 |
| Solution coverage | 0.768 | | | 0.601 |
| Non-covered cases | TAT | | | CAN, TAN, FIJ |

(1.A). One out of the ten surviving dyadic federations had territorially non-concentrated groups, a nationalised party system and was of long duration (1.B). Two out of the ten surviving dyadic federations had an inclusive executive, an equal economic distribution and lasted over time (1.C). This confirms the importance of territorial heterogeneity and shows that it is usually combined with another stabilising mechanism—electoral proportionality or a nationalised party system. In addition, the territorially concentrated cases with a nationalised party system have also been of long duration, which is something that the territorially concentrated cases with a proportional electoral system will probably be in a few years. These two paths are perfectly consistent and cover together 70% of the cases. In two cases, however, none of these factors was present (Canada and Tanzania). Instead, their survival occurred in the presence of inclusive executives and an equal distribution of economic resources between groups, in addition to the fact that they had been of long duration. Finally, there is one surviving case which corresponds to none of these constellations—Trinidad and Tobago—and which is surprising insofar as its only stabilising factors were territorial heterogeneity and long duration (2.A). These two factors achieve a high sufficiency across all cases $(7/7)^{23}$ and even cover 70% of the surviving federations. But given that they are present only in a single case, we are cautious with overinterpreting their sufficiency and suggest a deeper investigation of the stability of Trinidad and Tobago, which is beyond the scope of the current analysis.

Figure 3.1, below, provides some additional information on the situation of the cases vis-à-vis the three main solution formulas. Guyana, Fiji, Northern Ireland and Suriname are the most typical cases for solution 1.A in that they were full members of both the conjunction and the outcome. Belgium and Bosnia and Herzegovina are still typical cases but have a slightly lower (though positive) membership in the conjunction. Solution 1.B and 1.C have no most typical cases (i.e. no full conjunction members), but Saint Kitt and Nevis, Canada and Tanzania are respective typical cases. As noted above, Trinidad and Tobago is the only case that is covered by none of these three solutions and is therefore deviant in coverage. Finally, Cyprus, Czechoslovakia, the Federation of Malaysia, Senegambia and Serbia and Montenegro are negative cases because they did not survive and can therefore not provide relevant information for the analysis of survival, except for their presence as logical counterfactuals. These cases are analysed in the following sub-section.

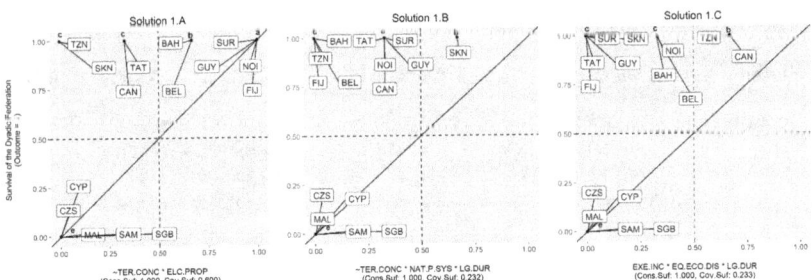

**Fig. 3.1** XY-Plot for the paths of the main solution explaining the survival of dyadic federations (Outc. = 1). a = most typical cases, b = typical cases, c = deviant cases in coverage, d = deviant cases in consistency, e = negative (irrelevant) cases

23 The consistency of sufficiency does not reach 1.000 because of some deviance in degree.

## When Have Dyadic Federations Failed?

The analysis of necessary and sufficient conditions for the breakup of dyadic federations (outcome = 0), summarised in Table 3.7, below, suggests that four conditions appear *a priori* to be close to necessary for the outcome to occur, while none is sufficient on its own. Concerning necessity, one can see that most dyadic federations that broke up had a regionalised party system (5/5), were of short duration (5/5), had an unequal economic distribution between communities (5/5) and had territorially concentrated communities (4/5). While all of these conditions thus seem to be important for understanding when dyadic federations break up, one should note that the first three have low relevance of necessity scores (probably because of the limited diversity of their distribution), while the last one has a contradicting case. None of these conditions can therefore be considered truly necessary. Furthermore, no single condition is on its own sufficient to explain the breaking apart of a dyadic federation.

Two constellations can be identified when looking for the combination of conditions under which dyadic federations have broken apart, as we can see in Table 3.8 below.[24] Four out of the five of these dyadic federations had territorially concentrated groups, a regionalised party system, an unequal economic distribution between groups and were of short duration (1.A). Together, these factors achieve (almost)[25] perfect sufficiency (4/4). The only case not covered by this solution is Cyprus because its groups used to be territorially non-concentrated. The evidence suggests

**Table 3.7**  Consistency and coverage scores for conditions' necessity and sufficiency for explaining the breakup of dyadic federations (Outc. = 0)

| Analysis | Condition[a] | Consistency | Coverage | RoN | PRI |
|---|---|---|---|---|---|
| Necessity | ~NAT.P.SYS | 1.000 | 0.405 | 0.265 | – |
|  | ~LG.DUR | 0.934 | 0.668 | 0.476 | – |
|  | ~EQ.ECO.DIS | 0.934 | 0.482 | 0.515 | – |
|  | TER.CON | 0.800 | 0.632 | 0.788 | – |
| Sufficiency | – | – | – | – | – |

[a]Only conditions whose consistency of necessity or sufficiency exceeds 0.75 are presented

[24] The minimisation process of solution 1.A relied on one and that of 1.B on two simplifying assumptions. They were based on the directional expectation that conditions (1,0,0,0,0,0) → outcome(0).

[25] The consistency of sufficiency does not reach 1.000 because of some deviance in degree.

**Table 3.8**  Minimised conjunctions explaining the breakup of dyadic federations (Outc. = 0)

| Solution | 1 | |
|---|---|---|
| Path | A | B |
| Territorial concentration | ● | |
| Electoral proportionality | | ⊗ |
| Nationalised party system | ⊗ | ⊗ |
| Executive inclusiveness | | |
| Equal economic distribution | ⊗ | ⊗ |
| Duration of the union | ⊗ | ⊗ |
| Consistency | 0.918 | 0.901 |
| Raw coverage | 0.734 | 0.600 |
| Unique coverage | 0.268 | 0.134 |
| Covered cases | CZS, MAL, SGB, SAM | CYP, MAL, SGB |
| Contradictory cases | BAH (in degree) | BAH (in degree) |
| Solution consistency | 0.929 | |
| Solution coverage | 0.868 | |
| Non-covered cases | – | |

that the breaking apart of the latter occurred in the presence of a disproportional electoral system, a regionalised party system, an unequal economic distribution between groups and a (rather) short duration (1.B, which were also present in the Malaysian and Senegambian cases). However, one should note that the Cypriot case is somewhat particular insofar as both its dominant groups were kin-minorities of larger external states—Greece and Turkey—and that these states had a major responsibility for the escalation of tensions between Greek and Turkish Cypriots (enforcing at some point the territorial homogeneity). The proposed solution therefore has to be read jointly with this external kin-state influence.

Figure 3.2, below, provides some additional information on the situation of the cases vis-à-vis the two solution formulas. Czechoslovakia, the Federation of Malaysia and Serbia and Montenegro are the most typical cases for solution 1.A in that they are both full members of the conjunction and the outcome. Senegambia is also typical but has a slightly lower (though positive) membership in the conjunction. Cyprus, as explained before, is deviant in coverage because it is not covered by the conjunction. Bosnia and Herzegovina is a negative case but slightly deviates in consis-

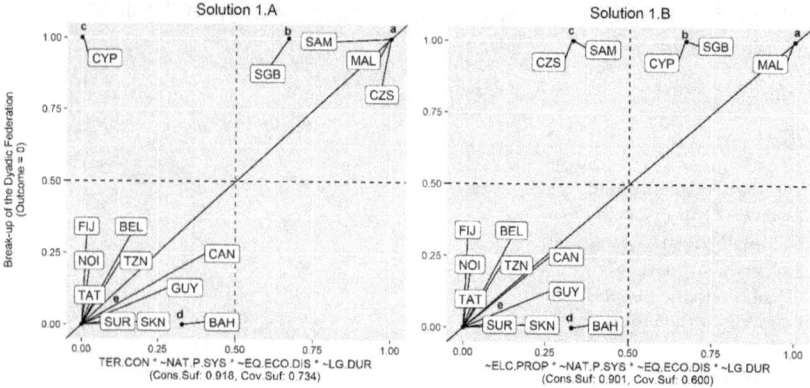

**Fig. 3.2** XY-Plot for the paths of the main solution explaining the breakup of dyadic federations (Outc. = 0). a = most typical cases, b = typical cases, c = deviant cases in coverage, d = deviant cases in consistency, e = negative (irrelevant) cases

tency because it has partial membership in the conjunction (0.33).[26] The remaining cases are negative in both the outcome and conjunction. For solution 1.B, the Federation of Malaysia is the most typical case, while Cyprus and Senegambia are typical. Malaysia and Czechoslovakia are not covered. Bosnia and Herzegovina deviates again slightly in consistency.

## CONCLUSION

This chapter has brought to light and further explored in the presence or absence of which factors dyadic federal projects have succeeded (i.e. survived) and in which they have failed (i.e. broken apart). By mapping the factors that seem crucial for their stability, we provided an expanded and updated account of the institutional, geographic and economic contexts of dyadic federations. By systematically comparing the importance of these factors with a *fuzzy-set Qualitative Comparative Analysis* of all democratic dyadic federations, past and present, the chapter also offered a unique

---

[26] In some way, the Bosnian case confirms the importance of kin-state influence already underlined for Cyprus. Here, however, kin-state presence served stability since Serbia is one of the guarantors of the Dayton peace agreement, together with the external conditionality ensured by the European Union.

comprehensive comparative assessment in a field that has tended to focus on single case studies or on small-n comparisons.

Our results inform the broader literature on federalism, national diversity and democracy by showing, like Duchacek (1988, 31), that federalism is not *per se* an institutional arrangement likely to fail in bipolar polities, as suggested by Watts (2008, 184), for example. Overall, the analysis shows that federal projects with two major communities can succeed if geographical factors such as the territorial dispersion of the dominant groups play in its favour and when institutional arrangements (i.e. a proportional electoral system or a national party system) either ensure fair political representation for both communities or prevent polities from being conceived in exclusively sub-national terms. In the absence of territorial dispersion, other institutional arrangements such as executive inclusiveness and an equal economic distribution between groups appear to be crucial in preventing the breakup of the federation. In general, dyadic federations that survive tend to do so for many years and one can reasonably expect that if a dyadic federal project lasts a few (~20) years, it will last many years. By contrast, the analysis shows that a bipolar federal project is likely to fail in the absence of stabilising institutional arrangements (i.e. electoral proportionality and a national party system) and, more particularly, when economic resources are unequally distributed between communities and when these communities are clearly territorially separable. The duration of the union is, again, of importance because the dyadic federations that failed did so at their very beginning.

To be clear, based on these findings, we are not arguing that the survival of a dyadic federation is inherently a good thing. Instead we argue that, under the aforementioned conditions, federalism can be a successful institutional arrangement for a bipolar polity when its survival as a state is desired or without a viable alternative.

These findings have several implications for existing and future studies. First, the findings reaffirm the necessity for political scientists to pay attention to the geographic particularities of the territory they are studying (Coakley 2012). That the stabilising potential of political geography is often imposed rather than chosen can be interpreted as yet another paradox of democratic peace. Second, the findings cut through the debate between consociationalists and centripetalists in that both approaches could probably live with our findings. It appears indeed that group-based (executive inclusiveness), cross-group (national party systems) and mixed accommodative mechanisms (electoral proportionality) all contribute to the stability of dyadic federations, and that even for the latter, consociationalism and centripetalism might be 'rather friends than foes' (Bogaards 2019). Third, the 'political economy of regionalism' (Keating 2013) is a concept that can very well be applied to the study of dyadic federation when an equal distribution of economic resources is envisioned as a stabilising factor preventing both greed and grievance (Gurr 1993, 2015). Finally, the analysis shows that there seems to be something like a 'seven-year itch' for dyadic federations. Among the five failed federations identified in this study, four broke up within seven years (Czechoslovakia, the Federation of Malaysia, Senegambia and Serbia and Montenegro). Only Cyprus made it a little longer (14 years) and may have perhaps remained intact longer without external kin-state influence (cf. *supra*).

Before fully concluding this study, two further considerations are necessary. First, while the explanation of when dyadic federations survived relied on a rather solid set of cases that was well distributed on the different conditions, the number of cases explaining when dyadic federations broke up is somewhat limited. Therefore, counterfactual reasoning for this group of cases was not possible in some instances and the accompanying conclusions should thus be interpreted accordingly. Secondly, the cases under study are not immutable realities and even if political engineering solutions are path-dependent (Pierson 2000), this does not discount the possibility of exogenous shocks or of endogenous conditions changing extremely quickly and deeply. After all, between Duchacek's study in 1988 and today, some cases have evolved quite dramatically. Needless to say it is also quite possible that other cases might also evolve in the future.

It is not necessary, though, to wait for these changes to occur in order to continue studying dyadic federations. In light of the present findings, future studies might for instance want to dig further into particular cases like Trinidad and Tobago (to explain why this federation did not break up despite what one would have expected from a comparative perspective). Additionally, this study's findings also open the possibility for a comparison with non-dyadic federations or bipolar polities without federal power-sharing agreements with the aim of assessing the prospects of dyadic federalism vis-à-vis alternative institutional arrangements or contexts. We hope that this chapter has paved some of the way to these and other potential studies on the prospects of federalism and power-sharing arrangements in deeply diverse democracies.

# APPENDIX

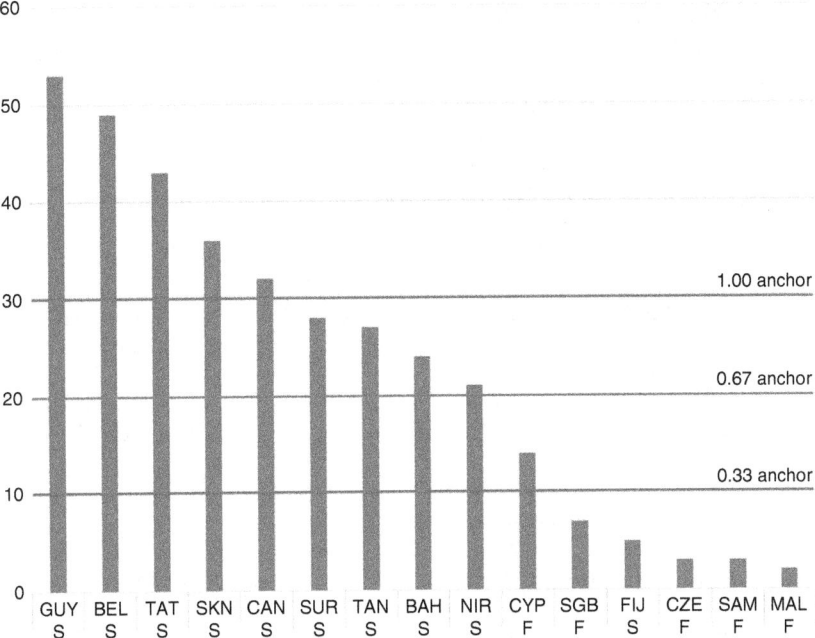

**Fig. 3.3** Number of years that the cases remained intact as of today. S = succeeded, F = failed

# REFERENCES

Anderson, Benedict. 1983. *Imagined Communities: Reflections on the Origin and Spread of Nationalism*. London and New York: Verso.

Bahcheli, Tozun, and Sid Noel. 2013. The Quest for a Political Settlement in Cyprus: Is a Dyadic Federation Viable? *Publius: The Journal of Federalism* 44 (4): 659–680.

Beaufays, Jean. 1988. Belgium: A Dualist Political System? *Publius: The Journal of Federalism* 18 (2): 63–73.

Berg-Schlosser, Dirk, Gisèle De Meur, Benoît Rihoux, and Charles C. Ragin. 2009. Qualitative Comparative Analysis (QCA) as an Approach. In *Configurational Comparative Methods. Qualitative Comparative Analysis (QCA) and Related Techniques*, ed. Benoît Rihoux and Charles C. Ragin, 1–18. Thousand Oaks: Sage Publications.

Bieber, Florian. 2002. Aid Dependency in Bosnian Politics and Civil Society: Failures and Successes of Post-War Peacebuilding in Bosnia-Herzegovina. *Croatian International Relations Review* 8 (26/27): 25–29.

———. 2003. The Challenge of Institutionalizing Ethnicity in the Western Balkans: Managing Change in Deeply Divided Societies. *European Yearbook of Minority Issues Online* 3 (1): 89–107.

Bogaards, Matthijs. 2019. Consociationalism and Centripetalism: Friends or Foes? *Swiss Political Science Review* 25 (4): 519–537.

Bryant, Rebecca. 2011. *The Past in Pieces: Belonging in the New Cyprus*. Philadelphia and Oxford: University of Pennsylvania Press.

Burgess, Michael. 2006. *Comparative Federalism: Theory and Practice*. London: Routledge.

Caluwaerts, Didier, and Min Reuchamps. 2015. Combining Federalism with Consociationalism: Is Belgian Consociational Federalism Digging Its Own Grave? *Ethnopolitics* 14 (3): 277–295.

Cameron, Greg. 2019. Zanzibar in the Tanzania Union. In *Secessionism in African Politics*, ed. Lotje de Vries, Pierre Englebert, and Mareike Schomerus, 179–205. Cham: Palgrave Macmillan.

Coakley, John. 2012. *Nationalism, Ethnicity and the State: Making and Breaking Nations*. London and Thousand Oaks: Sage.

Deschouwer, Kris. 2012. *The Politics of Belgium: Governing a Divided Society, Comparative Government and Politics Series*. 2nd ed. Houndmills: Palgrave Macmillan.

Duchacek, Ivo D. 1988. Dyadic Federations and Confederations. *Publius: The Journal of Federalism* 18 (2): 5–31.

Elazar, Daniel Judah. 1988. Introduction. *Publius: The Journal of Federalism* 18 (2): 1–3.

Erk, Jan, and Alain-G. Gagnon. 2000. Constitutional Ambiguity and Federal Trust: The Codification of Federalism in Belgium, Canada and Spain. *Regional & Federal Studies* 10 (1): 92–111.

Fournier, Bernard, and Min Reuchamps, eds. 2009. *Le fédéralisme en Belgique et au Canada. Comparaison sociopolitique, Ouvertures sociologiques*. Bruxelles: De Boeck Université.

Fraenkel, Jon. 2006. Power Sharing in Fiji and New Caledonia. In *Globalisation and Governance in the Pacific Islands: State, Society and Governance in Melanesia*, ed. Stewart Firth. Canberra: Australian National University Press.

Fraenkel, Jon, and Bernard Grofman. 2006. Does the Alternative Vote Foster Moderation in Ethnically Divided Societies? The Case of Fiji. *Comparative Political Studies* 39 (5): 623–651.

Fraser, John M. 2003. Serbia and Montenegro: How Much Sovereignty? What Kind of Association? *International Journal* 58 (2): 373–388.

Freedom House. 2018. *Freedom in the World 2018. Democracy in Crisis*. Freedom House. Accessed 16 October 2018. https://freedomhouse.org/report/freedom-world/freedom-world-2018.

Gagnon, Alain-G, ed. 2006. *Le fédéralisme canadien contemporain: fondements, traditions, institutions, Paramètres*. Montréal: Presses de l'Université de Montréal.

Gallagher, Michael. 2018. *Least Squares Index*. Trinity College Dublin. Accessed 16 October 2018. https://www.tcd.ie/Political_Science/people/michael_gallagher/ElSystems/Docts/lsq.php.

Gordon, Roger H., and Julie Berry Cullen. 2012. Income Redistribution in a Federal System of Governments. *Journal of Public Economics* 96 (11–12): 1100–1109.

Guelke, Adrian. 2012. *Politics in Deeply Divided Societies*. Cambridge: Polity Press.

Gurr, Ted Robert. 1993. Why Minorities Rebel: A Global Analysis of Communal Mobilization and Conflict since 1945. *International Political Science Review* 14 (2): 161–201.

———. 2015. *Why Men Rebel*. New York: Routledge.

Hale, Henry E. 2004. Divided We Stand: Institutional Sources of Ethnofederal State Survival and Collapse. *World Politics* 56 (2): 165–193.

Hinds, David. 2011. *Ethno-politics and Power Sharing in Guyana: History and Discourse*. Washington: New Academia Publishing.

Hoefte, Rosemarijn. 2013. *Suriname in the Long Twentieth Century: Domination, Contestation, Globalization*. New York: Palgrave Macmillan.

Horowitz, Donald L. 1993. Democracy in Divided Societies. *Journal of Democracy* 4 (4): 18–38.

Hughes, Arnold. 1992. The Collapse of the Senegambian Confederation. *Journal of Commonwealth & Comparative Politics* 30 (2): 200–222.

Hulsey, John, and Dejan Stjepanović. 2017. Bosnia and Herzegovina: An Archetypical Example of an Ethnocracy. In *Regional and National Elections in Eastern Europe*, ed. Arjan Schakel, 35–58. London: Palgrave Macmillan.

Innes, Abby. 1997. The Breakup of Czechoslovakia: The Impact of Party Development on the Separation of the State. *East European Politics and Societies* 11 (3): 393–435.

Josey, Alex. 2013. *Lee Kuan Yew: The Crucial Years*. Singapore: Marshall Cavendish.

Karmis, Dimitrios, and Alain-G. Gagnon. 1996. Fédéralisme et identités collectives au Canada et en Belgique: des itinéraires différents, une fragmentation similaire. *Canadian Journal of Political Science/Revue canadienne de science politique* 29 (3): 435–468.

Keating, Michael. 2013. The Political Economy of Regionalism. In *The Political Economy of Regionalism*, ed. John Loughlin and Michael Keating, 17–40. London and New York: Routledge.

Keil, Soeren. 2016. *Multinational Federalism in Bosnia and Herzegovina*. London and New York: Routledge.

Kim, Julie. 2006. *Serbia and Montenegro Union: Background and Pending Dissolution (CRS Report)*. Washington: Congress of the United States of America.

Lederach, John Paul. 1997. *Sustainable Reconciliation in Divided Societies*. Washington, DC: U.S. Institute of Peace Press.

Leslie, Peter M. 1988. Bicommunalism and Canadian Constitutional Reform. *Publius: The Journal of Federalism* 18 (2): 115–129.

Lijphart, Arend. 1977. *Democracies in Plural Societies. A Comparative Exploration*. New Haven and London: Yale University Press.

———. 1995. Self-Determination versus Pre-Determination of Ethnic Minorities in Power-Sharing Systems. In *The Rights of Minority Cultures*, ed. Will Kymlicka, 275–287. New York: Oxford University Press.

———. 2004. Constitutional Design for Divided Societies. *Journal of Democracy* 15 (2): 96–109.

Macek-Mackova, Emanuela. 2011. Challenges in Conflict Management in Multiethnic States–The Dissolution of Czechoslovakia and Serbia and Montenegro. *Nationalities Papers* 39 (4): 615–633.

Midgett, Douglas. 2005. The Nevis Secession Vote: The Search for Explanations. *Journal of Eastern Caribbean Studies* 30 (4): 77–86.

Milne, Robert Stephen. 1988. Bicommunal Systems: Guyana, Malaysia, Fiji. *Publius: The Journal of Federalism* 18 (2): 101–113.

Nassor, Aley Soud, and Jim Jose. 2014. Power-Sharing in Zanzibar: From Zero-Sum Politics to Democratic Consensus? *Journal of Southern African Studies* 40 (2): 247–265.

Oberschall, Anthony. 2007. *Conflict and Peace Building in Divided Societies: Responses to Ethnic Violence*. London: Routledge.

Özgür, Ergün, Nur Köprülü, and Min Reuchamps. 2019. Drawing Cyprus: Power-Sharing, Identity and Expectations among the Next Generation in Northern Cyprus. *Mediterranean Politics* 24 (2): 237–259. https://doi.org/1 0.1080/13629395.2017.1404720.

Pierson, Paul. 2000. Increasing Returns, Path Dependence, and the Study of Politics. *American Political Science Review* 94 (2): 251–267.

Premdas, Ralph R. 1998. *Secession and Self-determination in the Caribbean: Nevis and Tobago*. Kingston: University of the West Indies Press.

———. 2002. Identity in an Ethnically Bifurcated State: Trinidad and Tobago. In *Ethnonational Identities*, ed. Steve Fenton and Stephan May, 176–197. London: Palgrave Macmillan.

Ragin, Charles, and Benoît Rihoux, eds. 2009. *Configurational Comparative Methods: Qualitative Comparative Analysis (QCA) and Related Techniques*. Thousand Oaks: Sage.

Reilly, Benjamin. 2001. *Democracy in Divided Societies: Electoral Engineering for Conflict Management, Theories of Institutional Design*. Cambridge: Cambridge University Press.

Reuchamps, Min. 2007. La parité linguistique au sein du conseil des ministres. *Res Publica* 49 (4): 602–627.

———. 2011. *L'avenir du fédéralisme en Belgique et au Canada. Quand les citoyens en parlent, Diversitas*. Bruxelles: P.I.E.-Peter Lang.

———. 2013. Structures institutionnelles du fédéralisme belge. In *Le fédéralisme belge: Enjeux institutionnels, acteurs socio-politiques et opinions publiques*, ed. Régis Dandoy, Geoffroy Matagne, and Caroline Van Wynsberghe, 29–61. Louvain-la-Neuve: Academia-L'Harmattan.

———, ed. 2015. *Minority Nations in Multinational Federations: A Comparative Study of Quebec and Wallonia, Routledge Series in Federal Studies*. Abingdon and New York: Routledge.

Reuchamps, Min, and François Onclin. 2009. La fédération belge. In *Le fédéralisme en Belgique et au Canada. Comparaison sociopolitique*, ed. Bernard Fournier and Min Reuchamps, 21–40. Bruxelles: De Boeck Université.

Reynolds, Andrew, and Ben Reilly. 1999. *Electoral Systems and Conflict in Divided Societies*. Washington, DC: National Academies Press.

Richmond, Edmun B. 1993. Senegambia and the Confederation: History, Expectations, and Disillusions. *Journal of Third World Studies* 10 (2): 172–194.

Roeder, Philip G., and Donald S. Rothchild, eds. 2005. *Sustainable Peace: Power and Democracy after Civil Wars*. Ithaca and London: Cornell University Press.

Ruane, Joseph, and Jennifer Todd. 1996. *The Dynamics of Conflict in Northern Ireland: Power, Conflict and Emancipation*. Cambridge: Cambridge University Press.

Ryan, Selwyn. 2002. Power Sharing in the Caribbean: The Search for Equity and Security. *Caribbean Dialogue* 8 (1/2): 1–63.

Salih, Halil Ibrahim. 2013. *Reshaping of Cyprus: A Two-State Solution*. Bloomington: Xlibris.

Schmitt, David E. 1991. Problems of Accommodation in Bicommunal Societies. *Journal of Conflict Studies* 11 (4): 7–18.

Schneider, Carsten Q., and Claudius Wagemann. 2012. *Set-Theoretic Methods for the Social Sciences. A Guide to Qualitative Comparative Analysis*. Cambridge: Cambridge University Press.

Singh, Chaitram. 2008. Re-democratization in Guyana and Suriname: Critical Comparisons. *European Review of Latin American and Caribbean Studies* (84): 71–85.

Stroschein, Sherrill. 2003. What Belgium Can Teach Bosnia: The Uses of Autonomy in Divided House States. *Journal of Ethnopolitics and Minority Issues in Europe* 3: 1–30.

Taylor, Rupert. 2009. *Consociational theory: McGarry and O'Leary and the Northern Ireland conflict.* London: Routledge.

Trimikliniotis, Nicos, and Umut Bozkurt. 2012. *Beyond a Divided Cyprus: A State and Society in Transformation.* Basingstoke: Palgrave Macmillan.

Watts, Ronald L. 2000. Federalism and Diversity in Canada. In *Autonomy and Ethnicity. Negotiating Competing Claims in Multi-ethnic States,* ed. Yash Ghai. Cambridge and New York: Cambridge University Press.

———. 2008. *Comparing Federal Systems.* Montreal and Kingston: McGill-Queen's University Press.

## CHAPTER 4

# Assessing the Spanish State's Response to Catalan Independence: The Application of Federal Coercion

*Lucía Payero-López*

## INTRODUCTION

This chapter focuses on the territorial dimension of the ongoing constitutional crisis in Spain. The crisis began in 2010 when the Constitutional Court ruled on the reform of the Catalan Statute of Autonomy.[1] Many Catalans interpreted this ruling as an unwarranted interference in regional autonomy and started to believe that within the current constitutional framework no deepening in self-government would ever be possible. As a

---

[1] A statute of autonomy is the 'basic institutional rule' (Article 147.1 of the Constitution) of an autonomous community, in which the assumption of legislative and executive powers by the regional institutions is established. As part of the state legal system—they are organic acts (Article 147.3 of the Constitution)—, statutes of autonomy are subordinate to the Constitution. The amendment of a statute of autonomy requires both the approval from the regional legislature and from the central Parliament.

---

L. Payero-López (✉)
University of Granada, Granada, Spain
e-mail: payero@ugr.es

© The Author(s) 2020
A.-G. Gagnon, A. Tremblay (eds.), *Federalism and National Diversity in the 21st Century*, Federalism and Internal Conflicts,
https://doi.org/10.1007/978-3-030-38419-7_4

result, support for independence increased exponentially in Catalonia and a number of political initiatives were taken in order to hold a referendum on Catalan independence. Since Spanish political and judicial institutions prevented the referendum from taking place, a majority in the Catalan Parliament decided to seek to unilaterally *disconnect* from Spain. On the basis of Catalan law—deemed unconstitutional from the Spanish standpoint—a consultation was called on October 1, 2017 and, in compliance with its results, independence was then declared. The response of the central authorities consisted in applying an exceptional mechanism established in Article 155 of the Spanish Constitution: *federal coercion*.

What is federal coercion? Why was federal coercion implemented? How has federal coercion been applied to combat Catalan nationalism? What are the consequences of the application of federal coercion? In addressing these questions, this chapter is divided into four parts. Part 1 provides a contextualisation of the territorial dimension of the constitutional crisis which has afflicted Spain since 2010. Part 2 explains how and why Article 155 was applied in Catalonia in 2017. Part 3 argues that the actual application of Article 155 severely affected the territorial Constitution and the right to autonomy and, accordingly, outlines a series of excesses committed by the Agreement of the Council of Ministers and the Senate. In light of this argument, Part 4 of this chapter shows what this particular interpretation of Article 155 reveals about Spanish political culture and constitutionalism at the outset of the twenty-first century.

## HISTORICAL CONTEXT

Spain's constitutional crisis affects not only the territorial organisation of the state, but also the parliamentary system, the monarchy, and the economic dimensions that are part and parcel of the constitution (i.e. the pillars of the welfare state and the protection of social rights). However, and as noted above, this chapter focuses exclusively on the constitutional crisis as it relates to Spain's territorial constitution.[2]

---

[2] It is significant to note that the territorial constitution was not defined in the text adopted in 1978, as Pérez-Royo has pointed out (2018, 215). On the contrary, the territorial constitution was established by means of the statutes of autonomy. In the Constitution there is a 'constituent commitment (…) by which the right to autonomy of the nationalities and regions of which it [the state] is composed [as enshrined in Article 2 of the Constitution] is recognised. [However], that commitment had still to be developed. Just after the Constitution came into effect, between 1979 and 1981, the first Autonomic Agreements were signed and the organisation of the state was set up within the scope and limits determined by the

This facet of the constitutional crisis is the culmination of a number of successive developments, the first of which took place in 2006. At this point in time, the Catalan Statute of Autonomy, originally promulgated in 1979, was reformed in a three-fold process: first, a draft statute was passed by the Catalan legislature; second, the Spanish Parliament approved the draft statute after having introduced a number of substantial changes[3]; third, the people of Catalonia ratified the bill in a region-wide referendum.[4] All the while, the *Partido Popular*, the country's main right-wing party, refused to take part in this process. Consequently, when the statute entered into force, the *Partido Popular* immediately challenged it before the Constitutional Court.[5] When the Constitutional Court issued its ruling in 2010,[6] it specified the correct interpretation of many of the statute's Articles, but also declared other Articles to be unconstitutional.

Constitution.' In Pérez-Royo's opinion, Autonomic Agreements had a constituent nature only from a material point of view, but not from a formal one. That is the central reason why 'the legitimacy of origin of the State of the Autonomies is weak. (…) During the first three decades of its existence, this lack of legitimacy of origin was compensated for by its strong legitimacy of exercise, particularly because those matters closely connected with the welfare state (health and education) fell within the Autonomous Communities' remit (…). Economic crisis in 2008 led also to a crisis of the welfare state, which negatively affected the State of the Autonomies. As the legitimacy of exercise had weakened, the absence of a legitimacy of origin suddenly emerged, which seriously reduced chances of finding a solution to the constitutional problems that confront Spain at the moment' (2018, 215–216).

[3] In fact, changes were introduced by the Constitutional Commission in the Congress of Deputies. Once the bill had been approved by the majority of deputies (those belonging to the *Partido Socialista Obrero Español, Convergència i Unió, Iniciativa per Catalunya Verds, Izquierda Unida, Partido Nacionalista Vasco, Coalición Canaria*, and *Bloque Nacionalista Galego*), the Senate passed it with no modifications. It is interesting to note that amendments were so significant that *Esquerra Republicana de Catalunya*, one of the political parties that had led the initiative to amend the Statute of Autonomy in the Catalan legislature, finally voted down the bill in the Congress of Deputies and campaigned for a no vote in the referendum. This party argued that the text passed in Catalonia had been denaturalised.

[4] Organic Act 6/2006, July 19, on the reform of the Statute of Autonomy of Catalonia. English version available at: https://web.gencat.cat/en/generalitat/estatut/estatut2006/.

[5] The *Partido Popular* had previously appealed the decision adopted by the *Mesa* (Bureau)—the *Mesa* is 'a collective body, which includes the President and representatives of various political groups, that organises the parliamentary affairs from an administrative point of view' (Ferreres 2013, 105)—in the Congress by which the proposal of reforming the Statute of Autonomy of Catalonia was accepted for consideration. The *Partido Popular* argued that the proposal was in fact an attempt to reform the Constitution covertly. The argument was rejected by the Constitutional Court Auto 85/2006, March 15 (available at: http://hj.tribunalconstitucional.es/eu/Resolucion/Show/20719).

[6] Constitutional Court Judgment (CCJ for short) 31/2010, June 28. English version available at: https://www.tribunalconstitucional.es/ResolucionesTraducidas/31-2010,%20 of%20June%2028.pdf.

Catalans understood this ruling to be a direct attack against Catalonia's self-government and started to demand a referendum on independence.[7] And, in December 2012, *Convergència i Unió*, the right-wing leaning nationalist party governing in Catalonia at the time, signed a governability accord with *Esquerra Republicana de Catalunya*, a left-wing nationalist party in Catalonia, whereby both parties committed themselves to call an independence referendum in 2014.[8]

Following that, the Catalan Parliament requested that power to call a referendum be delegated to it by the Congress of Deputies (i.e. the lower house of the Spanish legislature) given that, according to the Spanish Constitution, referendum calls fall within the state's jurisdiction (Article 149.1, 32nd). The request was rejected[9] and, as a result, the Catalan legislature adopted a number of legislative initiatives with a view to hold the independence referendum.

In September 2014, the Catalan Parliament passed the *Act of non-referendum popular consultations* in order to circumvent the state's jurisdiction on matters of referenda.[10] Following this, the Government of Catalonia issued Decree 129/2014 on September 27, 2014 thus calling for a 'non-referendum popular consultation' to decide the political future of Catalonia.[11] The 'non-referendum popular consultation' vote took

[7] As Pérez-Royo has remarked, the CCJ 31/2010 broke the territorial compact that was at the basis of the Constitution (2011). According to the territorial Constitution, the referendum was the final step for the reform of the statute of autonomy; nonetheless, once the Constitutional Court altered that procedure, the referendum became the first step of a new process in which the relationship between Catalonia and the rest of Spain would be redefined. That is why the so-called right to decide—an individual right, aimed to call a referendum and founded on the state legal framework (the Constitution, where freedom of speech and the right to political participation are recognised, and the CCJ 42/2014, March 25)—is now a sine qua non for many people in Catalonia, even for those who are not in favour of independence. For an extensive analysis of the right to decide, see Barceló et al. (2015).

[8] Available at: https://file.lavanguardia.com/extl/file01/2012/12/18/54356471159-url.pdf.

[9] Journal of Sessions of the Congress of Deputies no 192, April 8, 2014 (available at: http://www.congreso.es/public_oficiales/L10/CONG/DS/PL/DSCD-10-PL-192.PDF).

[10] Act 10/2014, September 26, of non-referendum popular consultations and other forms of citizen participation, passed by the Catalan Parliament (available at: https://www.boe.es/diario_boe/txt.php?id=BOE-A-2015-2743).

[11] Decree 129/2014, September 27, for the call of a popular consultation on the political future of Catalonia, enacted by the President of the Catalan Government (available at: https://portaljuridic.gencat.cat/eli/es-ct/d/2014/09/27/129).

place on November 9, 2014 (commonly referred to as 9-N), at which point citizens were asked two interrelated questions: 'Do you want Catalonia to become a state? If so, do you want that state to be independent?' In total, 2,305,290 votes were cast with 80.8% of the total number of votes answering 'yes' to both questions.[12]

Despite these results, and as I have argued elsewhere (Payero 2015), the consultation lacked the legal guarantees of a referendum and it therefore, in actuality, bore more resemblance to an opinion poll. In the three years that followed the vote at the 'non-referendum popular consultation,' a series of sudden developments further contributed to Spain's current constitutional crisis and led to the Spanish government's decision to implement federal coercion.

First, the 2015 regional election, held on September 27, was promoted by nationalist parties in Catalonia as a plebiscite on independence; at the election, pro-independence nationalist parties gained the majority of seats in the regional legislature (although they did not obtain the majority of votes),[13] which granted them a fair amount of leeway to pave the path for *disconnection* with the rest of Spain. Second, in November 2015, the Catalan Parliament approved a motion to initiate negotiations with the central government in Spain in order to create an independent state in the form of a republic in Catalonia.[14] Third, and due to the failure of these negotiations to actually take place, the Catalan Parliament passed two bills, the Act on the referendum of self-determination[15] and the Act on the juridical transition,[16] in September 2017. Fourth, a referendum was then

[12] Official data are available at: http://www.participa2014.cat/resultats/dades/cs/escr tot.html.

[13] The alliance *Junts pel Sí* and *Candidatura d'Unitat Popular-Crida Constituent* obtained 72 seats out of 135, but only the 47.8% of votes.

[14] Resolution 1/XI of the Catalan Parliament on the beginning of the political process in Catalonia as a consequence of the electoral results on September 27, 2015 (available at: http://www.parlament.cat/document/activitat/153122.pdf).

[15] Act 19/2017, September 6, on the referendum of self-determination (English version available at: http://exteriors.gencat.cat/web/.content/00_ACTUALITAT/notes_context/Law-19_2017-on-the-Referendum-on-Self-determination.pdf). It was declared unconstitutional on October 17, 2017 by the CCJ 114/2017 (English version available at: https://www.tribunalconstitucional.es/ResolucionesTraducidas/Ley%20referendum%20ENGLISH.pdf).

[16] Act 20/2017, September 8, on the juridical transition and founding of the Republic (English version available at: http://exteriors.gencat.cat/web/.content/00_ACTUALITAT/notes_context/Law-20_2017-on-Juridical-Transition.pdf). The Constitutional Court outlawed

held on October 1, 2017 (known as 1-O) during which 2,044,038 Catalans (or close to 91% of total votes cast) opted for secession.[17] Fifth, and in compliance with the Act on the referendum,[18] Carles Puigdemont, President of the Government of Catalonia, addressed the Catalan legislature to ask for a suspension of the declaration of independence which had been signed on October 10, 2017 and that expressed, albeit in a symbolic manner,[19] the government of Catalonia's adherence to the will of the people; in suspending the declaration, Puigdemont's government aimed to initiate a period of dialogue with the Spanish government. However, instead of engaging in a dialogue with the government of Catalonia, the Spanish central government resorted to implementing *federal coercion* on that very same day; this meant that it imposed direct rule on Catalonia for seven months (from October 27, 2017 to June 2, 2018). In response to the central government's decision, the majority of the Catalan legislature formally declared independence, but with no legal or political effects.[20]

## What Is Federal Coercion?

Federal coercion is an institution that is viewed (see Ridao 2018) as a tool that plural states—both federal and regional—can use in exceptional cases either to ensure that sub-state entities meet constitutional obligations and/or to safeguard the general interest of the state. Federal coercion

it by the CCJ 124/2017, November 8 (English version available at: https://www.tribunalconstitucional.es/ResolucionesTraducidas/Ley%20transitoriedad%20ENGLISH.pdf).

[17] Official data are available at: https://estaticos.elperiodico.com/resources/pdf/4/3/1507302086634.pdf?_ga=2.177408613.1521946470.1566584123-414068493.1566584122.

[18] Article 4.4 of the Act on the referendum stated: 'If the count of votes validly cast gives a result of more affirmative than negative votes, this shall mean the independence of Catalonia. To this end, the Parliament of Catalonia shall, within two days of the proclamation of the results by the Electoral Commission, hold an ordinary session to issue the formal declaration of independence of Catalonia and its effects and resolve upon the commencement of the constituent process.'

[19] English version available at: http://www.cataloniavotes.eu/wp-content/uploads/2017/10/27-Declaration-of-Independence.pdf. Puigdemont's speech can be read here: http://exteriors.gencat.cat/ca/ambits-dactuacio/afers_exteriors/delegacions_govern/franca/actualitat/noticia/Compareixenca-MHP-Parlament.

[20] An indication of this lack of effects of the declaration of independence was the fact that even the Spanish flag remained waving at the head office of the *Generalitat* in Barcelona, while thousands of people rallied to celebrate the birth of the new republic.

therefore potentially involves a number of concurrent measures that the central state can adopt against regional political and administrative bodies with the aim of forcing them to comply with the obligations that the Constitution or other laws impose on all regions, provided of course that a specific region has actually violated these obligations (Ballart 1987).

In Spain—a regionally plural state where some powers have been devolved to the autonomous communities[21]—federal coercion is contained in Article 155 of the Constitution.[22] Article 155 reads as follows:

1. If a Self-governing Community does not fulfil the obligations imposed upon it by the Constitution or other laws, or acts in a way that is seriously prejudicial to the general interest of Spain, the Government, after having lodged a complaint with the President of the Self-governing Community and failed to receive satisfaction therefore, may, following approval granted by the overall majority of the Senate, take all measures necessary to compel the Community to meet said obligations, or to protect the abovementioned general interest.

[21] The distribution of powers between the central state and the autonomous communities is established in Articles 148–149 of the Constitution. Each autonomous community can include in its respective statute of autonomy the particular competences it is going to exercise provided that Articles 148–149 of the Constitution are respected. Most autonomous communities have actually assumed the maximum level of powers available.

[22] Article 155 is a provision directly inspired by Article 37 of the German Constitution. Article 37 of the German Constitution reads: '(1) If a Land fails to comply with its obligations under this Basic Law or other federal laws, the Federal Government, with the consent of the Bundesrat, may take the necessary steps to compel the Land to comply with its duties. (2) For the purpose of implementing such coercive measures, the Federal Government or its representative shall have the right to issue instructions to all Länder and their authorities.' In fact the German influence was explicitly mentioned during the elaboration of the Spanish Constitution. Pérez-Llorca, deputy of *Unión de Centro Democrático* (the party in office at that time) in the constituent period of sessions, expressly admitted that Article 155 'is a quasi literal translation of a provision of the Constitution of the Federal Republic of Germany' (Journal of Sessions of the Congress of Deputies, no 91, June 16, 1978, p. 3416—available at: http://www.congreso.es/public_oficiales/L0/CONG/DS/C_1978_091.PDF). Most scholars agree on the similarities between both provisions (for instance, García-Torres 1984; Ballart 1987; Gil-Robles 1999; Fernández-Rodera 2003; Vírgala 2005; Ridao 2018; Lafuente 2018; Albertí 2018). In Vírgala's words, 'the Spanish model (…) can be included, with certain differences [divergences that are put forward in his article], in the model of the German federal execution' (2005, 59).

2. With a view to implementing the measures provided for in the foregoing paragraph, the Government may issue instructions to all the
   authorities of the Self-governing Communities.[23]

The Spanish government decided to activate Article 155 immediately
after a majority in the Catalan Parliament signed the symbolic declaration
of independence on October 10, 2017. In order to comply with the
requirements of this provision, the Spanish central government sent a letter to President Carles Puigdemont on October 11 wherein he was asked
whether or not independence had actually been declared in Catalonia.[24]
The letter provided the Catalan President with a five-day window to
respond and it noted that silence would be interpreted as a response in the
affirmative. The letter also ordered that Puigdemont revoke a declaration
of independence (assuming independence had been declared) and restore
constitutional order within three days.

Although the Catalan President issued two letters in response,[25] it was
the central government's opinion that he had failed to answer their letter
in a clear manner; it was therefore decided by the central executive to continue to apply federal coercion in the form of Article 155. On October 21,
the Council of Ministers approved the 'necessary measures'[26] to compel

---

[23] The procedure to implement Article 155 is developed in Article 189 of the Standing
Orders of the Senate (*Texto Refundido del Reglamento del Senado aprobado por la Mesa del
Senado, oída la Junta de Portavoces,* on May 3, 1994). English version available at: http://
www.senado.es/web/conocersenado/normas/reglamentootrasnormassenado/detalles-
reglamentosenado/index.html?lang=en.

[24] The petition can be read here: https://www.lamoncloa.gob.es/consejodeministros/
Documents/11102017-requerimiento.pdf.

[25] Puigdemont sent a letter to Rajoy on October 16, 2017 with a couple of requests: first,
the end of political and judicial repression in Catalonia; second, an appointment aimed to
conclude an agreement on the Catalan conflict (available at: https://www.elnacional.cat/
es/politica/carta-puigdemont-rajoy_202215_102.html). The letter was answered by the
Spanish Prime Minister on the same day (available at: https://www.lamoncloa.gob.es/presi-
dente/actividades/Documents/2017/161017RespuestaRajoy.pdf), and there was even a
second letter written by Puigdemont on October 19, 2017 in which he threatened to vote
the declaration of independence in the Catalan Parliament—whose effects had been suspended at that time—should attempts of dialogue be thwarted and repression continue
(available at: https://estaticos.elperiodico.com/resources/pdf/9/4/1508399971849.
pdf?_ga=2.40447137.2081363125.1559406558-1242467289.1559406557).

[26] Order PRA/1034/2017, October 27, by which the Agreement of the Council of
Ministers of October 21, 2017 is published (available at: https://www.boe.es/buscar/doc.
php?id=BOE-A-2017-12328).

Catalonia to meet constitutional obligations and to comply with the general interest of Spain under Article 155. These measures (e.g. removal from office of the Catalan President and his cabinet, dissolution of the Catalan Parliament, suppression of a number of regional institutions) were ratified by 'the overall majority of the Senate,'[27] which included not only the majority seat-holding *Partido Popular* but also the *Partido Socialista Obrero Español* and *Ciudadanos-Partido de la Ciudadanía* (a right-wing and populist Spanish nationalist party).

Measures adopted by virtue of Article 155 included the removal from office of the President of Catalonia and his cabinet,[28] whose functions were assumed by the President of Spain—subsequently by the Vice-President of Spain—and by the rest of the Ministers of the central government, respectively.[29] The Catalan legislature was also dissolved and a regional election was called for December 21, 2017.[30] In addition, the central government removed a number of regional institutions, such as the Advisory Council for the National Transition, the Public Diplomacy Council of Catalonia, and the territorial Delegations of the Government of Catalonia abroad[31]; the only exception to this clampdown was

[27] Resolution of October 27, 2017, of the Presidency of the Senate, by which the Agreement of the Senate in Plenary Sitting, where the measures requested by the government under Article 155 of the Constitution are passed, is published (available at: https://www.boe.es/buscar/doc.php?id=BOE-A-2017-12327).

[28] Royal Decree 942/2017, October 27, in which, by virtue of the measures authorised by the Senate in Plenary Sitting regarding the *Generalitat* of Catalonia under the basis of Article 155 of the Constitution, the President of the *Generalitat* of Catalonia, Mr. Carles Puigdemont i Casamajó, is dismissed (available at: https://www.boe.es/diario_boe/txt.php?id=BOE-A-2017-12332); Royal Decree 943/2017, October 27, in which, by virtue of the measures authorised by the Senate in Plenary Sitting regarding the *Generalitat* of Catalonia under the basis of Article 155 of the Constitution, the Vice-President of the *Generalitat* of Catalonia and the members of the Council of Government of the *Generalitat* of Catalonia are dismissed (available at: https://www.boe.es/diario_boe/txt.php?id=BOE-A-2017-12333).

[29] Royal Decree 944/2017, October 27, by which several organs and authorities are entrusted with the enforcement of the measures imposed on the Government and the Administration of the *Generalitat* of Catalonia that were authorised by the Agreement of the Senate in Plenary Sitting, October 27, 2017 (available at: https://www.boe.es/buscar/doc.php?id=BOE-A-2017-12329).

[30] Royal Decree 946/2017, October 27, on the call for election to the Parliament of Catalonia and its dissolution (available at: https://www.boe.es/buscar/doc.php?id=BOE-A-2017-12330).

[31] Royal Decree 945/2017, October 27, by which several measures on the organisation of the *Generalitat* of Catalonia are adopted, and a number of high-ranking officials of the *Generalitat* of Catalonia are dismissed, by virtue of the measures authorised by the Senate in

Catalonia's Delegation to the European Union. The measures also meant that all the administrative acts of the *Generalitat* (i.e. the Catalan institutional system around which Catalonia's self-government is organised, comprising the Catalan Parliament, the President of Catalonia, and the Executive Council of Catalonia) would need to be pre-authorised. Administrative or parliamentary provisions published in the Official Gazette of the *Generalitat* of Catalonia or in the Official Bulletin of the Catalan Parliament without first being authorised or in contravention of the Resolution of October 27, 2017 of the Senate would not come into effect.

## How Has Article 155 Been Applied?

The Constitutional Court explicitly stated that Article 155 is an 'extraordinary mechanism of coercion' (CCJ 49/1988, March 22, Legal Basis 31st).[32] Accordingly, most legal scholars (e.g. Ballart 1987; Gil-Robles 1999; Calafell 2000; Álvarez 2016; Vintró 2019) argue that the institution of federal coercion should be seen as a last resort (i.e. ultima ratio) and that its implementation must be reduced to only the strict and necessary measures that can force an autonomous community to comply with the constitutional or legal obligations it is infringing and, at that, for only the minimum time required. In this sense, Article 155 does not confer unlimited powers on the central government to adopt any and all measures it deems necessary (Urías 2019).

The Spanish central government has offered its own interpretation of the application of federal coercion; the Spanish President has in fact stated that the government has implemented a 'soft' version of Article 155 (De-la-Hoz et al. 2017).[33] This chapter disputes this interpretation and

plenary sitting regarding the *Generalitat* of Catalonia under the basis of Article 155 of the Constitution (available at: https://www.boe.es/buscar/doc.php?id=BOE-A-2017-12334).

[32] On the contrary, a small group of academics holds that Article 155 is an ordinary mechanism by which the state could monitor the acts of the autonomous communities (García-de-Enterría 1983; García-Torres 1984). However, the Constitutional Court declared such interpretation—contained in the controversial *Proyecto de Ley Orgánica de Armonización del Proceso Autonómico* (Organic Bill of Harmonisation of the Autonomic Process, passed by the Congress of Deputies and the Senate on July 29, 1982)—unconstitutional (CCJ 76/1983, August 5).

[33] Even then, those media with a right-wing leaning criticised the government for the softness perceived in the implementation of federal coercion. See, for instance, *El Mundo* (2018).

argues, by contrast, that when one examines the procedure of federal coercion's application and the content of the measures of federal coercion, it becomes clear that the Spanish government has applied a particularly *hard* version of Article 155.

## The Procedure

A number of possible excesses in the actual application of federal coercion in Catalonia in 2017 come to light when examining the request made to the Catalan President on October 11, 2017, the Agreement of the Council of Ministers, and the Agreement of the Senate. In order to understand these excesses, it is necessary to refer back not only to the two provisions of Article 155 of the Constitution (highlighted above) but also to Article 189 of the Standing Orders of the Senate, which deals with the procedure to apply Article 155 of the Constitution. Article 189's five provisions are listed in Table 4.1.

### The Request to the Catalan President

The request made by the government to the Catalan President was probably beyond the pale given that measures to be adopted in case the petition was dismissed were absent. According to several scholars (Ballart 1987; Gil-Robles 1999; Vírgala 2005; Ridao 2018[34]; Albertí 2018; Vintró 2019), these measures should have been detailed in the letter, since the President of the autonomous community must be given the opportunity to conduct its defence on fair and equal terms. What is more, the previous request does not constitute 'a mere formal requisite;' it should be a 'warning,' as well as an 'opportunity for dialogue that eventually may lead to an agreement' (Albertí 2019, 103)—something that was explicitly proposed (by Puigdemont in his first letter) to and rejected by Mariano Rajoy, the then Spanish Prime Minister.

---

[34] Ridao particularly stresses the importance that the omission of the dissolution of the Catalan Parliament and the call of snap elections entailed, since they are exclusive powers of the regional President (2018). Carles Puigdemont might have decided to exercise them before October 27, 2017, which would have almost certainly prevented the Agreement of the Council of Ministers from being adopted and then approved by the Senate.

**Table 4.1**   Article 189 of the Standing Orders of the Senate

189.1 'If the Government, in the cases contemplated in Article 155.1 of the Constitution, requires the Senate's approval of the measures referred therein, it shall have to submit to the Speaker of the House a document indicating the contents and the scope of the proposed measures, as well as justify that the relevant petition to the President of the Autonomous Community has been made and further that the latter has failed to comply with the petition.'

189.2 'The Bureau of the Senate shall refer this document and the supporting documentation to the General Committee on Autonomous Communities, or else, shall create a joint Committee under the provisions established in Section 58 of the present Standing Orders.'

189.3 'The Committee, without prejudice to the provisions of Section 67, shall request, by the intermediary of the Speaker for the Senate, from the President of the Autonomous Community, the submission, within a term to be fixed, of all past records, data and allegations it may consider fit and, if deemed advisable, the appointment of the person who shall deputise to these effects.'

189.4 'The Committee shall table a reasoned proposal on whether it is advisable or not to grant the approval requested by the Government, with the conditions or the modifications which should be made, if necessary, in connection with the envisaged measures.'

189.5 'The Plenary Sitting of the House shall submit to debate the said proposal, with two turns pro and two turns against, of 20 minutes each, and speeches, lasting also 20 minutes, to be made by the Spokesmen of the Parliamentary Groups who wish to take the floor. Upon conclusions of the debate, a counting of the votes on the proposal in question shall be made, and the approval of the resolution shall only be granted if the result is a favourable vote by the absolute majority of the Senators.'

## The Agreement of the Council of Ministers

In all probability, the Agreement of the Council of Ministers[35] did not meet certain procedural requirements. First, and putting this Agreement in relation to the previous request, the events which warranted the resort to Article 155 were not clearly defined,[36] since there was no full coincidence

---

[35] Order PRA/1034/2017, October 27, by which the Agreement of the Council of Ministers of October 21, 2017 is published.

[36] The Constitution contemplates two different situations which can prompt the government to apply Article 155: the breach of constitutional or legal obligations, and the attack against the general interest of Spain. Scholars disagree on this point, where two positions can be distinguished. First, some authors hold that both situations can be considered as just one, since any violation of the general interest is in fact an infringement of the Constitution or the

between the legal violations mentioned in the request sent to Puigdemont on October 11 and those contained in the Agreement of the Council of Ministers 10 days later. Although Puigdemont was only asked whether independence had been declared—which, strictly speaking, is not a request—the Council of Ministers then made reference to the whole pro-sovereign process, and even added illegal/contrary-to-the-general-interest actions, including the flight of companies,[37] decrease in car sales, and fall in economic activity. In all likelihood, this course of action not only left the Catalan government defenceless for not having the opportunity to respond to the accusation, but also justified the resort to federal coercion on the basis of actions that in those days had already been suspended, nullified, or made void by the Constitutional Court[38] or the autonomic institutions.

Second, although Puigdemont answered the request of the Spanish government on two occasions (October 16 and 19), the Council of Ministers found his response to be both inadequate and insufficient and, in turn, the activation of Article 155 was maintained by the Senate. Despite the Catalan President willingness to open a period of dialogue and negotiation—although 'the President of the Catalan government did not answer in the restrictive terms that the Spanish government asked (...), there were elements [in his two letters] to consider that the request had been addressed' (Vintró 2019, 173)—the Council of Ministers rejected Puigdemont's reasoning with no argument whatsoever (Ridao 2018).

state laws (Albertí 1985; Ballart 1987). Second, for other academics there are two diverse cases in Article 155, which leads them to defend the adoption of different and more serious measures in case the general interest of Spain is breached (Cruz Villalón 1984; García Torres 1984). In the particular case this chapter analyses, both the central government and the Senate assumed that the two situations had occurred: the Catalan authorities ignored their constitutional and legal obligations, and their actions seriously damaged the general interest of Spain.

[37] However, it is not mentioned that the central government favoured this flight with the enactment of the Royal Decree-law 15/2017, October 6, of urgent measures on mobility of economic agents within the national territory (available at: https://www.boe.es/diario_boe/txt.php?id=BOE-A-2017-11501).

[38] For instance, the Act on the referendum of self-determination and the Act on the juridical transition are mentioned. The former had been declared unconstitutional on October 17, 2017 (CCJ 114/2017), while the operation of the latter had been suspended at that time by virtue of Article 161.2 of the Constitution, which reads: 'The Government may appeal to the Constitutional Court against provisions and resolutions adopted by the bodies of the Self-governing Communities, which shall bring about the suspension of the contested provisions or resolutions (...).'

## The Agreement of the Senate[39]

The Senate may have also breached several procedural rules. First, according to Article 189.1 of the Standing Orders of the Senate (see Table 4.1), the High Chamber should have checked that the formal requirements preceding the approval of coercive measures had been followed. However, the Senate did not make any objection to the lack of justification of Puigdemont's so-called 'failure' to comply with the government's petition.

Second, Article 189.3 (see Table 4.1) was likely infringed, since Puigdemont, as well as submitting 'all past records, data and allegations considered as relevant,' decided to appoint Ferran Mascarell, the delegate of the Catalan government in Madrid, to stand in for him at the Joint Commission of both the General Commission on Autonomous Communities and the Constitutional Commission.[40] However, the Joint Commission did not allow Mascarell to take part in the proceedings,[41] following a decision adopted by the *Mesa* (Bureau) and the *Junta de Portavoces* (Board of Spokespeople) of the Senate.[42] This decision left the *Generalitat* of Catalonia defenceless and transformed 'what should have been a discussion between the Senate and the Catalan government (…) in a parliamentarian debate' (Ridao 2018, 189) with two senators appointed to represent the *Generalitat* of Catalonia. The reason for prohibiting Mascarell's intervention has never been adequately justified—it has simply been adduced that Mascarell was not a member of the *Generalitat* and therefore ineligible in the first place (Albertí 2019).[43]

---

[39] Resolution of October 27, 2017, of the Presidency of the Senate, by which the Agreement of the Senate in Plenary Sitting, where the measures requested by the government under Article 155 of the Constitution are passed, is published.

[40] Allegations of the President of the *Generalitat* regarding the request made by the Spanish Government to the Senate in relation to Article 155 of the Constitution (Official Bulletin of the *Cortes Generales*, Senate, no 165, October 27, 2017. Available at: http://www.congreso.es/public_oficiales/L12/SEN/BOCG/2017/BOCG_D_12_165_1373.PDF).

[41] In Albertí's words, the negative of the Senate was a 'gratuitous burden' on the *Generalitat* of Catalonia (2018, 31).

[42] The *Junta de Portavoces* 'consists of spokespeople of all the parliamentary groups (each group has one spokesperson), together with the representatives of the Government. It is a political organ which organises the contacts between the legislative assembly and the executive branch, and fixes the parliamentary agenda' (Ferreres 2013, 105).

[43] On the basis of the speech delivered by one of the senators who opposed to the participation of Mascarell in the debate, Vintró speculates on 'resentment' (2019, 176) as the authentic reason that warranted the decision, given that Puigdemont did not attend the session

Third, and as a direct result of the vagueness of the enabling events contained in the Agreement of the Council of Ministers (events that amounted to the breach of Catalonia's constitutional obligations and were seriously prejudicial to the general interest of Spain), the measures adopted to redress the situation it created were equally imprecise. Due to this vagueness, the Senate even had to authorise the central government to adopt new measures in the future (Section II, subsection h of the Resolution of the Presidency of the Senate, October 27, 2017).

## The Content: Measures Adopted under the Aegis of Article 155

The two main measures adopted by the Council of Ministers and then approved by the Senate can be said to be unconstitutional for a few key reasons. The following sub-sections briefly explore both of these measures beginning with the destitution of the Catalan government and then moving onto the dissolution of the Catalan Parliament.

### *The Catalan Government*

Scholars (e.g. Sosa 1979; García-Torres 1984; Ballart 1987; Gil-Robles 1999; Álvarez 2016; Ridao 2018; Albertí 2019; Vintró 2019) generally agree that the central government's capacity to issue instructions to the authorities of the autonomous community, as contained in Article 155.2 of the Constitution, does not also allow the central government to remove these authorities from office. By all appearances then, the application of federal coercion in Catalonia followed the opinion of a minority group of academics who believe that 'the only limit that can be imposed on the measures adopted by the Senate is the suppression or unlimited suspension of the right to autonomy in a part of the Spanish territory (*Liquidation* in Germany or Direct Rule in Ulster)' (Vírgala 2005, 103).[44]

---

despite of having been personally invited to be there. In this sense, Senator Barreiro (*Partido Popular*) justified the negative of his parliamentary group to allow the representative appointed by Puigdemont to intervene in the debate on the following basis: 'it is a matter of respect to this House' (Journal of Sessions of the Senate no 183, October 26, 2017, p. 3— available at: http://www.congreso.es/public_oficiales/L12/SEN/DS/CO/DS_C_12_183.PDF).

[44] See also Cruz-Villalón (1984).

This very strict 'Italian reading of Article 155' (Albertí 2018, 19) is debatable for three reasons. First, Article 155.2 can only be applied if the authorities of the autonomous community are still in office to comply with the instructions that have been issued (García-de-Enterría and Fernández 2008; Ridao 2018). Consequently, it can be argued that in the absence of autonomic authorities no possibility of issuing instructions to the authorities of autonomous communities does exist.

Second, the removal of the Catalan government denaturalised the principle of autonomy contained in Article 2 of the Constitution,[45] as well as the parliamentary model of the autonomous communities designed in the so-called *constitutional bloc*.[46] Regarding the right to autonomy, the Constitutional Court has stated that autonomous communities enjoy political autonomy rather than simply being endowed with mere administrative autonomy (CCJ 25/1981, July 14, Legal Basis 3rd). One of the aspects of this political autonomy is the regional legislature's power to elect the President of the autonomous community from among its members (Article 152.1 of the Constitution and 67.2 of the Statute of Autonomy of Catalonia) as well as its capacity to dismiss this person. In brief:

> The President of the *Generalitat*'s term of office ends with renewal of Parliament following elections, the passing of a motion of censure or the defeat of a vote of confidence, death, resignation, permanent physical or mental disability acknowledged by Parliament rendering him or her unfit for office, or a confirmed criminal sentence rendering him or her unfit to hold any public office. (Article 67.7 of the Statute of Autonomy of Catalonia)

Consequently, the removal of the members of the Catalan government by the Spanish government and the assumption of their functions by the central authorities may actually entail a 'de facto suspension of the autonomy that is recognised to the Catalan Parliament, and of the powers

---

[45] Article 2 of the Constitution reads: 'The Constitution is based on the indissoluble unity of the Spanish Nation, the common and indivisible homeland of all Spaniards; it recognises and guarantees the right to self-government of the nationalities and regions of which it is composed and the solidarity among them all.'

[46] The expression *constitutional bloc* is used to make reference to the set of norms that, along with the Constitution, are used to delimit reserved from devolved matters, and also to determine the constitutionality of an act (Rubio-Llorente 1989). Statutes of autonomy are included in the constitutional bloc.

conferred on the President to appoint the members of his or her government' (Ridao 2018, 191). This would run contrary to Article 2 of the Constitution, whose 'materialisation requires that the higher institutions of an autonomous community are always preserved from any intervention of the state in the procedural regime of its bodies' (Vintró 2019, 170).

As for the parliamentary model of the autonomous communities, it is important to note that the regional government's legitimacy rests on the political support that the parliamentary majority confers on it.[47] This is why the Parliament elects and removes the President and also why the President exclusively is able to dissolve the Parliament and call for election whenever it fits his or her political interest (Article 75 of the Statute of Autonomy of Catalonia). As such, power relies both on parliamentary confidence vested in the President and the President's accountability to the regional legislature.

Third, given that the Statute of Autonomy is an organic act which epitomises the territorial compact between the state and the autonomous community, it cannot be modified or repealed by means of the unilateral will of one of the parties—in this case, the state. The procedure to reform the Statute of Autonomy of Catalonia is contained in Articles 222–223 of this institutional norm. Therefore, 'state government's instructions cannot alter the content of the basic institutional norm of Catalonia, in the sense that one of the powers of the President of the *Generalitat*, as stated in the Statute of Autonomy, is transformed without due reform of the Statute' (Ridao 2018, 190). Ultimately, Article 155 cannot be used either to revise the constitution or the constitutional bloc (Albertí 2018).

### The Catalan Parliament

In terms of comparative law, certain constitutions include mechanisms of federal coercion by which the central authorities are entitled to dissolve or take control of the self-governing organs of the sub-state regions in the

---

[47] This is the essence of the parliamentary system as contained in Article 152.1 of the Constitution: 'In the case of Statutes passed by means of the procedure referred to in the foregoing section [as it is the case of Catalonia], the institutional self-government organisation shall be based on a Legislative Assembly elected by universal suffrage under a system of proportional representation which shall also assure the representation of the various areas of the territory; an Executive Council with executive and administrative functions and a President elected by the Assembly among its members and appointed by the King (…).'

exceptional case that they breach the principle of federal loyalty.[48] One example that can be cited is Italy.[49] By contrast, other constitutions only authorise the central government to adopt those measures that are strictly necessary to compel the sub-state territory to meet its constitutional obligations, in particular by issuing enforceable instructions to the authorities of the *renegade* region. Such is the case of Germany (Article 37 of the German Constitution).

When applying Article 155, a German reading, rather than an Italian one,[50] should be made for three main reasons. First, this point was specifically discussed during the constituent debates. *Alianza Popular* (the right-wing party which was later re-founded as the *Partido Popular*) proposed that the intervention of an autonomous community was included in the Spanish Constitution.[51] However, the amendment was not passed by the majority in the Congress. *Unión de Centro Democrático* proposed two similar amendments in which the dissolution of the regional Assembly was included,[52] but they were equally rejected by most Deputies and Senators.

---

[48] Two authors who link inextricably federal coercion to federal loyalty are Álvarez (2008, 2016) and Arroyo (2015).

[49] Article 126 of the Italian Constitution reads: 'The *Regional Council* may be *dissolved* and the *President of the Executive* may be *removed* with a reasoned decree of the President of the Republic in the case of acts in contrast with the Constitution or grave violations of the law. The dissolution or removal may also be decided for reasons of national security. Such decree is adopted after consultation with a committee of Deputies and Senators for regional affairs which is set up in the manner established by a law of the Republic (…)'—italics added.

[50] Several scholars (Entrena 1985; Urías 2019) have explained that Article 155 'follows the federal example and not the Italian model, typical from regional states, in which the Regional Council may be dissolved by a decree of the President of the Republic' (Entrena 1985, 2313).

[51] The proposed text read as follows: 'In serious cases, the Government shall be able to approve the intervention of an Autonomous region, and the Cortes shall be informed immediately. Measures may include: the suspension of one or more of its self-governing bodies, the appointment of a Governor General vested with extraordinary powers. The intervention shall be accorded by a motivated Decree and automatically give rise to a debate on the question of confidence in the Congress. The Decree must detail the period of intervention, which will be connected to an election call.'

[52] Amendment no 736, presented by Deputy Ortí, added a third section to Article 155 (at that time, numbered 144) with the following text: '(3) The King, at the proposal of the President of the Government, after deliberation of the Council of Ministers and having consulted with the Presidents of the Congress and the Senate, shall be able to decree the dissolution of the regional Assembly for the commission of actions contrary to the Constitution, for seriously violating the law, or for reasons of state security' (available at: http://www.congreso.es/constitucion/ficheros/enmiendas/enmcongreso.pdf). Senator Ballarín proposed

Considering the parliamentary debates, and taking into account that the Constitutional Court has stated that they 'can help to interpret the scope and meaning of constitutional Articles and provisions included in the constitutionality bloc' (CCJ 8/2013, January 17, Legal Basis 8th), in Spain few scholars admit the possibility of dissolving the Parliament when Article 155 is activated (Cruz-Villalón 1984; Satrústegui 2017). Most academics, on the contrary, reject that measures can affect the ordinary functioning of the regional legislature (see, for instance, García-Torres 1984; Ballart 1987; Gil-Robles 1999; Ridao 2018).

Second, the principle of legality is consistent with a restricted conception of the powers conferred on the central state when applying Article 155. In those countries where the intervention into regional autonomy is allowed, the extent and limits of such capacity is detailed in the Constitution: for instance, the Italian Constitution quite literally mentions the possibility of removing the President of the regional government and dissolving the regional Parliament.[53] Given the profound and negative impact that these two measures—the removal of the region's government and the dissolution of its Parliament—have on the right to autonomy, explicit mention in the Constitution to them seems a minimal requirement.

Third, and in line with a restrictive interpretation of this exceptional mechanism, most scholars consider that the application of federal coercion should be guided by the *proportionality test* (Cruz-Villalón 1984; Entrena 1985; Albertí 1985; Gil-Robles 1999; Calafell 2000; Álvarez 2016; Ridao 2018; Vilajosana 2019). Proportionality includes a three-fold test: suitability, necessity, and proportionality understood in a strict sense. This means that, first, 'the measures (...) must be restricted to' (Albertí 2019, 115) compel the autonomous community to comply with its constitutional and legal obligations, or to protect the general interest—and this objective needs to be:

the amendment no 957, which read: '(3) Regional bodies may be dissolved if the measures adopted are not complied with, or for reasons of national security (...)' (available at: http://www.congreso.es/constitucion/ficheros/enmiendas/enmsenado.pdf).

[53] Other Constitutions specifically include the possibility of dissolving regional legislatures and calling elections (Article 100 of the Constitution of Austria) only, or of removing also the regional government (Article 234 of the Constitution of Portugal), when applying federal coercion.

determined in the previous request that the state government addresses to the President of the autonomous community; second, measures must be necessary to achieve this goal, in the sense that not only should they be suitable, but also that no other less serious or invasive means reasonably exist; third, measures have to be proportional in a strict sense to the aim that justifies them, so that the right to autonomy encounters the minimum possible interference. (Ibid.)

Considering these three arguments, the dissolution of the Catalan Parliament by the central government may have infringed upon the right to autonomy (Article 2 of the Constitution), the parliamentary model of Catalonia (Article 152 of the Constitution in relation to Articles 55, 57, 67, 74–75 of the Statute of Autonomy of Catalonia), and, perhaps most importantly, the right to political participation (Article 23 of the Constitution[54]). The right of the citizens of Catalonia to political participation through representatives, who were democratically elected in 2015, was arguably breached since a political party that amounts to a minority in Catalonia decided to dissolve the Parliament and call a snap election (active suffrage). Furthermore, the right of elected representatives to hold office was also affected (passive suffrage); more specifically, the early dissolution of the Parliament deprived them from parliamentary privileges (inviolability, legal immunity, jurisdiction of the *Tribunal Superior de Justicia de Catalunya*—High Court of Justice of Catalonia—over them). As Albertí (2018) has pointed out, Article 155 may not limit individual rights and liberties, which can only be suspended under the conditions established in Articles 55 and 116 of the Constitution.

Finally, it can also be argued that the proportionality test has not been observed here. Regarding suitability, it is debatable that federal coercion is an appropriate way to respond to the Catalan question. Article 155 contains a legal mechanism to force an autonomous community to comply with its constitutional obligations. However, the challenge posed by Catalonia was not of a legal nature; rather, it has a political character. More specifically, as Pérez-Royo (2017) has remarked, Catalonia is creating a 'constituent problem.' Constituent problems can only be tackled by

[54] Article 23 reads as follows: '(1) Citizens have the right to participate in public affairs, directly or through representatives freely elected in periodic elections by universal suffrage. (2) They also have the right to accede under conditions of equality to public functions and positions, in accordance with the requirements laid down by the law.'

means of negotiation and dialogue, but never by resorting to coercion which, by definition, is 'opposed to the integration of Catalonia within the state.'

As for necessity, the election held in December 2017 proved its inability for the purpose of restoring constitutional order: the majority of seats in the regional legislature were obtained by pro-sovereign parties, and the new President belongs to Puigdemont's political party. So things are more or less at the same point, except for the feeling of resentment a significant part of Catalan society harbours now—which certainly makes the possibility of reaching an agreement with the central state even more difficult.

Last, it is arguable that the dissolution of the Catalan Parliament and the removal of the Catalan government are proportional measures to be taken in order to revoke a unilateral declaration of independence. As some scholars have pointed out, the Constitution includes other mechanisms to force an autonomous community to comply with its constitutional obligations which are 'more respectful of the right to autonomy' (Vilajosana 2019, 147), namely the annulment of laws by the Constitutional Court, and the possibility to ask for the suspension of their effects until the ruling is delivered (Articles 153 and 161 of the Constitution).[55] The measures adopted in October 2017 may possibly be understood as a total suspension of the right to autonomy in Catalonia: the government was dismissed, the regional administration was forced to yield to the authority of the central administration, and the Catalan Parliament, although formally subsisted, was de facto subordinated to the power of the Spanish government (Ridao 2018).

---

[55] Article 153 establishes: 'Control over the bodies of the Self-governing Communities shall be exercised by: (a) The Constitutional Court, in matters pertaining to the constitutionality of their regulatory provisions having the force of law (…).' Article 161, for its part, reads: '(1). The Constitutional Court has jurisdiction over the whole Spanish territory and is entitled to hear: (a) against the alleged unconstitutionality of acts and statutes having the force of an act (…). (2) The Government may appeal to the Constitutional Court against provisions and resolutions adopted by the bodies of the Self-governing Communities, which shall bring about the suspension of the contested provisions or resolutions, but the Court must either ratify or lift the suspension, as the case may be, within a period of not more of five months.'

## Spanish Political Culture and Constitutionalism

The actual application of Article 155 in Catalonia brings to light five aspects of Spanish political culture and constitutionalism that deserve attention. First of all, it seems that the main constitutional interest that merits protection is the unity of the Spanish Nation, understood as a *meta-right* in Barceló's (2019) words. The logic that guided the implementation of federal coercion in Catalonia answered a Schmitt's reading of Article 155, an extreme which has been noted by Vilajosana (2019). According to Vilajosana, the application of federal coercion in Catalonia was based on a conception of national unity as the exclusive basis of the whole legal system of the state. In this context, the exceptional situation is defined and declared by the sovereign who, in Schmitt's terms (1985), also decides when the return to normality has occurred. Furthermore, the scope of the political is delimited by the distinction between *friends* and *enemies* (Schmitt 1996); measures typical of *prerogative state*—in line with Fraenkel's thesis of the dual state[56]—are devoted to enemies and, as a result, 'democracy is conceived of in a sense that citizens' will is not given priority and unity finds no limit in fundamental rights' (Vilajosana 2019, 151).

Second, it is clear that top priority has been placed on ensuring the unity of Spain, even when rights or other constitutional principles may be at stake. The reason for attaching more weight to national unity than to fundamental rights, such as political participation,[57] is that the Constitution, where those rights are recognised and guaranteed, is ultimately based on the indissoluble unity of the Spanish nation (see Article 2). Vilajosana has called this the 'hypostasis of unity' (2019, 151) which is to say the conception of unity as an absolute reality that does not need to be weighted with other constitutional principles. In this sense, Article 155 has produced a series of outcomes that affect other rights significantly. For instance, the

[56] Fraenkel (2006) differentiates a normative state (*Normenstaat*) from a prerogative state (*Massnahmenstaat*). The scope of politics cannot be regulated by norms, rather measures control it. When applying measures, public officers exercise their powers discretionally. What is important to note is that aspects confined to normality are decided from the prerogative state, and also that in a real state, normative and discretionary aspects coexist. Therefore, 'a state will be closer to the ideal of the rule of law as fewer measures typical from a prerogative state contains' (Vilajosana 2019, 140).

[57] For example, see the restrictive interpretation of referenda held by the Constitutional Court (CCJ 103/2008, September 11). English version available at: https://www.tribunal-constitucional.es/ResolucionesTraducidas/103-2008,%20of%20September%2011.pdf.

possibility of debating the independence of Catalonia has been precluded,[58] even in Parliament, which suggests a violation of freedom of speech and parliamentary privilege. Additionally, members of the Catalan government and Parliament were deprived of their parliamentary privilege and inviolability by means of their removal, which may represent an infringement of due process and the right to the natural judge (the *Tribunal Superior de Justicia de Catalunya* rather than the Constitutional Court). And, a collective imaginary prone to justify almost any action taken against pro-independence nationalists has been created, which may amount to the deterioration of the rule of law and criminal guarantees. In brief, the excessive resort to the judiciary to deal with a political issue like the Catalan crisis is tilting the separation of powers and undermining the international image of Spanish judges. For instance, political leaders are still in prison charged for rebellion[59] even after a German Court ruled that former President Puigdemont could not face rebellion charges—which made the Constitutional Court of Spain drop the European arrest warrant, although Puigdemont could be prosecuted for misuse of public funds.[60]

---

[58] A detailed account of the interferences that individual rights and liberties faced before and after 1-O, with particular reference to freedom of speech, can be found in Barceló (2019).

[59] More than 100 Professors in Criminal Law signed a manifesto in November 2017 to denounce a number of abuses in the trial against the Catalan nationalist leaders. First, acts attributed to them do not constitute rebellion because violence, an essential element of that offence, was absent. Second, rebellion crimes do not fall within the remit of the *Audiencia Nacional* (a special and exceptional High Court with jurisdiction over the whole territory of Spain in some specific matters). Third, the judge Carmen Lamela was arguably too severe when applying law, in particular because she ordered pre-trial detention (Álvarez-García et al. 2017).

[60] The European arrest warrant (EAW) is 'a judicial decision issued by a Member State with a view to the arrest and surrender by another Member State of a requested person, for the purposes of conducting a criminal prosecution or executing a custodial sentence or detention order' [Article 1.1 of the Council Framework Decision of June 13, 2002 on the European arrest warrant and the surrender procedures between Member States (2002/584/JHA)]. When Puigdemont fled Spain just after declaring the independence of Catalonia, the Constitutional Court issued an EAW against him based on the offences of rebellion and misuse of public funds. On March 25, 2018 Puigdemont was arrested in Germany pursuant to the EAW. The *Oberlandesgericht* (Higher Regional Court) in Schleswig-Holstein ruled that Puigdemont could only be surrendered to face the charge of misuse of public funds, but not that of rebellion because 'the act on which the European arrest warrant is based does not constitute an offence under the law of' Germany (Article 4.1). The decision of the German Court led the Constitutional Court to withdraw the EAW against Puigdemont, while the rest of his deposed cabinet are in jail—except those *consellers* who also abandoned Spain—and being prosecuted for

Third, the Constitution and the rest of the legal order are being used as a tool to combat Catalan nationalism. In line with the political atmosphere prevailing those days,[61] the implementation of Article 155 in Catalonia actually meant a genuine *punishment* for the series of legal and constitutional infringements recorded on the Agreement of the Council of Ministers. However, it is relevant to stress that those normative acts were not in force at that time—including the Declaration of Independence—, so no legal effects could be produced. That is why it can be asserted that a *general lawsuit* against independence was brought, which combined political and judicial means. In this holistic sense, the application of Article 155 in Catalonia can be better understood if it is connected with the rest of measures adopted by the Spanish political and judicial institutions to fight Catalan nationalism, namely: dirty war launched by the Department of the Interior (Operation Catalonia),[62] violent repression against the voters on 1-O, criminal proceedings against Catalan nationalist leaders, resort to the Constitutional Court to suspend the operation and make void any

rebellion. Given that democratic legitimacy of the members of the government derives from that of the President, who receives it in the investiture session from the majority vote of the MPs, only the President is individually responsible for the government action. Any act which could be considered rebellion would be included within the government action. Therefore, as the President has been discharged for rebellion, the public prosecutor should drop charges against the members of his government.

[61] The political atmosphere brought to mind echoes of a *war* between two factions: Spaniards against Catalans. That is why, according to the Spanish Secretary of the Interior, José-Ignacio Zoido (*Partido Popular*), '6000' Spanish anti-riot police officers were deployed in Catalonia with the aim of preventing citizens from voting on October 1, 2017 (Journal of Sessions of the Senate no 210, January 18, 2018, p. 13—available at: http://www.congreso. es/public_oficiales/L12/SEN/DS/CO/DS_C_12_210.PDF); additionally, in many cities hundreds of people went to see them off at police stations chanting *¡A por ellos, oé!* (Go for them!), a war cry often heard on football pitches (El Mundo 2017).

[62] Operation Catalonia was a conspiracy aimed at stopping political dissent in Catalonia and, more specifically, the independence movement. It was carried out between 2011 and 2016, while Jorge Fernández-Díaz (*Partido Popular*) was the Spanish Secretary of the Interior. It consisted of a series of actions of a political, police, and intelligence nature that intended to minimise social support for independence by means of discrediting it as a political option. In particular, political leaders were accused of corruption (Report of the Commission of Inquiry on the Operation Catalonia, Official Bulletin of the Catalan Parliament no 498, September 1, 2017—available at: https://www.parlament.cat/document/actualitat/232293.pdf).

legal and non-legal initiative on the Catalan sovereign process, financial intervention of the *Generalitat* from September 2017,[63] and so on. In light of what has been explained, it can be argued that Article 155 was not used to restore breached constitutional order; rather an alternative political option was imposed (Ridao 2018; Vintró 2019)—and the new option was in a clear minority in Catalonia.[64]

Fourth, despite the endless references made to the need of respecting the legal order as a necessary precondition for the operation of democracy,[65] the truth is that the rule of law and democracy are taken in a very narrow sense. In Spain, it is generally believed that law and democracy can be used interchangeably; more specifically, that the current Constitution epitomises democracy (Payero 2016). However, even accepting the democratic nature of the 1978 Constitution, not all its contents present the maximum degree of democracy: for instance, the territorial model cannot be equated with fundamental rights and liberties.[66] Moreover, the Spanish democracy is not militant (CCJ 48/2003, March 12, Legal Basis 7th)—formal respect of the Constitution is required, but it is not necessary to show an enthusiastic adherence to the content of the Constitution—, so it is legitimate to propose any reform of the Constitution or, even, the opening of a new constituent process without being considered an *enemy* of the state. As for

---

[63] Order HFP/886/2017, 20 September, by which credits are declared to be unavailable in the 2017 Catalan Regional Budget (available at: https://www.boe.es/diario_boe/txt.php?id=BOE-A-2017-10741)—abolished on December 27, 2017.

[64] In the regional election held on December 21, 2017, *Partido Popular* only obtained 4 seats (out of 135) and the *Partit dels Socialistes de Catalunya* obtained 17 seats. The winner was *Ciudadanos*, with 36 seats; however, the sum of *Junts per Catalunya* (34 seats), *Esquerra Republicana de Catalunya* (32 seats) and *Candidatura d'Unitat Popular-Crida Constituent* (4 seats) amounted to an overall majority. Thus, Quim Torra (*Junts per Catalunya*) was inaugurated President of the *Generalitat* (May 17, 2018), after the failed attempts to invest Jordi Sànchez and Jordi Turull, both in custody awaiting trial. As can be seen, political parties that voted in favour of Article 155 in the Senate are in a minority in the Catalan legislature (57 seats out of 135).

[65] For example, the previous request that the Council of Ministers sent to Puigdemont on October 11, 2017 read: 'The democratic state cannot exist without the rule of law, a state in which all public authorities are subject to the law.'

[66] As Aragón has pointed out, although the Constitution 'cannot be legitimate without democracy [or without fundamental rights], it can be legitimate with a bigger or smaller people. For democratic constitutional theory (…), the configuration of the people (its external limits as a human group different from other peoples) and its territorial dimension are facts that law regulates, but they do not provide any justification for law—or, in other words, they do not confer legitimacy on law' (1989, 54).

the rule of law, this concept 'often has limited purchase' when dealing with constituent problems like the one posed by Catalonia: 'legal orders presuppose a constituent power (the Spanish constitution bases itself on the Spanish people as a whole). But if another vision of a *pouvoir constituant* gathers sufficient allegiance, it might just as well create a constitutional order of its own—an alternative legality that will compete with the previous one for dominance. (...) [In the case that an independence movement arises], whether the "rule of law" can make a claim to obedience (...) will depend on the quality of the law it protects, and democratic constitutions typically have a relatively strong claim. Still, mere reliance on this claim might be a self-defeating strategy' (Torbisco and Krisch 2014). Time and again, Spanish politicians have often tempted to adopt this simplistic approach when dealing with the Catalan question, mistaking the rule of law for the rule *by* law (Núñez-Seixas 2018).

Finally, the refusal to respond to Puidgemont's overture for discussion shows that political culture in Spain is not used to dialogue and negotiation, which are both interpreted as expressions of weaknesses or, even worse, acts of treason. This is particularly salient when one of the parties is a peripheral region (Catalonia, the Basque Country),[67] but can also be observed whenever a coalition government needs to be formed—particularly if the left could seize power.[68] The formation of a new executive in

[67] During the negotiations aimed to pass the state budget, Pedro Sánchez met Quim Torra, the President of the *Generalitat*, in Pedralbes (December 20, 2018). After the meeting, a document containing 21 points to be agreed on was released to the press (Proposal of the government of Catalonia to the summit with the government of Spain: A state agreement to resolve the conflict between Spain and Catalonia—available at: https://drive.google.com/file/d/1H-YXFqIGA-baBUyoqkG6A7oAGMAJ_Jsh/view). Point 3 was particularly contentious—'It is necessary an international mediation in order to facilitate a negotiation on equal terms—'; so much so that references to 'the inferior position of Spain' (ABC 2019), 'humiliation' (Cruz and Oms 2019), and even 'treason' (La Razón 2019) could be read in certain newspapers.

[68] Alfredo Pérez-Rubalcaba (*Partido Socialista Obrero Español*) coined the term 'Frankenstein government' to discredit the possibility of constituting a left-wing government with *Unidos Podemos* and other nationalist parties in 2016 (EFE 2016). *Partido Popular* and *Ciudadanos* liked the formula and several of their representatives have used it afterwards—see, for instance, Mariano Rajoy (Journal of Session of the Congress of Deputies, no 126, May 31, 2018, p. 16), Rafael Hernando (Journal of Sessions of the Congress of Deputies, no 127, June 1, 2018, p. 5), Inés Arrimadas (ABC 2018) or Albert Rivera (Journal of Sessions of the Congress of Deputies, no 2, July 22, 2019, p. 39).

Catalonia (June 2, 2018) put an end to the formal application of federal coercion; nevertheless, exceptionality continues. Catalan politicians in prison faced enormous difficulties to exercise their rights to political participation as we saw in the last elections—regional, state-wide, and to the EU Parliament—(Barceló 2019), and the mere possibility of forming a government in Spain with the support of Catalan nationalist parties is being used as a political tool to oppose it.

In short, it seems that Article 155 has become a *state of mind* and a style of doing politics in Spain.[69] A process of recentralisation was carried out during the first decade of the new century (Requejo and Klaus-Jürgen 2011),[70] a centripetal tendency that was reinforced by the economic crisis. Autonomous communities were blamed for the debt of the state, which aroused animosity towards self-rule as a way forward. The explosion of the Catalan pro-sovereign movement helped to feed Catalan-phobia among important sectors of Spaniards, which was capitalised by right-wing parties. Moreover, the *Partido Popular* government waved the national flag while reducing civil rights.[71] This authoritarian policy was not vigorously contested in the streets; conversely, most citizens gave priority to national cohesion over democracy and the respect of fundamental rights and liberties. Even in Catalonia, *Ciudadanos* won the regional election in December 2017, although they did not obtain an absolute majority. Article 155 does not inspire politicians with fear any more in Spain: other autonomous communities were threatened by the *Partido Popular* government (the Basque Country, Navarre, Castile-La Mancha), and now this party is out of office its leader, Pablo Casado, has urged the *Partido Socialista Obrero Español* government to adopt even wider measures—including the inter-

---

[69] On December 12, 2017, while direct rule was operating in Catalonia, Senator Jon Iñarritu (*EH-Bildu*, a left-wing Basque nationalist party) asked the then Secretary of the Interior, José-Ignacio Zoido, whether a number of powers would be transferred to the Basque Country and Navarre. Zoido, instead of directly responding the question, warned him that 'Article 155 is applicable to everybody' (Journal of Sessions of the Senate no 53, December 12, 2017, p. 27—available at: http://www.congreso.es/public_oficiales/L12/SEN/DS/PL/DS_P_12_53.PDF).

[70] For instance, the Act 39/2006, December 14, for the Promotion of Personal Autonomy and Care for People in a Situation of Dependency, was criticised for invading devolved matters (Lasagabaster 2007; Aguado 2012).

[71] Particular relevance bears the Organic Act 4/2015, March 30, on Public Safety, popularly known as 'Gag Law,' which has been severely criticised for curtailing 'freedom of expression, peaceful assembly and information' (Amnesty International 2018, 340).

vention of *Televisió de Catalunya* (the public broadcasting network)[72] and the suppression of the model of language immersion at school—under the aegis of Article 155 (Herrera 2018).

However, facts—stubborn as they are—show that neither the resort to Courts nor the active imposition of a unitary vision of Spain is able to resolve the Catalan problem. Negotiation is still a path to be explored. The new government in Spain might decide the timing is right to revert to the ancient tradition of pactism (Gagnon 2014) so that the territorial compact is re-established on mutually accepted terms.[73]

## References

ABC. 2018. El PNV pide a Sánchez que convoque elecciones 'en 2020 o a finales de 2019'. *ABC*, June 2. https://www.abc.es/espana/abci-directo-san-chez-toma-posesion-cargo-201806021001_directo.html.

———. 2019. Elecciones, una emergencia nacional. *ABC*, February 6. https://www.abc.es/opinion/abci-elecciones-emergencia-nacional-201902052345_noticia.html.

Aguado, Vicenç. 2012. El régimen jurídico de las prestaciones de los servicios sociales. In *El marco jurídico de los servicios sociales en España*, ed. Antonio Ezquerra, 47–85. Barcelona: Atelier.

Albertí, Enoch. 1985. La resolución de conflictos entre el Estado y las Comunidades Autónomas. In *El sistema jurídico de las Comunidades Autónomas*, ed. Eliseo Aja, 456–475. Madrid: Tecnos.

———. 2018. Qüestions constitucionals entorn de l'aplicació de l'article 155 CE al conflicte de Catalunya. *Revista d'estudis autonòmics i federals* 27: 11–40.

[72] The Senate specifically rejected the proposal of the Council of Ministers to supersede the *Generalitat* in the exercise of powers on the broadcasting public service of Catalonia (Section II, subsection b of the Resolution of the Presidency of the Senate, October 27, 2017).

[73] This chapter was written before the Constitutional Court rulings on Article 155 were published. During the proofreading process, the Court released the rulings 89/2019 and 90/2019, July 2, 2019 which almost completely endorsed the interpretation of Article 155 made by both the Spanish government and the Senate. Nevertheless, the main thesis argued in this chapter holds firmly. Part 3 of this chapter maintains a stricter interpretation of Article 155 than the one contained in the Agreement of the Senate—which the Court has found to be in accordance with the Constitution—, but it does fit the wide limits set by the Court. As well as some problems that the reasoning of the Court presents—apodictic in some passages, as Ridao has observed (2019)—, this loose exegesis of Article 155 reveals a number of deficiencies in the political understanding of democracy, the rule of law, constitutionalism, and fundamental rights that are quite worrying, as explained in Part 4.

————. 2019. La aplicación del art. 155 CE a Cataluña: un instrumento inadecuado e ineficaz para la resolución del conflicto constitucional de Cataluña. In *Crisis institucional y democracia (A propósito de Cataluña)*, ed. Iñaki Lasagabaster, 101–120. Valencia: Tirant lo Blanch.

Álvarez, Leonardo. 2008. La función de la lealtad en el Estado autonómico. *Teoría y Realidad Constitucional* 22: 493–524.

————. 2016. La coerción estatal del art. 155 CE en la estructura del Estado autonómico. *Teoría y Realidad Constitucional* 38: 277–304.

Álvarez-García, Francisco-Javier, et al. 2017. Legalidad y proceso penal. *El Diario*, November 9. https://www.eldiario.es/tribunaabierta/Legalidad-penal-proceso-independentista_6_706289383.html.

Amnesty International. 2018. *Amnesty International Report 2017/18. The State of the World's Human Rights*. London: Amnesty International. https://www.amnesty.org/download/Documents/POL1067002018ENGLISH.PDF.

Aragón, Manuel. 1989. *Constitución y democracia*. Madrid: Tecnos.

Arroyo, Antonio. 2015. Unidad, lealtad y coerción federal (o estatal) en Alemania y España. *Revista Jurídica de la Universidad Autónoma de Madrid* 31: 51–70.

Ballart, Xavier. 1987. *Coerció estatal i autonomies. Estudi de l'article 155 de la Constitució de 1978*. Barcelona: Escola d'Administració Pública de Catalunya.

Barceló, Mercé. 2019. Crisis constitucional del Estado o cuando la 'unidad de España,' como metaderecho, se impone a los derechos fundamentales de la ciudadanía. In *Crisis institucional y democracia (A propósito de Cataluña)*, ed. Iñaki Lasagabaster, 151–191. Valencia: Tirant lo Blanch.

Barceló, Mercé, et al. 2015. *El derecho a decidir. Teoría y práctica de un nuevo derecho*. Barcelona: Atelier.

Calafell, Vicente-Juan. 2000. La compulsión o coerción estatal (estudio del artículo 155 de la Constitución española). *Revista de Derecho Político* 48–49: 99–146.

Cruz, Marisa, and Oms, Javier. 2019. Pedro Sánchez humilla al Estado al aceptar un mediador con Torra. *El Mundo*, February 6. https://www.elmundo.es/espana/2019/02/05/5c597203fc6c83655a8b4577.html.

Cruz-Villalón, Pedro. 1984. Coerción estatal. In *Diccionario del sistema político español*, ed. José-Juan González-Encinar, 56–62. Madrid: Akal.

De-la-Hoz, Cristina, et al. 2017. El Gobierno se limitará al 'despacho de asuntos ordinarios' de la Generalitat. *El Independiente*, October 23. https://www.elindependiente.com/politica/2017/10/23/gobierno-asuntos-ordinarios-generalitat/.

EFE. 2016. Rubalcaba: un acuerdo con Podemos sería una 'investidura frankenstein'. *El Diario*, July 13. https://www.eldiario.es/politica/Rubalcaba-acuerdo-Podemos-investidura-frankenstein_0_536847238.html.

El Mundo. 2017. Todos '¡a por ellos, oé!' *El Mundo*, September 26. https://www.elmundo.es/espana/2017/09/26/59ca03d922601df7168b46b0.html.

————. 2018. Un 155 útil, pero demasiado leve. *El Mundo*, March 5. https://www.elmundo.es/opinion/2018/03/05/5a9c3630ca4741b56d8b468b.html.

Entrena, Rafael. 1985. Artículo 155. In *Comentarios a la Constitución*, ed. Fernando Garrido-Falla, 2nd ed., 2311–2316. Madrid: Civitas.

Fernández-Rodera, José-Alberto. 2003. A vueltas con el artículo 155 de la Constitución. Su relación con los estados excepcionales. *Actualidad Jurídica Aranzadi* 603: 1–5.

Ferreres, Víctor. 2013. *The Constitution of Spain. A Contextual Analysis.* Oxford and Portland: Hart.

Fraenkel, Ernst. 2006. *The Dual State. A Contribution to the Theory of Dictatorship.* Clark: The Lawbook Exchange.

Gagnon, Alain-G. 2014. *Minority Nations in the Age of Uncertainty: New Paths to National Emancipation and Empowerment.* Toronto: University of Toronto Press.

García-de-Enterría, Eduardo. 1983. *La ejecución autonómica de la legislación del Estado.* Madrid: Civitas.

García-de-Enterría, Eduardo, and Tomás-Ramón Fernández. 2008. *Curso de derecho administrativo.* Vol. I. 14th ed. Cizur Menor: Thomson-Civitas.

García-Torres, Jesús. 1984. El artículo 155 de la Constitución española y el principio constitucional de autonomía. In *Organización territorial del Estado (Comunidades Autónomas) (vol. 2)*, VVAA, 1189–1303. Madrid: Instituto de Estudios Fiscales.

Gil-Robles, José-María. 1999. Artículo 155. El control extraordinario de las Comunidades Autónomas. In *Comentarios a la Constitución española de 1978, tomo XI*, ed. Óscar Alzaga, 499–518. Madrid: Edersa.

Herrera, Elena. 2018. El 155, un artículo ambiguo que PP y Ciudadanos agitan para pedir la intervención de Catalunya. *El Diario*, October 5. https://www.eldiario.es/politica/Cataluna-Casado-Rivera_0_820668845.html.

La Razón. 2019. El mediador, una traición a España. *La Razón*, February 6. https://www.larazon.es/opinion/editorial/el-mediador-una-traicion-a-espana-CN21799957.

Lafuente, José-María. 2018. El art. 155 de la Constitución española: examen doctrinal y comparado. *UNED. Revista de Derecho Político* 102: 79–121.

Lasagabaster, Iñaki. 2007. La Ley de Promoción de la Autonomía Personal y Atención a las Personas en Situación de Dependencia: una reflexión desde la perspectiva competencial. *Revista d'Estudis Autonòmics i Federals* 4: 129–158.

Núñez-Seixas, Xosé-M. 2018. *Suspiros de España. El nacionalismo español, 1808–2018.* Barcelona: Crítica.

Payero, Lucía. 2015. The 'Citizen Participation Process' in Catalonia: Past, Present and Future. *Liverpool Law Review* 36 (3): 237–256.

————. 2016. ¿Por qué Cataluña no puede autodeterminarse? Las razones del Estado español. In *El encaje constitucional del derecho a decidir. Un enfoque polémico*, ed. Jorge Cagiao and Gennaro Ferraiuolo, 183–217. Madrid: Los Libros de la Catarata.

Pérez-Royo, Javier. 2011. La STC 31/2010 y la contribución de la jurisprudencia constitucional a la configuración de un Estado compuesto en España: elementos de continuidad y ruptura, e incidencia en las perspectivas de evolución del Estado autonómico. *Revista catalana de dret públic* 43: 121–149.

————. 2017. La tercera mayor estupidez: el 155. *Ara*, October 25. https://www.ara.cat/es/javier-perez-royo-tercera-mayor-estupidez-155_0_1894010794.html.

————. 2018. Anexo. ¿Reforma constitucional o periodo constituyente? In *Constitución: la reforma inevitable. Monarquía, plurinacionalidad y otras batallas*, ed. Antón Losada and Javier Pérez-Royo, 211–286. Barcelona: Roca Editorial de Libros.

Requejo, Ferran, and Nagel Klaus-Jürgen, eds. 2011. *Federalism beyond Federations. Asymmetry and Processes of Resymmetrisation in Europe*. Surrey and Burlington: Ashgate.

Ridao, Joan. 2018. La aplicación del artículo 155 de la Constitución a Cataluña. Un examen de su dudosa constitucionalidad. *Revista Vasca de Administración Pública* 111: 169–203.

————. 2019. Les sentències del Tribunal Constitucional sobre l'aplicació a Catalunya de l'article 155 de la Constitució. *Blog Revista catalana de dret públic*, July 17. https://eapc-rcdp.blog.gencat.cat/2019/07/17/les-sentencies-del-tribunal-constitucional-sobre-laplicacio-a-catalunya-de-larticle-155-de-la-constitucio-joan-ridao/.

Rubio-Llorente, Francisco. 1989. El bloque de constitucionalidad. *Revista Española de Derecho Constitucional* 27: 9–37.

Satrústegui, Miguel. 2017. Un instrumento para la defensa del Estado: el artículo 155 de la Constitución. In *Retos del Estado y de la Administración en el siglo XXI: Libro Homenaje a Tomás de la Quadra-Salcedo*, ed. Luciano-José Parejo and José Vida, vol. 2, 1859 1894. Valencia: Tirant lo Blanch.

Schmitt, Carl. 1985. *Political Theology. Four Chapters on the Concept of Sovereignty*. Chicago: The University of Chicago Press.

————. 1996. *The Concept of the Political*. Chicago: The University of Chicago Press.

Sosa, Francisco. 1979. El control de las Comunidades Autónomas por el Estado en la Constitución española. *Documentación Administrativa* 182: 149–164.

Torbisco, Neus, and Krisch, Nico. 2014. Using Spanish Law to Block Catalonia's Independence Consultation May Simply Encourage Catalans to Construct Their Own 'Alternative Legality'. *LSE Blog European Politics and Policy (EUROPP)*, November 4. https://blogs.lse.ac.uk/europpblog/2014/11/04/using-spanish-law-to-block-catalonias-independence-consultation-may-simply-encourage-catalans-to-construct-their-own-alternative-legality/.

Urías, Joaquín. 2019. El artículo 155 CE: alcance y límites de una excepción constitucional. *Revista catalana de dret públic*, special issue: 101–114.

Vilajosana, Josep-Maria. 2019. El Estado dual en España: contexto y justificación de la aplicación del artículo 155 CE. *Revista catalana de dret públic*, special issue: 137–155.

Vintró, Joan. 2019. L'article 155 de la Constitució: configuració jurídica general i aplicació a Catalunya. *Revista catalana de dret públic*, special issue: 156–181.

Vírgala, Eduardo. 2005. La coacción estatal del artículo 155 de la Constitución. *Revista Española de Derecho Constitucional* 73 (January–April): 55–110.

# PART II

# The Stalled Emergence of Multinational Federalism

## CHAPTER 5

# Origins and Consequences of American Multicultural Federalism: Constitutional Patriotism, Territorial Neutrality, and National Polarization

*John Kincaid*

## INTRODUCTION

This chapter deals with an exceptional case in the study of multinational federalism and explains why the United States became a multicultural federation[1] rather than a multinational federation. The chapter also discusses the long-term consequences of American multicultural federalism. In deciding not to impose culturally homogenizing policies on a heterogeneous society, the founders opted instead to foster national unity around

---

[1] This chapter uses the terms multicultural and multiculturalism in a broad sense, that is, in reference to a diversity of cultural preferences that may or may not find territorial expressions and may or may not be the result of a specific political project as understood in some of the literature (e.g., Kymlicka 1995).

---

J. Kincaid (✉)
Department of Government and Law, Lafayette College, Easton, PA, USA
e-mail: kincaidj@lafayette.edu

A.-G. Gagnon, A. Tremblay (eds.), *Federalism and National Diversity in the 21st Century*, Federalism and Internal Conflicts,
https://doi.org/10.1007/978-3-030-38419-7_5

the Constitution (i.e., through constitutional patriotism) and thus to allow expressions of cultural preferences across constituent territories (i.e., resulting from territorial neutrality). As a result, the chapter argues, multicultural federalism has been a double-edged sword. On one edge, federal tolerance of territorial and non-territorial expressions of diverse cultural preferences has fostered national unity. On the other edge, some of the most ardent expressions of such preferences, especially those pivoting on racism, provoke moral approbation that generates calls for federal intervention that trigger ferocious national polarization.

## One People, One Nation

The United States, which is the modern world's original federal republic, was the first major colony to overthrow colonial rule, thereby becoming 'the first "new nation"' (Lipset 1963, 2). The inhabitants of the 13 colonies undertook their revolt against colonialism as a single people. As President Abraham Lincoln put it in his 1863 Gettysburg Address, 'our fathers brought forth on this continent, a new nation.'

A single identity began to be forged as a result of what Americans call the French and Indian War of 1754–1763 (or Seven Years' War or *Guerre de la Conquête*) as well as the much-hated Royal Proclamation of 1763 forbidding European settlement west of the Appalachians. Many colonists increasingly identified as English, partly to assert what they regarded as their rights as Englishmen. The Declaration and Resolves of the First Continental Congress of 1774, which strongly opposed the 1774 Quebec Act, referred variously to the colonists as 'English colonists,' 'inhabitants of the English colonies,' and 'good people of the several colonies of New-Hampshire...' with the other colonies listed serially in recognition of each colony's separate status. However, the document's resolutions referred to the colonies collectively as 'America' and then asserted 'American rights' and the existence of 'Americans' (Tansill 1927, 1–5). Two years later, the Declaration of Independence (1776) announced that the time had arrived 'for one people to dissolve the political bands which have connected them with another,' although the statement was more aspirational than factual in 1776 (Burlingame 1960, 157).

The country's first constitution, the Articles of Confederation of 1781, created a weak general government but nevertheless gave formal recognition to a single polity called 'The United States of America' (Article I) and committed the 13 states to a 'perpetual Union' (Preamble and Article

XIII). Seven years later, in contrast to the preamble to the Articles, which lists all the confederating states, the preamble to the U.S. Constitution of 1788 does not list the federating states. It opens simply with the phrase 'We the People of the United States.' Two of the mottos on the Great Seal of the United States summarize the American approach to federal union: e pluribus unum, out of many, one (i.e., a single union inhabited by a diverse but single people), and novus ordo seclorum, a new order of the ages (i.e., the American federal era).

In *Federalist* 2, John Jay expressed a common sentiment of the founders when he referred to Americans as 'a band of brethren.' The 13 states, he contended, were 'one connected, fertile, wide spreading country' housing 'one united people ... descended from the same ancestors, speaking the same language, professing the same religion, attached to the same principles of government, very similar in their manners and customs, and who' fought 'side by side' to establish 'their general Liberty and Independence.'

Sociologically, the demographic make-up of the United States provided a foundation for the concept of one people. In contrast to Livingston's notion of a 'federal society' (Livingston 1952), the 1790 U.S. census showed 66.3 per cent of the U.S. population identifying as English. At 19.3 per cent, black residents were the next largest group, but most of them were slaves and, thus, politically impotent. Among other whites, 5.6 per cent were Scottish, 4.5 per cent German, 2.0 per cent Dutch, 1.6 per cent Irish, 0.4 per cent French, and 0.3 per cent other. Religiously, 74.7 per cent of all congregations in 1776 were Reformed Protestant (Stark and Finke 1988, 43), which has its roots in covenant or federal theology (Elazar and Kincaid 2000). Anglicans were another 15.3 per cent, 8.1 per cent were other Protestants, Roman Catholics made up 1.7 per cent, and 0.2 per cent were Jews. Thus, Jay's statement about American homogeneity while rhetorical hyperbole was not far off the mark.

There was a practical urgency as well to the founders' emphasis on one nation, one people. The United States was the only independent nation on a hemisphere dominated by the colonial superpowers of the late eighteenth century: Great Britain, France, Spain, Portugal, and Russia. The founders feared that a weak United States would be unable to counter efforts by the great powers to interfere in American affairs and sow divisions within the union. They also feared that 13 independent nations, or two or more confederations, would become 'entangled in all the pernicious labyrinths of European politics and wars' (*Federalist* 7) and replicate the divisions and perennial warfare of the Old World.

To solidify union and enhance defence capacity, the founders advocated robust economic development, which, in their view, could be achieved only by establishing a single, common market free of internal trade barriers. For these reasons, the two principal sets of powers delegated to the federal government by the Constitution concern (1) interstate and foreign commerce and (2) defence and foreign affairs. Many of the Constitution's framers regarded these federal powers as being essential, strong, and exclusive. Otherwise, the Constitution is silent about such domestic matters as education, transportation, policing, and marriage and family law.

The Constitution seeks to foster unity in many other ways. Among these is the guaranteed equal representation of the states in the Senate, the requirement that members of Congress be inhabitants of the states they represent, the admission of new states on an equal footing with the original states, a prohibition on Congress changing any state's boundaries without its consent, and a guarantee that Congress not award any regulatory or fiscal preferences 'to the Ports of one State over those of another.' In these respects, the Constitution establishes a general symmetry among the constituent political communities conducive to citizen perceptions of equitable unity.

Non-exclusion provisions open the federal government to current and future social diversities. Anticipating immigration, the Constitution ensures that naturalized citizens can be elected to the U.S. House of Representatives after seven years of citizenship and to the U.S. Senate after nine years. By statute, the most common length of residency prior to citizenship was five years. By prohibiting any religious test for any federal office, the Constitution opened federal service to adherents of all religions (in contrast to religious tests for public office in many of the states).

Article I, Section 10 prohibits states from abridging fundamental citizen rights, waging trade or armed wars against each other, or engaging in military or diplomatic activities injurious to the union. In turn, the full-faith-and-credit and privileges-and-immunities clauses in Article IV ensure substantial mobility across state lines. The constitutional jurisdiction of the federal courts is designed partly to foster unity by allowing them to settle controversies between two or more states, between citizens of different states, and between states or citizens and foreign states or citizens. The Constitution also obligates the federal government to 'guarantee to every State in this Union a Republican Form of Government' (Article IV, Section 4).

National and individual liberty were among the founders' principal political objectives, and they deemed unity to be essential for liberty. Alexander Hamilton especially painted a stark portrait of a Hobbesian war of all against all that would be spawned by disunion and destroy liberty. He wrote 'that if these States should either be wholly disunited, or only united in partial confederacies,' they 'would have frequent and violent contests with each other' (*Federalist* 6).

In summary, establishment of a perpetual union encompassing a diverse but single people was of paramount concern to the founders of the United States. This single people called 'Americans' was, for the founders, defined by the Declaration of Independence and the federal Constitution and allegiance to them, not by a language, race, religion, or blood-based nationality. In contrast to many states where 'the consciousness of nationality often preceded the existence and the institution of a state' (Lukacs 2005), in the United States, the 'nation-state' preceded full consciousness of nationality.

## TERRITORIAL NEUTRALITY AND DEMOCRACY

Consequently, federal land policies, as well as the Constitution's interstate mobility clauses, fostered territorial neutrality with respect to non-native settlers, making state and local jurisdictions open theatres for immigrants' cultural performances. Whatever sociocultural group constitutes the majority in a particular territorial jurisdiction can establish a democratic government that reflects the inhabitants' political, socioeconomic, and cultural preferences. However, no majority can assert perpetual authority or exclude 'foreigners'; the reigning majority is vulnerable to displacement by a new majority formed by incoming and outgoing migrants. A 'state may be created for the good of its people, but it is defined by its territory, and 'its people' are defined by the territory in which they live' (Laycock 1992, 316–317).

Territorial neutrality was underwritten by the Continental Congress's Public Lands Resolution of 1780 and by the land ordinances of 1784, 1785, and 1787 enacted by the Confederation Congress. The new U.S. Congress adopted those policies because the U.S. Constitution (Article IV, Section 3) gives Congress plenary authority over U.S. territories. All four acts managed disposition of the Northwest territories (today, the states of Ohio, Indiana, Illinois, Michigan, Wisconsin, and northeastern Minnesota) ceded to the union by the seven states that had claimed those territories. The 1780 resolution and 1784 ordinance provided for settlement of the territories and their formation into 'republican states' eligible to 'become members of the Federal Union' and to enjoy 'the same rights of sovereignty, freedom and independence as the other States' (quoted in Hill 1988, 43). Congress also sought to create states roughly equal in geographic size (Stein 2008). The 1785 ordinance mandated a rectangular land-survey creating a continuous grid of 36-square-mile townships (93.24 square kilometres), each divided into 36 one-square-mile sections (640 acres or 259 hectares). Land was sold for a dollar an acre, often with a 640-acre minimum. The rectangular survey covers 69 per cent of the land area of the 48 contiguous states and partially covers another 9 per cent (Carstensen 1988). The survey was extended to Alaska. The straight lines that demarcate all or a portion of the boundaries of all U.S. states except Hawaii highlight this territorial neutrality.

Section 16 of each 36-square-mile section was set aside to support public education as organized by the section's settlers. Congress declined to designate a section for religion. The religion receiving support would have been decided by a majority of the residents of the 36-square-mile section. Rejection of such land grants did not reflect fear of religious nationalism but of creating discord on the frontier among competing religious groups.

The Northwest Ordinance of 1787 prohibited slavery and provided for federal-government appointment of a governor, secretary, and three judges for territories having less than 5000 free, white, male inhabitants. When a territory reached 5000 free, male residents, the inhabitants could elect a legislature; reaching 60,000 such inhabitants, the residents could petition to enter the union as a co-equal state. The federal Enabling Act of 1802 established the procedure for admitting the first new territorial state, Ohio, in 1803 and subsequent states. Residents must elect a constitutional convention to decide whether to join the union and, if so, draft a state constitution, although most territories first held a statehood referendum. The constitution is submitted to the U.S. Congress. The Enabling Act's only requirements were that the state constitution be 'republican' and not violate the Northwest Ordinance.

Although movies portray the nineteenth-century territories as the 'wild West,' the rectangular system fostered a rather '*mild* West' (Carstensen 1988, 39) by facilitating orderly and relatively non-litigious settlement. The system permitted local expressions of political, socioeconomic, and cultural preferences based on the citizens and immigrants who settled various sections, as well as a diversity of preference expressions across the sections, while also denying settler groups an ability 'to claim national rights on the ground of settlement before the establishment of U.S. authority' (Glazer 1977, 73).

These lands, of course, were not empty. The grid survey was laid atop Indian lands to benefit settlers of European stock with little regard for Indian land claims. The prevailing European attitude was well captured by Tocqueville: 'Although the huge territories ... were inhabited by many native tribes, one can fairly say that at the time of discovery they were no more than a wilderness' ([1835] 1969, 30). This attitude towards native peoples was not peculiar to the United States; the decimation of indigenous peoples and thefts of their lands occurred everywhere in the Western Hemisphere as well as in Australia and New Zealand.

Territorial neutrality underlies what Brownson called 'territorial democracy' ([1865] 1972, 210). In the United States, he noted, political powers and rights are vested in places, not estates, nations, or peoples, and all residents of a place are entitled to participate in its governance. The concept was revived by Kirk (1974) who argued that while the federal union is a republic, states and localities are territorial democracies that sustain associational life against the pressures of mass society and protect liberty against government centralization (Russello 1994). Elazar (1984, 1994) emphasized territorial democracy's role in fostering territorial pluralism. For Elazar: people gain representation in government through 'their ability to capture political control of territorial political units' and when 'one interest declines ... and a new one arises, the new one can gain some voice in the system' (Elazar 1984, 47); furthermore, specific groups often settled in specific jurisdictions to establish specific communities and '[this] territorial distribution of power has served to mitigate the effects of great national diversity by allowing subnational territorial communities to interpret national demands in such a way as to reflect their own local values as well' (Elazar 1994, 67).

Territorial democracy was empowered by very constrained federal power (except for federal assaults on slavery and polygamy during the second half of the nineteenth century) for about the first 150 years of U.S. history. The United States was a federation of 'island communities' up through the nineteenth century (Wiebe 1975), although those communities were connected to national commerce (Hoganson 2019). Even today, despite tremendous centralisation since the 1960s (Kincaid 2012), the United States ranks the third highest for regional authority among the seven federations scored on the regional authority index (Hooghe et al. 2008) and is the world's ninth most decentralized country (with Switzerland being the only federation more decentralized than the United States) according to the World Bank (Ivanyna and Shah 2012).

## A Multicultural Federation

As such, the U.S. Constitution established by necessity and default a de facto multicultural federal system almost ideally suited as well to multinational or plurinational federalism insofar as the Constitution delegates only limited powers to the general government and reserves to the states all of the powers so jealously guarded or desired by the constituent 'nations' of multinational or plurinational federations. To further guarantee those powers, the U.S. Constitution created a dual constitutional arrangement that did not abrogate or regulate the extant state constitutions. Except when a state constitutional provision contradicts the federal Constitution, the U.S. Constitution and state constitutions are co-equally sovereign within their respective spheres of authority.

Most important, the police power is reserved to the states. In American law, the police power is the authority of government to make all necessary laws governing the health, safety, welfare, and morals of its citizens. Whereas the federal government possesses delegated powers (although Congress and presidents later claimed some inherent powers), the states' police power is inherent and plenary. Consequently, because the federal Constitution is silent about such important matters as citizenship, language, health, education, marriage, welfare, and culture, there were few contradictions between the federal Constitution and state constitutions and statutes on cultural matters until the late-nineteenth to mid-twentieth centuries, at which point Congress and the Supreme Court entered these domestic fields on grounds of interstate commerce and individual-rights protection.[2]

---

[2] The Constitution also places insignificant limits on states' tax powers. States enact income, sales, property, and many other taxes and fees. They have broad leeway to use taxes to regulate behaviour. No federal constitutional limits inhibit state borrowing. Consequently, state and local citizens have wide fiscal and police powers to enact and finance their political, socioeconomic, and cultural preferences.

## Citizenship

The 1788 Constitution did not even define a 'citizen.' Citizenship was left to the states until the Fourteenth Amendment to the Constitution of 1868. Before the amendment, states conferred citizenship, which was then recognized by the federal government (Schuck and Smith 1985). The Fourteenth Amendment was necessitated by a pre-Civil War U.S. Supreme Court ruling (*Dred Scott* 1857) that defined black residents as non-citizens and non-persons. However, after 1868, states retained substantial authority over immigration until the federal government asserted virtually exclusive power over immigration through Supreme Court rulings (especially *Chae Chan Ping*, 1889) and Congress's Immigration Act of 1891.

## Language

The federal Constitution mandates no official languages. Given the demographic prevalence of English, the framers perhaps saw no need to address language. Indeed, the United States has long been a language graveyard. However, Pennsylvania's legislature translated the draft Constitution into German during the ratification campaign of 1787–1788 because one-third of the state's residents were German. In New York, a pro-Constitution interest group translated the document into Dutch (Mulligan et al. 2016).

The federal government faced no consequential language challenge until majority French-speaking Louisiana sought admission to the union in 1812. However, the French majority desired quick incorporation in order to gain self-governing powers not available under imperial Spanish and Napoleonic rule and thus exercised no political leverage to privilege French. Congress mandated that Louisiana's constitution require laws and official documents to be published in the language 'in which the Constitution of the United States is written,' but not exclusively (Ward 1997, 1293). Up to the Civil War (1861–1865), Louisiana issued documents in English and French; its legislature operated bilingually; and some officials spoke only French. The 1845 constitution recognized French language rights, and an 1847 law authorized bilingual instruction in public schools. However, the post-Civil-War 1868 constitution banned non-English legal publications, and in 1921, English was declared the state's official language. Nevertheless, French again achieved a special status in 1968, and Louisiana's current (1974) constitution provides: 'The right of the people to preserve, foster, and promote their respective historic linguistic and cultural origins is recognized' (Art. XII, Sec. 4). Louisiana also maintained its civil law system while the other 49 states rest on the common law.

When New Mexico joined the union in 1912, its constitution allowed bilingual governance and other accommodations for its large Hispanic population. The legislature ceased publishing laws in English and Spanish in 1949, although Spanish still has a special status in state law. Today, Hawaii has two official languages, English and Hawaiian, which were specified in a 1978 amendment to the state's constitution because Hawaiian had been banned in 1896 after white residents had overthrown the native government of Queen Lili'uokalani. Alaska has 20 official native languages in addition to English. Nineteen states have no official language.

Some critics (Kymlicka 1995; Frymer 2017) contend that Puerto Rico is not a state because Congress refuses to admit a Spanish-speaking state. Language is a barrier to statehood for some Americans, but three other barriers are more decisive. First, a majority of Puerto Ricans has never voted on a clear question to join the union. Second, Republicans resist admission because Puerto Rico would be solidly Democratic. Third, Puerto Rico would be the 29th largest state in terms of population (much larger than Alaska, Hawaii, and 19 other states) and entitled to about four members of the U.S. House of Representatives plus two senators. All other new U.S. states entered the union with smaller populations posing much lower political threats to the relative positions of the extant states. Puerto Rico, therefore, occupies an asymmetric position. Its residents are U.S. citizens with self-governing authority over their own polity, but they have not, to date, requested statehood or independence (Garrett 2013).

The federal government did not enter the language field nationwide until 1923, when the U.S. Supreme Court struck down laws in about 23 states that mandated English-only instruction in public and private schools (*Meyer* 1923). In a related cultural case, the court vacated an anti-Catholic Oregon law that required all children to attend public schools (*Pierce* 1925). Thirty-one states have declared English their official language, with 28 states doing so since 1983 in reaction to growing Hispanic populations and perceptions of 'politically correct' multicultural efforts to institutionalize bilingualism.[3] However, these state laws are mostly symbolic

---

[3] These laws have been passed with a number of specific justifications. For example, the California Official English law was framed as a response to the institutionalization of 'cultural

because the U.S. Civil Rights Act of 1964, Voting Rights Act of 1965, Bilingual Education Act of 1968, and other statutes provide extensive federal protections for languages and rights for non-English speakers, especially with respect to voting (e.g., non-English ballots) and interactions with all governments. More recently, four states (New Mexico, Oregon, Rhode Island, Washington) have passed English Plus resolutions that encourage instruction in English and a second language for all children (Tremblay 2019, pp. 180–181).

### Religion

The federal Constitution requires federal neutrality on religion. The document prohibits any religious test for federal offices (Article VI), and the First Amendment (1791) forbids the federal government from establishing any religion or abridging the free exercise of religion. Until the U.S. Supreme Court reinterpreted the First Amendment in 1934, moreover, it did not apply to the states. In 1788, five states had an established Anglican church and four had an established congregational church. These establishments continued beyond 1791 until the states disestablished their churches. Otherwise, some form of state support of religion continued until as late as 1875 in North Carolina and 1877 in New Hampshire.

Religious groups that predominate in a particular territorial jurisdiction, such as Mormons in Utah, can put their cultural stamp on that jurisdiction. Likewise, in Hamtramck, Michigan, which was previously French, then German, then Polish, and now Muslim, the Muslim call to prayers has been broadcast on the city's streets since 2004. Voters elected a majority-Muslim city council in 2015, although on Paczki Day (the Tuesday before Lent), Muslims crowd into bakeries to buy Polish pastries called 'paczki.' In 1984, after followers of Bhagwan Shree Rajneesh moved into Antelope, Oregon, they took over the municipal government and changed the city's name to Rajneesh (Abbott 1990).

pluralism' (Tatalovich 1995, p. 119), while the Colorado law was articulated as a means to prevent the creation of parallel English-speaking and Spanish-speaking communities (p. 155). Official English laws in Idaho, Iowa, and Missouri were defined by their main proponents as instruments of immigrant integration (Tremblay 2019, p. 179).

## *Family Law and Education*

Family law and education are other important cultural powers reserved to the states. Marriage law, however, experienced an early federal intervention because the new Republican Party, established in 1854, pledged to 'extinguish the twin relics of barbarism – slavery and polygamy' (Kincaid 2003). Because family law is reserved to the states, Mormons, who practised polygamy and had migrated to the Salt Lake basin in Utah to escape persecution, expected their territory to be admitted to the union with polygamy. However, beginning with the Morrill Anti-Bigamy Act of 1862, the federal government mounted a political, legal, economic, and partly militarized campaign to rid the Mormon territory of polygamy, which was portrayed as female slavery. After the Mormon church renounced polygamy in 1890, a reduced-size Mormon territory entered the union as Utah in 1896. Otherwise, the federal government did not disturb state marriage laws until 1967, when it struck down mostly southern state laws prohibiting marriage between blacks and whites (*Loving* 1967). The most substantial intervention occurred in 2015, when the U.S. Supreme Court voided all constitutional and statutory prohibitions of same-sex marriage (*Obergefell* 2015) present in a majority of states on the ground the bans violated the 'equal protection of the laws' clause of the Fourteenth Amendment (1868) to the U.S. Constitution.

Elementary and secondary education experienced little federal intervention until 1954 when the U.S. Supreme Court struck down mostly southern state laws mandating racial segregation in public schools (*Brown* 1954). The ruling sparked massive resistance, sometimes violent, from many white southerners from 1954 to the mid-1960s. This resistance provoked further federal involvement such that the federal government is now deeply entrenched in elementary and secondary education (e.g., Driver 2018) compared to Canada (Wallner 2014), although still far from something comparable to Australia's national curriculum (Reid and Price 2018).

## PROTECTING THE SOUTH'S PECULIAR INSTITUTION

The *Brown* ruling unveils a major reason for the U.S. Constitution's reservation of the police power and so many other powers to the states. Southern delegates to the Constitutional Convention of 1787 wanted to shield their 'peculiar institution' of slavery from federal interference. Even if slavery had been absent from the continent, the U.S. Constitution would still have reserved most domestic powers to the states because delegates from the northern states also wanted to protect their states' self-governing prerogatives, but no region was more insistent on thoroughgoing protection than the South, especially because southerners recognized that slavery was an anathema to many northerners.

Slavery was inextricably entwined with all the police powers exercised by the southern states, such that potential federal interventions into domestic matters seemingly remote from slavery triggered slippery-slope fears of federal pretexts for striking at slavery. For example, the federal government's campaign against polygamy could not begin until southerners had resigned from Congress when their states seceded from the union. Even though southerners abhorred polygamy, they refused to support anti-polygamy legislation out of fear that federal interference with polygamy would legitimize federal interference with slavery.

Territorial neutrality and democracy also reached a tragic apogee because of slavery. Before 1861, continual political battles occurred over the admission of new free and slave states. Both northerners and southerners wanted to maintain a balance of power in Congress between free and slave states. In 1854, the Kansas-Nebraska Act allowed settlers of those territories to vote on whether the territories would join the union as free or slave states and, thereby, alter the balance of power in Congress. Pro- and anti-slavery advocates poured into the territories, sparking considerable violence (Goodrich 2004). Kansas entered the union as a free state in 1861 after six southern states had seceded from the union. Nebraska joined the union in 1867.

As a result of slavery being the key pillar of the South's culture and growing northern opposition to slavery during the antebellum period, white southerners increasingly defined their territory as a separate nation. The existence of slavery in the contiguous states of the South helped southern whites define themselves as a separate nation—something that would not likely have occurred if slavery were dispersed among non-contiguous states. By the outbreak of the Civil War in 1861, many white southern elites conceptualized themselves as 'a separate nation ... a nation with its own people, existing within a nation' (Lee 2015). For them, it was from the Puritan or Roundhead versus the Cavalier or Norman heritage in England that sprang 'the two nationalities that now divide the empire of the American continent.' This notion 'drew a strong line of separation between distinct peoples and alien communities' (Moore 1862, 9), such that 'the present conflict in America is not a *civil* strife, but a war of *Nationalities*' (Moore 1861, 76). In this respect, the United States was a de facto binational federation.

Although some abolitionists urged northern secession so as to free those states from the taint of association with the southern slave states, most northerners did not forge a comparable regional 'national' identity. They rallied around the federal Constitution and the union, and they defined the southern secessionists as rebels against the Constitution's legitimate authority. Northern reactions, especially those of the Republicans, to the Kansas-Nebraska Act (1854), the Supreme Court's 1857 *Dred Scott* ruling, and the Civil War produced a major constitutional change in the nature of American federalism—the Fourteenth Amendment in 1868. The Republicans' leader, Lincoln, was appalled by the idea that the principles of territorial neutrality and democracy could be used to justify the right of anyone to vote on whether to enslave other human beings. Slavery, he argued, is 'a vast moral evil' (Lincoln 1858b, 461) for which no person has a right to vote. The underlying implication of the Fourteenth Amendment, therefore, is that certain fundamental human rights should not be subject to subnational democratic decision-making and that the federal government is obligated to intervene in states' domestic affairs in order to guarantee protection of such rights nationwide. The Fourteenth Amendment is directed squarely at the states, and Section 5 gives Congress authority to enforce the amendment's provisions in the states. Thus, federal neutrality on states' cultural preferences came to an official end in 1868 with an expectation by many northerners that the federal government would crush odious cultural manifestations of territorial neutrality and democracy.

However, this amendment was a dead letter for nearly a century. The federal government sought to reconcile the southern states to the union quickly, during the course of which it not only acquiesced but also endorsed the South's racial segregation policies (*Plessy* 1896) and black disenfranchisement that sprang up after the 1865–1877 period of Reconstruction (Bateman et al. 2018). The pre-war principle of federal neutrality and non-interference with respect to territorial jurisdictions and local democracies was strongly reasserted after the war as Republicans ceased to insist on black rights protection and as the solidly Democratic South allied with northern and western Democrats to wield more power in Congress, thereby holding at bay federal disturbances of the South's cultural preferences for about seventy years. Consequently, a measure of party polarisation in the U.S. Congress shows a sharp decline of polarization beginning at about 1906 and reaching a low point by 1930. The period from 1930 to about 1976 was one of historically low polarization and high bipartisanship in Congress (Moshowitz et al. 2017).

## CENTRALIZATION AND POLARIZATION

The civil-rights and equality revolutions associated with the 1960s considerably discredited and narrowed federal tolerance of territorially based multiculturalism because many of the territorial expressions of cultural preferences came to be viewed as anti-liberal (except for Indian tribes). Whereas 1960s' 'new left' revolutions elsewhere, as in Canada, often ushered in support for liberal expressions of territorial multiculturalism under the banner of anti-colonial self-determination, the self-determination struggles of minority groups in the United States led to calls for the federal government to centralize power and liberate 'oppressed' peoples from the tyranny of parochial state and local governments.

As before the Civil War, race has been a fundamental fault line. The contemporary fault began opening when President Harry Truman desegregated the U.S. armed forces in 1948, provoking some conservative southern Democrats to bolt the party and form the States' Rights Democratic Party (Dixiecrats), whose presidential candidate won four southern states in 1948. The U.S. Supreme Court's 1954 *Brown* ruling mandating racial desegregation of public schools incited massive southern resistance. Richard M. Nixon pursued a southern strategy in 1968 to pull the Democratic South into the Republican Party. Rising racial resentment among white Republican voters, which reached a record level in 2016, set the stage for Donald Trump's election to the presidency (Abramowitz 2018, 136–137).

Abortion became the second fundamental fault line after the U.S. Supreme Court struck down the laws in 30 states that prohibited abortion and the laws in 20 states that limited abortion (*Roe* 1973). Although nearly two-thirds of Americans have consistently supported the court's ruling since 1973, about one-third have opposed it vehemently. The court's later decision to void all state constitutional provisions and statutes prohibiting same-sex marriage (*Obergefell* 2015) aggravated this fault line, even though about 60 per cent of Americans supported same-sex marriage in 2015, which increased to 67 per cent by 2018 (McCarthy 2018).

Because of the profound political and societal changes occurring since the early 1960s, some observers contend that the United States no longer needs federalism because the country is no longer divided between free and slave states or among other subnational cultural identities (Feeley and Rubin 2008). The United States is now a single economic and cultural unit whose citizens no longer identify as New Yorkers, Virginians, and the like. There is much truth to this observation. Territorially speaking, there has been a tremendous socioeconomic convergence of the country's regions since the 1950s, especially an upward convergence of the South. Interstate migration, along with immigration since 1965, has also made the 50 states look increasingly similar than dissimilar. Federal policies imposed on the states have also increased uniformity.

Non-territorially speaking, however, the theory that federalism is now superfluous presupposes a national consensus on important cultural values. There is no such national consensus, as is evident in the rise of political polarization and cultural warfare (Hunter 1991), which has been underway since about 1968. The centralization of power and nationalization of cultural issues previously governed by the states could soon produce a national dissensus characterized by hyper-polarization.

As a result, the meaning of the U.S. Constitution as the nation's defining document is now embedded in white-heat conflict. Many of the triggers of polarization have been U.S. Supreme Court rulings interpreting the federal Constitution so as to strike down state laws mandating such policies as racial segregation and prayer and Bible-reading in public schools and prohibiting such practices as abortion and same-sex marriage.

Many Americans who support political leaders like Donald Trump believe the federal Constitution is being misused by unelected elites who are violating federal neutrality and depriving them of their rights to territorial democracy. As conservative commentator Patrick Buchanan put it (2017, 112), 'Brown v. Board of Education had taken the issue of school desegregation away from the states and Congress, and imposed Warren Court ideology on America, leading to decades of racial conflict that no civil-rights act ever produced. In the same way, Roe drove a wedge through America and ignited a culture war that is with us yet.' Consequently, the 2018 confirmation of Brett Kavanaugh for a seat on the U.S. Supreme Court to replace an often liberal justice was bitterly contentious. By contrast, from 1789 to 1965, 68 per cent of Supreme Court appointments were confirmed by acclamation in the Senate. None of the 18 justices (through Neil Gorsuch in 2017) appointed since 1965 have been approved by acclamation.

In short, so long as race, abortion, marriage, and other cultural matters were diffused across the landscape of territorial democracy under state regulation, national unity was high and polarization low, but the centralization of these local matters in the hands of the federal government necessarily polarized national politics. A fundamental question, therefore, is whether the American political system can reduce polarization in the face of the political impossibility of restoring most nationalized cultural issues to the states.

## Concluding Observations

The United States has never aimed to be multinational or plurinational in the contemporary sense of those terms. Several reasons account for this exceptionalism: (1) none of the original 13 states identified as a distinct 'national' polity set apart from the other states in terms of language, religion, nationality, or race; (2) none of the original states was a colony or former colony of a powerful rival of Great Britain; (3) the founders and most residents of the original states regarded themselves as at least a potentially single people by 1776; (4) the founders emphasized unity as an urgent need because the new nation was the only independent polity in a hemisphere otherwise controlled by the imperial superpowers of the 1780s; (5) the founders deemed unity essential for establishing an 'empire of liberty' (Jefferson 1780); and (6) no politically consequential demand for a multinational arrangement emerged in U.S. history.

Nevertheless, the United States was, and still is, multicultural in important ways (Kincaid 2016). This multiculturalism is expressed territorially and non-territorially. Although the founders did not use a language of multiculturalism comparable to that used today (Kymlicka 1995; Modood 2013), they recognized the assets and liabilities of cultural diversity among the states. They structured the U.S. Constitution to accommodate diverse cultural preferences by minimizing federal interference with the political and cultural affairs of the constituent states but allowing market and political forces to mitigate cultural establishments.

The founders' expectation was that the unity of the nation inhabited by a single people consisting of immigrants and their descendants would be achieved mainly through allegiance to the federal Constitution—or what was later termed 'constitutional faith' (Levinson 1988) and 'constitutional patriotism' (Müller 2006)—more than identification with a language, religion, race, or nationality. The American people exist only so long as the federal Constitution exists, which is why the Constitution occupies a sacred status rarely found in other federations.

Fostering such allegiance required substantial federal neutrality towards social diversity. This diversity was accommodated territorially by treating territory as neutral, such that whichever cultural group constituted a territory's majority could define its cultural life until interstate migration brought a new majority into power on that territory. Legally, 'State lines are all that distinguish one state from another and the people of one state from another' (Brilmayer 1991, 219).

Allowing expressions of cultural preferences across constituent territories fostered national unity around the Constitution because the federal government avoided imposing culturally homogenizing policies on a heterogeneous society. This system failed catastrophically in the early 1860s when the country polarized violently over slavery. Eleven southern states seceded from the union precisely because they feared the federal government was about to abrogate neutrality by moving to abolish slavery. It was northern accommodation of the slavocracy that had enabled creation of the union in 1788. For many northerners, though, slavery had become morally abhorrent, and by the 1860s, many believed, like Abraham Lincoln, that: 'A house divided against itself, cannot stand ... this government cannot endure, permanently, half slave and half free' (Lincoln 1858a, 197). Today, the political polarization that has characterized American national politics since the 1960s (Schier and Eberly 2016) can be attributed significantly, though not entirely, to federal impositions of culturally homogenizing policies on a still territorially heterogeneous society. Race is again a fault line in this polarization, but other fault lines, especially marriage and family policies, exacerbate that polarization.

Consequently, multiculturalism has been a double-edged sword for American federalism. On one edge, federal tolerance of territorial and non-territorial expressions of diverse cultural preferences has fostered national unity. On the other edge, some of the most ardent expressions of such preferences, especially those pivoting on racism, provoke moral approbation that generates calls for federal interventions that trigger centralization and polarization.

National polarization is re-territorializing diversity among the 50 states as mirror images of that polarization, as reflected in the division between blue (Democratic) states and red (Republican) states. In 2019, only two state legislatures were split between the two parties; otherwise, 30 legislatures had Republican majorities and 18 legislatures had Democratic majorities. Republicans controlled both the governorship and the legislature in 22 states; Democrats did so in 13 states. These two groups of states are almost as polarized as were free and slave states 159 years ago. Recent research also points to increased geographical and cultural self-segregation of like-minded people, mostly along liberal and conservative lines (Bishop 2009; Putnam 2015). Consequently, contemporary expressions of territorial democracy are less culturally diverse than the expressions that emerged during most of U.S. history and are also, unlike the past, more ideological than cultural.

Voters' religious beliefs are a major fuel of this polarization. The United States is one of the world's most religious countries, and a conservative, fundamentalist version of Christianity has taken root in recent decades, especially in red Republican states, particularly in the South. Loosely known as 'evangelical Christians,' these believers are politically active. About 80 per cent of white evangelicals voted for Trump in 2016. Pew polling concludes that 39 per cent of Americans are highly religious, 32 per cent, somewhat religious, and 29 per cent, non-religious (Alper 2018). Although the non-religious category is growing, religious activists will continue fuelling national polarization for the foreseeable future.

However, non-territorial multiculturalism, or what is often called 'identity politics,' flourishes nationwide and is most closely associated with liberals and Democrats. This multiculturalism is constitutionally sustained by the U.S. Bill of Rights and state constitutional declarations of rights that give citizens broad scope to express their cultural identities in civil society and to have those expressions protected against discrimination in the private and public sectors. This protection includes religious identities, such as the right of Muslim women to wear a hajib in workplaces and in public spaces, such as Congress and other government places. Sikh members of the U.S. military can wear a dastaar. Some aspects of this multiculturalism fuel polarization as certain identity groups align with one party and as voters of white European descent reject some contemporary expressions of identity.

The principal exception to the above developments is the reassertions since the early 1970s of territorial autonomy for indigenous peoples. There are 573 sovereign tribal nations in the United States. Congress enacted a series of statutes from 1975 to 1994 restoring important elements of tribal sovereignty and other Indian rights. The federal government treats the tribes on a government-to-government basis, thus making them a part of the intergovernmental system even though they are not constituent governments in the federal system because they are not parties to the federal Constitution. Although the U.S. Supreme Court has been less sympathetic to tribal sovereignty than Congress, and some justices would redefine tribes as 'clubs,' American Indians enjoy more territorially sovereign self-governance and rights protection than do Canada's First Nations and are more protected from invasive state legislation than First Nations are shielded from provincial legislation (Borrows 2016).

Contemporary legitimations of multinational federalism, at least in western federations, require minority 'nations' to adhere to the principles of liberal democratic welfare states, but because American federalism was created when the enslavement of African peoples was deemed legitimate, the union has had to struggle continually with illiberal cultural territories in its midst. Consequently, aside from the absence of a truly culturally distinct jurisdiction like a Quebec or Flanders, notions of multinational federalism ring alarm bells for most Americans.

## References

Abbott, Carl. 1990. Utopia and Bureaucracy: The Fall of Rajneeshpuram, Oregon. *Pacific Historical Review* 59 (1): 77–103.

Abramowitz, Alan I. 2018. *The Great Alignment: Race, Party Transformation, and the Rise of Donald Trump.* Yale University Press.

Alper, Becka A. 2018. From the Solidly Secular to Sunday Stalwarts, A Look at Our New Religious Typology. https://www.pewresearch.org/fact-tank/2018/08/29/religious-typology-overview/, accessed 11 June 2019.

Bateman, David A., Ira Katznelson, and John S. Lapinski. 2018. *Southern Nation: Congress and White Supremacy after Reconstruction.* Princeton: Princeton University Press.

Buchanan, Patrick J. 2017. *Nixon's White House Wars: The Battles that Made and Broke a President and Divided America Forever.* New York: Crown Forum.

Bishop, Bill. 2009. *The Big Sort: Why the Clustering of Like-Minded America Is Tearing Us Apart.* New York: Mariner Books.

Borrows, John. 2016. *Freedom and Indigenous Constitutionalism.* Toronto: University of Toronto Press.

Brilmayer, Lee. 1991. *Conflict of Laws: Foundations and Future Directions.* Boston: Little, Brown.

*Brown* v. *Board of Education* of Topeka, 347 U.S. 483 (1954).

Brownson, Orestes A. 1972 [1865]. *The American Republic: Its Constitution, Tendencies and Destiny.* Edited by Americo D. Lapati. New Haven: College and University Press.

Burlingame, Roger. 1960. *The American Conscience*. New York: Alfred A. Knopf.

Carstensen, Vernon. 1988. Patterns on the American Land. *Publius: The Journal of Federalism* 18 (4): 31–39.

*Chae Chan Ping* v. *United States*, 130 U.S. 581 (1889).

*Dred Scott v. Sandford*, 60 U.S. (19 How.) 393 (1857).

Driver, Justin. 2018. *The Schoolhouse Gate: Public Education, the Supreme Court, and the Battle for the American Mind*. New York: Pantheon.

Elazar, Daniel J. 1984. *American Federalism: A View from the States*. 3rd ed. New York: Harper & Row.

———. 1994. *The American Mosaic*. Boulder: Westview.

Elazar, Daniel J., and John Kincaid, eds. 2000. *The Covenant Connection: From Federal Theology to Modern Federalism*. Lanham, MD: Lexington Books.

Feeley, Malcolm M., and Edward Rubin. 2008. *Federalism: Political Identity and Tragic Compromise*. Ann Arbor: University of Michigan Press.

Frymer, Paul. 2017. *Building an American Empire: The Era of Territorial Expansion and Political Expansion*. Princeton: Princeton University Press.

Garrett, R. Sam. 2013. *Puerto Rico's Political Status and the 2012 Plebiscite: Background and Key Questions*. Washington, DC: Congressional Research Service.

Glazer, Nathan. 1977. Federalism and Ethnicity: The Experience of the United States. *Publius: The Journal of Federalism* 7 (4): 71–87.

Goodrich, Thomas. 2004. *War to the Knife Bleeding Kansas, 1854–1861*. Lincoln, NE: Bison.

Hill, Robert S. 1988. Federalism, Republicanism, and the Northwest Ordinance. *Publius: The Journal of Federalism* 18 (4): 41–52.

Hoganson, Kristin L. 2019. *The Heartland: An American History*. New York: Penguin.

Hooghe, Liesbet, Arjan Schakel, and Gary Marks. 2008. Appendix B: Country and Regional Scores. *Regional and Federal Studies* 18 (2–3): 259–274.

Hunter, James Davison. 1991. *Culture Wars: The Struggle to Define America—Making Sense of the Battles Over the Family, Art, Education, Law, and Politics*. New York: Basic Books.

Ivanyna, Maksym, and Anwar Shah. 2012. *How Close Is Your Government to Its People? Worldwide Indicators on Localization and Decentralisation*. Policy Research Working Paper 6138. Washington, DC: The World Bank, March.

Jefferson, Thomas. 1780 [1950]. Letter to George Rogers Clark. In *The Papers of Thomas Jefferson*, ed. Julian P. Boyd, Charles T. Cullen, John Catanzariti, Barbara B. Oberg, et al., V 4: 238. Princeton: Princeton University Press.

Kincaid, John. 2003. Extinguishing the Twin Relics of Barbaric Multiculturalism—Slavery and Polygamy—From American Federalism. *Publius: The Journal of Federalism* 33 (1): 75–92.

———. 2012. The Rise of Coercive Federalism in the United States: Dynamic Change with Little Formal Reform. In *The Future of Australian Federalism*, ed. Gabrielle Appleby, Nicholas Aroney, and Thomas John, 157–179. Cambridge: Cambridge University Press.

———. 2016. Territorial Neutrality and Cultural Pluralism in American Federalism: Is the United States the Archenemy of Peripheral Nationalism? *Swiss Political Science Review* 22 (4): 565–584.

Kirk, Russell. 1974. The Prospects for Territorial Democracy in America. In *A Nation of States: Essays on the American Federal System*, ed. Robert A. Goldwin, 2nd ed., 43–66. Chicago: Rand McNally.

Kymlicka, Will. 1995. *Multicultural Citizenship: A Liberal Theory of Minority Rights*. Oxford: Oxford University Press.

Laycock, Douglas. 1992. Equal Citizens of Equal and Territorial States: The Constitutional Foundations of Choice of Law. *Columbia Law Review* 92 (2): 249–337.

Lee, Harper. 2015. *Go Set a Watchman*. New York: Harper.

Levinson, Sanford. 1988. *Constitutional Faith*. Princeton: Princeton University Press.

Lincoln, Abraham. 1858a [1973]. A House Divided. In *The Political Thought of American Statesmen*, ed. Morton J. Frisch and Richard G. Stevens, 197–203. Itasca, IL: F. E. Peacock.

———. 1858b [1929]. Speech at Chicago. In *A Source Book of American Political Theory*, ed. Benjamin Fletcher Wright, 460–461. New York: Macmillan.

Lipset, Seymour Martin. 1963. *The First New Nation: The United States in Historical and Comparative Perspective*. New York: Basic Books.

Livingston, William S. 1952. A Note on the Nature of Federalism. *Political Science Quarterly* 67 (1): 81–95.

*Loving v. Virginia*, 388 U.S. 1 (1967).

Lukacs, John. 2005. *Democracy and Populism: Fear and Hatred*. New Haven: Yale University Press.

McCarthy, Justin. 2018. Two in Three Americans Support Same-Sex Marriage. *Gallup*. https://news.gallup.com/poll/234866/two-three-americans-support-sex-marriage.aspx, accessed 24 October 2018.

*Meyer v. Nebraska*. 1923. 262 U.S. 390

Modood, Tariq. 2013. *Multiculturalism: A Civic Idea*. Cambridge: Polity.

Moore, J. Quitman. 1861. The Belligerents. *De Bow's Review* 31 (1): 69–77.

———. 1862. Southern Civilization; or, The Norman in America. *De Bow's Review* 32 (1–2): 1–19.

Moshowitz, Daniel J., Jon C. Rogowski, and James M. Snyder, Jr. 2017. *Parsing Party Polarisation in Congress*. Paper Presented at https://scholar.harvard.edu/files/rogowski/files/npat-paper.pdf, accessed 23 October 2018.

Müller, Jan-Werner. 2006. On the Origins of Constitutional Patriotism. *Contemporary Political Theory* 5 (1): 278–296.

Mulligan, Christina, Michael Douma, Hans Lind, and Brian Quinn. 2016. Founding-Era Translations of the U.S. Constitution. *Constitutional Commentary* 31 (1): 1–53.

*Obergefell v. Hodges*, 135 S. Ct. 2584 (2015).

*Pierce, Governor of Oregon, et al. v. Society of the Sisters of the Holy Names of Jesus and Mary*, 268 U.S. 510 (1925).

*Plessy v. Ferguson*, 163 U.S. 537 (1896).

Putnam, Robert. 2015. *Our Kids: The American Dream in Crisis*. New York: Simon & Schuster.

Reid, Alan, and Deborah Price, eds. 2018. *The Australian Curriculum: Promises, Problems and Possibilities*. Canberra: Australian Curriculum Studies Association.

*Roe v. Wade*, 410 U.S. 113 (1973).

Russello, Gerald J. 1994. Russell Kirk and Territorial Democracy. *Publius: The Journal of Federalism* 34 (4): 109–124.

Schier, Steven E., and Todd E. Eberly. 2016. *Polarised: The Rise of Ideology in American Politics*. Lanham, MD: Rowman & Littlefield.

Schuck, Peter H., and Rogers M. Smith. 1985. *Citizenship Without Consent: Illegal Aliens in the American Polity*. New Haven: Yale University Press.

Stark, Rodney Stark, and Roger Finke. 1988. American Religion in 1776: A Statistical Portrait. *Sociological Analysis* 49 (1): 39–51.

Stein, Mark. 2008. *How the States Got Their Shapes*. New York: HarperCollins.

Tansill, Charles C., ed. 1927. *Documents Illustrative of the Formation of the Union of American States*. Washington, DC: Government Printing Office.

Tatalovich, Raymond. 1995. *Nativism Reborn? The Official Language Movement and the American States*. Lexington, KY: University Press of Kentucky.

Tocqueville, Alexis de. 1969 [1835]. *Democracy in America*. Edited by J.P. Mayer and Translated by George Lawrence. Garden City, NY: Doubleday Anchor Books.

Tremblay, Arjun. 2019. *Diversity in Decline? The Rise of the Political Right and the Fate of Multiculturalism*. Cham, Switzerland: Palgrave Macmillan.

Wallner, Jennifer. 2014. *Learning to School: Federalism and Public Schooling in Canada*. Toronto: University of Toronto Press.

Ward, Roger K. 1997. The French Language in Louisiana Law and Legal Education: A Requiem. *Louisiana Law Review* 57 (4): 1283–1324.

Wiebe, Robert H. 1975. *The Segmented Society: An Introduction to the Meaning of America*. New York: Oxford University Press.

## CHAPTER 6

# 'Nested Newness' and the Quality of Self-Government: The Case of the Hong Kong Special Administrative Region

*Susan J. Henders*

## INTRODUCTION

The chapter explores how 'nested newness' (Mackay 2014) has shaped the quality of minority territorial autonomy provided by the Hong Kong Special Administrative Region (HKSAR). This arrangement was established in 1997, when the south China coastal territory was incorporated into the People's Republic of China (PRC) after more than 150 years of British colonial rule. It is now clear that Hong Kong's post-handover autonomy arrangement has inadequately recognized, accommodated, and politically empowered this distinct territorial community to be self-governing in the sense of having the authority and power to protect and develop the distinct collective identity claimed by many of its residents. It has also failed adequately to advance socioeconomically and politically inclusive citizenship, resulting in a decentralization process that institutionalizes and protects the values, preferences, and power of capitalist and

S. J. Henders (✉)
York University, Toronto, ON, Canada
e-mail: henders@yorku.ca

© The Author(s) 2020
A.-G. Gagnon, A. Tremblay (eds.), *Federalism and National Diversity in the 21st Century*, Federalism and Internal Conflicts,
https://doi.org/10.1007/978-3-030-38419-7_6

131

other establishment elites allied with the PRC central government, at the expense of most residents.

The chapter illuminates how these outcomes are produced by a *nested* decentralization process. It uses and builds on MacKay's gendered concept of 'nestedness newness' as a means of clarifying 'the promise and limit of new institutions' such as those established during the decentralization of state architectures (2011, 550–551). Specifically, the analysis considers how three dimensions of nestedness can help account for the quality of self-government that results from decentralization: (1) how the HKSAR has been shaped by how the autonomy arrangement emerged and developed within the evolving inter-state and political economy structures in world order; (2) how it was shaped by the interplay of old and new institutions, actors, and power configurations; and (3) how it interacted with coincident, sequenced processes. In this case the sequenced processes included democratization and state- and nation-building. Drawing from the feminist institutionalist literature, the chapter argues that a focus on nested newness offers an account of some of the conditions in which minority territorial autonomy arrangements become strong-holds for conservative elites wishing to constrain how a minority community exercises its self-governing authority (see Vickers et al. 2010, 233–234; Henders 2010, 224–228; 2018). For Hong Kong, this limits the community's ability to protect and develop cherished values and (re)produces internally exclusionary citizenship that is classed, gendered, and ethnicized/racialized as well as marginalizing residents based on their immigration status. Examining nested newness can also help identify prospects for such a situation becoming entrenched.

The chapter first briefly situates Hong Kong within the context of comparative studies of federal/federalising polities and of minority territorial communities. It then introduces nested newness as an analytical concept, before using the latter to assess the quality of self-government available through the minority autonomy arrangement in Hong Kong to date. The conclusion offers openings for considering the comparative implications of the findings as well as for understanding the mounting public political mobilization against HKSAR and PRC government autonomy policies evident during the 2019 anti-extradition bill protests at the time of writing.

## 'MINORITY' STATUS AND SEMI-FEDERAL STRUCTURES

On the face of it, Hong Kong does not easily fit into the conversations in the present book. Its distinct identity is normally not claimed as 'nationness' except by some dissidents, much persecuted by central and HKSAR authorities in recent years (see Ngok 2017; Chan 2019; Veg 2017). Hong Kong people are not recognized as a minority nationality within the PRC constitution and laws, but rather regarded as part of the ethnic Han majority. When scholars discuss the distinct identity and values of Hong Kong, they generally give less attention to the Cantonese language and ethnicity of most residents compared to the territory's unique colonial history; its entrepot position in global and regional trade and commerce and associated capitalist institutions and ethos; its liberal institutions and values as well as democratic sentiments; and its outward-looking cultural orientation. Indeed, it is these latter three elements that the autonomy arrangement recognizes and attempts to protect. Nevertheless, since the handover, more residents and new movements have begun publicly contesting and resisting the rising power of Mandarin Chinese, or *Putonghua*, and simplified Chinese written characters in Hong Kong (Liu 2017). The present analysis treats Hong Kong as a minority territorial community, not because residents are an objectively identifiable substate group based on ethnolinguist or other markers of difference, but because of the claims of most residents that they have a distinct collective identity in the PRC context. Following Brubaker (2002), the analysis sees minorities or majorities, whether defined ethnically or in some other way, as contingent and contextual processes; it regards them,

> not as substances or things or entities or organisms or collective individuals—as the imagery of discrete, concrete, tangible, bounded and enduring 'groups' encourages us to do—but rather ... in terms of practical categories, cultural idioms, cognitive schémas, discursive frames, organizational routines, institutional forms, political projects and contingent events. (167–168)

Public opinion polls show that since the handover—and especially from 2008 for the generation born around 1997 and educated since—the identity *Heunggongyahn* 香港人, or Hongkonger, has strengthened and rarely is accompanied by a political identification with the Chinese nation; state-determined understandings of Chinese culture and identity are also widely repudiated by Hong Kong residents (see Veg 2017).

Further, the PRC's formally unitary state architecture suggests that an analysis of Hong Kong offers little to a discussion of contemporary federalisms. However, as argued elsewhere (Henders 2013), the PRC state architecture has 'hybrid' elements that open up points of comparison. Among these hybridities, emergent since the opening of the PRC economy to global capitalism in the early 1980s and early 1990s, are what He has called 'semi-federal' formal features, of which the Hong Kong and SARs are key examples (He 2007, 3, 13). Zheng argues that behavioural and informal federal characteristics have also created de facto policy discretion and bargaining space for substate authorities based on shared norms and reciprocity, although unevenly evident across space and function (2007, 99–107). These hybrid features emerged as a mechanism of market creation and involved the central government delegating to lower-level governments both institutional functions and some authority to make reforms and experiment (Montinola et al. 1995). Consequently, the PRC's hybrid state architecture has provided more economic than political autonomy for substate authorities, including Hong Kong. Moreover, decentralization has remained weakly institutionalized; there are few formal checks on recentralizing power, as has been evident since President Xi Jinping ascended to paramount PRC leader status from 2012 (Guo 2017; Hu 2017, 456–457).

Although its self-government has weakened since 1997, Hong Kong still has the most wide-ranging and deepest formal autonomy of the PRC substate authorities. The 'high degree of autonomy' promised for 50 years from 1997 is specified in Art. 2 of the Basic Law of the Hong Kong SAR (1990; hereafter BL), a PRC statute that elaborates on the 1984 Sino-British Joint Declaration (hereafter JD). The latter established an agreement on the British departure and parameters for the territory's future autonomy within the PRC. Compared with the units of formal federations, the functional range of Hong Kong's de jure competencies and its fiscal and financial autonomy under the BL are extensive (see Henders 2013; He 2007, 7–8). The HKSAR has formal autonomy in all functional policy areas except foreign affairs and defence; a separate legal system based on British-era statutes and the common law; courts with final adjudication power; and separate fiscal, monetary, and customs regimes. Its separate regional citizenship norms include the incorporation of key international human rights agreements into local law (the International Covenant on Civil and Political Rights as well as the International Covenant on Economic, Social and Cultural Rights). Therefore, residents have rights and freedoms unprotected elsewhere in the PRC. The autonomy arrangement promises an executive and legislature made up of Hong Kong permanent residents, with the eventual goal of a Legislative Council and Chief Executive elected by universal adult suffrage (BL Art. 3, 45, 68). Hong Kong also has authority to run its own economic and cultural external affairs, including by signing agreements with states, regions, and intergovernmental organizations where permitted for non-sovereign entities. These provisions give Hong Kong a distinct multi-level governance architecture in PRC terms.

However, the territory's political autonomy is shallow and missing many of the protections afforded the units of formal federations. The HKSAR's final decision-making authority is limited by PRC government vetoes, without constitutionalist protections such as a division of competencies protected in a legally binding constitution adjudicated by an autonomous judiciary. The Standing Committee of the PRC National People's Congress (NPC), not Hong Kong courts, has authority to interpret the BL and the NPC itself must approve all BL amendments (BL Art. 158, 159). Laws must be annulled if the NPC Standing Committee returns them for nonconformity with BL provisions concerning matters under central government jurisdiction or concerning HKSAR-central government relations (BL Art. 17). The 12-person Committee for the Basic Law, which advises the NPC on the BL, is not an independent committee able strongly to defend Hong Kong's autonomy nor its residents' civil rights and freedoms. Its advisory powers are highly circumscribed and its six Hong Kong members central government appointed (Ip 2015; Cheng 2007, 257–259; BL Appendix). The PRC has no regionally representative, democratically elected second legislative chamber, an important feature protecting the preferences of substate units in some federations. Hong Kong representatives to the NPC are chosen by a small number of mostly pro-PRC Hong Kong elites, rather than universal suffrage. Moreover, the central government appoints the HKSAR Chief Executive after nomination by a committee of Hong Kong elites (BL Art. 15, Ch. IV). Finally, the HKSAR legislature is only partly elected by universal suffrage and is dominated by pro-PRC elites, as detailed later (BL Annex II: Method for the Formation of the Legislative Council of the Hong Kong Special Administrative Region and Its Voting Procedures).

## NESTED NEWNESS

These institutional weaknesses undoubtedly contribute to the failures of the autonomy arrangement to protect the territory's distinct identity and values and to its exclusionary citizenship outcomes. Mackay's concept of nested newness, within the feminist institutionalism literature, deepens our understanding of why this is the case. As interpreted in the present analysis, nested newness offers a dynamic account that provides insights into the wider historical, institutional, and structural contexts of emergent and evolving minority autonomy arrangements, looking both at their environments within particular states and in wider world order. Specifically, Mackay's concept provides the basis for situating new institutions established during the decentralization of state architectures within the context of historically evolving structures of the inter-state system and the political economy in world order; interactions between established and new institutions, organizations, material conditions, power distributions, actors, and values; and sequenced, coincident processes, such as state- and nation-building and democratization.

Mackay's understands nested newness as a *gendered* concept, drawing attention to the ways that new institutions, like the old, are not gender neutral (Mackay 2014, 553). She uses nested newness to explain why the introduction and consolidation of new institutions do not necessarily foster women-friendly reforms, illustrating this with a case study of devolution in the United Kingdom focused on Scotland. Elsewhere, I have used nested newness to account for the gendered outcomes of the HKSAR autonomy arrangement, looking at its effects on women's equality and rights (Henders 2018). However, nested newness also offers broader analytical insights. Feminist institutionalist frameworks shed light on 'temporality, relationality, and contextuality in political developments' (Mackay 2011, 193), even where women's agency and equality or other aspects of gendered power are not the only or even the main analytical concern (see Krook and Mackay 2011).

Thus, beyond shedding important light on gendered patterns of inclusion/exclusion associated with minority autonomy arrangements, nested newness illuminates effects associated with class, ethnicity, racialization, and immigration status differences and other fields of hierarchical power, including their interactions. It allows for examination of the degrees to which autonomy arrangements both empower minority territorial communities and produce inclusive citizenship for differently empowered individuals within those communities. It does so by paying attention to the spatial and structural embeddedness of decentralization processes in wider environments, where they interact with institutions, processes, and unequal fields of power through time. Nested newness also *historicizes* minority autonomy arrangements, conceptualizing decentralization *as a process*, shaped by interactions between 'the new and the old' and with other simultaneous processes (Mackay 2014, 551–552). Newness's dynamic analytical framework, paired with an understanding of minority territorial communities as claims marked by contestation and uneven distributions of power within and vis-à-vis the outside, enables assessment of who benefits from decentralization processes within federal or hybrid states at particular times and why. Nested newness also provides analytical tools for considering the conditions in which the power hierarchies associated with autonomy arrangements may be challenged and with what potential consequences (see Vickers et al. 2010, 233–234; Henders 2010, 224–228; 2018). Informed by feminist thinking even while not focusing exclusively on women-friendly outcomes, the present analysis shares Mackay's view that we should assess the quality of sub-state self-government that results from institutional changes within federal or hybrid state architectures in terms of whether it advances inclusive citizenship on two axes, both for the minority territorial community vis-à-vis the majority community and central state as well as for the more vulnerable minority community residents. As Mackay (2011, 554) states: 'Nested newness, then, is a way of alerting us to the complexities of creating new institutions—for all institutional designers, but perhaps particularly so for feminist designers for whom their "new" seeks to challenge rather than conform to the wider status quo.'

## Nested Newness and the Hong Kong Autonomy Arrangement

The analysis examines three dimensions of the nested newness of the HKSAR as it emerged and has evolved from the early 1980s, each of them consequential for the quality of self-government over time. These include: how the autonomy arrangement has been shaped by the evolving world order context, particularly the interacting structures of the inter-state system and global political economy; how pre-1997 legacies have moulded the newer elements, referring to patterns of continuity and change in organizations, institutions, material structures, power distributions, actors, and values; and how the autonomy arrangement has interacted with and been shaped by coincident, sequenced processes, namely struggles over democratization in Hong Kong and PRC state- and nation-building with respect to the territory. These interacting processes have made decentralization in Hong Kong a triple transition.

### The World Order Context: The Inter-State System and Global Political Economy

Most broadly, the Hong Kong decentralization process has been nested in the processes, structures, and institutions of world order integral to its genesis, related to capitalist globalization and the inter-state system. This is evident in the two goals that motivated post-Mao PRC authorities to agree to the autonomy arrangements for Hong Kong and for Portuguese-administered Macau under Deng Xiaoping's 'one country, two systems' policy. The first was the desire to complete national unification by ending what they regarded as vestiges of European colonialism, making the boundaries of the de facto state coincide with the nation as idealized by the nationalist model of the modern territorial state. The second was the desire to modernize the PRC economy and society through selective integration into global capitalism.

The inter-state system in which the autonomy arrangement emerged has shaped it in several ways. It is unclear whether PRC decisions concerning Hong Kong were influenced by the general, if spatially uneven, trend since WWII of changes in state architectures that strengthened formal federalism and quasi-federal features of some states. These changes were sometimes impelled by territorialized minority claims and were promoted in recent decades by some inter-state organizations as 'best practices' or 'minimum standards' if not actual international legal norms (see Erk and Swenden 2010, 2–5; Kymlicka 2007, 379). The JD did not constitute Hong Kong as a minority territory, but in terms of a dispute between the UK and PRC governments 'left over from the past,' a territory that the PRC wanted to 'recover' and over which it would '[resume] the exercise of sovereignty,' a territory the UK would 'restore' to the PRC.

Nevertheless, other developments in inter-state norms and practices evidently influenced the autonomy arrangement. Because of a desire to be regarded as a system-maintaining inter-state participant so as to advance its developmental and nationalist goals, PRC authorities first formalized their autonomy plan for Hong Kong in the JD, an international agreement registered with the United Nations. The use of this international legal form reflected post-WWII growth in the use of international agreements by states in their mutual dealings. Further, the JD provision that the major international human rights treaties would apply to the territory after 1997 was consistent with the post-WWII trend towards the internationalization of human rights, that is, the increasing recognition that how a government treats its citizens is of legitimate international concern. Although somewhat unusual in comparative terms, the autonomy arrangement's provision to Hong Kong of significant self-rule in external economic and cultural affairs reflected the historical practice of permitting the participation of non-sovereign and sub-state governments in some inter-state organizations and international agreements, even if such governments still lack the high degree of international legal personality afforded sovereign states (Davis 1989). These concessions to and use of prevailing inter-state institutions and practices by the post-Mao government aimed to reassure Hong Kong people and global and Hong Kong investors that its commitments to the territory were trustworthy. Thus, drawing from findings in the feminist work on state architectures (see Sawer and Vickers 2010, 9–12; Haussman 2005; Mackay 2010a, 2010b; Vickers 2013, 2), the timing of Hong Kong autonomy arrangement vis-à-vis developments in the inter-state system mattered. The nature of inter-state norms and practices in the period of the HKSAR's emergence shaped the international dimension of the territory's multi-level governance architecture in ways that influence the quality of self-government, including inclusive citizenship, as discussed further below.

The political economy dimension of the world order context has also shaped these outcomes. The concept of 'graduated sovereignty' developed by Aihwa Ong (1999, 217–218; 2000) aids in theorizing the relationship between the PRC's position in and policy goals vis-à-vis global capitalism and its decision to establish the HKSAR and make other changes to its state architecture and sovereignty practices. Developed to understand the emergence in some southeast Asian states of special economic zones and other alterations to sovereignty in the 1980s and 1990s, graduated sovereignty refers to practices states used to manage their relationships with neoliberal global capitalism in an effort to capture its benefits while controlling its threats and risks. It involves employing territorially differentiated legal regimes marked by calibrated levels of state sovereignty and control as well as the differential governing of portions of the population according to their specific relationship to global markets. Applied to Hong Kong, the concept of graduated sovereignty locates in PRC efforts to attract and manage global capital both the genesis of the autonomy arrangements for Hong Kong and Macau as well as the simultaneous establishment of special economic zones and areas initially along the PRC coast. In the post-Mao period, Hong Kong evolved from being a transnational conduit for goods for a largely isolated command economy, to the PRC's main source of external investment and major transshipment, financial, legal, and other international business services hub as China opened to global capitalism. Increasingly, also, PRC businesses have used Hong Kong as a base for their own outward expansion. The autonomy arrangement was designed to protect the rule of law and other distinct liberal institutions that underpin this role and the economic advantages Hong Kong brought to the PRC economy. Business analysts debate the extent to which the PRC government still sees Hong Kong's international financial centre role in particular as worth protecting (see Rezvani 2019; Prasad 2019).

Yet, unlike in the southeast Asian special economic zones, and also unusual among contemporary minority autonomous territories in federal states, Hong Kong was not already governed by the state that granted it an autonomy arrangement. Rather, it was brought under de facto PRC rule for the first time as the arrangement was being implemented (although the PRC had always claimed sovereignty over the territory). Therefore, graduated sovereignty was not merely a means of articulating with global capitalism, but additionally a means of smoothing a significant state- and nation-building process vis-à-vis the territory. It provided a territorially specific legal regime and calibrated PRC state sovereignty and control to permit the HKSAR to deviate from mainland laws and institutions for 50 years. The aim was to facilitate rule over and the winning of the loyalties of people accustomed to liberal institutions; an outward-oriented capitalist economy; a majority Cantonese language and culture; and strong ties to the outside world, including significant numbers of residents with 'foreign' nationality and the widespread use of English. Hong Kong residents' claim to a distinct character, born of the territory's liminal position between empires, cultures, and globally contending ideologies and forms of economic organization, conflicted sharply with the PRC's authoritarian, Communist one-party political system, still largely command economy (when the JD was signed), state-defined Chinese nationalism and official *Putonghua* language. Additionally, distrust in the Communist PRC government was high, as most Hong Kong people either had fled the political and economic turmoil of the mainland over the decades or were the off-spring of such individuals.

In terms of the differential governing of population based on their specific relationship to global markets associated with graduated sovereignty, the HKSAR's distinct formal citizenship regime internally differentiates rights depending on residents' assumed value for capitalist accumulation, shaped by migration and racist assumptions (see Sautman 2004, 104). The regional citizenship regime continues British-era citizenship norms preferencing those considered capital generators; it also incorporated new PRC nationality norms based on *jus sanguinis* (status is acquired from the parent) and a stronger preferencing of ethnic Chineseness, in keeping with PRC government understandings of the nation. The old and the new interact to produce a regional citizenship regime where formal rights are allocated in classed, racialized or ethnicized, and gendered ways. The regime grants the most rights and status to Hong Kong ethnic Chinese individuals. Next come recent mainland migrants, especially those better-educated individuals deemed important for capital accumulation, and then other east Asians and those from the West considered similarly valuable. Among those with the least rights and status are most south Asians, even if they have lived in Hong Kong for generations, and the approximately 370,000 domestic workers, most from the Philippines or Indonesia and most women (ibid., 103–104).

Access to permanent residency rights illustratives how the regional citizenship regime differentially governs the population. Permanent residency accords a right of abode and some political rights. Hong Kong-born individuals and some of their offspring born elsewhere have a right to the status. Others may apply after living in the territory continuously for seven years. Under the BL (Art. 24), newcomers who are PRC nationals, unlike those who are not, can acquire permanent residency if they are Hong Kong born, even if their parents are not permanent residents. Access to permanent residency is also relatively easy for wealthier, better-educated, mostly male internationally mobile managers, even if they are not ethnic Chinese. By contrast, foreign domestic workers are excluded from permanent residency even when they have met the seven-year residency requirement. Although middle- and upper-class families rely on the care work of these individuals, it is deemed less value to capitalism (Wu, Ka-Ming 2003, 136, 141; Lam and Tong 2006; Chang and Ling 2000). Consequently, foreign domestic workers have an insecure status in Hong

Kong, with few political channels to challenge the government policies that perpetuate their inadequate remuneration and poor employment and political rights (Leung and RainLily 2015, 4, 9–10).

Ethnicized and racialized understandings of belonging further restrict regional citizenship rights, effectively excluding non-Chinese from holding the highest HKSAR offices. Only permanent residents with PRC nationality and no 'foreign' right of abode can serve in such top positions as Chief Executive, Executive Council or Legislative Council members, Chief Justice of the Court of Final Appeal, and Committee for the Basic Law members (BL Art. 44, 55, 67, 90). PRC law only grants citizenship to non-Chinese who are close relatives of Chinese, live in China and renounce their 'foreign' citizenship (Sautman 2004, 111–112). Later analysis will discuss the Hong Kong's substantive citizenship regime, where socioeconomic exclusion affects even the ethnic Chinese majority, but disproportionately harms women, poorer mainland newcomers, and non-ethnic Chinese without European ancestry.

### Pre-1997 Legacies and Their Interactions with the New

As the discussion of the autonomy arrangement's world order context has begun to demonstrate, the quality of collective self-government and inclusive citizenship under the HKSAR has been shaped by the interaction of pre-decentralization and post-1997 institutions, organizations, values, material conditions, actors, social relations, and power hierarchies related to class, gender, racialization, and ethnicization as well as immigration status. This interplay of the new and the old should be inherent in autonomy arrangements to the extent that they are designed to protect some existing features of minority societies. The quality of self-government under the HKSAR has particularly been shaped by the interaction of the British-era and new political economies and their related institutions, as it has contributed to perpetuating stark socioeconomic inequalities and undemocratic political institutions dominated by business and other establishment elites (see Poon 2011).

Regarding capitalist legacies, the BL gives quasi-constitutional status to pre-1997 laissez-faire and oligopolistic capitalist norms, policies, and political power. It requires HKSAR governments to maintain 'expenditure within the limits of revenue,' keep taxes low and hold prudent fiscal reserves; they must maintain Hong Kong as a free port and continue the land-lease system that underpins one of the developed world's worst property wealth disparities (BL Art. 107, 108, 111, 114, 120–123). The BL also protects the continued application after 1997 of Hong Kong laws that provide restrictive labour rights and protections and of international labour conventions selected to reinforce the established minimalist approach to labour standards (BL Art. 8, 39).

Together, these norms legitimate limited government economic regulation and public spending as well as the continuation of the pre-1997 residual approach to public social protection and the latter's restrictive eligibility criteria (see Chan 1998). The timing mattered here too, as the establishment of the HKSAR coincided with the economic recession that followed the 1997 Asian Financial Crisis. This caused the new HKSAR government to deepen already establish laissez-faire norms and policies in a manner similar to neoliberal restructuring elsewhere (Lee 2005).

The interaction of the old and new political economies has resulted in the institutionalizing and further normalizing of an established laissez-faire capitalist ethos and norms that have marginalized most residents economically. Income polarization, already increasing in the decades before 1997 and among the worst in the developed world, has continued to worsen. Women have been disproportionately represented in the ranks of the poor and especially the working poor (Oxfam, Hong Kong 2016, 2–3, 14) as they lack equal employment opportunities, remuneration, and work conditions despite educational attainment levels similar to men (Lee 2003, 5; DeGolyer 2013, 13; Kennett et al. 2013, 88). Racialized ethnic minorities, especially those of South Asian descent, are also disproportionately poor and socially and politically marginalized (Kapai 2015, Ch. 3, 13–17, Key Observations and Recommendations, 4; Ng 2018). This gendered and racialized marginalization is normalized by established discourses of Hong Kong identity that naturalize reliance on families, neighbourhoods, and communities for social protection and care. This particularly burdens women, who do most of the unpaid, underpaid, and precarious care work. When these established discourses of Hong Kong identity also represent self-sufficiency and family centredness as ethnic Chinese, they further contribute to exclusion by constituting non-ethnic Chinese residents as other (Lee 2003, 4–5; Kennett et al. 2013, 37). Poorer ethnic Chinese newcomers from mainland PRC are also disproportionately marginalized by the Hong Kong political economy institutionalized in the autonomy arrangement. They experience considerable social stigma and exclusion based on racialization and class, even though most are ethnic Chinese with relatively easy access to permanent residency and many are women married to or in long-term relationships with Hong Kong men (Kennett et al. 2013, 110–111, 120–123; Pun and Wu 2004; Lee et al. 2016).

Pre-1997 capitalist legacies have also been altered through interaction with new actors, institutions, structures, and processes linked to the PRC's growing economic and political power internationally and in Hong Kong. At the heart of Hong Kong's political system since its founding during the opium trade is a business-government alliance. This alliance began to shift with the JD and was reconfigured after 1997 (Ngok 2009, 498–499). Internationally oriented capital, once aligned with the British colonial government, has declined in relative power, while the power of PRC-oriented capital has increased. The PRC state has used patronage appointments to mainland political bodies and access to mainland business opportunities to secure allies among Hong Kong capitalists and other elites, incorporating them into the 'nation' (Mathews et al. 2008, 1, 15, 18; Holliday et al. 2004, 261). Political parties and civil society groups and movements now fall mainly into two camps, or are perceived as such: an establishment, or pro-PRC, camp, including the powerful reconfigured government-business alliance, and an opposition, pan-democratic, one. The pan-democratic camp has lost influence in formal government processes and, relatively speaking, gets little overt support from business, although pan-democratic parties have rarely challenged the established political economy. This political dualism has been complicated by the rise since 2010 of 'localist' movements and more recently new political parties demanding self-determination or independence for the territory, which PRC and HKSAR authorities have attempted to suppress (see Veg 2017).

The effects in Hong Kong of the interaction of the new and old political economy are broadly consistent with arguments that in the neoliberal context of recent decades, multicultural accommodation policies—including minority autonomy arrangements—have mainly served markets (e.g., Hale 2011, 2005). This has happened either because they push ethnic minority and indigenous individuals to become or remain transnationally competitive market actors, or at least not market inhibitors (Mitchell 2004, 123–124, cited in Kymlicka 2013, 110–111), or because they strengthen international economic competitiveness through protecting minority cultures and languages (ibid., 109–110). The key question is the extent to which minority autonomy arrangements enable or permit policy choices that deviate from market norms, such as to expand socioeconomic citizenship.

There is little political space for this in the HKSAR. Post-1997 political institutions significantly institutionalize undemocratic, business-dominated

British-era institutions, reinforced by the PRC government's own undemocratic political preferences. The BL and other policies have decolonized political institutions in the sense of putting Hong Kong ethnic Chinese into most senior executive, administrative, judicial, and legislative positions. At the same time, the BL provides for continuation of an executive-led, undemocratic and establishment elite-dominated political system. Due to late British-period reforms, some legislators are directly elected by universal suffrage, currently 35 seats in geographic constituencies and 5 from a slate of District Councillors. However, the other 30 legislators are chosen by 'traditional functional constituencies' with small electorates composed of occupational, social, and political interest-based groups where businesses, professional, and other establishment and pro-PRC elites dominate. Business and other establishment and pro-PRC elites also dominate the 1200-member Election Committee that chooses the Chief Executive for appointment by PRC central authorities (see Scott et al. 2017). The functional constituency system and Election Committee exclude most Hong Kong people from meaningful political representation by choosing these senior office-holders based on a classed and gendered definition of 'function.' Women, people who do precarious or poorly remunerated work, as well as those who do unpaid social reproductive labour and the unemployed have not been allocated traditional functional constituency seats (Hong Kong Women's Coalition for Beijing '95 1997; Young and Law 2004; Migrants Rights International 2003). Although only a few women have ever held a traditional functional constituency seat, not a single woman secured one in the 2012 and 2016 elections. Women have done somewhat better in competing for directly elected seats, gaining up to 20 per cent, still far from parity (Legislative Council Secretariat c.2009, 2 at Table 2).

Within this complex of continuity and change, the question of whether and how the territory's political system should be democratized has been hugely contentious. The HKSAR and PRC governments have delayed implementation of the BL promise of the eventual direct election of the Chief Executive and entire Legislative Council by universal adult suffrage (Art. 45, 68). Since the British years, there has been ongoing and strengthening pro-democratization political mobilization, as many residents came to see a democratic political system as necessary to shore up Hong Kong's autonomy and liberal institutions. The protesters who occupied major streets for 79 days in the 2014 Occupy Central and Umbrella Movement civil disobedience action demanded democracy to protect the territory's distinct culture and core shared values (e.g., rule of law; civil rights and freedoms and equality; anti-corruption). These had been strengthened in the last British years under pressure from feminist and other rights activists and pan-democratic political parties (see Fischler 2003). However, many 2014 protesters also saw democratization as necessary to challenge business and other establishment interests with a stake in blocking the building of a more socioeconomically equitable society (see Lo 2015, 111–112; Kaeding 2017, 161–63, 169, 170 at n. 2). Hong Kong capitalists fear a democratic political system would create electoral pressure for pro-poor, even pro-middle class policies that would threaten elite privileges and capital accumulation. The PRC central government worries that a democratic Hong Kong would more strongly challenge its policies, provide a channel for the 'foreign' influence it blames for political mobilization in the territory, and serve as a dangerous precedent for the mainland.

With democratization stalled, Hong Kong's political system now stands between 'electoral authoritarianism' and 'liberal authoritarianism' (Fong 2017), and the autonomy arrangement is still a power base for business and other pro-PRC establishment interests. Prospects for eventual democratization depend partly on whether more moderate business interests might arise and become convinced that such reforms are necessary to protect the core liberal values and institutions that underpin Hong Kong's economic competitive advantage within the PRC and internationally. Notably, several local and international business groups were publicly critical of the 2019 bill that would have permitted extradition to the PRC and that sparked massive, ongoing public protests in the territory. Business people, like other residents, feared the policy would expose individuals transferred to the mainland to arbitrary detention, unfair trial without due process, and torture. Business successfully lobbied the HKSAR government for changes to the proposal, and after massive popular demonstrations in June 2019 the government eventually withdrew the entire bill. Whether moderate business interests also could be convinced to support policies meaningfully to reduce socioeconomic inequalities is much less certain.

Finally, the status-quo-oriented, exclusionary political economy of Hong Kong's autonomy arrangement is reinforced by the international legal context of its emergence and development. As is argued elsewhere drawing from feminist institutionalist insights (Henders in press), the autonomy arrangement unfolded when international human rights standards had become relatively robust, including with respect to gender, ethnic, and racial equality. UN treaty bodies charged with monitoring government compliance with international human rights agreements both before and after 1997 have provided Hong Kong civil society organizations with some international political spaces and resources for drawing international attention to HKSAR government shortcomings as to rights protection (see Davis 1995). They have taken advantage of the public 'naming and shaming' used by UN treaty bodies to induce governments to improve their compliance with civil and political rights treaty obligations (see Petersen 2003, 42; Lim 2015, 44–45; Kennett et al. 2013, 94–95). However, the international dimension of multi-level governance provides less support for civil society groups pushing to strengthen socioeconomic rights and citizenship within the autonomy arrangement. As A. Claire Cutler (2001) argues, embedded in international law are assumptions that tend to reinforce the existing political economy, namely Westphalian state-centrism, legal positivism and 'public' understandings of the nature of authority. Consequently, international law tends to obscure the importance of non-state actors and of private, informal, and economic power in the contemporary global political economy. This helps explain why international socioeconomic rights are not regarded as justiciable (see Marsh 2016; Choukroune 2005), including in Hong Kong.

Another dimension of nestedness shaping the quality of self-government is its sequencing and interaction with coincident processes of democratization and PRC state- and nation-building, to which the analysis now turns.

### The Triple Transition

The emphasis of nested newness on the temporality, relationality, and contextuality of decentralization in federal or hybrid state architectures focuses attention to how decentralization may be shaped by coincident processes and their sequencing. As is argued elsewhere (Henders in press), Hong Kong's decentralization has been a triple transition. It has occurred simultaneously and interacted with two other major political processes: the PRC state's attempts through state- and nation-building to bring the territory under its rule and turn residents' orientations and loyalties towards it; and democratization, currently stalled.

The creation and operation of any autonomy arrangement involves state- and nation-building by the central/federal state vis-à-vis the sub-state territory, with its inherent tensions. Arguably, such tensions have been particularly intense in Hong Kong because the territory was brought under de facto PRC rule for the first time in 1997 and because there have been especially marked differences in institutions, socio-cultural and economic conditions, and organization as well as identities and values between the territory and the mainland. PRC state- and nation-building since 1997 have involved policies that have increased mainland economic and political influence in Hong Kong, eroded liberal institutions and democratization prospects, and decreased the scope for dissent given central government expectations that residents behave as PRC patriots. These policies have triggered political resistance from large sectors of Hong Kong society and growing political mobilization, evidenced by the anti-government protests ongoing since June 2019. The central and HKSAR governments have backed off on, delayed or moderated some policies many residents saw as bringing illiberal and arbitrary mainland norms and practices into Hong Kong, but only after major public protests and other forms of extra-parliamentary political mobilization. This occurred with the 2019 extradition bill; a 2014 proposal to allow direct election of the Chief Executive but using a candidate selection method that ensured a pro-PRC winner; a 2012 national education curriculum policy deemed an attempt to brainwash students; and a 2003 national security bill widely seen as eroding civil rights and freedoms. While these strategic government retreats have helped protect liberal institutions in the short term, they have not resolved the political disfunctions of the autonomy arrangement and its inability to provide meaningful and inclusive collective self-government. At the time of writing there were mounting tensions between HKSAR police, criticized for using rubber bullets and other 'brutal' techniques, and anti-government protesters, who have been increasingly confrontational and in some cases have resorted to violence. With their present composition, norms, and authority, the executive and legislature have failed to provide much needed political solutions.

Democratization would be but a first step towards such solutions, but is unlikely in the foreseeable future given the interactions and sequencing of decentralization with PRC state- and nation-building. In a comparative analysis, Filippov and Shvetsova (2013, 167–168) argue that federalism is less likely to foster democratic consolidation where institutions and processes only weakly integrate the sub-state territory and the state. This is because the central-local bargaining and related tensions typical of federal state architectures are more likely to be politically destabilizing in circumstances where a sub-state territory is weakly integrated with a state. In these circumstances, political incumbents are likely to try to undermine democratic consolidation in an attempt to lessen political instability. This finding can only be applied cautiously to a context where democratization itself is at issue in a minority autonomy arrangement within a hybrid state architecture. However, it suggests that conditions in Hong Kong may be especially inhospitable for democratization. Given the relative newness of the PRC state- and nation-building process and the marked institutional and social asymmetries between Hong Kong and the mainland, integrative conditions are particularly weak. Following Filippov and Shvetsova's logic, the tensions associated with normal central-local bargaining should be especially sharp. The incumbents—the PRC central and HKSAR governments and Hong Kong's politically dominant establishment elites—are very likely to block democratization, fearing it will increase political instability and further weaken integration, alongside concerns about it weakening the established unequal political economic order.

Comparative analysis of the interaction and sequencing of political processes also suggests weak to moderate prospects for transforming the autonomy arrangement into one supportive of more socioeconomically inclusive citizenship. Kymlicka argues that prospects for substantive citizenship are greater where 'a threshold level of democratic citizenization' (2013, 117) predates the introduction of neoliberal policies. When sequenced in this way, the negative effects of the neoliberal policies are more likely to be buffered by constitutional rights protections and electoral and representative politics (ibid. 2013, 99–100, 114–115). Using Kymlicka's logic, prospects for strong substantive citizenship in Hong Kong are weak as constitutional rights protections did not predate neoliberal policies and the territory's political system is still undemocratic. The administration of Chief Executive Carrie Lam has taken small steps to increase the affordable housing supply and slightly increase social protection spending, but the established political economic order remains, protected by the autonomy arrangement.

## Conclusions

This chapter has examined the Hong Kong case to show how MacKay's gendered understanding of nested newness can account for the quality of self-government resulting from decentralization processes. The HKSAR has thus far served as a power base for government, capitalist, and other establishment elites with a vested interest in constraining how the territory's self-governing authority is exercised, limiting both the community's ability to protect and develop shared, cherished core values and to advance internally inclusive socioeconomic citizenship for those marginalized by intersecting class, gender, ethnicized, racialized, and immigration status hierarchies. Nested newness draws attention to the effects on emergent minority autonomy arrangements of key temporal, relational, and contextual factors: the world order in which the HKSAR was negotiated and implemented, especially the late twentieth- and early twenty-first-century inter-state and global capitalist systems; interactions between British-era and new institutions, organizations, material conditions, power distributions, social relations, values, and actors; and the sequencing of decentralization with coincident processes, in this case state- and nation-building and democratization. To be clear, feminist institutionalism, and Mackay's gendered concept of nested newness, shed light on gendered exclusion and inclusion as effects of the nested newness of minority autonomy arrangements. However, as the foregoing discussion has shown, these insights that can be extended to understand nested newness's broader effects on collective self-rule and dimensions of inclusive citizenship beyond gender alone. The analysis illuminates the conditions that shape the potential for minority autonomy arrangements to advance the protection of the collective identities and values of territorial communities claimed to be distinct, but also that affect their ability to make new choices about inclusive socioeconomic citizenship as conditions and values evolve.

The analysis has focused attention on the political economy context of evolving minority autonomy arrangements. This dimension is particularly evident in the Hong Kong case, as the application of the 'one country, two systems' policy to the territory explicitly aimed to reproduce its system of capitalist accumulation even while advancing the PRC's national unification goals. However, the nested newness concept more generally underscores the need to incorporate political economy analysis into the study of multinational accommodation within federal and hybrid state architectures. It offers an analytical framework for considering how late capitalism in specific places and moments effects state architectures and other policies concerning the accommodation of territorialized cultural differences. At the same time, nested newness as well as Hong Kong's experience suggests that self-government quality is not reducible to the evolving effects of capitalist social relations and power alone. Much will also depend on how these interact with other dimensions of the autonomy arrangement's evolving historical, institutional, and structural context. Not least, nested newness emphasizes the element of time. Hong Kong is only promised autonomy for 50 years, and 2047 is well within the lifetime of the territory's young generation of increasingly politically mobilized residents.

## POSTSCRIPT

As I write from Hong Kong several months after submitting the present chapter, pan-democratic candidates have just swept the territory's District Council elections, held November 24, 2019. The turnout of 71.2 per cent of registered voters was a historic record for any Hong Kong election. The District Councils are the territory's only almost fully directly elected bodies. However, they are advisory and mainly deal with local matters like garbage collection and bus stop locations. Going into the polls, they were largely controlled by relatively well-resourced, pro-establishment politicians benefitting from the local organizing of pro-Beijing groups. Nevertheless, as nested newness reminds us, timing matters. The elections occurred when nearly six months of anti-government demonstrations triggered by the now formally withdrawn extradition bill had been in a particularly disruptive and violent phase. The economy was officially in recession. Protester demands had expanded to include a demonstrator amnesty, withdrawal of the designation of some protests as riots, an independent inquiry into alleged police brutality and misconduct, and democratization. Voters, including some who thought the protesters had gone too far, widely repudiated the government.

Police-protester clashes intensified in mid-November after a protester's death, but also due to mounting anger over the government's failure to provide a political way forward. Instead, the government relied on police, apparently authorized to use what many residents regarded as disproportionate violence against protesters. Demonstrators blocked access to some university campuses, major roads and public transport. Daily life was seriously disrupted for days. Schools were closed; as universities became major front lines, post-secondary classes were also cancelled. One campus saw a pitched battle between police and protesters; another experienced a days-long standoff and the violent clashes spilled into nearby neighbourhoods. As I write, a few dozen protesters are still inside that campus, surrounded by a police cordon and concerned residents. Many protesters have been seriously injured, as have some police, journalists, politicians, and residents (one of whom died). The authorities have increasingly denied permission for legal demonstrations. Consequently, the District Council polls became a referendum on the government's handling of the crisis. With pan-democrats reported to have won just under 60 per cent of the popular vote and 347 of 452 seats, they have effectively wrested control of 17 of 18 of the local bodies from establishment and pro-Beijing politicians.

The day after the election, Chief Executive Lam said in a statement that the 'SAR government will humbly listen to the public and reflect thoroughly' (Cheng 2019a). PRC officials did not directly address the pandemocratic landslide, reiterating that halting violence and restoring stability remained priorities and that Hong Kong was still an SAR within the PRC (SCMP Staff 2019). At this crucial point in the evolution of Hong Kong's autonomy arrangement, the nested newness analytical framework points to three key contextual, temporal, and structural factors shaping events and, ultimately, the quality of self-government possible.

First, the evolving global political economy in which the autonomy arrangement is embedded—characterized by the PRC's growing economic and political power in Hong Kong and beyond—has continued to influence government responses to protester demands. Local and international business associations and elites widely and publicly criticized the extradition bill, a key factor in its eventual withdrawal. However, the business-government alliance institutionalized in the autonomy arrangement has not openly fractured. As the protests went on, the territory's powerful business tycoons largely backed the government's hardline, no concessions strategy.

Some business-related actors were more willing than others to push back publicly, despite the reliance of so many on PRC money, directly or indirectly. In recent weeks, some office workers in the central financial district held almost daily lunch-hour anti-government demonstrations in support of protesters. Back in July, the American Chamber of Commerce in Hong Kong called on the HKSAR government to end the violence and promote reconciliation. Underscoring the importance of Hong Kong's liberal institutions to capitalism, it said that a survey of its members found concern that the protests could permanently damage the territory's reputation as an international business hub characterized by the free flow of information and rule of law (Tsang 2019). The HKSAR government continued to reject protester demands for an independent inquiry into police conduct. However, the American Chamber said its members supported '[s]etting up an internationally credible independent inquiry into all aspects of recent unrest over the bill, a move that will demonstrate fairness and justice under the rule of law' (American Chamber of Commerce in Hong Kong 2019).

A legacy of the context in which the autonomy arrangement arose, two sets of norms are still evidently in tension in the territory's 'one country, two systems': the norms of traditional territorial state sovereignty that legitimate PRC state- and nation-building and the liberal norms that instead internationalize Hong Kong's status, and that are desired by many residents and valued by many businesses. Accordingly, the PRC government has declared to be illegal foreign interference the US *Hong Kong Human Rights and Democracy Act* passed by Congress in recent days. Effectively an expansion of the 1992 United States–Hong Kong Policy Act that permits the US to treat post-1997 Hong Kong separately from the rest of the PRC for trade and economic controls purposes, the new Act provides for sanctions against individuals or entities considered to have violated freedoms guaranteed in Hong Kong by the Basic Law.

Time, and the interacting new and old, have been the second dimension of nested newness of particular relevance at this juncture in the evolution of Hong Kong's autonomy arrangement. The protests have brought to the fore new and newly empowered actors, namely the police and the demonstrators, many of the latter school- and university-aged individuals. To be clear: these actors are empowered, but not symmetrically. The police, who used more powerful weapons and tactics as the protest continued, recently changed their motto from 'We Serve with Pride and Care' to 'Serving Hong Kong with Honour, Duty and Loyalty' (Cheng 2019b). Wearing professional grade protective clothing, often full anti-riot gear, they have deployed tear gas, pepper spray, water cannon, rubber bullets, and sometimes live ammunition; there have also been reports of semi-automatic weapons and machine guns stored at the front lines. Meanwhile, protesters, typically armed with masks, umbrellas, and other makeshift garb, have sometimes wielded bricks, petrol bombs, and metal poles, and occasionally arrows and corrosive acid (Leung 2019). Protester-police interactions with each other have weakened the HKSAR government's legitimacy and power; they have pushed into greater prominence the District Councils. There, large numbers of new voters have helped to elect significant numbers of new, younger-generation pan-democratic politicians. Moreover, despite their restricted formal policy role, these pan-democratic District Councils will affect the political balance in upcoming higher-level elections: District Councils select 117 of the 1,200 Election Committee members who choose the Chief Executive; electors choose five District Councillors as legislators. All of these new and newly empowered actors could have longer-term consequences for more established actors in Hong Kong's autonomy arrangement.

However, the local election alone will not resolve the political and socioeconomic exclusion that helped propel people into the streets. What began as massive, peaceful demonstrations against the extradition bill over time widened into a struggle for meaningful autonomy for Hong Kong, the protection of residents' rights and freedoms as well as democratization. In the last weeks, protesters have been as little inclined to accept concessions as has been the governments.

The triple transition that characterizes Hong Kong's autonomy process still makes democratization a risky proposition for the PRC government. The protests have further underscored how weakly integrated into the rest of the PRC many Hong Kong residents are and want to be, even though those advocating for independence remain a minority. Through the protests, the central government has continued to prioritize the strengthening of state- and nation-building in the territory, especially through stronger national patriotic education and more aggressive national security laws. When, just days before the election, local judges ruled unconstitutional a HKSAR emergency regulation banning protesters from wearing masks, a central government official stated that only the NPC Standing Committee had the authority to interpret the Basic Law, failing to mention the scope that Hong Kong courts have under the Basic Law Art. 158 to make such interpretations on their own when adjudicating cases involving Basic Law provisions within the limits of the HKSAR's autonomy.

Yet, so far the Standing Committee has left the Hong Kong courts to adjudicate as the HKSAR government attempts to defend the anti-mask regulation. Protesters and police did not clash on polling day. Voters were given their say. Demonstrators and police remained relatively restrained the next day amid reports that protesters still at one campus were in some cases refusing to eat. The calling of an independent inquiry into police conduct and other government concessions could contribute to de-escalation and to building political conditions more conducive to political dialogue on democratization, socioeconomic exclusion, and the protection of the territory's distinct identity and institutions. Meanwhile, the wider contextual, temporal, structural, and processual nestedness of Hong Kong's autonomy arrangement will continue to constrain its evolution and the quality of self-government it provides.

Hong Kong
November 25, 2019

## References

American Chamber of Commerce in Hong Kong. 2019. *Fix Hong Kong's Protest Pain Now or Risk Permanent Scars: AmCham Survey.* Hong Kong: American Chamber of Commerce in Hong Kong. July 26. https://www.amcham.org.hk/.

Cheng, Kris. 2019a. *Hong Kong District Council Election: Democrats Take Control of 17 out of 18 Councils in Landslide Victory.* Hong Kong Free Press, November 25. https://www.hongkongfp.com/.

Cheng, Kris. 2019b. Hong Kong Police Drop 'Pride and Care' Motto, Now Vow to Serve with 'Honour, Duty and Loyalty'. *South China Morning Post,* November 20. https://www.hongkongfp.com/.

Leung, Christy. 2019. Police Respond to More Menacing Mob Attacks by Bringing Out Lethal Anti-Riot Weapons Not Used Earlier in Unrest. *South China Morning Post,* November 20. https://www.scmp.com/.

SCMP Staff. 2019. Hong Kong Election Result Draws Cautious Response from China. *South China Morning Post,* November 25. https://www.scmp.com/.

Tsang, Denise. 2019. American Chamber of Commerce Urges Government to Step Up Reconciliatory Efforts to Save City's Reputation from Permanent Damage. *South China Morning Post,* October 15. https://www.scmp.com/.

## References

*Basic Law of the Hong Kong Special Administrative Region.* 1990. Hong Kong: Government of the Hong Kong Special Administrative Region. http://www.basiclaw.gov.hk/en/basiclawtext/index.html.

Brubaker, Rogers. 2002. Ethnicity Without Groups. *European Journal of Sociology/ Archives européennes de sociologie* 43 (2): 163–189.

Chan, Chak-Kwan. 1998. Welfare Policies and the Construction of Welfare Relations in a Residual Welfare State: The Case of Hong Kong. *Social Policy & Administration* 32 (3): 278–291.

Chan, Holmes. 2019. In Full: Hong Kong Leader Carrie Lam Submits Report to Beijing on Banning Pro-Independence Party, Makes Doc Public. *Hong Kong Free Press,* April 18. https://www.hongkongfp.com/2019/04/18/just-hong-kong-leader-carrie-lam-submits-report-beijing-banning-pro-independence-party-makes-doc-public/.

Chang, Kimberley A., and L.H.M. Ling. 2000. Globalization and Its Intimate Other: Filipina Domestic Workers in Hong Kong. In *Gender and Global Restructuring: Sightings, Sites, and Resistances,* ed. Marianne H. Marchand and Anne Sisson Runyan, 27–44. Abingdon: Routledge.

Cheng, Peter T.Y. 2007. Toward Federalism in China? The Experience of the Hong Kong Special Administrative Region. In *Federalism in Asia,* ed. Baogang He, Brian Galligan, and Takashi Inoguchi, 242–265. Cheltenham: Edward Elgar.

Choukroune, Leila. 2005. Justiciability of Economic, Social, and Cultural Rights: The UN Committee on Economic, Social and Cultural Rights' Review of China's First Periodic Report on the Implementation of the International Covenant on Economic, Social and Cultural Rights. *Columbia Journal of Asian Law* 19 (1): 30–49.

Cutler, A. Claire. 2001. Critical Reflections on the Westphalian Assumptions of International Law and Organization: A Crisis of Legitimacy. *Review of International Studies* 27 (3): 133–150.

Davis, Michael C. 1989. *Constitutional Confrontation in Hong Kong: Institutional Implications of the Basic Law*. London: Macmillan.

———., ed. 1995. *Human Rights and Chinese Values: Legal, Philosophical, and Political Perspectives*. Hong Kong: Oxford University Press.

DeGolyer, Michael E. 2013. *The Changing Faces of Hong Kong Women in the Community and National Context, 1994–2010*. February. Hong Kong: Civic Exchange and the Women's Foundation.

Erk, Jan, and Wilfried Swenden. 2010. The New Wave of Federalism Studies. In *New Directions in Federalism Studies*, ed. Jan Erk and Wilfried Swenden, 1–15. Abingdon: Routledge.

Filippov, Mikhail, and Olga Shvetsova. 2013. Federalism, Democracy, and Democratization. In *Federal Dynamics: Continuity, Change, and the Varieties of Federalism*, ed. Arthur Benz and Jorg Broschek, 167–184. Oxford: Oxford University Press.

Fischler, Lisa. 2003. Women's Activism During Hong Kong's Political Transition. In *Gender and Change in Hong Kong: Globalisation, Postcolonialism and Chinese Patriarchy*, ed. Eliza W.Y. Lee, 49–77. Vancouver: University of British Columbia Press.

Fong, Brian. 2017. In-Between Liberal Authoritarianism and Electoral Authoritarianism: Hong Kong's Democratization Under Chinese Sovereignty, 1997–2016. *Democratization* 24 (4): 724–750.

Guo, Gaogang. 2017. China's Administrative Governance Reform in the Era of 'New Normal'. *Journal of Chinese Political Science* 22 (3): 357–373.

Hale, Charles. 2005. Neoliberal Multiculturalism: The Remaking of Cultural Rights and Racial Dominance in Central America. *PoLAR Political & Legal Anthropology Review* 28 (1): 10–28.

———. 2011. *Resistencia Para Que?* Territory, Autonomy and Neoliberal Entanglements in the 'Empty Spaces' of Central America. *Economy and Society* 40 (2): 184–210.

Haussman, Melissa. 2005. *Abortion Politics in North America*. Boulder and London: Lynne Rienner.

He, Baogang. 2007. Democratization and Federalizations in Asia. In *Federalism in Asia*, ed. Baogang He, Brian Galligan, and Takashi Inoguchi, 1–32. Cheltenham: Edward Elgar.

Henders, Susan J. 2010. *Territoriality, Asymmetry, and Autonomy: Catalonia, Corsica, Hong Kong, and Tibet*. New York: Palgrave Macmillan.
———. 2013. Assessing Hybridity in the People's Republic of China: The Impact of Post-Mao Decentralization. In *Routledge Handbook of Regionalism and Federalism*, ed. John Loughlin, John Kincaid, and Wilfried Swenden, 371–386. London: Routledge.
———. 2018. Territorial Autonomy, Nationalisms, and Women's Equality and Rights: The Case of the Hong Kong Special Administrative Region. In *Gendering Nationalism: Intersections of Nation, Gender and Sexuality in the 21st Century*, ed. Jon Mulholland, Nicola Montagna, and Erin Sanders-McDonagh, 337–356. Basingstoke: Palgrave.
———. in press. 'Nested Newness' and the Engendering of Regional Autonomy: Women's Rights and Equality in Hong Kong. In *Handbook on Gender, Diversity and Federalism*, ed. Jill Vickers, Cheryl Collier, and Joan Grace. Cheltenham: Edward Elgar.
Holliday, Ian, Ma Ngok, and Ray Yep. 2004. After 1997: The Dialectics of Hong Kong Dependence. *Journal of Contemporary Asia* 34 (2): 254–270.
Hong Kong Women's Coalition for Beijing '95. 1997. Alternative Report on Women in Hong Kong. In *EnGendering Hong Kong Society: A Gender Perspective of Women's Status*, ed. Fanny M. Cheung, 385–394. Hong Kong: Chinese University Press.
Hu, Xiaobo. 2017. China's New Normal: Challenges to Old Politics of Economic Reforms China's Administrative Governance Reform in the Era of 'New Normal'. *Journal of Chinese Political Science* 22 (3): 449–460.
Ip, Eric C. 2015. Prototype Constitutional Supervision in China: The Lessons of the Hong Kong Basic Law Committee. *Asian Journal of Comparative Law* 10 (2): 323–342.
Kaeding, Malte Philipp. 2017. The Rise of 'Localism' in Hong Kong. *Journal of Democracy* 28 (1): 157–171.
Kapai, Puja. 2015. *Status of Ethnic Minorities Report, 1997–2014*. Hong Kong: Zubin Foundation and Centre for Comparative and Public Law, Faculty of Law, University of Hong Kong. https://www.hku.hk/press/press releases/detail/13284.html.
Kennett, Patricia, Chan Kam Wah, Chung Kim Wah, Pun Ngai, and Lucille Lok Sun Ngan. 2013. *Governance and Citizenship in East Asia: Beijing, Hong Kong, Taipei, and Seoul*. Research Report Series. June 20. Hong Kong: Centre for Social Policy Studies, Department of Applied Social Sciences, Hong Kong Polytechnic University.
Krook, Mona, and Fiona Mackay. 2011. Introduction: Gender, Politics, and Institutions. In *Gender, Politics, and Institutions: Towards a Feminist Institutionalism*, ed. Mona Krook and Fiona Mackay, 1–20. Houndmills: Palgrave Macmillan.

Kymlicka, Will. 2007. National Cultural Autonomy and International Minority Rights Norms. *Ethnopolitics* 6 (3): 379–393.

———. 2013. Neoliberal Multiculturalism. In *Social Resilience in the Neoliberal Era*, ed. Peter A. Hall and Michèle Lamont, 99–125. Cambridge: Cambridge University Press.

Lam, Wai-Man, and Irene L.K. Tong. 2006. Political Change and the Women's Movement in Hong Kong and Macau. *Asian Journal of Women's Studies* 12 (1): 7–35.

Lee, Eliza Y.W. 2003. Introduction: Gender and Change in Hong Kong. In *Gender and Change in Hong Kong: Globalisation, Postcolonialism and Chinese Patriarchy*, ed. Eliza W.Y. Lee, 3–22. Vancouver: University of British Columbia Press.

———. 2005. The Renegotiation of the Social Pact in Hong Kong: Economic Globalisation, Socio-Economic Change, and Local Politics. *Journal of Social Policy* 34 (2): 293–310.

Lee, Siu-Yau, Isabella F.S. Ng, and Kee-Lee Chou. 2016. Exclusionary Attitudes Toward the Allocation of Welfare Benefits to Chinese Immigrants in Hong Kong. *Asian and Pacific Migration Journal* 25 (1): 41–61.

Legislative Council Secretariat. c.2009. *Fact Sheet: Woman Participation in the Legislative Council, the District Councils, the Public Sector Advisory and Statutory Bodies, the Government of Hong Kong and Selected Overseas Legislatures, FS12/09-10*. Hong Kong: Legislative Council Secretariat. http://www.legco.gov.hk/yr09-10/english/sec/library/0910fs12-e.pdf.

Leung Lai-Ching and RainLily. 2015. *The Effectiveness of the 'We Stand Program for Female Migrant Workers and Ethnic Minority Women': A Research Report*. April. Hong Kong: RainLily.

Lim, Adelyn. 2015. *Transnational Feminism and Women's Movements in Post-1997 Hong Kong: Solidarity Beyond the State*. Hong Kong: Hong Kong University Press.

Liu, Juliana. 2017. Cantonese v Mandarin: When Hong Kong Languages Get Political. *BBC News*, June 29. https://www.bbc.com/news/world-asia-china-40406429.

Lo, Sonny. 2015. *Hong Kong's Indigenous Democracy: Origins, Evolution and Contentions*. Houndmills: Palgrave Macmillan.

MacKay, Fiona. 2010a. Descriptive and Substantive Representation in New Parliamentary Spaces: The Case of Scotland. In *Representing Women in Parliament: A Comparative Study*, ed. Marian Sawer, Manon Tremblay, and Linda Trimble, 171–187. London: Routledge.

———. 2010b. Devolution and the Multilevel Politics of Gender in the United Kingdom: The Case of Scotland. In *Federalism, Feminism, and Multilevel Governance*, ed. Melissa Haussman, Marian Sawer, and Jill Vickers, 155–168. Farnham: Ashgate.

———. 2011. Conclusion: Towards a Feminist Institutionalism? In *Gender, Politics, and Institutions: Towards a Feminist Institutionalism*, ed. Mona Krook and Fiona Mackay, 181–196. Houndmills: Palgrave Macmillan.

———. 2014. Nested Newness, Institutional Innovation, and the Gendered Limits of Change. *Politics and Gender* 10 (4): 549–571.

Marsh, Luke. 2016. The Strategic Use of Human Rights Treaties in Hong Kong's Cage-Home Crisis: No Way Out? *Asian Journal of Law and Society* 3: 159–188.

Mathews, Gordon, Eric Kit-wai Ma, and Tai-lok Lui. 2008. *Hong Kong, China: Learning to Belong to a Nation*. London: Routledge.

Migrants Rights International. 2003. *MRI and Migrant Forum in Asia (MFA) Symposium, Asian Migrant Workers: Issues, Needs and Responses*. Parallel Event of the 59th Session of the Commission on Human Rights, Palais des Nations, Geneva, April 7. http://www.migrantwatch.org/mri/whats_new/mri_mfa_symposium.htm.

Mitchell, Kathryn. 2004. *Crossing the Neoliberal Line: The Pacific Rim Migration and the Metropolis*. Philadelphia: Temple University Press.

Montinola, Gabriella, Yingyi Qian, and Barry R. Weingast. 1995. Federalism, Chinese Style: The Political Basic for Economic Success in China. *World Politics* 48 (1): 50–81.

Ng, Kang-Chung. 2018. Close to One in Five Ethnic Minority Individuals in Hong Kong Are Living in Poverty, Government Report Shows. *South China Morning Post*, February 8. Updated February 9. http://www.scmp.com/news/hong-kong/community/article/2132469/close-one-five-ethnic-minority-individuals-hong-kong-are.

Ngok, Ma. 2009. Reinventing the Hong Kong State or Rediscovering It? From Low Interventionism to Eclectic Corporatism. *Economy and Society* 38 (3): 492–519.

———. 2017. The China Factor in Hong Kong Elections: 1991 to 2016. *China Perspectives* 3: 17–26.

Ong, Aihwa. 1999. *Flexible Citizenship: The Cultural Logics of Transnationality*. Duke University Press.

———. 2000. Graduated Sovereignty in South-East Asia. *Theory, Culture and Society* 17 (4): 55–75.

Oxfam, Hong Kong. 2016. *Report on Women and Poverty (2001–2015)*, September. Hong Kong: Oxfam. http://www.oxfam.org.hk/content/98/content_31064en.pdf.

Petersen, Carole J. 2003. Engendering a Legal System: The Unique Challenge of Postcolonial Hong Kong. In *Gender and Change in Hong Kong: Globalisation, Postcolonialism and Chinese Patriarchy*, ed. Eliza W.Y. Lee, 23–48. Vancouver: University of British Columbia Press.

Poon, Alice. 2011. *Land and the Ruling Class in Hong Kong*. 2nd ed. Singapore: EnrichProfessional.

Prasad, Eswar S. 2019. Why China No Longer Needs Hong Kong. *New York Times*, July 3. https://www.nytimes.com/2019/07/03/opinion/hong-kong-protest.html.

Pun, Ngai, and Wu Ka-Ming. 2004. Lived Citizenship and Lower-Class Chinese Migrant Women: A Global City Without its People. In *Remaking Citizenship in Hong Kong: Community, Nation, and the Global City*, ed. S. Ku by Agnes and Pun Ngai, 139–154. London: Routledge.

Rezvani, David A. 2019. Extradition Law Won't Be Worth the Resultant Loss of Market Confidence in Hong Kong. *South China Morning Post*, June 12. https://www.scmp.com/comment/opinion/article/3013895/extradition-law-wont-be-worth-resultant-loss-market-confidence-hong.

Sautman, Barry. 2004. Hong Kong as a Semi-Ethnocracy: 'Race,' Migration and Citizenship in a Globalized Region. In *Remaking Citizenship in Hong Kong: Community, Nation, and the Global City*, ed. Agnes S. Ku and Ngai Pun, 115–138. London: Routledge.

Sawer, Marion, and Jill Vickers. 2010. Introduction: Political Architecture and its Gender Impact. In *Federalism, Feminism and Multilevel Governance*, ed. Melissa Haussman, Marian Sawer, and Jill Vickers, 3–18. Farnham: Ashgate.

Scott, Brendan, Robert Olsen, Adrian Leung, and Yue Qiu. 2017. How China Holds Sway Over Who Leads Hong Kong. *Bloomberg Politics*, February 28. https://www.bloomberg.com/graphics/2017-hk-election/.

Veg, Sebastian. 2017. The Rise of 'Localism' and Civic Identity in Post-Handover Hong Kong: Questioning the Chinese Nation-State. *China Quarterly* 230 (June): 323–347.

Vickers, Jill. 2013. Is Federalism Gendered? Incorporating Gender into Studies of Federalism. *Publius* 43 (1): 1–23.

Vickers, Jill, Melissa Haussman, and Marian Sawer. 2010. Conclusion. In Federalism, Feminism and Multilevel Governance, ed. Melissa Haussman, Marian Sawer, and Jill Vickers. Farnham: Ashgate.

Wu, Ka-Ming. 2003. Discourse on *Baau Yih Naai* (Keeping Concubines): Questions of Citizenship and Identity in Postcolonial Hong Kong. In *Gender and Change in Hong Kong: Globalisation, Postcolonialism and Chinese Patriarchy*, ed. Eliza W.Y. Lee, 133–150. Vancouver: University of British Columbia Press.

Young, Simon N. M., and Anthony Law. 2004. *A Critical Introduction to Hong Kong's Functional Constituencies*. Hong Kong: Civic Exchange. http://www.hkhrm.org.hk/resource/A_critical_introduction_to_HK_FC.pdf.

Zheng, Yongnian. 2007. *De Facto Federalism in China: Reforms and Dynamics of Central-Local Relations*. Hackensack: World Scientific.

## CHAPTER 7

# Federalism, Democracy and National Diversity in Twenty-First Century China: Reinterpreting Hong Kong's Autonomy, Subverting its Democracy

*Jean-François Dupré*

## INTRODUCTION

Hong Kong was handed over from British to Chinese sovereignty in 1997. It was, at the time, promised a high degree of autonomy for a period of at least 50 years, during which democratic institutions would be established and consolidated. However, recent and ongoing developments demonstrate that the process of integration into the authoritarian state is already well under way, just two decades after the Handover. Not only has the democratisation process been halted, but democracy is also arguably receding (Fong 2017). Yet, the Handover did not take the form of an all-out invasion by China. Unlike an outright institutional takeover, the national absorption of Hong Kong has operated by way of institutional conversion (Mahoney and Thelen 2010; Tsai 2006). More precisely,

J.-F. Dupré (✉)
Institute of Sociology, Academia Sinica, Taipei, Taiwan
e-mail: jfdupre@connect.hku.hk

© The Author(s) 2020
A.-G. Gagnon, A. Tremblay (eds.), *Federalism and National Diversity in the 21st Century*, Federalism and Internal Conflicts,
https://doi.org/10.1007/978-3-030-38419-7_7

China has managed to extend its grip on Hong Kong's political apparatus by nurturing the interests for compliance already embedded in the system and by pushing for its own interpretation of Hong Kong's constitutional order. This has enabled Beijing to rule Hong Kong indirectly through the local establishment.

Given that the People's Republic of China (PRC) is an authoritarian (if not totalitarian) state with little credible commitment to human rights or for the legal or constitutional orders in place (other than as tools to further the interests of the ruling Communist Party), its treatment of Hong Kong should not come as a surprise. In fact, it was probably overly optimistic to believe that China would uphold its promises regarding Hong Kong's autonomy and its eventual democratisation. Hope of Hong Kong exercising a meaningful level of autonomy, self-government and democracy rested largely on the assumption that China itself would eventually democratise. At the same time, Hong Kong's experience should not be taken lightly, nor should it be discarded as inapplicable to democratic settings.[1]

This chapter investigates the politics of federalism, democracy and national diversity in China, tracing the process through which the central and local governments have furthered national integration and authoritarianisation in Hong Kong. It argues that these joint processes were enabled not by a sudden and drastic institutional takeover by China, but by an incremental process of institutional conversion in which institutions governing Hong Kong's autonomy and democratisation were brought to serve objectives that seem contrary to their stated purposes. Beijing and the local establishment carried out this institutional conversion process in part by reframing and reinterpreting institutions and their purposes, as well as by taking advantage of power asymmetries entrenched in institutions. This was itself enabled by a weakly defined constitutional order, the lack of a tradition of multilevel governance and an institutional setting that was designed to facilitate elite co-optation by the establishment.

This chapter is divided into four sections. The first section sketches out the historical institutionalist theoretical premises that inform the analysis. The second section highlights the main characteristics of Hong Kong-China relations and delineates the parameters of Hong Kong's autonomy regime as enshrined through the Basic Law—Hong Kong's constitution.

---

[1] Arguably, China has done little that couldn't be done in a democracy; parallels have, for instance, been made with Spain's handling of self-determination claims in Catalonia (see Lecours and Dupré 2018).

The third section discusses how Hong Kong's constitutional framework and political system have been designed and used by Beijing so as to facilitate elite co-optation and indirect rule. The fourth section investigates the process of incremental institutional change more directly, with a focus on the authoritarianisation process under way.

## THEORETICAL FRAMEWORK AND CENTRAL ARGUMENT

The more materialist accounts of historical institutionalism have highlighted the relation between institutions and strategies—a relation that is usually thought to be mediated by interests (Immergut 1998). In other words, rational actors act in ways that can maximise their interests, but alternatives for action are determined by institutions in place, such as rules, laws or other mechanisms (Hall 2010, 217). Although materialist accounts remain predominant in historical institutionalism, ideational factors have also featured as important determinants of institutional change (Blyth et al. 2016; Lieberman 2002). For instance, instead of conceptualising institutional change as formal amendments to rules or to organisational structures (Hall and Taylor 1996, 938), some have highlighted the fact that institutional change can consist in reinterpreting institutions (Mahoney and Thelen 2010; Tsai 2006). Essentially, such processes of informal institutional change correspond to institutional conversion. As Mahoney and Thelen explain, 'Conversion occurs when rules remain formally the same but are interpreted and enacted in new ways' (2010, 17). In highlighting the agency involved in this process, they argue that the 'gap between the rules and their instantiation [...] is produced by actors who actively exploit the inherent ambiguities of the institutions. Through redeployment, they convert the institution to new goals, functions, or purposes' (17–18).[2]

Institutional change is also deeply influenced by issues of power distribution (Hall and Taylor 1996; Mahoney and Thelen 2010). In particular, Mahoney and Thelen emphasise the role of power asymmetries, together with the potential for coalition building embedded in institutions, as

---

[2] Similarly, March and Olsen (2004, 10) observe that 'Rules, laws, identities and institutions provide parameters for action rather than dictate a specific action, and sometimes actors show considerable ability to accommodate shifting circumstances by changing behavior without changing core rules and structures'. This, in turn, draws attention to the social constructedness of institutions and of their political consequences (see Blyth 2002; Hay 2008).

important determinants of institutional change: 'actors with different endowments of resources are normally motivated to pursue the creation of different kinds of institutions. And the institutions that are actually created often reflect the relative contributions of—and often conflict among— these differentially motivated actors' (2010, 8). Since dominant groups often have disproportionate influence over the implementation or interpretation of institutions, power asymmetries and their potential for co-optation can make it easier for dominant coalitions to enact institutional change, be it formally or informally. Consequently, the relationship between institutions, interests and power distributions implies that opportunistic actors can easily be co-opted by vesting interests into a given institutional framework.

Temporality is another central concern for new institutionalists, particularly in the realm of historical institutionalism. To historical institutionalists, political events are interrelated in a path-dependent fashion (della Porta and Keating 2008, 10), so that institutions link to political outcomes in sequence patterns that can be either self-reinforcing or reactive (Mahoney 2000; Mahoney et al. 2016). On the one hand, self-reinforcing sequences link institutions to political outcomes in a somewhat predictable and linear manner in that 'each step in a particular direction makes it more likely that a unit will continue to follow that same direction' (Mahoney et al. 2016, 83). On the other hand, reactive sequences appear less linear, being 'marked by *backlash processes* in which *reversals can take place*' (Mahoney et al. 2016, 85).

If self-reinforcing sequences can be associated with stability, reactive ones are often associated with conflict and change (Mahoney 2000, 526). In some contexts, interrelated institutions can produce sequence patterns that appear both reactive and self-reinforcing at the same time, at least at different levels of analysis. For instance, as we shall see in the remainder of this chapter, institutions governing elections in Hong Kong appear to have generated dynamics typical of reactive sequences, leading to legislative stalemate and dysfunctionality. In the context of Hong Kong's ingrained power asymmetries, however, this has worked to the benefit of the establishment, thus reinforcing the system of electoral authoritarianism at a more macro level.

Indeed, issues of interpretation and power asymmetries have been crucial to institutional change in Hong Kong. While designed so as to give the impression that the system would (or at least *could*) become increasingly competitive and that a variety of interests would be protected, Hong

Kong's political system has deeply institutionalised pro-Beijing interests to the detriment of others. It is in large part this power component that has enabled the process of institutional conversion. Just like Hong Kong's autonomy regime was interpreted so as to actualise and accelerate national integration, the democratisation process—cautiously framed as a process of 'political reform' towards 'universal suffrage'—has been used not to liberalise Hong Kong, but to further authoritarianise it. Overall, what is being perceived as radical change has, for the most part, proceeded incrementally and ideationally and has featured subtle changes in the interpretation of rules and their application, together with a realignment of interests, vis-à-vis institutions whose design remains fundamentally unchanged.

## HONG KONG-CHINA RELATIONS: THE INSTITUTIONAL CONTEXT

Although the Chinese constitution of 1982 mentions that 'All power in the People's Republic of China belongs to the people' (Article 2), and that 'The state organs of the People's Republic of China apply the principle of democratic centralism' (Article 3), China is in fact a 'democratic dictatorship' (Article 1), or, more straightforwardly, a one-party dictatorship. As a previous (and, by some accounts,[3] present) empire, China has been built through conquest, inevitably making it a multinational state. In fact, Article 4 of the constitution recognises the plurinational character of China on the basis of which five so-called autonomous regions have been established. These regions and the national groups that inhabit them, however, enjoy little meaningful autonomy. On the contrary, some of these regions, like Tibet and Xinjiang, are probably the most tightly policed, controlled and politically oppressed areas of the country.

Constitutionally, China is a unitary state. Administratively, it is divided into 22 provinces, 4 municipalities, 5 autonomous regions and 2 special administrative regions (SARs). Although provinces and autonomous regions have legislative powers, in practice the scope of their legislative autonomy is limited. The central government can compel local governments to make laws and enforce policies designed at state level, just as they can override local legislation. Informally, however, some aspects of centre-region relations are reminiscent of federalism. Despite the lack of formal

---

[3] See, for instance, Terrill (2003) and Snelder (2014).

federal structures, principles and mechanisms, there are areas in which local governments can negotiate and bargain with the state, particularly within the economic and fiscal arenas (Zheng 2007). However, in the past decade—especially since the accession to power of strongman Xi Jinping to Communist Party Secretary in 2012 and to President in 2013—there has been a noticeable trend towards recentralisation rooted in fear that the party would eventually lose control over local administrators and civil society (Overholt 2017).

While depictions of China as a quasi- or de facto federal state are perhaps less convincing than they were a decade ago, two regions exist that (at least on paper and in comparison to the provinces and autonomous regions) enjoy a substantial degree of autonomy and for whom relations with Beijing are reminiscent of federal arrangements: Hong Kong and Macau.[4] In addition to constituting the only sub-polity (alongside Macau) that has the potential to entertain federal relations with Beijing, Hong Kong is also the only polity that has democratic potential.[5] Moreover, Hong Kong can make a strong claim for nationhood. As defined by Anthony Smith (2001, 13), a nation is 'a named human community occupying a homeland, and having common myths and a shared history, a common public culture, a single economy and common rights and duties for all members'.

Many in China (and even in Hong Kong) would dispute Hong Kong's national character, arguing that Hong Kong's place is and has always been in the Chinese 'homeland'. After all, the bulk of Hongkongers trace their

[4] Constitutionally, Macau's autonomy status as SAR is almost identical to Hong Kong's. However, as a tiny city of just over 600,000 inhabitants (about 12 times smaller than Hong Kong) whose economy is heavily reliant on the gambling and entertainment industries, the previous Portuguese colony is in many ways even more idiosyncratic than Hong Kong. The processes of co-optation and authoritarianisation described in this chapter in reference to Hong Kong are to a large extent applicable to Macau, although the latter also features its own dynamics, which were also reinforced by different colonial models, legal systems, socio-political institutions and practices. From Beijing's perspective, the 'One Country, Two Systems' formula has worked better in Macau than in Hong Kong, precisely because civil society and democracy (among others) were arguably less developed in the former, enabling Beijing to exercise a higher degree of control over the region from the very beginning (see Lo 2007; Yu 2013).

[5] After all, the eventuality of democratisation is inscribed into Hong Kong's constitution, and Hong Kong democratic parties and organisations have thrived in ways not witnessed in Macau, let alone other parts of China, where calls for democracy are considered subversive and firmly suppressed.

origins to China, with a large proportion of Hong Kong residents (or their close ancestors) having fled to the British colony in the context of the communist takeover in the mid-twentieth century. At the same time, it is precisely this experience of exile from China and of refuge in the British colony that has made Hong Kong nothing short of a homeland for Hongkongers, especially for Hong Kong-born youths who have little or no direct connection with the Chinese Mainland. Similarly, although many aspects of Hong Kong culture stem from Chinese culture (including most of its fundamental myths and folk beliefs), Hong Kong's distinctive political institutions, legal system, core values, collective memory, popular culture and more are certainly characteristic of a distinct society or nation as defined by Anthony Smith. Indeed, as we will see later, Hong Kong nationalism has become an important ideology, especially among Hong Kong's youth.

The Handover of 1997 saw Hong Kong's status change from British Dependent Territory to SAR of the PRC. It is worth noting that the Handover was entirely engineered by the Chinese and British governments, and that the local population was never called on to express itself regarding its future. Thus, the Handover consisted of a rare process of decolonisation that was accompanied not by a process of national emancipation but instead by a forced 'return' to an alleged motherland under a vaguely defined principle of 'One Country, Two Systems' (OCTS). Given the lack of popular endorsement, the Handover was little more than a recolonisation process. At the same time, the Handover played a major role in the creation and activation of a (proto-)national identity in Hong Kong. For one, the experience may have crystallised this sense of sharing a common space and history in a society that was hitherto essentially one of refuge and immigration.

The terms of the Handover were set in 1984 through the Sino-British Joint Declaration. The Joint Declaration stated that 'The Hong Kong Special Administrative Region will enjoy a high degree of autonomy, except in foreign and defence affairs which are the responsibilities of the Central People's Government' (Article 3.2), and that 'The current social and economic systems in Hong Kong will remain unchanged, and so will the life-style' (Article 3.5). The Joint Declaration also mandated the adoption of the Hong Kong Basic Law—Hong Kong's constitution. The Basic Law was drafted between 1985 and 1990 by a committee made up of Chinese and Hong Kong officials, businessmen and representatives of various sectors (a majority of which were, quite conveniently, easily co-optable by the state), itself working under the auspices of the Standing Committee of the National People's Congress (SCNPC), China's rubber-stamp legislature. It was adopted in 1990 and came into effect on July 1, 1997.

As Cheung (2007, 249) points out, '[the] design of the OCTS model is fundamentally different from other federalist models'. Cheung mentions that, in some respects, Hong Kong's level of autonomy is higher than most substate entities worldwide. For instance, Hong Kong enjoys the status of separate customs territory, has its own currency, and maintains an independent common law system, in addition to preserving its lawmaking and policymaking organs (Cheung 2007, 246). In other respects, however, Hong Kong's autonomy status is fragile. As Susan Henders (2010, 138) puts it, 'the wide functional autonomy of the HKSAR was undergirded by uneven political autonomy'. Article 2 of Hong Kong's Basic Law stipulates that Hong Kong's ability to 'exercise a high degree of autonomy and enjoy executive, legislative and independent judicial power' is merely 'authorise[d]' by China's National People's Congress. Moreover, Beijing has almost total oversight over the formation and leadership of Hong Kong's executive and has massive indirect influence on the constitution of the legislature, casting doubts on whether Hong Kong's executive and legislative powers are exercised independently from each other and from Beijing. Finally, Article 5 mentions that 'The socialist system and policies shall not be practised in the Hong Kong Special Administrative Region, and the previous capitalist system and way of life shall remain unchanged for 50 years', suggesting that Hong Kong's autonomy status may be set to expire in 2047 (Cheung 2007, 246).

## CONSTITUTIONAL ORDER AND POWER ASYMMETRIES: HONG KONG'S AUTONOMY AND ITS PRACTICE

Among the many fundamental problems with the constitutional arrangement set up by Beijing, four stand out. The first problem is that concepts and terms were not appropriately defined in the framework; more precisely, terminology appears to have been kept ambiguous so as to allow for a maximum of flexibility in interpretation. For instance, in official discourses, the Basic Law is usually represented as embodying the principle of OCTS, which supposedly entails 'a high degree of autonomy' and 'Hong Kong People ruling Hong Kong' (Constitutional and Mainland Affairs

Bureau 2007). But what exactly is the nature of the two systems? Does the term refer purely to two economic systems (a planned economy and a free market), or to two comprehensive political regimes encompassing issues of human rights and freedoms and state-society relations? What exactly is meant by a 'high degree of autonomy'? Would Hong Kong enjoy genuine self-government, or would the degree of its autonomy merely be higher than that of other polities within China? Does 'Hong Kong people ruling Hong Kong' refer to *the Hong Kong people* ruling Hong Kong democratically in accordance with the concept of popular sovereignty, or does it merely mean that the state would rule Hong Kong indirectly through Hong Kong permanent residents working on behalf of Beijing? Throughout the first decade following the Handover, the steady (though not linear) growth in confidence in the OCTS arrangement in Hong Kong seemed to hinge on the popular impression that Hong Kong enjoyed meaningful autonomy from Beijing, except for foreign and military affairs. Beijing's strategy has been to play on the terms' ambiguity until sociopolitical conditions enabled it to push for its own interpretation more forcefully.[6]

A second, similar problem has applied to the issue of democratisation or 'political reform'. In addition to delineating the contours of Hong Kong's autonomy regime, the Basic Law appears to enshrine the eventuality of democratisation, mentioning that 'The ultimate aim is the selection of the Chief Executive by universal suffrage upon nomination by a broadly representative nominating committee in accordance with democratic procedures' (Article 45), and that 'The Legislative Council of the Hong Kong Special Administrative Region shall be constituted by election' (Article 68). But what exactly is universal suffrage? How representative would the nominating committee be? Representative of what? Would democratic procedures be modelled on liberal democratic standards of free and fair elections, or on China's 'democratic dictatorship' and 'democratic centralism'? Once again, ambiguity paid off and the system worked considerably well as long as expectations were kept on the positive side. However, Beijing's disingenuousness was exposed in its 2014 Chief Executive election package, according to which Hong Kong people finally got to elect

---

[6] Beijing has used such strategies extensively. For an account of China's use of 'deliberate ambiguity' in a different context, see Ang (2019).

their Chief Executive by 'universal suffrage', albeit among a list of candidates indirectly vetted by Beijing.[7]

A third problem was the lack of a precedent for the OCTS arrangement, and by the same token, of a tradition that could inform its workings. In this regard, particularly problematic was the fact the SCNPC—an unelected legislature designed to rubberstamp central government decisions, rather than an independent judiciary—was given the final power of interpretation over Hong Kong's Basic Law. Although the British government undertook to monitor Hong Kong's situation in its capacity as signatory of the Joint Declaration, it had little actual influence on China-Hong Kong relations after the Handover. In other words, even if a potentially workable institutional framework had been laid out, there was no guarantee that China would respect it or that its interpretation would align with that of the United Kingdom and other international actors. Was it really conceivable that a tiny enclave of economic liberalism would be called upon to govern itself and democratise as part of a communist, authoritarian powerhouse? A general belief in the tenets of 'modernisation theory' (Lipset 1959), according to which China would inevitably be absorbed by the 'third wave' of democratisation (Huntington 1991), provided much of the basis for optimism.

Finally, a fourth problem lay in the high potential for co-optation embedded in Hong Kong's institutions. In many ways, the making of Hong Kong's post-Handover political order highlights the nexus between institutions, interests and coalitions. In preparation for the Handover, Beijing not only set up Hong Kong's constitutional order, it also put in place incentives for a favourable alignment of interests and power relations that would enable it to rule Hong Kong indirectly through Hong Kong's local elite. Already in the 1960s and 1970s, Beijing exerted significant influence on specific segments of Hong Kong's grassroots movements, mainly through the activities of leftist and anti-colonial organisations. In the early 1980s, economic reforms in China and economic restructuring in Hong Kong created ideal circumstances for the co-optation of Hong Kong's capitalist elite by China (Fong 2014, 197–199). Hong Kong's capitalist class had maintained particularly close ties with the highly corporatist colonial regime, but increasing calls for democratisation within civil society, especially from the 1980s onwards, threatened their highly privileged status (Fong 2014, 198). Interests vested in this coalitional order

[7]For details of the proposed arrangement, see South China Morning Post (2014).

also made for a rather paradoxical ideological and identity realignment between Hong Kong's capitalist class and the communist regime. While concentrating its co-optation efforts on prominent firms for their 'demonstration effect' (Wong 2012), China also extended the range of co-optation strategies to include, for instance, the appointment of other strategically relevant elites to a diverse array of committees and state organs, such as the National People's Congress and the Basic Law Drafting Committee (Fong 2014, 199).

Power asymmetries have been central to these co-optation strategies and to the process of incremental institutional change in Hong Kong. In the legislature, these asymmetries have been embodied by Functional Constituencies (FCs)—voting constituencies reserved for a variety of interest groups, but dominated by business interests. Currently, half of the legislature's 70 seats are reserved for FCs. Of these 35 FC seats, only five are elected on the basis of universal suffrage—that is, by anyone who does not have the right to vote in other FCs, or who opts out of the FC in which they have vote-granting membership. The remaining 30 seats are elected by individual members of the FC, by corporate entities or by a mixture of both. For instance, as of 2018, 85,705 voters were registered in the Educational Constituency, for the most part education professionals (Voter Registration 2018). The Insurance Constituency, however, is not directly open to individual voters working in the industry; instead, only 127 bodies are registered (ibid.).

Although the government has defended the continuation of FCs under the 'principle of balanced participation',[8] about half of those constituencies are deeply entrenched in business interests (for instance, Commercial, Industrial, Finance, etc.). By contrast, legislators in Geographical Constituencies (GCs), which account for the remaining half of the seats, are elected by universal suffrage following a proportional representation system. Overall, these asymmetries have given pro-establishment candidates an advantage in elections. For instance, in the 2016 Hong Kong legislative election, they only managed to win 17 out of 35 seats in GCs (49 per cent) but ended up controlling 61 per cent of all seats by grabbing 26 out of 35 seats in FCs (74 per cent). This power imbalance has been instrumental in the process of institutional conversion that has seen Hong Kong's democratisation process transformed into one of authoritarianisation.

---

[8] See, for instance, Hong Kong Government (2010).

## REDEFINING AUTONOMY, SUBVERTING DEMOCRACY

The dynamics of incremental institutional conversion in the context of power asymmetries in Hong Kong are best exemplified by the process of political reform. It is only in the 1980s that the colonial government put forward some modest initiatives for the democratisation of the district boards and the legislative council,[9] setting up—among others—the first FCs. Although the Chinese government agreed to enshrine the eventuality of universal suffrage in the Basic Law, it was also opposed to the democratisation initiatives put forward by the colonial administration, especially in the 1990s, believing that they went against the spirit of the Joint Declaration of 1984. The Chinese and British governments had agreed to leave Hong Kong's system essentially unchanged, but the colonial administration now seemed to be accelerating the pace of reforms in the run-up to the Handover. Beijing sought to design a system that seemed to show potential for democratic politics, but in which pro-Beijing interests would be sure to dominate. FCs and indirect voting mechanisms—themselves a legacy of British colonialism—were an integral part of this system.

With these institutions firmly in place, Beijing oversaw the 'incremental' path to universal suffrage,[10] making sure its interests would not be affected by democratic expansion. In addition to using power asymmetries to exercise its control indirectly, namely, through local pro-establishment politicians, one of Beijing's strategies was to use the political reform process to divide the opposition. It did so by presenting, in concert with the local establishment, blueprints for reform that were highly divisive in nature.[11] In 2005, for instance, the government presented a proposal for a limited political reform that merely expanded the scope of indirect voting, thus still ruling out pan-democrats as top contenders for power. Initially, moderate democrats showed some willingness to support the proposal, but they were ultimately convinced by more radical ones to vote against it.

---

[9] The legislative council is Hong Kong's parliament, and its members are endowed with lawmaking powers for the whole HKSAR. District boards, now referred to as district councils, are responsible for district-level affairs.

[10] Articles 45 and 68 of the Basic Law, referring to Chief Executive and legislative elections, stress that election methods 'shall be specified in the light of the actual situation in the Hong Kong Special Administrative Region and in accordance with the principle of gradual and orderly progress'.

[11] Reform proposals have been issued and negotiated regularly since the Handover. For a brief overview of the reform process, see Ng (2015).

The rift was particularly strong between the Democratic Party—at the time this faction's largest party—and other opposition parties. The Democratic Party had indeed adopted a moderate position underscored by a longer term strategy, showing greater willingness to negotiate with the government—which many in Hong Kong saw as a propensity to compromise on its own principles. The following decade saw the multiplication and increasing radicalisation of opposition parties. When, in 2010, the establishment employed the same strategy of dividing the opposition, the Democratic Party ended up supporting the government's blueprint, which further widened the gap between the party and more radical alternatives (see Kwong 2016; Lo 2010; Ma 2011).

On the reform plan, the Decision of 31 August 2014, in which the Chinese leadership unveiled its reform package for the 2017 Chief Executive election, was a wake-up call. The package, which boasted the advent of universal suffrage, still required the preliminary screening of all candidates by a committee dominated by pro-Beijing interests, thus once again barring any pan-democrat from taking part in the race. In practice, the proposal was akin to having the population vote by universal suffrage on candidates selected, albeit indirectly, by Beijing. It became clear to the public and to observers that Beijing had been pushing for a consolidation of electoral authoritarianism (Fong 2017), not democracy. Some democrats—led by university professors Benny Tai Yiu-ting and Chan Kin-man and by reverend Chu Yiu-ming—had tried to pressure Beijing to grant Hongkongers 'real universal suffrage', threatening to occupy Hong Kong's Central district if they didn't (South China Morning Post, n.d.). The Occupy Central movement, which evolved into a sit-in that came to be known as the Umbrella Movement between September and December 2014, brought no concession from the establishment. The package was eventually voted down by pan-democrats, who feared endorsing it would convey a willingness to compromise their ideals and settle for what they saw as a 'fake democracy' (Phillips 2015). Since that date, the political reform process has for all practical purposes been put on indefinite hold.

The August Decision also had another significant and probably unintended effect: the emergence of a new form of Hong Kong nationalism expressed through calls for enhanced autonomy or Hong Kong independence (Lecours and Dupré 2018). Up to the early 2010s, Hong Kong was seldom, if at all, conceptualised as a nation. Indeed, Hongkongers were generally considered devoid of a national identity—whether Chinese or Hongkongese—or at the very least lukewarm to identity issues (Mathews et al. 2008). A number of events in the 2010s contributed to Hongkongers' national awakening. Most significant were events surrounding the Moral and National Education curriculum that was being planned for gradual introduction in primary schools from the Fall of 2012. Largely decried as a brainwashing device aimed at instilling a blind sense of patriotism in Hong Kong's youth, the curriculum gave rise to large scale protests which played an important role in the development of a new Hong Kong solidarity and national identity. In turn, the combined effect of the protests against the National Education curriculum and the Umbrella Movement led to the formation, between 2015 and 2016, of self-determinationist and independentist parties (Lecours and Dupré 2018). The formation of a new nationalist or 'localist' faction would further fragment the pan-democratic camp, which is now usually referred to more broadly as the 'anti-establishment' camp.

The rise of Hong Kong nationalism was used by Beijing and the local establishment as an opportunity to accelerate the authoritarianisation process. Prior to Hong Kong's legislative election of September 2016, the government had already rejected the candidacy of openly pro-independence party leaders under the pretext that Hong Kong independence went against Article 1 of the Basic Law, which states that Hong Kong 'is an inalienable part of the People's Republic of China'. Nonetheless, some candidates from more moderate 'localist' parties were allowed to take part in the election, of whom six were elected.[12] In November, Beijing took unilateral action to disqualify two of them—Yau Wai-ching and Baggio Leung—on the basis that they distorted their oath of allegiance and threw insults at China during their swearing-in ceremony (BBC News 2016). It did so by requesting an interpretation on oath-taking requirements from the SCNPC. Although the Hong Kong government had already launched a legal challenge in local courts, the SCNPC delivered its own interpretation first, thereby forcing the ousting of the two legislators (ibid.). The ruling was particularly controversial in that the president of Hong Kong's legislature, himself from the pro-establishment camp, had already agreed to allow the duo to retake their oath; Hong Kong's executive and the SCNPC were therefore bypassing what were seen as legislative procedures to expel democratically elected legislators.

---

[12] They were Cheng Chung-tai (Civic Passion), Sixtus Baggio Leung Chung-hang (Youngspiration), Yau Wai-ching (Youngspiration), Nathan Law (Demosistō), Lau Siu-lai (Democracy Groundwork) and Eddie Chu Hoi-dick (Land Justice League).

Needless to say, direct, unsolicited involvement from an undemocratic legislative body over matters that would otherwise be considered internal Hong Kong affairs (although Beijing would argue that secessionist activities are a matter of national security) is enough to raise doubts on the SAR's autonomy status. Similarly, the use of legal arguments and mechanisms to achieve political means can raise questions on the nature of judicial independence and on a regime's adherence to liberal standards of governance. Even without direct involvement from the SCNPC, recent developments suggest an increased use of the law and of legal arguments in Hong Kong's process of authoritarianisation (Dupré 2019a). In July, 2017, four more opposition legislators who had altered their oath were retrospectively disqualified following a legal challenge launched by Hong Kong's executive (BBC News 2017). Having stripped the opposition of their veto-enabling powers, the establishment rushed to change rules on legislative procedures so as to prevent some of the delaying tactics democrats had been pushed to resort to due to their institutional marginalisation (Cheng 2017a). The post-2016 period was also marked by a wave of prosecutions of protestors who took part in protests and civil disobedience movements from 2014 onwards. Although the upsurge of prosecutions echoes the sharp rise in such movements in recent years, some have identified an escalation in the severity of charges and sentences sought (Cheng 2017b). In April, 2019, nine Occupy Central leaders and organisers were ultimately convicted on charges ranging from 'conspiracy to commit public nuisance' to 'incitement to commit public nuisance', as well as the widely contested charge of 'incitement to incite public nuisance' (Holmes Chan 2019).

Other recent controversies testify to a continuing escalation of the establishment's divisive, provocative and—to the extent that it seems to make a point of flouting public opinion—increasingly authoritarian approach. Examples of these dynamics include, but are not limited to: threats to introduce a controversial National Security Law (Cheung 2018a); the assertion by Beijing that the Joint Declaration 'no longer has any practical significance' despite the fact that it is lodged with the United Nations (Sergeant 2017); Beijing's refusal to endorse previous financial secretary John Tsang (Chung and Ng 2017), a relatively popular and moderate pro-establishment figure, and the subsequent 'election' of the least popular candidate but Beijing favourite and hardliner, Carrie Lam, as Chief Executive in 2017 (South China Morning Post 2017); arrangements for Chinese laws to be applied on Hong Kong segments of a newly opened Mainland-Hong Kong Express Rail Link, which are widely seen as unconstitutional by the legal community (Cheng 2018); the much contested appointment of a Beijing loyalist openly supportive of Mandarin[13] and national education as undersecretary of education (Lam and Chiu 2017); an upcoming law criminalising acts of disrespect towards the Chinese National Anthem and mandating its singing in schools (Chung 2019); and a controversial extradition bill that risked expanding—though once again indirectly—the scope of China's legal jurisdiction over Hong Kong by allowing the SAR government to extradite suspects—either Chinese fugitives or foreign nationals in transit through Hong Kong—to Chinese authorities (Sherry Chan 2019).

These events have been accompanied by acts and statements suggesting further curtailments of political rights may be under way. In the summer of 2018, the government invoked national security as a pretext to ban the pro-independence Hong Kong National Party (itself barred from the electoral process), which was effectively done in September of that year (BBC News 2018). But the regime's strategy has not been limited to barring radical opponents and organisations. Instead, it is now also intimidating moderate segments of the opposition. In March, 2018, some senior officials and representatives from Hong Kong and China implied that candidates calling for an end to the Communist Party leadership in China may eventually be barred from taking part in local elections on the basis that it allegedly contravenes the Chinese constitution, which is now more resolutely being depicted as not only applicable to Hong Kong, but even considered *above* the Basic Law (Cheung 2018b). Since calls for China's democratisation have been at the basis of even the most moderate democratic organisations in Hong Kong, such as the Democratic Party, such statements seem to signal that the ideational spectrum permissible in the political arena may soon be unprecedentedly restricted. When these threats become a reality and the advocacy of democracy becomes a ground for exclusion from the electoral process, the joint processes of national absorption and authoritarianisation can be deemed complete.

---

[13] Hong Kong is a predominantly Cantonese-speaking society, and many have grown linguistically insecure in the face of Mandarin hegemony in China.

## CONCLUSION

This chapter has argued that recent changes widely interpreted as a recession in both autonomy and democracy in Hong Kong were made possible not by an outright institutional takeover by China but instead by a subtler process of incremental institutional conversion. This process was carried out by reinterpreting Hong Kong's autonomy status and constitutional order, as well as by using Hong Kong's democratisation process as an opportunity to divide the opposition and strengthen the establishment's grip on Hong Kong's political system and society. As can be expected, this process of institutional conversion has led to the emergence of a more radical ideology—that of Hong Kong nationalism—embodied in an independence movement. This movement, however, is both a result of institutional conversion and a driver of its acceleration and intensification.

The strategies used by anti-establishment forces in the absence of favourable external conditions have so far been largely counterproductive. While the institutional framework in place would have required a high degree of unity, foresight and coordinated strategy on the part of pan-democrats, they have instead grown increasingly fragmented and confrontational, sometimes placing their alleged principles over sound strategy. Still, it is difficult to tell whether any significant concessions could have been obtained from a more conciliatory strategy. For instance, had democrats accepted the reform blueprint of 2014, there may have been hope for the election of a more moderate Chief Executive capable of maintaining the status quo rather than accelerating the authoritarianisation process. On the other hand, democrats would have granted legitimacy to a deeply flawed system while still having to cope with an antagonistic executive—this time one of their own choosing.

In the end, the apparent consolidation of electoral authoritarianism in Hong Kong has proceeded—at least in part—in response to changes in society. The more radical anti-establishment figures—especially Hong Kong nationalists—have sought to test the limits of the system, only to see them recede further. Or perhaps they have simply exposed limits that were already implicit in the system. Many decry the regime's clampdown on Hong Kong independence advocacy [and, increasingly, the mere discussion of it (Chiu 2018)] as an attack on various rights and freedoms promised in the Basic Law, including free speech and academic freedom. Whether this actually represents a *retreat* of rights and freedoms previously enjoyed, however, may be up to debate. The establishment *did* use the independence movement as an opportunity to impose a new (and somewhat arbitrary) 'red-line', but to the extent that discourses on Hong Kong nationalism and independence were simply non-existent less than a decade ago (and were thus never demonstrably tolerated), it is not entirely clear that these restrictions constitute a departure from previous government policy.

In this sense, the process of institutional conversion should perhaps be more accurately understood as a process of institutional reinforcement rather than one of institutional change proper. While democrats see autonomy and democracy receding, Beijing and Hong Kong's establishment are merely reinforcing a system meant to promote Hong Kong's integration into China and the strengthening of electoral authoritarianism. Once again, institutional ambiguities have been central to these perceptions of institutional change and reinforcement, and both sides have sought to frame and define institutions in ways that support their interests and objectives. Power asymmetries, however, have given the establishment the upper hand. To the extent that the influence of Beijing and the establishment over institutions can increasingly be considered hegemonic, the potential for the actualisation of Hong Kong's autonomy, its democratisation and the recognition of its national distinctiveness remain grim.

At the time of writing this chapter, new dynamics appear to be emerging in the opposition. Planned amendments to Hong Kong's extradition ordinance that would have enabled the government to extradite suspects to China—thus enabling the central government to extend its legal jurisdiction over Hong Kong indirectly—have brought about a wave of unprecedented protests in the summer of 2019.[14] Although the protests have succeeded in defeating the extradition bill, the movement has grown to encompass demands for more fundamental regime change. The lack of a clear leadership among protesters has enabled the formation of a broader anti-government coalition, with pan-democratic lawmakers occupying the formal political arena, and more radical groups—including Hong Kong nationalists, who have been ejected from formal political channels—taking charge of street politics and sometimes engaging in intense clashes with the police. In the context of an intensifying Sino-American trade war and a straining of China's relationships with many other countries, protesters have sought to enlist support from the international community in

---

[14] For more information on this movement, see New York Times Editorial Board (2019), The Guardian Editorial (2019) and Sherry Chan (2019).

constraining the range of options available to Beijing. The government, however, has remained unmovable. As clashes between protesters and the police have intensified—leading to thousands of arrests—Beijing has not ruled out the possibility of deploying its troops to crush the movement (Dupré 2019b). Should the dynamics of institutional reinforcement laid out in this chapter subsist, the movement is unlikely to succeed. On the contrary, the conflict is likely to be settled by force and followed by sustained repression, marking another victory for the system.

## REFERENCES

Ang, Yuen Yuen. 2019. Demystifying Belt and Road. *Foreign Policy*, 22 May. https://www.foreignaffairs.com/articles/china/2019-05-22/demystifying-belt-and-road (Last accessed 3 August 2019).

*Basic Law of the Hong Kong Special Administrative Region of the People's Republic of China*. 1990. Hong Kong: The Consultative Committee for the Basic Law. https://www.basiclaw.gov.hk/en/basiclawtext/index.html (Last accessed 29 May 2019).

BBC News. 2016. Hong Kong pro-independence lawmakers disqualified from office. 15 November. https://www.bbc.com/news/world-asia-china-37984118 (Last accessed 4 August 2019).

———. 2017. Hong Kong Court Disqualifies Pro-Democracy Lawmakers. 14 July. https://www.bbc.com/news/world-asia-40604363 (Last accessed 4 August 2019).

———. 2018. Hong Kong Government Bans Pro-Independence Party. 24 September. https://www.bbc.com/news/world-asia-45623556 (Last accessed 5 August 2019).

Blyth, Mark M. 2002. *Great Transformations: Economic Ideas and Institutional Change in the Twentieth Century*. Cambridge: Cambridge University Press.

Blyth, Mark, Oddny Helgadottir, and William Kring. 2016. Ideas and Historical Institutionalism. In *The Oxford Handbook of Historical Institutionalism*, ed. Orfeo Fioretos, Tulia G. Falleti, and Adam Sheingate, 142–162. Oxford: Oxford University Press.

Chan, Holmes. 2019. Leading Hong Kong Umbrella Movement Activists Found Guilty of Public Nuisance. *Hong Kong Free Press*, 9 April. https://www.hongkongfp.com/2019/04/09/breaking-hong-kong-umbrella-movement-activists-handed-verdicts-public-nuisance-trial/ (Last accessed 29 May 2019).

Chan, Sherry Yuen Yung. 2019. Hong Kong's Protests Aren't Just About the Extradition Bill Anymore. *The Diplomat*, 25 July. https://thediplomat.com/2019/07/hong-kongs-protests-arent-just-about-the-extradition-bill-anymore/ (Last accessed 5 August 2019).

Cheng, Kris. 2017a. Hong Kong Legislature Passes Controversial House Rule Changes Taking Powers from Lawmakers. *Hong Kong Free Press*, 15 December. https://www.hongkongfp.com/2017/12/15/legislature-passes-controversial-house-rule-amendments-taking-powers-lawmakers/ (Last accessed 4 August 2019).

———. 2017b. You're All Under Arrest: How Hong Kong's Gov't Changed Its Policy on Political Protests. *Hong Kong Free Press*, 1 July. https://www.hongkongfp.com/2017/07/01/youre-arrest-hong-kongs-govt-changed-policy-political-protests/ (Last accessed 29 May 2019).

———. 2018. Joint Checkpoint Deal Has No Constitutional Foundation; Legislature Has No Authority to Enact It, Says Bar Assoc. *Hong Kong Free Press*, 14 March. https://www.hongkongfp.com/2018/03/14/joint-checkpoint-deal-no-constitutional-foundation-legislature-no-authority-enact-says-bar-assoc/ (Last accessed 29 May 2019).

Cheung, Peter. 2007. Towards China's Federalism? The Case of Hong Kong. In *Federalism in Asia*, ed. Baogang He, Brian Galligan, and Takashi Inoguchi, 242–265. Cheltenham: Edward Elgar Publishing.

Cheung, Tony. 2018a. No Timetable on National Security Law, Hong Kong Leader Insists, but Officials Working to Create 'Favourable Conditions'. *South China Morning Post*, 17 April. https://www.scmp.com/news/hong-kong/politics/article/2142063/no-timetable-national-security-law-hong-kong-leader-insists (Last accessed 4 August 2019).

———. 2018b. People Who Chant 'End One-Party Dictatorship' Slogal Are Breaking the Law and Should Be Banned from Seeking Political Office, Says Wang Guangya. *South China Morning Post*, 25 April. https://www.scmp.com/news/hong-kong/politics/article/2143260/people-who-chant-end-one-party-dictatorship-slogan-are (Last accessed 5 August 2019).

Chiu, Peace. 2018. Hong Kong Students Cautioned About Independence Debate as Academic Year Begins. *South China Morning Post*, 3 September. https://www.scmp.com/news/hong-kong/education/article/2162579/hong-kong-students-cautioned-about-independence-debate (Last accessed 5 August 2019).

Chung, Kimmy. 2019. How National Anthem Law Is Being Applied More Strictly in Hong Kong than in Beijing. *South China Morning Post*, 7 June. https://www.scmp.com/news/hong-kong/politics/article/3013586/how-national-anthem-law-being-applied-more-strictly-hong (Last accessed 5 August 2019).

Chung, Kimmy, and Joyce Ng. 2017. Beijing 'Doesn't Trust John Tsang Because He Ignored Its Warning Not to Run' in Hong Kong Chief Executive Election. *South China Morning Post*, 25 March. https://www.scmp.com/news/hong-kong/politics/article/2081850/beijing-doesnt-trust-john-tsang-because-he-ignored-its (Last accessed 4 August 2019).

Constitution of the People's Republic of China. 1982. http://www.fmcoprc.gov.hk/eng/syzx/tyflsw/t944932.htm (Last accessed 23 January 2020).

della Porta, Donatella, and Michael J. Keating. 2008. Introduction. In *Approaches and Methodologies in the Social Sciences: A Pluralist Perspective*, ed. Donatella della Porta and M.J. Keating, 1–15. Cambridge: Cambridge University Press.

Dupré, Jean-François. 2019a. Debunking Hong Kong's Rule of Law Myth: There Is No Rule of Law Without Democracy. *Centre on Constitutional Change blog*, 7 August. https://www.centreonconstitutionalchange.ac.uk/blog/debunking-hong-kongs-rule-law-myth-there-no-rule-law-without-democracy (Last accessed 12 August 2019).

———. 2019b. Will the People's Liberation Army Be Deployed in Hong Kong? No. A Police State Would Serve Beijing Better. *Taiwan Sentinel*, 30 July. https://sentinel.tw/will-the-peoples-liberation-army-be-deployed-in-hong-kong/ (Last accessed 12 August 2019).

Fong, Brian C.H. 2014. The Partnership Between the Chinese Government and Hong Kong's Capitalist Class: Implications for HKSAR Governance, 1997–2012. *China Quarterly* 217: 195–220. https://doi.org/10.1017/S0305741014000307.

———. 2017. In-Between Liberal Authoritarianism and Electoral Authoritarianism: Hong Kong's Democratization Under Chinese Sovereignty, 1997–2016. *Democratization* 24 (4): 724–750. https://doi.org/10.1080/13510347.2016.1232249.

Hall, Peter A. 2010. Historical Institutionalism in Rationalist and Sociological Perspective. In *Explaining Institutional Change: Ambiguity, Agency, and Power*, ed. James Mahoney and Kathleen Thelen, 204–223. Cambridge: Cambridge University Press.

Hall, Peter A., and Rosemary C.R. Taylor. 1996. Political Science and the Three New Institutionalisms. *Political Studies* 44: 936–957. https://doi.org/10.1111/j.1467-9248.1996.tb00343.x.

Hay, Colin. 2008. Constructivist Institutionalism. In *The Oxford Handbook of Political Institutions*, ed. Sarah A. Binder, R.A.W. Rhodes, and Bert A. Rockman, 56–74. Oxford: Oxford University Press.

Henders, Susan J. 2010. *Territoriality, Asymmetry, and Autonomy: Catalonia, Corsica, Hong Kong, and Tibet*. New York: Palgrave Macmillan.

Hong Kong Government. 2010. LCQ4: The Legislative Council Functional Constituencies. *Press Releases*, 10 March. https://www.info.gov.hk/gia/general/201003/10/P201003100172.htm (Last accessed 3 August).

Huntington, Samuel P. 1991. *The Third Wave: Democratization in the Late Twentieth Century*. Norman: University of Oklahoma Press.

Immergut, Ellen M. 1998. The Theoretical Core of the New Institutionalism. *Politics and Society* 26 (1): 5–34. https://doi.org/10.1177/0032329298026001002.

Kwong, Ying-ho. 2016. The Growth of 'Localism' in Hong Kong: A New Path for the Democracy Movement? *China Perspectives* (3): 63–68. https://journals.openedition.org/chinaperspectives/7057 (Last accessed 29 May 2019).

Lam, Jeffie, and Peace Chiu. 2017. Pro-Beijing School Principal Named Hong Kong's New Education Undersecretary Despite National Education Fears. *South China Morning Post*, 1 August. https://www.scmp.com/news/hong-kong/politics/article/2104961/pro-beijing-school-principal-named-hong-kongs-new-education (Last accessed 5 August 2019).

Lecours, André, and Jean-François Dupré. 2018. The Emergence and Radicalization of Self-Determination Claims in Hong Kong and Catalonia: A Historical Institutionalist Perspective. *Ethnicities* (Online First). https://doi.org/10.1177/1468796818785937.

Lieberman, Robert C. 2002. Ideas, Institutions, and Political Order: Explaining Political Change. *American Political Science Review* 96 (4): 697–712. https://doi.org/10.1017/S0003055402000394.

Lipset, Seymour M. 1959. Some Social Requisites of Democracy: Economic Development and Political Development. *American Political Science Review* 53: 69–105. https://doi.org/10.2307/1951731.

Lo, Sonny S.H. 2007. One Formula, Two Experiences: Political Divergence of Hong Kong and Macao Since Retrocession. *Journal of Contemporary China* 16 (52): 359–387. https://doi.org/10.1080/10670560701314214.

———. 2010. *Competing Chinese Political Visions: Hong Kong vs. Beijing on Democracy*. Oxford: Praeger.

Ma, Ngok. 2011. "Hong Kong's Democrats Divide." Journal of Democracy 22(1): 54-67. https://www.journalofdemocracy.org/articles/hong-kongs-democrats-divide/ (Last accessed 29 May 2019).

Mahoney, James. 2000. Path Dependence in Historical Sociology. *Theory and Society* 29: 507–548. https://doi.org/10.1023/A:1007113830879.

Mahoney, James, and Kathleen Thelen. 2010. A Gradual Theory of Institutional Change. In *Explaining Institutional Change: Ambiguity, Agency, and Power*, ed. James Mahoney and Kathleen Thelen, 1–37. Cambridge: Cambridge University Press.

Mahoney, James, Khairunnisa Mohamedali, and Christoph Nguyen. 2016. Causality and Time in Historical Institutionalism. In *The Oxford Handbook of Historical Institutionalism*, ed. Orfeo Fioretos, Tulia G. Falleti, and Adam Sheingate, 71–88. Oxford: Oxford University Press.

March, James G., and Johan P. Olsen. 2004. *The Logic of Appropriateness*. ARENA Working Paper (Centre for European Studies, University of Oslo) 04/09. http://www.sv.uio.no/arena/english/research/publications/arena-working-papers/2001-2010/2004/04_09.html (Last accessed 29 May 2019).

Mathews, Gordon, Eric Kit-wai Ma, and Tai-lok Lui. 2008. *Hong Kong, China: Learning to Belong to a Nation*. London: Routledge.

New York Times Editorial Board. 2019. A Movement, and a Country, Torn by Protests. *New York Times*, 4 July. https://www.nytimes.com/2019/07/04/opinion/hong-kong-protests-china-beijing.html (Last accessed 2 August 2019).

Ng, Kang-chung. 2015. The Road to Universal Suffrage: A Timeline of Hong Kong's Journey to Votes for All. *South China Morning Post*, 22 April (Last accessed 10 August 2019).

Overholt, William H. 2017. *China's Crisis of Success*. Cambridge: Cambridge University Press.

Phillips, Tom. 2015. What Will Hong Kong's Political Reform Vote Mean? *The Guardian*, 16 June. https://www.theguardian.com/world/2015/jun/16/hong-kong-political-reform-vote-fake-democracy (Last accessed 4 August 2019).

Sergeant, Gray. 2017. Britain Should Speak Up—Don't Let China Get Away with Ripping up Hong Kong's Handover Treaty. *Hong Kong Free Press*, 8 July. https://www.hongkongfp.com/2017/07/08/britain-speak-dont-let-china-get-away-ripping-hong-kongs-handover-treaty/ (Last accessed 29 May 2019).

*Sino-British Joint Declaration on the Question of Hong Kong*. 1984. http://www.cmab.gov.hk/en/issues/joint.htm (Last accessed 29 May 2019).

Smith, Anthony D. 2001. *Nationalism: Theory, Ideology, History*. Cambridge: Polity Press.

Snelder, Julian. 2014. The History of the New Chinese Empire. *The Interpreter*, 17 December. https://www.lowyinstitute.org/the-interpreter/history-new-chinese-empire (Last Accessed 2 August 2019).

South China Morning Post. 2014. Full Text: NPC Standing Committee Decision on Hong Kong 2017 Election Framework. 31 August. https://www.scmp.com/news/hong-kong/article/1582245/full-text-npc-standing-committee-decision-hong-kong-2017-election (Last accessed 3 August 2019).

———. 2017. Carrie Lam Wins Hong Kong Chief Executive Election, with 777 Votes. 6 June. https://www.scmp.com/news/hong-kong/politics/article/2082192/live-decision-day-arrives-hong-kong-race-its-next-leader (Last accessed 4 August 2019).

———. n.d. What Is Occupy Central? 10 Key Facts About Hong Kong's Pro-Democracy Movement. https://www.scmp.com/article/1604649/what-occupy-central-10-things-you-need-know (Last accessed 3 August 2019).

Terrill, Ross. 2003. *The New Chinese Empire And What It Means for the United States*. New York: Basic Books.

The Guardian Editorial. 2019. The Guardian View on Hong Kong's Crisis: The People Have Spoken. *The Guardian*, 17 June. https://www.theguardian.com/commentisfree/2019/jun/17/the-guardian-view-on-hong-kongs-crisis-the-people-have-spoken (Last accessed 2 August 2019).

Tsai, Kellee S. 2006. Adaptive Informal Institutions and Endogenous Institutional Change in China. *World Politics* 59: 116–141. https://doi.org/10.1353/wp.2007.0018.

Voter Registration (Hong Kong Government). 2018. Voter Registration Statistics: Functional Constituency. https://www.voterregistration.gov.hk/eng/statistic20183.html (Last accessed 29 May 2019).

Wong, Stan Hok-wui. 2012. Authoritarian Co-optation in the Age of Globalisation: Evidence from Hong Kong. *Journal of Contemporary Asia* 42 (2): 182–209. https://doi.org/10.1080/00472336.2012.668348.

Yu, Eilo Wing-yat. 2013. Macao's 'One Country, Two Systems': High Autonomy or Intervention? In *Negotiating Autonomy in Greater China Hong Kong and Its Sovereignty Before and After 1997*, ed. Ray Yip, 207–241. Copenhagen: Nordic Institute of Asian Studies Press.

Zheng, Yongnian. 2007. *De Facto Federalism in China: Reforms and Dynamics of Central-Local Relations*. Singapore: World Scientific.

# PART III

# Recognizing and Accommodating National and Other Diversities: Success or Failure?

## CHAPTER 8

# Internal Migration in Asian Multinational Countries: Attitudes, Challenges and Institutions

*Isabelle Côté and Mira Raatikainen*

## INTRODUCTION

This chapter answers three questions: (1) What factors shape local attitudes towards internal migrants? (2) How do sub-national and national actors recognise and accommodate the challenges of national diversity resulting from increased levels of population mobility? (3) Does federalism matter in cases of sub-national migration governance?

Discussions on multinational federalism touch on several forms of diversity including national diversity and polyethnic diversity, the latter of which is a by-product of international migration (Kymlicka 1995). These

I. Côté (✉)
Memorial University of Newfoundland, St. John's, NL, Canada
e-mail: icote@mun.ca

M. Raatikainen
The Norman Paterson School of International Affairs, Carleton University,
Ottawa, ON, Canada
e-mail: mira.raatikainen@carleton.ca

© The Author(s) 2020
A.-G. Gagnon, A. Tremblay (eds.), *Federalism and National Diversity in the 21st Century*, Federalism and Internal Conflicts,
https://doi.org/10.1007/978-3-030-38419-7_8

187

discussions tend, however, to overlook the dynamics of *internal* migration, by which we mean the phenomenon of citizens relocating within a country's borders. This oversight is particularly glaring given the sheer number of internal migrants in many multinational states, the contribution of internal migration to developing local ethnic heterogeneity in these states and the recent spur of opposition—if not outright hostility—to internal migration from ethnically distinct 'native' or 'local' populations—that is, what Myron Weiner (1978) dubbed 'Sons of the Soil' (SoS) conflicts.[1]

This chapter investigates these three central questions by exploring the academic literature, official reports and media coverage on internal migration in multinational federations in Asia, where 'Sons of the Soil' (Weiner 1978) conflicts are most prominent (Fearon and Laitin 2011, 200).[2] As opposed to unitary states, where power is by all accounts generally centralised, federal states are characterised by a union of partially self-governing provinces or states operating under a central federal government, giving their constituent parts more leeway to pass locally specific regulations. Consequently, we would expect federations to be uniquely designed to experience local opposition to internal migration.

This chapter focuses on India and Malaysia, two of the most prominent multinational federations in Asia,[3] before drawing parallels and establishing

---

[1] The focus on international migration is not unique to discussions on multinational federalism. Migration scholars have long paid attention to the socio-economic implications of international migration for both the host and home regions. Since the attacks on 11 September 2001, a burgeoning literature has emerged that explores how international migration may also threaten national security by challenging state capacity and control (see Mitchell 2018). Yet compared to refugees and other international migrants, the political impacts of internal migrants on host regions have gone largely unnoticed.

[2] To be clear, "Sons of the Soil" or SoS conflicts are not confined to Asia. Scholars have examined the rise of these conflicts throughout Africa (Dunn 2009; Mitchell 2011; Lynch 2011; Green 2012), former Soviet Republics (Kolstø and Blakkisrud 2013) and throughout parts of Western Europe (Geschiere 2009), among other places.

[3] The Indian Federation is not only the world's largest democracy, it is also one of the most religiously and linguistically diverse countries in the world. The year 2018 estimates put India's population at 1.3 billion, which consists mainly of Hindus, Muslims, Christians and Sikhs (CIA Factbook 2018). India's population is divided into 29 states and 7 union territories and its constitution lists 22 languages as 'recognized languages', with Hindi (43.6%), Bengali (8%), Marathi (6.9%) and Telugu (6.7%) making up the largest language groups (CIA Factbook 2018). However, the latest census puts the number of languages spoken across the country at nearly 20,000—evidence of significant diversity in India (Bajwa 2018). The Malaysian Federation consists of 13 federal states and 3 federal territories. Malaysia has a population of roughly 31 million, which is made up of locally born Malays (55%), Chinese

contrasts with China, a multinational unitary state with a long history of internal population movements (IOM 2017). This cross-country comparison allows us to explore, at a preliminary level, whether the political challenges of internal migration are ubiquitous to multinational countries regardless of the nature of their political arrangements, while examining the roles played by various sub-national and national actors in addressing the challenges of migration-induced ethnic heterogeneity.

This chapter is divided into three sections: first, it introduces internal migration as a key driver of national diversity in multinational states. Second, it provides an overview of the theoretical rationales that underscore recent opposition to internal migration across the three cases; in so doing, it shows that rather than being driven purely by economic or nativist concerns, attitudes towards internal migration are shaped by the relative position of the migrant population vis-à-vis that of the local population. Third, it explores national and sub-national responses to the challenges of national diversity resulting from internal migration. In brief, it shows that, while opposition to internal migration may not be unique to a given political system, political decentralisation facilitates the creation and implementation of local barriers to mobility, such as bylaws, registration lists and nativist parties.

## Logics of Opposition to Internal Migration in Multinational States

Scholars are only starting to investigate the political impacts of population movements (see Weiner and Teitelbaum 2001; Goldstone et al. 2012). Still, most of the literature focuses on international migration and its potential for threatening international security (e.g., Teitelbaum and Winter 1998) or national security (e.g., Weiner and Russell 2001). These trends are surprising given that the global number of internal migrants greatly surpasses the global number of international migrants. According to recent estimates, there are 760 million internal migrants worldwide (IOM 2018, 2), as opposed to 258 million international migrants (UN

(24%) and Indians (7%). However, these groups are further refined into those who are considered *bumiputeras* ("Sons of the Soil") (13%) and those who are not (Pillai 2015, xviii–xix). The various ethnic groups are not distributed evenly across the country; for example, peninsular Malaysia is dominated by Malays while the Island of Borneo is dominated by different *bumiputera* groups, such as the Kadazan-Dusun and Iban (Pillai 2015, xix).

2017, 3). This estimated total number of internal migrants includes the 300 million people classified as internal migrants in India (Deshingkar 2006, 3), the 253 million Chinese internal migrants (Zhao et al. 2018, 19) and the 6 million internal migrants in Malaysia (which constitutes approximately 20% of the country's total population) (UNESCO 2016b).

Internal migration can take very different forms: it includes movements as disparate as the forced resettlement of people affected by China's Three Gorges Dam, internally displaced people (IDPs) who have been forced to relocate after a natural disaster and (largely voluntary) mass relocation of rural people to urban areas. Revolutionary changes in transportation and telecommunications are expected to make it even easier for people to relocate in the future, further underscoring the importance of understanding migration dynamics. As several countries are calling for the removal of structural and cultural barriers to internal population movements in an effort to create a nation-wide labour and resource market,[4] we can only expect the internal migration to continue—if not increase—in years to come.

In multinational countries, it is not unusual for internal migrants to belong to an ethnic group different from that of the majority population of the host region. A brief examination of migration patterns in China's northwestern region illustrates this difference. Over the years, Han Chinese—that is, the majority ethnic group in China—have accounted for nearly 95% of all internal migrants to the Xinjiang Uyghur Autonomous Region (Iredale et al. 2001, 176). As a result of these large population inflows, the proportion of Han Chinese in this region has increased exponentially, from a meagre 5% in 1941 to 40.48% in 2010, while the proportion of Uyghurs has dropped sharply, from 80% to 45.84% (Côté 2015a, 137).[5] Meanwhile, some Uyghurs have also relocated to Han-populated coastal cities in Eastern China, though in smaller number (Baranovitch 2003).

Internal population movements, relocating people in and out of ethnic homelands and urban areas, represent an important source of local diversity and ethnic heterogeneity—sometimes more so than international migration. The 2010 Chinese National Census revealed that there were

---

[4] See MacMillan and Grady 2007 for a Canadian example.

[5] Considering that Chinese population censuses at the provincial level do not account for military and military-related personnel or the sizeable number of temporary migrants who have relocated *en masse* to Xinjiang in recent years following the introduction of favourable economic and trading opportunities, it is probable that the Han share of the population is even higher.

only 600,000 foreigners living in China, a very modest number given the country's total population and the 113.8 million people who belong to one of China's 55 national minorities (NBSC 2011). What is more, the impact of international migration is often limited to the country's largest cities. The situation is similar in Malaysia, where international migration is estimated at 1.8–3.2 million foreign workers, most of whom reside in the capital of Kuala Lumpur (Ramchandani 2018). Much like in China, the number of international migrants pales in comparison to the 13.5 million who belong to one of Malaysia's ethnic minority groups and who can, through internal migration, alter local demographics.

Domestic population movements are not always welcomed with open arms by the host communities; they sometimes face significant opposition. Opposition to internal migration tends to fall under two categories: (1) opposition for reasons of economic resource scarcity or (2) opposition due to identity differences. Bhavnani and Lacina (2018) describe the complex and somewhat contradictory logic undergirding the first form of opposition. They argue that while internal migration is a potential source of economic growth, financial gains, increased government accountability and better policy for the host communities, these gains are not always realised, as local governments—who benefit from population influxes by seeing their tax revenues increase—often fail to use this new financial windfall to mitigate the impact sudden population growth has on receiving communities. Under these circumstances, internal migration becomes a major point of contention given how an ever-growing population is left to compete for an ever decreasing share of the proverbial resource pie. As migrants often lack a political voice in their new host communities,[6] politicians can then 'ignore' them at little to no cost to their political capital, pandering instead to those 'natives' to the area and introducing policies promoting local interests (Côté and Mitchell 2016). Communities where local resources are scarce and those that are inadequately prepared or unwilling to direct resources to managing an increasingly diverse population would then be more likely to oppose internal migration and become a breeding ground for resentment, discrimination and violence.

---

[6]Although internal migrants are citizens of their new host community, city or state, they often face barriers to voting due to complex registration requirements (Deshingkar 2006). Besides, several—though certainly not all—internal migrants are poor and therefore marginalized, which limits their ability to organize and become a political force in the host communities (Fearon and Laitin 2011).

As previously noted, it is not unusual in large multinational countries for internal migrants to belong to a different ethnic group, to speak a different language or to practice a different religion than the local majority population. This can result in a "clash of national identity" (Teitelbaum and Winters 1998), where the identity and cultural traditions of the host society are perceived to be threatened by those of the migrant populations—a tension at the heart of today's nativist populism movements. This type of identity-based opposition to internal migration is rooted in an underlying logic which presumes that opposition will be strongest when incoming migrants are ethnically distinct from the local population and weaker (or non-existent) when migrants belong to the same ethnic group as the majority population of the host communities.

Another variant of identity-based opposition to internal migration is not rooted so much in concerns about the growing juxtaposition of several ethnic groups, but rather it points out that opposition is likely to occur when 'one ethnic group migrates into an area that is considered "homeland" by another ethnic group and challenges the dominance of the latter' (Goldstone 2002, 13–14). Based on this logic, the main factor affecting local response to internal migration is whether a host region is considered a homeland for a territorially concentrated and ethnically distinct population.[7]

Building on these insights, recent scholarship has bridged these strands of literature by exploring how migrants from different ethnic groups have access to different political, economic and social resources. Migrants belonging to a country's 'dominant ethnicity'—that is, the ethnic group that controls the economic, political and social levers of a country (cf. Kaufmann 2004)—often enjoy greater political participation, cultural recognition and access to economic and social resources than the local people. While there are numerous exceptions to the rule (see Bookman 1998), an ethnic group that constitutes *either* the majority of the population (e.g., Malays in Malaysia) *or* its largest ethnic group (e.g., Han Chinese in China) is typically the dominant ethnic group of a country. The arrival of highly competitive 'dominant migrants' is thus expected to generate or magnify group disparities between migrants and locals, spurring nativist resistance to migration or devising regulations meant to control who gains entry to 'their region' (see Côté 2015b).

---

[7] In the words of Monica Duffy Toft, 'No matter how barren, no territory is worthless if it is a homeland' (2003, 1).

## OPPOSITION TO INTERNAL MIGRATION IN ASIA

An empirical exploration of migratory dynamics in multinational Asian countries allows us to better illustrate the logics behind different forms of opposition to internal migration. Concerns over increased resource competition have abounded both in Malaysia (Sadiq 2009, 21) and India, especially in Mumbai, where local people have accused internal migrants of usurping job opportunities, residential space and amenities that, according to nativist parties, 'rightfully belong[ed] to the local Maharashtrian population' (Abbas and Varma 2014, 8). In Assam, tribal groups have also accused Hindu and Muslim migrants of 'plundering resources and taking away jobs' (Das and Siddiqui 2018).

Opposition to internal migration in India is also plagued by classist undertones, as exemplified by attempts to place limits on the mobility and residency rights of the poor. In India, locals often fail to see the economic benefits of incoming low-skilled workers, seeing them instead as a nuisance to public spaces and adding strain on limited resources (Dasgupta 2018). In Mumbai, concerns related to incoming migrants include both resource-based and cultural considerations. However, since 70% of incoming migrants to Mumbai are rural intra-state migrants from the same cultural group as the majority of the urban population (*Times of India* 2012), one can only ask whether these concerns apply specifically to rural migrants of lower income levels.

The forces behind opposition to migration are not limited to federal states; they are, in fact, present in several cases of rural-urban migration around the world as rural migrants are often viewed as poor and uncivilised. This is certainly the case in China—a fiercely unitary state—where rural migrants are viewed as 'dirty and poor' (Li 2006) and newcomers, whether labourers or beggars, are denigrated as 'rootless people who summoned up distaste and even alarm among the town's permanent residents' (Solinger 1999, 457). Such traditional discrimination against (rural) outsiders has persisted, despite the opening up of China's internal migration in the 1980s. For instance, in 1995, the Chinese Ministry of Labor considered establishing a system similar to international passports and visa requirements in order to curb trans-provincial migration and protect the rights of urban workers. Meanwhile, local authorities have been known to require that rural migrant workers obtain work permits in order to work in the city, 'as if they were foreign' (Solinger 1999, 466; Han 2010, 598).

A recent study by Singer and Quek (2017) shows that locals base their opinions on internal migrants by taking into account labour market considerations. This would seem to make sense as both incoming migrants and host populations largely belong to the same ethnic group in Eastern China[8] and therefore there is little room for basing opinions on ethnic or religious considerations. However, the importance of material self-interest and labour market considerations has not been reproduced in other studies. For example, Zhu (2018) finds that labour market considerations do not 'naturally' play a significant role in urban residents' attitude formation about internal migrants in China: only when respondents are prompted by the researcher to consider labour market implications do they acknowledge their importance (2018, 21).

Another factor affecting local attitudes towards inter-provincial migration in China is the now infamous *hukou* or household registration system. The *hukou* system, implemented in 1958, is a complex migration management system run by the Chinese central government to control internal migration flows (Song 2014, 201). Under the *hukou* system, all Chinese citizens are assigned a *hukou* based on their locality (urban or rural) and occupation (agricultural or non-agricultural), which affects where they may access public services. It is difficult for those with a rural *hukou* to obtain an urban *hukou* since the government aims to restrict rural-urban migration, and the *hukou* system is largely considered to be discriminatory towards rural Chinese (Liu 2005). The *hukou* system has been reformed on multiple occasions but to this day continues to dictate where rural, and to a lesser degree, urban, Chinese are allowed to live and join the labour market (South China Morning Post 2019).

The challenges of securing a new *hukou* have forced an estimated 200 million migrants to relocate, whether permanently or temporarily, without first obtaining residency rights—that is, earning them the label of non-*hukou* migrants or 'floating population' (People's Daily Online 2019). China's floating population is often depicted in unflattering terms as unskilled, uncivilised, with little knowledge of hygiene and as potential criminals (see Ping and Pieke 2003, 12). It is not surprising, then, that local attitudes towards internal migration in China vary tremendously based on whether migrants are part of the state's organised programmes

---

[8] Studies have shown that approximately 90% of internal migrants in China belong to the Han Chinese ethnic group (Iredale et al. 2001).

(most of whom are *hukou* migrants) or have moved of their own volition (non-*hukou* migrants) (Côté 2019, 94).

'When' (i.e., the point in one's life) members of the host communities have obtained their urban *hukou* also appears to shape local attitudes towards internal migration. In a 2016 study, Tse finds that those who have had an urban *hukou* from birth (i.e., passed down from their parents) and who have high education and income levels tend to be more hostile towards internal migrants (2016, 580). Meanwhile, those who have more recently gained their urban *hukou* and who have less education and income tend to be more welcoming towards internal migrants, despite being those most likely to compete for jobs with the newcomers. Consequently, a desire to preserve one's privileged position appears to also play a role.

It is important to point out that, compared to Malaysia and India, the Chinese *hukou* system limits the degree of job and resource competition between locals and migrants—a distinction derived from China's authoritarian system rather than from its unitary form of political arrangements. Although China is experiencing large-scale rural-to-urban migration, migrants arriving in urban centres do not compete for the same jobs or add pressures on the same public services. Indeed, those with rural *hukou*s have been barred from accessing public services and, in the past, were even blocked from some job opportunities, though these restrictions have recently been relaxed (Li 2006; Sheehan 2017).

To be sure, migrants are not always seen through an economic prism; on occasion, identity factors play as important a role. In India and Malaysia, resentment based on economic competition is certainly prevalent but appears to be affected by whether or not the respondents belong to the local minority or majority group. In a study of Mumbai (a prominently Hindu city with a small Muslim minority), Gaikwad and Nellis (2017) presented survey respondents with hypothetical in-migrant profiles that show the migrant's skill level and an insinuation as to which religion the hypothetical migrant belongs—done by assigning the hypothetical migrant either a commonly known Hindu or Muslim name. The authors find that respondents belonging to the majority Hindu group did not show racial bias and were more concerned with the migrant's skill level, preferring high-skilled migrants, while respondents belonging to the minority Muslim group were more welcoming to Muslim migrants of any skill level (Gaikwad and Nellis 2017, 464). This, they hypothesise, is due to the minority group's desire to bolster their co-ethnic base and find 'safety in numbers' (Gaikwad and Nellis 2017, 458).

The importance of the relative position of migrants vis-à-vis the host population is even more acute in Malaysia, where indigenous groups in the eastern provinces of Sabah and Sarawak have repeatedly asked for protections against the in-migration of Malays—the dominant ethnic group in Malaysia. Despite being a demographic minority in those regions, Malay migrants are still part of the national majority ethnic group, granting them preferential access to economic and political resources and causing suspicion and apprehension in the local population (Sadiq 2009). Within this particular context, protections fell short of their expectations; by 1989, the vast majority of central government departments were still run by West Malaysians, which is in striking contrast to the 'Borneonization' of the bureaucracy that was promised to Sabah and Sarawak when the British colonisers departed (Sadiq 2009, 24–25). While up-to-date statistics on the composition of the civil service in Sabah are not readily available, in 2012, two former civil servants challenged the state and federal governments in the courts, arguing that 'Borneonization' of the public service had not been carried out as outlined in the Malaysia Agreement of 1963[9] (The Borneo Post 2012).[10] In 2016, a policy panel on 'Borneonization' was established to study potential changes and make recommendations to the state and federal governments on the hiring and appointing of civil servants in Sabah (Free Malaysia Today 2016). In brief, the issue of 'Borneonization' is still pressing today and continues to make headlines on the island.

## THE ROLE OF SUB-NATIONAL AND NATIONAL ACTORS

When local opposition to internal migration emerges, sub-national actors are faced with a conundrum: they can give in to local demands and ask for greater control over who gets in 'their territory', or they can turn a blind eye to these concerns and continue promoting population movements, whether implicitly or explicitly. It is particularly difficult for sub-national units in federal/decentralised states to opt for the second option given that their political arrangements make it so that their constituent parts are responsive first and foremost to local populations. Recent studies have

[9] The Malaysia Agreement of 1963 formed the Malaysian Federation and outlines the special rights given to Sabah and Sarawak.

[10] Their case was eventually dismissed due to the court finding that the plaintiffs lacked standing on the matter.

shown that a country's degree of political decentralisation has been linked to the salience of anti-migrant and SoS policies (Dunn 2009; Bhavnani and Lacina 2018, 2019; Côté and Mitchell 2016, 2017). As Bhavnani and Lacina (2019) explain, 'political decentralisation pushed by international institutions such as the World Bank creates new tiers of subnational governance that can be easily captured by nativists'. The introduction or the presence of democratic elections may further fuel the nativist flames. With more power and spoils devolved to regional governments, fierce competition may emerge among candidates who then tap into whatever identity, rhetoric or source of grievance—including their identity as 'locals'—to mobilise supporters and maximise their chance of being elected (Côté and Mitchell 2017, 344).

If and when sub-national units respond to anti-immigration attitudes and try to assert greater control over 'who gets in', the tools at their disposal are fairly limited. On the one hand, they can resort to violence against migrants. For example, nativist political parties in India, most notoriously the Shiv Sena in Mumbai (Katzenstein 1973) and the anti-migrant Kannada Chaluvaligars in Bangalore (Weiner 1978), have routinely relied on aggression towards migrants as a means to deter in-migration to these cities, since transformations of the local voter base may result in political parties losing power (Bhavnani and Lacina 2018, 31). This indirect strategy of population control has been known to result in migrants' mass exodus from an area, but it does come with heavy costs as well as uncertain benefits (e.g., Davidson 2008).

Alternatively, if 'native' groups control some political levers locally, they may try to pass local regulations to (re)gain control over their territory. An illuminating—and rather rare—example of sub-national units putting legal barriers in place to limit internal migration can be found in the multiethnic federation of Malaysia. Upon joining the newly formed Malaysian federation in 1963, the eastern provinces of Sabah and Sarawak on the Island of Borneo demanded constitutional protections for their indigenous status, highlighting the need to limit the number of Malay people—the country's dominant ethnic group—moving to or taking up employment in their region. As a result of these demands, Article 159 of the Federal Constitution of Malaysia prohibits 'West Malaysians' from travelling to 'East Malaysia' without a permit or a passport, effectively creating a two-tiered citizenship in which one group is *more native* than the other (Sadiq 2009). Article 159 also saddled the federal government with the double duty to safeguard the special status of Malay people in Malaysia, which led to the practice of stacking public services throughout the country—including in Sabah and Sarawak—with Malay employees (Sadiq 2009, 24–25).[11] This indicates that, while constitutional protections for minority populations were granted, they were also undermined by the simultaneous promotion of Malay dominance. Despite these limitations, the introduction of legal barriers to movement from West Malaysia to the eastern provinces of Sabah and Sarawak reflect how local ethnic pluralism may in fact limit democracy for the sake of regional preservation.

In other cases, *informal* barriers to internal migration have been more prevalent than *formal* regulations. In the Republic of India, for instance, the constitution grants control over immigration to the federal level of government and, while it may not allow its constituent units to pass formal bylaws restricting population mobility, it grants states the right to control important aspects of everyday life, such as ration cards and access to services within their own borders (Dossani and Vijaykumar 2005, 5). Access to a ration card—a form of documentation necessary to prove not only one's Indian citizenship but also one's belonging to a state—are particularly important; without it, one cannot access banking systems, health services, voting stations, or, perhaps most importantly, food and oil rations (Deshingkar 2006, 94). It may be particularly challenging for poor, interprovincial migrants to obtain ration cards. Consequently, control over ration cards gives constituent Indian states significant power to try and manipulate the flow of migrants within India.

Constituent states can also indirectly affect internal population movements by ignoring federal regulations meant to protect migrant workers in their new place of residence. While India's federal government passed the 1979 Inter-State Migrant Workmen Act in an effort to address the dismal living conditions of migrant workers, the regulation has largely been ignored by state-level governments (Abbas and Varma 2014). Instead, several large cities like Mumbai, Delhi and Kolkata—where the influx of rural migrants has intensified housing pressures and led to the expansion of 'slum' dwellings—have instead started to consider rural employment

---

[11] The federal government's lack of interest in the special status or interests of Sabah and Sarawak and its preoccupation with promoting 'Malayness' across the country were clear in the 2018 election, in which the prime minister running for re-election called Sabah a 'fixed deposit', insinuating that Sabah was a sure victory for him and the Barisan Nasional Party (BNP), as it has been for the last 50 years (*The Straits Times* 2018). This, however, sparked a backlash from native Sabahans, who ended up voting for candidates of other parties who promised greater autonomy as well as greater returns from oil royalties.

programmes and other policies aimed at *preventing* people from migrating from their home states (Abbas and Varma 2014, 10).

This, however, does not mean that the central government of India is completely uninfluential or 'hands off' when it comes to internal migration matters. The state of Assam provides a recent and fascinating example of the relationship between internal migration and federal and state-level governments. In July, 2018, the Assamese government published a 'national citizenship registry' (NRC) listing every Indian citizen residing in the state (Schultz 2018). Although the NRC was meant to better distinguish internal migrants from international migrants, the difficulties in obtaining the documents necessary to prove one's citizenship have meant it has been criticised as an effort to exclude millions of poor minority Indian citizens—many of whom are internal migrants—from official citizenship (Abbas 2016, 160).

Efforts to update the NRC were headed by the Hindu nationalist Bharatiya Janata Party (BJP) in Assam,[12] but federal BJP support was also evident as the party, headed by Prime Minister Narendra Modi, promised as part of its 2019 federal election campaign to implement a country-wide NRC and deport those not included in the NRC once re-elected (*The Indian Express* 2018; Bhaumik 2018). In light of the BJP re-election, the NRC remains a hot topic in India and has sparked widespread concerns, both within and outside India (Borpujari 2018), about becoming, in effect, a tool to expel people for 'political reasons' (Das and Siddiqui 2018). At the very least, it shows how such informal tools can be used to bolster a voting base.[13]

National governments can also work to prevent inter-provincial migration by mitigating the factors motivating people to move in the first place, transferring resources from wealthier regions to poorer, less developed regions. This, however, does not seem to be the case in India. In 2016, *The Hindu* reported that the state of Jammu and Kashmir received a disproportionate amount of central government funds, whereas high outmigration states such as Uttar Pradesh and Bihar have received disproportionately low amounts of funds from the central government

[12] In fact, some claim that it is the promise of implementing the NRC that got BJP elected in Assam in the first place (Borpujari 2018).

[13] In the 2016 elections, for instance, BJP party leader Amit Shah promised citizenship to Hindus from Bangladesh—even those who arrived after the 1971 cut-off date (Seetharaman 2015).

(Raghavan 2016). To be sure, the politics of transfer funds are more nuanced than a simple comparison between funding amounts in a handful of states, one of which is politically unstable and in the middle of a border conflict. This brief point simply suggests that the national government of India may not, at the moment, be preoccupied with encouraging state-level population retention.[14]

One cannot write about governing internal migration in Asia without touching on China, home to the world's largest internal population movements (Zhao et al. 2018, 19). Unlike India, China is beginning to promote the benefits brought about by rural-to-urban migration. Instead of encouraging rural Chinese to stay put, the central government has made lofty promises to grant 100 million urban *hukous* to migrant workers by 2020 (Chan 2014, 4) in an effort to 'lift the percentage of people living in cities' (Xinhua 2018).[15] In order to receive one of the 100 million urban *hukous*, one must complete an application process that varies from region to region. Local governments in Shanghai, Beijing and Guangzhou have introduced points grading systems to assess education and income levels in allocating urban *hukous* to qualifying migrants (Sheehan 2017). In order to attract the 'best' internal migrants, cities like Shanghai have also held job fairs at which gaining employment comes with the promise of a Shanghai *hukou* (Daye and Deng 2019). After a relatively slow start to the programme[16]—only 30 million urban *hukous* had been granted in the first year of the initiative (Sheehan 2017)—the Chinese government announced that it was scrapping restrictions for medium-sized cities (1–3 million people) and easing restrictions on large cities (3–5 million people) for those with a new urban *hukou* (Daye and Deng 2019).

Despite recent relaxations in the *hukou* system, control over internal migration continues to fall squarely under the authority of the Chinese central government, and though provincial authorities may, to a limited extent, pass regulations *attracting* inter-provincial migration, any attempts at *curbing* migration are quickly denounced as anti-socialist, manifestation

[14] Although this may be changing, as the federal BJP is currently contemplating efforts to retain populations in rural areas, vowing to double farmer's income by 2022 (*The Times of India* 2018).

[15] That is one of the main goals of China's 13th Five-Year period (2016–2020) (Government of China 2016).

[16] Concerns over giving up rural land rights back home, were they to acquire an urban *hukou*, have precluded many potential rural migrants from partaking in this new initiative, though calls for reforms have been heard (Chan 2014).

of local nationalism, or worse, as 'national splittism' (Bulag 2002, 214). Several Tibetan and Uyghur respondents interviewed by Côté (2019, 92) indicated that while they disliked the mass migration of Han Chinese to Qinghai and Xinjiang, they could not voice their critiques of state-organised migration or they would be sent to prison or risk the death penalty. However, people relocating without the protective clout granted by a state-issued *hukou* were a much 'safer' migrant population to mobilise against, which explains why recent non-*hukou* migrants were those most targeted in the few SoS conflicts occurring in Chinese minority regions (Côté 2019, 94).

## CONCLUSION: DOES FEDERALISM MATTER?

The 'age of migration' has brought with it new challenges and obstacles to multinational states. Population movements—even those occurring within a country's borders—do not always occur smoothly and, as this chapter has shown, local opposition to internal migration does indeed take place. This chapter has also shown that attitudes towards internal migration are rarely driven purely by economic or nativist concerns; they seem instead to be shaped by the relative position of the migrant population vis-à-vis that of the local population.

When *local people* are in a comparatively advantageous position compared to newcomers and when their demographic dominance is not challenged, they tend to accept—or at least tolerate—internal migrants, so long as they do not put 'undue' pressure on already scarce local resources (e.g., fresh water supplies, land and housing). In cases where such pressure exists, poor migrants tend to bear the brunt of local resentment. Opposition to rural-urban migration in India and China are illustrative of these dis-criminative economic concerns. By contrast, when *internal migrants* are in an economically advantageous or dominant position compared to the local population, local people tend to oppose the in-migration of their fellow citizens out of 'nativist' concerns—for example, to preserve access to 'their' land, language and heritage. The migration of dominant Malays into the minority-populated provinces of Sabah and Sarawak illustrates this dynamic. And, as this chapter's brief discussion on China has shown, the challenges brought forth by internal migration are neither unique to federal states nor unique to democratic states, for that matter.

The Chinese unitary and authoritarian state has kept a tight grip on migration governance, preventing sub-national units from passing regulations meant to restrict access to 'their' region, though allowing local governments some leeway in devising policies meant to attract the most qualified internal migrants. This is not to say that local attitudes towards internal migration are necessarily more favourable in authoritarian states like China than in federal democracies like Malaysia and India. After all, migrants seen as 'less risky'—that is, non-*hukou* migrants—have been discriminated against in urban coastal areas and were also the targets of SoS attacks in China's Western minority regions. What this chapter points to, however, are the unintended consequences of authoritarianism in subduing or mitigating anti-migration mobilisation and preventing sub-national units from restricting population inflows, so long, at least, as internal migration bolsters China's main economic and political objectives as stated in its Five-Year Plans.

While opposition to internal migration may not be unique to a given political system, this chapter has nevertheless highlighted how federal states and other decentralised systems facilitate the creation and implementation of sub-national barriers to internal mobility as they grant their constituent parts substantial autonomy to respond to issues deemed locally important, such as migration controls. The Malaysian federation is a rare case where sub-national actors lobbied for legal barriers to limit internal migration from continental Malaysia, whereas in India, sub-national actors have relied on informal barriers to population mobility, such as registration lists and nativist parties. Even though managing internal migration in India and Malaysia has been largely in the hands of sub-national units, national governments have by no means been absent, adopting pro-urban or pro-rural policies shaping the context within which local governments operate as well as, incidentally, native-migrant relations. It is worth pointing out that recently decentralising unitary states like Indonesia have also experienced a surge in sub-national actors expressing their desire to better control inter-provincial migratory flows into 'their' provinces (e.g., Davidson 2008; Smith 2005; Somba 2009), which further suggests the importance of decentralisation practices for sub-national migration governance.

## References

Abbas, Rameez. 2016. Internal Migration and Citizenship in China. *Journal of Ethnic and Migration Studies* 42 (1): 150–168.

Abbas, Rameez, and Divya Varma. 2014. Internal Labor Migration in India Raises Integration Challenges for Migrants. *Migration Policy Institute*, March 3. https://www.migrationpolicy.org/article/internal-labor-migration-india-raises-integration-challenges-migrants.

Bajwa, Ramandeep. 2018. 19,596 Languages Spoken in India: Census. *International Business Times*, July 2. https://www.ibtimes.co.in/19569-languages-spoken-india-census-773726.

Baranovitch, Nimrod. 2003. From the Margins to the Centre: The Uyghur Challenge in Beijing. *The China Quarterly* 175: 726–750.

Bhaumik, Subir. 2018. Nearly Five Million in India's Assam at Risk of Citizenship Loss. *Al Jazeera*, March 28. https://www.aljazeera.com/news/2018/03/million-india-assam-risk-citizenship-loss-180328152649287.html.

Bhavnani, Rikhil R., and Bethany Lacina. 2018. *Nativism and Economic Integration Across the Developing World: Collision and Accommodation*. Cambridge, UK: Cambridge University Press.

———. 2019. The Backlash Against Internal Migration. *Center for the Advanced Study of India, University of Pennsylvania*, February 11. https://casi.sas.upenn.edu/iit/bhavnanilacina.

Bookman, Milica Z. 1998. *The Demographic Struggle for Power: The Political Economy of Demographic Engineering in the Modern World*. London: Frank Cass.

Borpujari, Priyanka. 2018. India's National Register of Citizens and Assam's Dilemma. *The Diplomat*, August 4. https://thediplomat.com/2018/08/indias-national-register-of-citizens-and-assams-dilemma/.

Bulag, Uradyn E. 2002. From Yeke-juu to Ordos Municipality: Settler Colonialism and Alter/Native Urbanization in Inner Mongolia. *Provincial China* 7 (2): 196–234.

Chan, Kam W. 2014. China's Urbanization 2020: A New Blueprint and Direction. *Eurasian Geography and Economics* 55 (1): 1–9.

CIA. 2018. *The World Factbook*. India. https://www.cia.gov/library/publications/the-world-factbook/geos/in.html.

Côté, Isabelle. 2015a. The Enemies Within: Targeting Han and Hui Migrants in Xinjiang. *Asian Ethnicity* 16 (2): 136–151.

———. 2015b. Horizontal Inequalities and Sons of the Soil Conflict in China. *Civil Wars* 17 (3): 357–378.

———. 2019. Internal Migration, Political Liberalization, and Violent Conflict in Authoritarian China. In *People Changing Places: New Perspective on Demography, Migration, Conflict and the State*, ed. Isabelle Côté, Matthew Mitchell, and Monica Duffy Toft, 86–104. New York: Routledge.

Côté, Isabelle, and Matthew I. Mitchell. 2016. Elections and Sons of the Soil Dynamics in Africa and Asia. *Democratization* 23 (4): 657–677.

———. 2017. Deciphering Sons of the Soil Conflicts: A Critical Survey of the Literature. *Ethnopolitics* 16 (4): 333–351.

Das, Krishna N., and Zeba Siddiqui. 2018. Indian State's Controversial Citizen's List Unites Modi Critics. *Reuters*, July 31. https://www.reuters.com/article/us-india-politics-religion/indian-states-controversial-citizens-list-unites-modi-critics-idUSKBN1KL1Y9.

Dasgupta, KumKum. 2018. Why India Must Safeguard the Rights of Internal Migrants. *Hindustan Times*, June 26. https://www.hindustantimes.com/analysis/why-india-must-safeguard-the-rights-of-internal-migrants/story-QFjoiT-S4IAFSFmgLfJYRPK.html.

Davidson, J.S. 2008. *From Rebellion to Riots*. Madison, WI: The University of Wisconsin Press.

Daye, Chu, and Deng Xiaoci. 2019. China Lowers Urban Hukou Thresholds. *Global Times*, April 8. http://www.globaltimes.cn/content/1145123.shtml.

Deshingkar, Priya. 2006. Internal Migration, Poverty, and Development in Asia: Including the Excluded. *IDS Bulletin* 37: 88–100.

Dossani, Rafiq, and Srinidhi Vijaykumar. 2005. *Indian Federalism and the Conduct of Foreign Policy in Border States: State Participation and Central Accommodation Since 1990* (Working Paper). Asia-Pacific Research Center, Stanford University.

Dunn, Kevin C. 2009. Sons of the Soil and Contemporary State Making: Autochthony, Uncertainty and Political Violence in Africa. *Third World Quarterly* 30 (1): 113–127.

Fearon, James D., and David Laitin. 2011. Sons of the Soil, Migrants, and Civil War. *World Development* 39 (2): 199–211.

Free Malaysia Today. 2016. PBS Sets up Panels on Devolution, Borneonisation. *Free Malaysia Today*, September 6. https://www.freemalaysiatoday.com/category/nation/2016/09/06/pbs-sets-up-panels-on-devolution-borneonisation/.

Gaikwad, Nikhar, and Gareth Nellis. 2017. The Majority-Minority Divide in Attitudes Toward Internal Migration: Evidence from Mumbai. *American Journal of Political Science* 61 (2): 546–472.

Geschiere, Peter. 2009. *The Perils of Belonging: Autochthony, Citizenship, and Exclusion in Africa and Europe*. Chicago, IL: University of Chicago Press.

Goldstone, Jack A. 2002. Population and Security: How Demographic Change Can Lead to Violent Conflict. *Journal of International Affairs* 56 (1): 3–21.

Goldstone, Jack A., Monica D. Toft, and Eric P. Kaufmann, eds. 2012. *Political Demography: How Population Changes Are Reshaping International Security and National Politics*. Boulder, CO and London, UK: Paradigm Publishers.

Government of China. 2016. China to Resolve Hukou Issue for 100 Million Rural Migrants (Press Release). *The State Council of the People's Republic of China*, October 11. http://english.gov.cn/policies/latest_releases/2016/10/11/content_281475463620362.htm.

Green, Elliott D. 2012. The Political Demography of Conflict in Modern Africa. *Civil Wars* 14 (4): 477–498.

Han, Dong. 2010. Policing and Racialization of Rural Migrant Workers in Chinese Cities. *Ethnic and Racial Studies* 33 (4): 593–610.

International Organization for Migration. 2017. *World Migration Report.* https://publications.iom.int/system/files/pdf/wmr2018en.pdf.

———. 2018. *World Migration Report.* https://www.iom.int/sites/default/files/country/docs/china/r5_world_migration_report_2018_en.pdf.

Iredale, Robyn, Naran Bilik, Suo Wang, Fei Guo, and Caroline Hoy, eds. 2001. *Contemporary Minority Migration, Education and Ethnicity in China.* Cheltenham: Edward Elgar Publishing Limited.

Katzenstein, Mary F. 1973. Origins of Nativism: The Emergence of the Shiv Sena in Bombay. *Asian Survey* 13 (4): 386–399.

Kaufmann, Eric P., ed. 2004. *Rethinking Ethnicity: Majority Groups and Dominant Minorities.* London, UK: Routledge.

Kolstø, Pal, and Helge Blakkisrud. 2013. Yielding to the Sons of the Soil: Abkhazian Democracy and the Marginalization of the Armenian Vote. *Ethnic and Racial Studies* 36 (12): 2075–2095.

Kymlicka, Will. 1995. *Multicultural Citizenship: A Liberal Theory of Minority Rights.* Oxford: Clarendon Press.

Li, Bingqin. 2006. Floating Population or Urban Citizens? Status, Social Provision, and Circumstances of Rural-Urban Migrants in China. *Social Policy and Administration* 40 (2): 174–195.

Liu, Zhiqiang. 2005. Institution and Inequality: The *Hukou* System in China. *Journal of Comparative Economics* 33 (1): 133–157.

Lynch, Gabrielle. 2011. The Wars of Who Belongs Where: The Unstable Politics of Autochthony on Kenya's Mt Elgon. *Ethnopolitics* 10 (3–4): 391–410.

MacMillan, Kathleen, and Patrick Grady. 2007. *Interprovincial Barriers to Internal Trade in Goods, Services and Flows of Capital: Policy, Knowledge Gaps and Research Issues.* Working Paper Series 2007–11 Prepared for Industry Canada, Micro-Economic Policy Analysis Branch. http://publications.gc.ca/site/eng/394952/publication.html.

Mitchell, Matthew I. 2011. Insights from the Cocoa Regions in Côte d'Ivoire and Ghana: Rethinking the Migration-Conflict Nexus. *African Studies Review* 54 (2): 123–144.

———. 2018. Migration, Sons of the Soil Conflict, and International Relations. *International Area Studies Review* 21 (1): 51–67.

National Bureau of Statistics of China (NBSC). 2011. Communiqué of the National Bureau of Statistics of People's Republic of China on Major Figures of the 2010 Population Census [1] (No. 1). http://www.stats.gov.cn/was40/gjtjj_en_detail.jsp?searchword=census&channelid=9528&record=7.

People's Daily Online. 2019. China's Floating Population Starts to Shrink. January 3. http://en.people.cn/n3/2019/0103/c90000-9534415.html.

Pillai, Patrick. 2015. *Yearning to Belong: Malaysia's Indian Muslims, Chitties, Portuguese Eurasians, Peranakan Chinese and Baweanese*. Singapore: ISEAS—Yusof Ishak Institute.

Ping, Huang, and Frank Pieke. 2003. *China Migration Country Study*. Paper Presented at the Regional Conference on Migration, Development and Pro-Poor Policy Choices in Asia, Dhaka, June 22–24, 2003.

Raghavan, Sharad. 2016. J&K Gets 10% of Central Funds with Only 1% of Population. *The Hindu*, July 24. https://www.thehindu.com/news/national/other-states/JampK-gets-1ofCentral-funds-with-only-1-of-population/article14506264.ece.

Ramchandani, Ariel. 2018. Forced Labor Is the Backbone of the World's Electronics Industry. *The Atlantic*, June 28. https://www.theatlantic.com/business/archive/2018/06/malaysia-forced-labor-electronics/563873/.

Sadiq, Kamal. 2009. When Being 'Native' Is Not Enough: Citizens as Foreigners in Malaysia. *Asian Perspective* 33 (1): 5–32.

Schultz, Kai. 2018. As India Clamps Down on Migration, Millions May Lose Citizenship. *The New York Times*, July 30.

Seetharaman, G. 2015. National Register of Citizens in Assam: Issue of Illegal Foreigners Continues to Be a Major Political One. *The Economic Times*, June 14. https://economictimes.indiatimes.com/news/politics-and-nation/national-register-of-citizens-in-assam-issue-of-illegal-foreigners-continues-to-be-a-major-political-one/articleshow/47657561.cms.

Sheehan, Spencer. 2017. China's Hukou Reforms and the Urbanization Challenge. *The Diplomat*, February 22. https://thediplomat.com/2017/02/chinas-hukou-reforms-and-the-urbanization-challenge/.

Singer, David A., and Kai Quek. 2017. *Attitudes Towards Internal and Foreign Migration: Evidence from a Survey Experiment in China*. Massachusetts Institute of Technology Research Paper No. 2017-28.

Smith, Claire Q. 2005. *The Roots of Violence and Prospects for Reconciliation: A Case Study of Ethnic Conflict in Central Kalimantan, Indonesia*. Social Development Papers, Conflict Prevention and Reconstruction (23). World Bank.

Solinger, Dorothy J. 1999. Citizenship Issues in China's Internal Migration: Comparisons with Germany and Japan. *Political Science Quarterly* 114 (3): 455–478.

Somba, Nethy D. 2009. Migration to Papua Should Be Restricted. *The Jakarta Post*, November 16.

Song, Yang. 2014. What Should Economists Know About the Current Chinese Hukou System? *China Economic Review* 29: 200–212.

South China Morning Post. 2019. Breaks of China's Floating Population. June 14. https://www.scmp.com/article/980385/brakes-chinas-floating-population.

Teitelbaum, Michael S., and Michael Winter. 1998. *A Question of Numbers: High Migration, Low Fertility, and the Politics of National Identity*. New York, NY: Hill & Wang.

The Borneo Post. 2012. 'Borneonisation' Case on July 23. *The Borneo Post*, June 19. https://www.theborneopost.com/2012/06/19/borneonisation-case-on-july-23/.

The Indian Express. 2018. NRC Will Be Implemented Across Country After 2019 Polls. BJP Vice President Om Mathur. *The Indian Express*, August 13. https://indianexpress.com/article/india/nrc-will-be-implemented-across-country-after-2019-polls-bjp-leader-5303712/.

The Straits Times. 2018. Malaysian Election: Sabah No Longer a Fixed Deposit for Malaysian PM Najib Says Party Rebel Shafie Apdal. *The Straits Times*, May 6. https://www.straitstimes.com/asia/se-asia/malaysia-election-sabah-no-longer-a-fixed-deposit-for-malaysian-pm-najib-says-party.

Times of India. 2012. 70% Migrants to Mumbai Are from Maharashtra. *Times of India*, 1 September 17. https://timesofindia.indiatimes.com/city/mumbai/70-migrants-to-Mumbai-are-from-Maharashtra/articleshow/16428301.cms.

———. 2018. Agriculture Budget Doubled to Help Double Farm Income by 2022: PM. *The Times of India*, June 20. https://timesofindia.indiatimes.com/business/india-business/agri-budget-doubled-to-help-double-farm-income-by-2022-pm/articleshow/64659053.cms.

Toft, Monica D. 2003. *The Geography of Ethnic Violence: Identity, Interests and the Indivisibility of Territory*. Princeton, NJ: Princeton University Press.

Tse, Chun W. 2016. Urban Residents' Prejudice and Integration of Rural Migrants into Urban China. *Journal of Contemporary China* 25 (100): 579–595.

———. 2016b. Overview of Internal Migration in Malaysia. https://bangkok.unesco.org/sites/default/files/assets/article/Social%20and%20Human%20Sciences/publications/malaysia.pdf.

United Nations Department of Social and Economic Affairs. 2017. *Population Facts*. December 2017. https://www.un.org/en/development/desa/population/publications/pdf/popfacts/PopFacts_2017-5.pdf.

Weiner, Myron. 1978. *Sons of the Soil: Migration and Ethnic Conflict in India*. Princeton, NJ: Princeton University Press.

Weiner, Myron, and Sharon S. Russell. 2001. *Demography and National Security*. New York, NY: Berghahn Books.

Weiner, Myron, and Michael S. Teitelbaum. 2001. *Political Demography, Demographic Engineering*. New York, NY: Berghahn Books.

Xinhua. 2018. Police to Help 100 Million Migrants Settle in Cities by 2020. *Xinhuanet*, January 26. http://www.xinhuanet.com/english/2018-01/26/c_136925024.htm.

Zhao, Liqiu, Shouying Liu, and Wei Zhang. 2018. New Trends in Internal Migration in China: Profiles of the New-Generation Migrants. *China and World Economy* 26 (1): 18–41.

Zhu, Boliang. 2018. Economic Considerations and Attitudes Towards Migrant Workers. https://ssrn.com/abstract=2819056.

## CHAPTER 9

# Immigration Federalism, Multinational States and Subnational Communities: Comparing Flanders and Quebec

## Catherine Xhardez

### Introduction

This chapter explores patterns of immigration federalism in subnational communities (SNCs)[1] in two states that fit the criteria of multinational federation: Flanders, a Dutch-speaking community in the Belgian state, and Quebec, the Francophone majority province of Canada. In federal states, the decentralisation of powers to substate governments has increased the involvement of subnational authorities in immigration policymaking. Federated entities now often deal with a large range of issues related to immigration regulation, such as immigrants' recruitment, selection, settlement or integration (Baglay and Nakache 2014b; Joppke and Seidle 2012;

---

[1] The adjective 'subnational' refers to the multilevel structure of the state and to the fact that entities exist below the state (national/federal) level. However, it does not imply a particular inferiority or a hierarchy between the governance levels (Barker 2015, 11).

---

C. Xhardez (✉)
Concordia University, Montreal, QC, Canada
e-mail: catherine.xhardez@sciencespo.fr

© The Author(s) 2020
A.-G. Gagnon, A. Tremblay (eds.), *Federalism and National Diversity in the 21st Century*, Federalism and Internal Conflicts,
https://doi.org/10.1007/978-3-030-38419-7_9

Spiro 2001). Immigration federalism refers to the involvement of different levels of government in immigration-related activities and can be broadly defined as 'the regulatory role that subnational territorial units, enjoying legislative powers, experience with regard to issues related to immigration policy' (Strazzari 2012, 96).

Both SNCs under examination in this chapter have exhibited a strong subnational identity as well as nationalist mobilisation (Erk 2002, 2014)[2] and have been confronted with a 'dilemma' generated by the arrival of newcomers.[3] Additionally, both SNCs possess a wide range of legislative powers and have developed extensive subnational immigration and/or immigrant integration policies. Despite these overarching similarities,[4]

---

[2] In Quebec, the *Parti Québécois* has long been the source of nationalist political mobilisation within the province, while the *Bloc Québécois* has served this function in the federal political arena. In Flanders, the mantle of nationalist political mobilisation has fallen to different political parties over the years: *Vlaams Belang* (Flemish Interest), *Volksunie* (People's Union) and *Nieuw-Vlaamse Alliantie* (New Flemish Alliance). Furthermore, in both cases, national mobilisation has been based on a sense of cultural insecurity, historical grievances and a quest for language recognition (Erk 2002).

[3] In multinational societies where subnational communities (SNCs) seek greater autonomy or are marked by nationalist mobilisation (Keating 1996, 2001; Guibernau 1999), immigration might be considered either a threat or an opportunity because the arrival of newcomers may alter the composition of multinational federations and disturb the balance of power between minority national and majority national communities (Carens 1995; Kymlicka 2001; Gagnon and Iacovino 2007; Zapata-Barrero 2009). For example, immigration might increase the relative demographic strength of the subnational community vis-à-vis the national majority community; yet, it might also weaken the subnational community's cultural or linguistic cohesion. In the literature, scholars have referred to this situation as a 'dilemma' (Barker 2015; Xhardez 2017) or a 'legitimation paradox' (Adam 2013a; Jeram et al. 2016). Consequently, immigration and immigrant integration are key areas for SNCs that seek to control their destinies (Kymlicka 2001; Barker 2015). The 'dilemma' generated by the arrival of newcomers in the two SNCs under examination in this chapter is, to some degree, rooted in a fear that immigrants would rather join 'the culturally more dominant side (Anglophone in Canada, Francophones in Belgium)' (Erk 2014, 226).

[4] To be clear, there are also important differences between the cases. For example, the electoral regimes of the SNCs differ: Flanders has a proportional representation system (Deschouwer 2012) while Quebec has a first-past-the-post electoral system (Blais 2008). There is also a difference in jurisdictional competence with regard to immigration: Quebec has its own devolved immigration policy whereas Flanders only has control over immigrant integration policies. Both SNCs also differ in terms of their demographic weight within their respective federation; Flanders represents a state-wide demographic majority (Swenden 2014, 245) whereas Quebec constitutes a demographic minority in Canada. These differences and their consequences on the immigration federalism debate are further discussed in this chapter's conclusion.

very little is known about the commonalities and differences in cross-national patterns of immigration federalism; in fact, research on immigration federalism (e.g., Varsanyi et al. 2012; Newton 2012; Gulasekaram and Ramakrishnan 2015; Rodriguez 2018; Jeram and Nicolaides 2018; Paquet 2019) tends to focus on North America and on intra-national analysis, pointing in some cases to significant differences across subnational units in the reasoning behind the shift to immigration federalism. Even less is known about how SNCs have approached the issue of immigration federalism, despite evidence that this issue might be of greater importance in multinational federations than it is on other federal democracies. Further, while there is precedent for comparative analysis of Belgian and Canadian models of federalism (see Karmis and Gagnon 1996; Fournier and Reuchamps 2009), the analytical focus has never been on immigration federalism. In addressing these lacunae, this chapter asks the three following questions:

1. Has the issue of immigration federalism been handled in similar or different ways in Flanders and Quebec?
2. Within each of these SNCs, what are the points of tension and/or convergence in debates over immigration federalism?
3. What are the key similarities and differences in approaches to immigration federalism in the two SNCs?

In answering these questions, this chapter explores how political actors have mobilised and constructed issues of immigration federalism at the subnational scale. More specifically, it explores the evolution of discourse employed by subnational political actors regarding immigration and immigrant integration management in the Flemish and Quebec parliaments, focusing on the time period between 1999 and 2014, and it analyses political parties' arguments for and against immigration federalism, using a longitudinal content analysis of parliamentary debates. The chapter finds that in each SNC, political actors promote different solutions to deal with immigration federalism: either cooperation or opposition to the central state. These actors also adopt different strategies to use immigration and immigrant integration regulation as a way of strengthening their claims for recognition and influencing the balance of power between the jurisdictions. The particularities of each case are subsequently categorised along three key dimensions: the centre-periphery cleavage, the balance of powers in the federation and the avenues for renegotiating the current arrangements.

## CASE SELECTION AND ANALYTICAL TIME-FRAME

Some background on each case's party system is necessary before proceeding. The main feature of the Quebec provincial party system is its polarisation around the national question (i.e., Quebec's place within or without Canada), with 'federalists' gravitating towards the *Parti Libéral du Québec* (PLQ) and the 'sovereignists' represented by the *Parti Québécois* (PQ) (Bélanger et al. 2018, 33; Montigny and Gélineau 2019). In Belgium, the party system is regionalised along linguistic lines and divided into a Flemish and a Francophone party system; in other words, political parties are not state-wide (De Winter 2006). With the exception of Brussels, the electorate of one side of the linguistic border cannot vote for political parties on the other side of the border (Pilet 2005) even though the federal government comprises political parties from both communities (De Winter et al. 2006). The parties are, however, vertically integrated: Flemish parties participate in regional as well as federal elections and parliaments (Deschouwer 2012).

This chapter focuses on discourse on immigration federalism between 1999 and 2014 in the Flemish Parliament and the Quebec National Assembly. As one can see in Tables 9.1 and 9.2, different political parties formed governments during this 15-year period in both Flanders and Quebec.

There are several important reasons for exploring this time frame. As we shall see in the following sections, major pieces of legislation devolving powers of immigration and immigrant integration were adopted in Quebec and Flanders, respectively, in the early 1990s. Consequently, the period under examination presents us with a trove of parliamentary documents concerning the merits of and opposition to immigration federalism (282 for Flanders and 237 for Quebec, totalling more than 12,000 pages of debates).

Additionally, this time period entailed a noticeable rotation in political power in both SNCs and along the left-right ideological spectrum. In Flanders, the 1999–2014 study period covers three five-year legislative sessions, each of which saw a different coalition form a government. In Quebec, the period covers five legislative sessions which includes changes in political leadership between the PQ and the PLQ as well as the brief electoral success of the *Action Démocratique du Québec* (ADQ) in 2007–2008 (Bélanger et al. 2013), a party considered to be an 'an anti-immigrant neoliberal nationalist party' (Hepburn 2011, 515). Given the different degrees of consistency/inconsistency between ideology, on the

**Table 9.1**  Flanders: Legislative sessions (1999–2014)

| Period | Governing party | Minister in charge |
|---|---|---|
| 1999–2004 | Liberals (VLD), Socialists (SP), Ecologists (Agalev), Regionalists (VU)[a] | Minister van Welzijn, Gezondheid en Gelijke Kansen (Minister for Welfare, Health and Equal Opportunities) 13.07.1999–23.05.2003: **Mieke Vogels** (Agalev) 24.05.2003–21.07.2004: **Adelheid Byttebier** (Agalev) |
| 2004–2009 | Christian Democrats & Nationalists (CD&V/N-VA) Socialists (sp.a/spirit); Liberals (VLD) | Minister van Binnenlands Bestuur, Stedenbeleid, Wonen en Inburgering (Minister for Local and Provincial Government, Urban Policy, Housing, and Civic Integration) 22.07.2004–12.07.2009: **Marino Keulen** (VLD) |
| 2009–2014 | Christian Democrats (CD&V); Socialists (sp.a) Nationalists (N-VA) | Minister van Bestuurszaken, Binnenlands Bestuur, Inburgering, Toerisme en Vlaamse Rand (Minister for Administrative Affairs, Local and Provincial Government, Civic integration, Tourism and Flemish 'periphery' of Brussels) 13.07.2009–24.07.2014: **Geert Bourgeois** (N-VA) |

[a]In 2001, the VU split into two political parties: Spirit and N-VA (Deschouwer 2009). Moreover, during the period analysed, several political parties changed their names: CVP (*Christelijke Volkspartij*) became CD&V (*Christen-Democratisch en Vlaams*) in 2001 (in a coalition with the N-VA from 2004 to 2008); VLD (*Vlaamse Liberalen en Democraten*) became Open VLDer in 2007; SP (*Socialistiche Partij*) became 'sp.a' (*Socialistiche Partij anders*) in 2001 (in a coalition with Spirit between 2002 and 2008); Agalev became Groen! in 2003; *Vlaams Blok* became *Vlaams Belang* in 2004

one hand, and immigrant-centred public policy, on the other (see Tremblay 2019), the 1999–2014 period therefore provides fertile ground for bringing to light different positions on immigration federalism.

Finally, the period under examination was also chosen because it marks the beginning of the so-called retreat from multiculturalism in the liberal state (Joppke 2004), a point in time when issues of immigration and immigrant integration have become focal points in most democracies and when, in some cases, we have seen the rise of new forms of assimilationist policies. In Flanders, these developments have entailed the widening of the Flemish subnational civic integration policy from its implementation in 2003 to its rebuilding in 2013[5] and several modifications to the federal nationality law (Caestecker et al. 2016). In Quebec, this period was

---

[5] The original decree (regional law) regulating civic integration in Flanders was passed in 2003 and implemented in 2004, amended several times (2006, 2008 and 2009) and finally replaced by a new decree in 2013. *Decreet van 28 februari 2003 betreffende het Vlaamse*

**Table 9.2**  Quebec: Legislative sessions (1999–2014)

| Period | Governing party | Minister in charge |
|---|---|---|
| 1999–2003 (36th legislative session) | Parti québécois (**PQ**) | Ministre des Relations avec les citoyens et de l'Immigration (Minister of Relations with Citizens and Immigration)<br>15.12.1998–06.10.2000: **Robert Perreault**<br>06.10.2000–08.03.2001: **Sylvain Simard**<br>08.03.2011–30.01.2002: **Joseph Facal**<br>30.01.2002–29.04.2003: **Rémy Trudel** |
| 2003–2007 (37th legislative session) | Parti libéral du Québec (**PLQ**) | 29.04.2003–18.02.2005: **Michelle Courchesne**<br>Ministre de l'Immigration et des Communautés culturelles (Minister of Immigration and Cultural Communities)<br>18.02.2005–18.04.2007: **Lise Thériault** |
| 2007–2008 (38th legislative session) | Parti libéral du Québec (**PLQ**) | 18.04.2007–10.08.2010: **Yolande James** |
| 2009–2012 (39th legislative session) | Parti libéral du Québec (**PLQ**) | 18.04.2007–10.08.2010: **Yolande James**<br>11.08.2010–19.09.2012: **Kathleen Weil** |
| 2012–2014 (40th legislative session) | Parti québécois (**PQ**) | 19.09.2012–23.04.2014: **Diane De Courcy** |

characterised by major debates relating to immigrants' *francisation* (Oakes and Warren 2009) as well as the debate over the 'reasonable accommodation' of immigrant minority communities—which culminated with the release of the Bouchard-Taylor Report in 2008 (Laxer et al. 2014)—and the debate over *la Charte des valeurs québécoises* (the Charter of Quebec Values), tabled by the PQ in 2013 and abandoned as a result of the 2014 provincial election (Iacovino 2015; C. Tessier and Montigny 2016; Gagnon and St-Louis 2016). One the aims of this chapter is to bridge the gap between discussions on these policy areas, traditionally the purview of multicultural studies, with the discussion on immigration federalism.

This chapter adopts a discursive institutionalist approach, 'taking ideas and discourse seriously' (Schmidt 2010). The choice of parliamentary debates from the multiple types of political discourse available for analysis (De Galembert et al. 2014) is justified because the parliamentary 'political arena' is the locus of both democratic discussion and decision-making (Vliegenthart 2007, 5) and due to the availability of information; parliamentary forums are consistently documented, and documents are

*inburgeringsbeleid; Decreet van 7 juni 2013 betreffende het Vlaamse integratie- en inburgeringsbeleid.*

accessible for analysis. Furthermore, parliamentary debates provide a clear insight into partisan positions on immigration and integration; parliaments 'feature opinions based on different ideologies' (Wodak and van Dijk 2000, 13) and actors must therefore officially justify their choices and their party's preferences (May 2016). Parliamentary speech allows members of parliament (MPs) 'to stake out a position and communicate it to their parties and to voters (...). Consequently, parliamentary speech is primarily an act of position-taking' (Proksch and Slapin 2015, 17) and, since speeches made in parliament are retained on record, they are 'normalised' and therefore set the tone regarding what may 'officially' be said about immigrants (Wodak and van Dijk 2000, 13).

This study's analysis of parliamentary debates captures the evolution of political actors' positioning and arguments, illustrating lines of convergence and divergence. The analysis of parliamentary debates helps to identify as well as contrast actors' 'foreground discursive abilities' (i.e., agents' abilities to change or maintain their institutions) (Schmidt 2008, 314). By looking at actors' ideas and discourse, this chapter discerns patterns and tensions that would not have been apparent from only examining the formal division of powers. By focusing only on public policy outcomes, this study would have been confronted with the 'gap-hypothesis' identified in the literature on migration, which is to say the 'gap between what parties say and what parties do' (Lutz 2019). To be sure, parliament is not necessarily the place where decisions are actually made due to the influence of the executive branch of government and the partisanship of representatives. However, parliament remains a mandatory and symbolic scene where different narratives regarding immigration federalism are expressed and confronted.[6]

## Immigration Federalism: A Brief History

This section describes the roles, powers and responsibilities of the two SNCs regarding immigration and immigrant integration. In so doing, it provides an overview of major constitutional, legal and political arrangements that embody immigration federalism in both polities.

---

[6] Focusing on political actors' arguments, computer-aided qualitative data analysis software (Atlas.ti) allowed for the consistent analysis of large amounts of texts, coding various quotations and developing networks of quotations (Kelle et al. 1995). While this method is exploratory and inherently contains a subjectivity factor (Gerring 2017, 20), the chapter includes a large number of quotations to illustrate and justify this analysis.

## Federalism, Immigration and Politics in Quebec

In Canada, the British North America Act of 1867 (BNAA) specifies that the federal level of government has full jurisdiction regarding 'naturalisation and aliens' (Section 91, 25) and that it is the sole authority responsible for granting and determining the conditions of access to citizenship. The federal level of government is also entitled to set admission requirements related to security, criminal and medical factors for newcomers entering Canada.[7] Nevertheless, Section 95 of the BNAA designates immigration as a concurrent jurisdiction of the provinces, but with federal paramountcy in case of conflict (Poirier 2009). This constitutional provision means that provinces can engage in immigration policymaking and it also introduces the possibility of asymmetry in the management of immigration between the different federated entities (Gagnon and Garon 2019).

Despite the existence of this provision, the provinces' interest in immigration matters has waxed and waned over time (Vineberg 1987; Hawkins 1988; Schertzer 2015; Paquet 2016) until the 1960s when, in the wake of the province's 'Quiet Revolution'—entailing inter alia a shift in the locus of power from a religious to a secular authority, the rapid expansion of the Quebec province-state and the assertion and political mobilisation of a new Francophone nationalism—Quebec became increasingly involved in this policy area.

Prior to the 1960s, Quebec had shown little interest in recruiting immigrants; newcomers were primarily seen as a 'potential threat to traditional French culture and institutions' (Carens 1995, 21) and as a 'Trojan horse' serving the economic and demographic interest of the province's Anglophone minority (Daniel 2006, 44). It was only in 1968 that Quebec created its own Immigration Ministry.[8] According to Fiona Barker (2010, 20–21), the ministry was created for three reasons: (1) Quebec's Francophone elites' perception that the province was facing a 'demographic crisis' undermining its Francophone character and its relative population weight in the Canadian federation, (2) a will to promote the Quebec province-state in an attempt to foster its recognition at the international level and (3) a desire to affirm the province-state's legitimacy by being more outward-looking and by moving away from hostility towards immigrants.

---

[7] Immigration and Refugee Protection Act, S.C. 2001, c. 27.

[8] Loi no. 75 créant un Ministère de l'Immigration du Québec (Assentiment royal 04.12.1968)/Bill 75 creating a Quebec Ministry of Immigration (Royal Assent 4.12.1968).

During the 1970s, three intergovernmental agreements expanded the Quebec government's involvement in immigration policy (Daniel 2006; Kostov 2008; Kelley and Trebilcock 2010; Baglay and Nakache 2014a). The *Lang-Cloutier Agreement of 1971* allowed Quebec to place provincial representatives in federal immigration offices abroad, but only in a counselling capacity. The *Andras-Bienvenue Agreement of 1975* increased Quebec's involvement in the immigration selection process by allowing provincial officers to meet all potential immigrants who hoped to settle in Quebec and by allowing provincial officers to offer recommendations to federal immigration officers regarding applicants. The *Cullen-Couture Agreement of 1978* enhanced Quebec's control over immigration into the province by instituting a joint decision-making process. This meant, more precisely, that 'any potential immigrants to Quebec must be reviewed by the Immigration Review Board of Quebec' (Tessier 1995, 225) before being selected by the federal government; apace with this change, the province adopted its own point system regulation for selecting immigrants, in the process giving greater importance to French language skills (Houle 2014, 124–127).

Throughout the 1980s and early 1990s, Quebec progressively reoriented its attention towards the positive contribution of immigration to economic and demographic development (Paquet 2016). *The Canada-Quebec Accord relating to Immigration and Temporary Admission of Aliens of 1991* (hereafter: the 1991 Agreement) gave unprecedented powers to the province.[9] Still in force as of the time of writing, the 1991 Agreement was part of a set of measures adopted in an attempt to ease tensions between Quebec and English-speaking Canada following the failure of the Meech Lake Accord in 1990 (Simeon 1990). The 1991 Agreement devolved significant powers to Quebec: the province would hereafter be autonomous in selecting not only refugees abroad (humanitarian immigration)[10] but also all immigrants (economic category) based on the use of a points system. The federal government retained its jurisdiction regarding asylum seekers, family reunification visas and admission to the country, as well as the power to define immigration categories.

---

[9] The 1991 Agreement is also known as the Gagnon-Tremblay/McDougall Accord.

[10] While the admission of refugees after an asylum claim is decided by the federal government, the province is responsible for the admission of government-assisted refugees and privately sponsored refugees. Quebec is the only Canadian province to have a prerogative regarding the selection of resettled refugees (Garnier 2018, 120).

As a result of this system, Quebec currently selects around 70% of the immigrants entering its territory (Labelle 2015). In addition, all settlement and integration services have been devolved to Quebec, allowing the province to develop its own policies and to promote 'interculturalism' (Gagnon et al. 2014), a model of immigrant integration that affirms the French language and a common public culture while allowing for the reasonable accommodation of cultural communities (Bouchard 2011). This approach to immigrant integration entails inter alia the provision of French language classes for non-Francophone immigrants as well as reception and integration services (offered by community agencies called *organismes communautaires*). The province receives financial transfers from the federal government for the implementation and administration of these programmes (Garon 2015).

The 1991 Agreement is favourable to Quebec in several ways: the Agreement does not contain a termination clause, it can only be amended if both parties agree to do so, and the total amount of annual financial transfers to Quebec is related to the general expenses of the federal government—not to the number of immigrants welcomed by the province—and cannot be reduced by the federal government (Reichhold 2016). It is debatable as to whether the Agreement has, in fact, led to the recognition of Quebec's special status as a 'distinct society' in Canada (Gagnon and Garon 2019) or whether it has been disruptive to the balance of the Canadian federation and in fundamental opposition to the country's constitutional principles (e.g., Kostov 2008). What is more clear is that the Agreement has been a trigger for other provinces to sign their own immigration and integration agreements with the federal government (Paquet 2016; Jeram and Nicolaides 2018) and that, as a result, it has also reduced the political and symbolic exceptionality of Quebec in immigration matters (Woehrling 2000).

Table 9.3 provides a summary of the major historical points (detailed above) in the development of intergovernmental immigration agreements between Canada and Quebec.

## Federalism, Immigration and Politics in Flanders

The repartition of jurisdictions in Belgium in the field of immigration and, in particular, in the area of immigrant integration must be understood within the country's more general framework of federalism by dissociation (Swenden et al. 2006; Adam 2013a; Romainville 2015). This type of federalism (the opposite of federalism by association) entailed the

**Table 9.3**  Intergovernmental immigration agreements between Canada and Quebec

| | |
|---|---|
| 1968 | Creation of the Quebec Ministry of Immigration |
| 1971 | The *Lang/Cloutier Agreement* authorises the presence of provincial orientation officers in federal immigration offices for counselling |
| 1975 | The *Andras/Bienvenue Agreement* allows Quebec to participate in recruitment trips and make recommendations to federal immigration officers, who have to take into consideration the opinion of the province before accepting or rejecting any applications for immigration to Quebec |
| 1978 | The *Cullen/Couture Agreement* establishes a joint decision-making process. Any immigrant willing to settle in Quebec has to be approved by the province, which has defined its own selection criteria (points system) |
| 1991 | The *Gagnon-Tremblay/McDougall Accord* transfers jurisdiction to Quebec for selecting and integrating immigrants to that province |

fragmentation the Belgian unitary state during the late stages of the twentieth century and resulted in the nearly unilateral transfer of certain powers from the federal government to the federated entities. Despite this process, the federal authority remains in charge of immigration policy (i.e., admissions, residence rights and removals) which is considered a 'residual power'.[11] Although the federal level is entirely responsible for determining who can enter the country and who can stay, policymaking over immigrant integration has gradually shifted to the subnational level.

Legislative and executive jurisdictions over immigrant integration have been transferred to different federal entities at three temporal points: 1974, 1980 and 1993. In 1974, jurisdiction over immigrant integration policy was assigned to the Walloon and Flemish Regions and initially framed as a power to welcome migrant workers (Adam 2013b, 552). In 1980, a state reform explicitly created a power regarding 'reception and integration of immigrants' (art. 5, §1, II, 3 of the Special Law of 8 August 1980 on Institutional Reforms) and gave the communities jurisdiction over this power (Clement and Van De Putte 2007; Strazzari 2012). In 1993, an asymmetrical transfer occurred: due to financial problems, the French Community transferred jurisdiction regarding migrant integration to both the Walloon Region and the French Community Commission of the Brussels-Capital Region while the other communities retained their own jurisdiction.

---

[11] The Belgian case also differs from the Canadian case in that immigration policies are strongly influenced and constrained by European or international law, for example regarding family reunification or asylum (Carlier 2010).

As a result of the three aforementioned transfers, jurisdiction over integrating immigrants in Belgium is divided according to the following asymmetrical distribution: the Flemish Community (in Flanders, the northern part of Belgium) has had legislative and administrative policymaking power for immigrant reception and integration since 1980; the Walloon Region (the southern, French-speaking part of the country) has handled immigrant integration since 1993; in Brussels (Belgium's bilingual region), both the Flemish Community (which also has jurisdiction over the Brussels territory) and the French Community Commission share jurisdiction over immigrant integration and have developed their own policies within the same territory (Xhardez 2016); and the German Community (in Eastern Belgium) has formal jurisdiction in the German-speaking region (Pommée 2017).

Despite these transfers, the federal state still retains powers that also have an effect (albeit indirect) on immigrant integration, such as power over citizenship acquisition (nationality), political rights (voting) and social rights (welfare) (Adam and Jacobs 2014, 68). Over recent decades, these issues have been the subject of important debates at the federal level, with Flemish and Francophone political elites regularly opposed over issues such as the enfranchisement of foreign residents (Teney and Jacobs 2007) and the opening of the nationality law (de Jonghe and Doutrepont 2012).

Subnational immigrant integration policies have slowly begun to diverge as a result of the gradual devolution of powers over immigrant integration and of emerging opposing views between communities. This has meant, more specifically, the development of very different policy frameworks in Flanders and Wallonia (Martiniello 1995; Martiniello and Rea 2004; Adam and Martiniello 2013; Adam et al. 2018).

Flanders has witnessed the most important policy development regarding immigrant integration over time. Prior to the 1990s, and despite decentralisation, Flemish political elites were relatively indifferent to the presence of immigrants or to the question of their integration (Barker 2007, 215). As Barker notes:

> In contrast to the Quebec experience, where the government asserted its powers over immigration in order to achieve particular nationalist goals, remarkably little concrete policy followed the recognition by Minister and bureaucrats that decentralization [sic] of integration policy placed them in a new situation of power. (2015, 90)

From the 1990s onward, the integration of immigrants has become progressively more politicised in Flanders due mainly to the electoral breakthrough of the far-right (Adam 2013a, 117–136). Despite this breakthrough (and perhaps in response to it), Flanders adopted a multicultural policy that entailed some recognition of cultural rights for immigrants (Jacobs 2004; Loobuyck and Jacobs 2010). However, since the early 2000s, compulsory civic integration trajectories for immigrants (*inburgering*) have been introduced, marking the beginning of a more assimilationist and interventionist policy (Adam 2013a, b) oriented towards individuals (Barker 2007, 215–216). This policy has increasingly insisted on teaching immigrants about 'Flemish norms and values' and the Dutch language (Ganty and Delgrange 2015). This policy shift is in line with the European 'civic integrationist turn' in immigrant integration policies (Kostakopoulou 2010; Goodman 2010, 2014; Joppke 2007, 2017).[12]

## FOR OR AGAINST IMMIGRATION FEDERALISM? DEBATES IN QUEBEC AND FLANDERS

The distribution of powers regarding immigration and immigrant integration is a sensitive issue in both Flanders and Quebec. It has been widely discussed during parliamentary debates and has featured opposing views from political parties in both SNCs. These discussions reveal, through the lens of immigration, how political actors view the relationship between the SNC and the central government.

### Quebec: Controlling Its Own Destiny?

Quebec political parties converge regarding past achievements but diverge when it comes to the future on the question of opposing or collaborating with the federal government in managing immigration and immigrant integration. In many of their interventions between 1999 and 2014, both main political parties (PQ and PLQ) highlight the benefits of the Canada-Quebec agreements. There are also clear differences between the two

---

[12] Ilke Adam identifies substate nationalism as a key variable that can explain these policy developments (Adam 2013b). Historically, compared to the other Belgian subnational entities in charge of immigrant integration, Flanders (through the Flemish Community) has developed more policy instruments, has devoted more budgetary means and has had more centralised integration policies (Adam et al. 2018).

political parties on how to follow up with this consensus and what institutional configuration would be ideal to manage immigration-related powers in the future.

The PLQ has praised the merits and the legacy of Canada-Quebec agreements in immigration matters. For example, in 2003, Monique Gagnon-Tremblay, the PLQ Minister (and Member of the National Assembly for Saint-François) for whom the 1991 Agreement is partially named after, stressed that the 'agreement is very important, it has given Quebec the lead in integration and *francisation* and the money necessary to integrate and *franciser* the immigrants'.[13] And two years earlier, Fatima Houda-Pepin (PLQ), highlighted the 'consensus ... beyond party lines'[14] of the 1991 Agreement, given that it 'delegates important responsibilities to Quebec' and allows the province to choose its immigrants and to develop its own integration policy.[15]

*Péquistes* (as PQ representatives have come to be known) have also been positive in their assessments of intergovernmental agreements on immigration policy. For instance, François Beaulne (PQ) stated that '[these agreements have] certainly been the subject of consensus over the past 20 years (...) it was the 1978 Cullen-Couture Agreement that opened the door to some control by Quebec over its immigration. This agreement was later strengthened under the leadership of Ms. Gagnon-Tremblay.'[16] And, Joseph Facal (PQ) has made a point of stressing Quebec's singularity in managing immigration, regarding not only the powers the province enjoys inside the Canadian federation but also regarding its political choices:

> No other government in Canada has chosen to devote to immigration and integration a such a level of resources and attention (...). It seems highly significant to me that Quebec, a francophone [sic] minority nation in North America, has chosen to make immigration one of the instruments of its collective development. It is an opening that blatantly contradicts the image of Quebec that is fearful and inward-looking that some people are trying to promote.[17]

---

[13] All translations are mine. Monique Gagnon-Tremblay (PLQ), June 11, 2003, *Assemblée nationale*, vol. 38, no. 5.

[14] Fatima Houda-Pepin (PLQ), May 8, 2001, *Commission culture*, vol. 37, no. 7.

[15] Yvan Bordeleau (PLQ), June 10, 2002, *Assemblée nationale*, vol. 38, no. 4; Kathleen Weil (PLQ), April 20, 2011, *Commission des relations avec les citoyens*, vol. 42, no. 8.

[16] François Beaulne (PQ), April 21, 1999, *Commission de la culture*, vol. 36, no. 4.

[17] Joseph Facal (PQ), May 8, 2001, *Commission de la culture*, vol. 37, no. 7.

This rhetorical line may suggest that PQ political elites are striving both to justify Quebec's special powers as well as to legitimate its policies by opposing the assumption that the nationalism challenging the nation-state is inherently anti-modern, illiberal (Hobsbawm 1992; Ignatieff 1994) and hostile to immigrants. However, while recognising that the 1991 Accord is particularly 'advantageous', the PQ wishes to 'go further'.[18]

The PQ's discourse regarding the management of immigration and integration is also, albeit implicitly, coloured by the party's antipathy towards the federal government in Ottawa. For Martin Lemay (PQ), the Party's position is clear: it claims full powers for the province, for political and symbolic reasons:

> The fact remains that for us, the *Parti Québécois*, our desire to repatriate all immigration powers will not surprise anyone. Assuming all powers are part of our political commitment. The future of our people depends, among other things, on an immigration policy that we must fully control. An agreement, however good it may be, is never worth the exclusivity of powers. In this case, symbolism is of great importance: therefore, we believe that the clearer the message is, the more efficient the integration will be.[19]

Antipathy towards Ottawa and the demand to be fully responsible for immigration is also evidenced in discourse over the management of financial transfers from the federal to the provincial government in accordance with the 1991 Agreement. During its time as official opposition (2003–2012), the PQ then criticised the PLQ government regarding the allocation of these transfers.[20] *Péquistes* demanded to know where money for immigration and integration services went and how it was used:

> Yes, it is federal money, but as long as we are in Canada, we pay taxes in Canada, we have an agreement and we receive (...) our money (...) and I think that we are entitled to wonder where that money goes.[21]

Additionally, *Péquistes* have critiqued the so-called dual integration model, a term that suggests competition and opposition between Canadian

[18] Emilien Pelletier (PQ), February 11, 2003, *Commission des relations avec les citoyens*, vol. 43, no. 2.

[19] Martin Lemay (PQ), September 18, 2007, *Commission de la culture*, vol. 40, no. 7.

[20] Lucie Papineau (PQ), April 6, 2004, *Assemblée nationale*, vol. 35, no. 58; Martin Lemay (PQ), June 8, 2007, *Commission de la culture*, vol. 40, no. 3.

[21] Martin Lemay (PQ), October 11, 2007, *Commission de la culture*, vol. 40, no. 14.

and the Quebec immigrant integration model.[22] More specifically, the federal multiculturalism approach has been presented as keeping Quebec from fully developing its own integration model, according to 'its needs and its aspirations':

> For decades, the *Parti Québécois* has opposed the concept of multiculturalism, a concept inserted into the Canadian Constitution. It is up to us to determine for ourselves the totality and content of our immigration, reception, integration and citizenship policies with a view to living a true sincere interculturality, with a desire for knowledge exchange and mutual recognition, which Canadian multiculturalism is far from fostering. In fact, it is antinomic to the integration of immigrants in Quebec.[23]

In response to these arguments, the PLQ has defended a more collaborative stance; its rhetorical valorisation of the 1991 Agreement may also be strategic in that the political party uses it as an 'example' of successful 'collaboration between Quebec and Ottawa'.[24] For example, on November 14, 2001, Yvan Bordeleau (PLQ) accused the PQ of 'trying to create conflicts and animosity or strained relationships (…) instead of working together, which was the spirit of the (…) McDougall-Gagnon-Tremblay Agreement'[25] while Benoît Pelletier (PLQ) promoted the federal framework as the optimal configuration for managing immigration, asserting that 'Quebec identity can flourish within the Canadian federal context'.[26] Additionally, PLQ Members of the National Assembly (MNAs) have stated that they are against the 'magic solution of sovereignty' and that while they oppose the transfer of immigration powers they are fine with the budgetary instruments contained in the 1991 Agreement.[27] Other PLQ MNAs have accused *Péquistes* of leveraging immigrant integration to

---

[22] Robert Perreault (PQ), September 13, 2000, *Commission de la culture*, vol. 36, no. 43; Louise Harel (PQ), May 15, 2007, *Assemblée nationale*, vol. 40, no. 4.

[23] Maka Kotto (PQ), February 9, 2011, *Assemblée nationale*, vol. 41, no. 170; see also: February 10, 2011, *Assemblée nationale*, vol. 41, no. 171; April 20, 2011, *Commission des relations avec les citoyens*, vol. 42, no. 8; May 3, 2011, *Commission des institutions*, vol. 42, no. 18.

[24] Fatima Houda-Pepin (PLQ), May 8, 2001, *Commission de la culture*, vol. 37, no. 7.

[25] Yvan Bordeleau (PLQ), November 14, 2001, *Assemblée nationale*, vol. 37, no. 56.

[26] Benoît Pelletier (PLQ), November 14, 2001, *Assemblée nationale*, vol. 37, no. 56.

[27] Pierre Marsan (PLQ), November 7, 2007, *Assemblée nationale*, vol. 40, no. 36; Kathleen Weil (PLQ), February 9, 2011, *Assemblée nationale*, vol. 41, no. 170; February 4, 2012, *Assemblée nationale*, vol. 42, no. 92.

promote Quebec's sovereignty both by influencing immigrant integration policy content (e.g., with the promotion of a formal Quebec citizenship) and by claiming more powers as a step towards their political project of separating from Canada.[28]

### *Flanders, or How to 'Dance on One Leg'*

In spite of criticising the actions of the central state, all three traditional Flemish political parties (Liberals, Christian Democrats and Socialists) highlight the need to work together with the federal level to manage immigrant integration. For example, the Flemish Liberals (VLD), who managed the immigrant integration portfolio between 2004 and 2009, regularly insist on the division of competences while underlining the need to better articulate each level's responsibilities. They reject any formal claim to managing immigration at the Flemish level since 'only separatism could bring this change, but the VLD is not in favour of it'.[29] Nevertheless, they sometimes acknowledge that 'it would be easier if everything was regulated by the same government, as it is in the Netherlands'.[30] The Flemish socialists (sp.a) agree and emphasise the need to collaborate with the central state (*samenwerken*).[31] For their part, the Christian Democrats (CD&V) tend to deplore the lack of connection between subnational integration and federal immigration policies, asserting that 'a congruent immigration policy and civic integration policy should be pursued',[32] meaning that the federal policy should be strengthened and better aligned with the Flemish one. For these political parties then, criticism of the federal level or the system as a whole does not lead to a claim for the transfer of power in immigration matters.

However, there are three parties that promote a different institutional approach; the far-right *Vlaams Blok/Belang* (VB), the nationalist *Nieuw-*

---

[28] See for example: November 14, 2001, *Assemblée nationale*, vol. 37, no. 56; July 9, 2003, *Commission de la culture*, vol. 38, no. 5; May 27, 2004, *Assemblée nationale*, vol. 38, no. 78.

[29] André Denys (VLD), January 28, 2003, *Commissie voor Welzijn, Volksgezondheid en Gelijke Kansen*, 1129-7; see also: Marino Keulen (VLD), December 6, 2004, *Commissie voor wonen, stedelijk beleid, inburgering en gelijke kansen*, 15–7.

[30] Marino Keulen (VLD), March 16, 2006, *Commissie voor wonen, stedelijk beleid, inburgering en gelijke kansen*, C180-WON14; December 6, 2004, *Commissie voor wonen, stedelijk beleid, inburgering en gelijke kansen*, 15–7.

[31] Chokri Mahassine (sp.a), February 23, 2005, *Vlaams Parlement*, 84.

[32] Cathy Berx (CD&V), December 19, 2006, *Vlaams Parlement*, 14, 15, 965, 1030.

*Vlaamse Alliantie* (N-VA) and the libertarian *Lijst Dedecker* (LDD) want to go further, demanding the grouping of integration and immigration powers at the Flemish level. The VB, which is in a permanent position of opposition because the '*cordon sanitaire*' prevents them from being part of the government (Erk 2005; Pauwels 2011), has consistently criticised actions in immigrant integration and immigration matters writ large, arguing that 'The limitation of Flemish competences is clear. It would be useful for Flanders, in the next round of state reform, to acquire full powers to manage the whole issue'.[33] For the VB, the current division of powers is flawed, or even 'schizophrenic'[34]; they claim that it undermines integration policy because the Flemish level has to 'bear the consequences' of the federal policy: 'in that sense, it is also a bit of a mop-up with the tap open' (*dweilen met de kraan open*).[35] This last expression is recurrent in the anti-immigration VB's rhetoric, asserting that 'any immigrant integration (*inburgering*) policy can only succeed if it is part of a global immigration policy'.[36] During the 2009–2014 legislative session, an MP from LDD joined this plea, criticising the situation as a form of 'counter-federalism' and calling for a transfer of jurisdictional authority ('regionalisation' in Belgian political vocabulary): 'Our group is also in favour of a regionalisation of immigration and asylum policy'.[37]

The N-VA shares this concern and advocates for Flanders becoming fully autonomous in these matters. As Kris Van Dijck (VU-N-VA) states: 'The problem of integration is not separate from a number of federal jurisdictions, such as nationality, voting rights and legal residence. We think that these areas should also become Flemish, otherwise the measures risk missing their point'.[38] Bart De Wever, leader of the N-VA, has often

---

[33] Marijke Dillen (VB), January 28, 2003, *Commissie voor Welzijn, Volksgezondheid en Gelijke Kansen*, 1129-7.

[34] Filip Dewinter (VB), October 6, 2009, *Commissie voor bestuurszaken, binnenlands bestuur, decreetsevaluatie, inburgering en tourism*, C4-BIN1.

[35] Joris Van Hauthem (VB), March 16, 2010, *Commissie voor bestuurszaken, binnenlands bestuur, decreetsevaluatie, inburgering en tourism*, C159-BIN13; see also for example Rob Verreycken (VB), December 6, 2004, *Commissie voor wonen, stedelijk beleid, inburgering en gelijke kansen*, 15-7; Win Van Dijck (VB), June 28, 2006, *Commissie voor wonen, stedelijk beleid, inburgering en gelijke kansen*, 850-8; Filip Dewinter (VB), June 30, 2010, *Vlaams Parlement*, 350.

[36] Rob Verreycken (VB), December 6, 2004, *Commissie voor wonen, stedelijk beleid, inburgering en gelijke kansen*, 15-7.

[37] Boudewijn Bouckaert (LDD), June 30, 2010, *Vlaams Parlement*, 350.

[38] Kris Van Dijck (VU-N-VA), February 12, 2003, *Vlaams Parlement*, 21.

employed the expression 'dancing on one leg'[39] (or 'running on one leg') to deride the current situation and to seek the transfer of jurisdictional authority:

> To pursue an integration policy without being able to control the immigration policy or the social legislation is like running on one leg. Several colleagues therefore argued in favour of a clear cooperation with the federal government, but Mr. De Wever argues in favour of a transfer of powers. He does not believe in this cooperation. (...) Federal policy is often synonymous with no policy. It is better to put these powers in one hand. Cooperation is not bad; the transfer of powers is better.[40]

To be clear, the N-VA have not suggested which alternative institutional configuration should be adopted, instead navigating the difficult waters between secessionist Scylla and 'confederalist' Charybdis (Beyens et al. 2017). During the 2009–2014 legislative session, a period in time that saw the N-VA directly managing the immigrant integration portfolio, the tone was a little bit softer. However, Geert Bourgeois, the N-VA's Minister in charge of civic integration between 2009 and 2014 (see Table 9.1), still pointed out the benefits of jointly managing immigration and integration powers: 'I am, of course, in favour of homogeneous packages of jurisdictions. In countries where all jurisdiction in terms of immigration, nationality legislation and regularisation policy are in one hand, it is easier to conduct a policy'.[41] The N-VA Minister regrets that 'Flanders is not turning all the knobs'—meaning that Flanders does not hold leverage over all immigration-related jurisdictions—and that instead the federal immigration policy progresses apart from Flanders.[42]

---

[39] In Dutch, "dansen op één been"; see, for example: Bart De Wever (N-VA), June 2, 2005, *Commissie voor wonen, stedelijk beleid, inburgering en gelijke kansen*, C225-WON18; March 16, 2006, *Commissie voor wonen, stedelijk beleid, inburgering en gelijke kansen*, C180-WON14.

[40] In Dutch, "lopen op één been"; Bart De Wever (N-VA), December 6, 2004, *Commissie voor wonen, stedelijk beleid, inburgering en gelijke kansen*, 15–7.

[41] Geert Bourgeois (N-VA), June 30, 2010, *Vlaams Parlement*, 350 (2009–2010); see also: March 16, 2010, *Commissie voor bestuurszaken, binnenlands bestuur, decreetsevaluatie, inburgering en tourism*, C159-BIN13; March 30, 2010, *Commissie voor bestuurszaken, binnenlands bestuur, decreetsevaluatie, inburgering en tourism*, C81-BIN14.

[42] In Dutch, the idiom used is 'we weten dat Vlaanderen niet aan alle knoppen draait'; Geert Bourgeois (N-VA), February 25, 2014, *Commissie voor bestuurszaken, binnenlands*

## LESSONS FROM THE FLANDERS-QUEBEC COMPARISON

What can we learn from the foregoing comparison? Although there do seem to be some interesting lines of convergence, there are also some important differences that must be noted.

First, in both SNCs, political parties' positions follow the lines of the centre-periphery cleavage[43] in claiming (or not) more immigration powers. Indeed, although the co-operative positioning in Quebec is quite different from the Flemish one, in both cases, the parties that defend more immigration decentralisation ('transfer', 'repatriation' or 'regionalisation') are the same ones that advocate for the periphery (the province or the region) by striving for an independent Quebec or for a Flemish state. Consequently, it is possible to make two observations. The first is that these parties follow a discursive strategy that casts the centre-periphery frame not only around the institutional debate but also over other policy areas (immigration in this case). This strategy is called 'issue *communautarisation*' in the Flemish case (Abts et al. 2019). The second is that the literature has highlighted that immigration is a key concern for this family of political parties, the so-called Stateless Nationalist and Regionalist Parties (SNRPs) (Hepburn 2009) in the development of their nation-building projects (Hepburn and Zapata-Barrero 2014; Jeram et al. 2016). Indeed, these parties call for the formal management of immigration in order to allow for a distinct approach reflecting the needs and interests of the SNC (Hepburn and Zapata-Barrero 2014, 10). In addition, they also put pressure on the central state by rhetorical means, since immigration can be used as a bargaining chip in intergovernmental negotiations. It has been the case in Quebec in the past. In Flanders, even when the transfer of immigration power has seemed improbable, immigration control has remained a strong rhetorical tool for the SNRPs to symbolically and politically support their goal of statehood.

Second, Quebec enjoys significant immigration powers compared to Flanders, but also in comparison with most SNCs worldwide. However, the weight and power of the SNCs in their respective federations varies

---

*bestuur, decreetsevaluatie, inburgering en tourism,* COM140-BIN9, October 16, 2013, *Commissie voor Brussel en de Vlaamse Rand,* COM28-BRU2.

[43] In the 'center-periphery' cleavage—initially framed by Stein Rokkan (1970/2009)—the 'center' represents the (central) state while the 'periphery' refers to the subnational community. In the context of party mobilisation, it opposes political parties advocating and mobilising for the 'periphery' to others (see Hepburn 2009).

substantially. Quebec is a minority nation, whereas Flanders is a demographic majority that has increased its powers within the Belgian state. Consequently, Flanders has the weight to influence federal politics and policies, which is much more difficult for Quebec inside the Canadian federation. Having no control at the subnational level over who can join the community, Flemish political elites have chosen to implement mandatory and extensive civic integration programmes, as well as a multilevel strategy to strengthen their integration policy (*inburgering*) by linking it to issues that are managed at the federal level. For example, Flanders implemented *inburgering* in 2000, at the same time as Belgian Nationality Law was liberalised to remove language and integration requirements (de Jonghe and Doutrepont 2012).

In reaction to this liberalisation, Flemish political elites repeatedly demanded a link (*koppel*) between *inburgering* and nationality acquisition, even though this lies outside subnational jurisdiction. After years of voicing their demands, Flemish political elites finally succeeded due to the vertical integration of political parties, with elites navigating between both regional and federal levels. In 2012, the federal nationality law was revised in a restrictive direction and the completion of a civic integration programme became one of the possible proofs of 'social integration' needed to acquire nationality in certain cases. This new condition was significant because only Flanders had a civic integration policy at the time (Adam et al. 2018). Such a strategy could not have been successful in Canada because Quebec does not enjoy the same strength at the federal level and is consequently blocked when proposing similar initiatives. To wit, the *Bloc Québécois*, which represents nationalist Québécois interests at the federal level, failed to introduce a French language requirement for Quebec residents seeking Canadian citizenship.[44]

Third, unlike Flanders, Quebec's power in immigration matters is not constitutionally recognised; rather it is based on an intergovernmental agreement, as is often the case in Canada (Poirier 2009). Could the 1991 Agreement be jeopardised or reopened? The accord does possess major political and symbolic force, even if it is financially very costly for the federal level. A denunciation of the Agreement by the federal government would probably be interpreted as a political 'attack' by the Quebec elites.

[44] See the most recent attempt at the House of Commons of Canada: Bill C-421, An Act to amend the Citizenship Act (adequate knowledge of French in Quebec), introduced by Mario Beaulieu (first reading, November 1, 2018).

However, the *Coalition Avenir Quebec* (CAQ), the political party that has formed a majority government following the 2018 provincial election, has reopened the discussion on institutional arrangements in matters of immigration. The party hopes to renegotiate the 1991 Agreement to allow the province to manage the family reunification programme, decrease immigration levels and implement language and values tests (Dion 2018; Chouinard 2018). On the Flemish side, immigrant integration powers were transferred as a result of a special law on institutional reforms; in the dissociative Belgian system, transfers are almost unilateral (from the federal authority to the federated entities). Regarding Flanders, Fiona Barker (2015, 160) states that:

> Flanders contrasts with Quebec in that its governments consistently made integration policy without reference to sub-state national autonomy goals or the broader politics of multinationalism in Belgium. Insulated institutionally by state reforms, Flemish policy makers seldom viewed immigration as linked to broader constitutional questions in the federalizing [sic] state. As such, Flemish governments did not construct an active integration policy approach until well after state reforms had empowered them to act in the area, and they never sought additional powers in associated areas such as immigration control.

Although Barker's diagnostic tells us a lot about the 1960–2000 time period (her focus), more recent parliamentary discourse demonstrates that some political forces do seek additional powers. To be sure, these statements concern a Flemish political arena in which speeches are harsher and do not have direct political consequences. However, the elites who embrace this position have become a major political force not only at the regional level but also at the federal level. For example, despite their critics of the Belgian state, the Nationalists were part of the federal governing coalition from 2014 to 2018 (Abts et al. 2019), as such they were able to influence the federal policy—particularly given that they managed the migration and asylum portfolio.[45] The far-right was the big winner in the 2019 Belgian elections and has become the second party of Flanders, just

---

[45] Theo Francken, a senior figure in the Flemish Nationalist party N-VA, was the state secretary for asylum and migration. However, the N-VA finally withdrew its support of the country's government coalition in December 2018 as the Nationalists refused to support the United Nations' Migration Pact which was going to be endorsed by the Belgian state, provoking the fall of the federal government.

behind the Nationalists; both parties focused their respective 2019 political campaigns on more restrictive immigration policies, especially as immigration was the top issue identified by Flemish voters (RepResent 2019).

To conclude, this chapter has sought to offer a cross-national perspective on immigration federalism and, as such, distinguishes itself from the largely intra-national analytical focus in the literature on immigration federalism. Its aim has been to further open up new avenues of inquiry and to provide a basis for future discussion. With the growing politicisation of immigration, the sensitivity of the debates around immigrant integration and the acuteness of the centre-periphery cleavage, there is no doubt that immigration federalism will become even more central in the politics of multinational federations.

## References

Abts, Koen, Emmanuel Dalle Mulle, and Rudi Laermans. 2019. Beyond Issue Diversification: N-VA and the Communitarisation of Political, Economic and Cultural Conflicts in Belgium. *West European Politics* 42 (4): 848–872. https://doi.org/10.1080/01402382.2019.1576407.

Adam, Ilke. 2013a. *Les Entités fédérées belges et l'intégration des immigrés: politiques publiques comparées.* Science Politique. Bruxelles, Belgique: Éditions de l'Université de Bruxelles.

———. 2013b. Immigrant Integration Policies of the Belgian Regions: Sub-State Nationalism and Policy Divergence after Devolution. *Regional & Federal Studies* 23 (5): 547–569. https://doi.org/10.1080/13597566.2013.789024.

Adam, Ilke, and Dirk Jacobs. 2014. Divided on Immigration, Two Models for Integration. The Multilevel Governance of Immigration and Integration in Belgium. In *The Politics of Immigration in Multi-Level States. Governance and Political Parties,* ed. Eve Hepburn and Ricard Zapata-Barrero, 65–85. London: Palgrave Macmillan UK.

Adam, Ilke, and Marco Martiniello. 2013. Divergences et convergences des politiques d'intégration dans la Belgique multinationale. Le cas des parcours d'intégration pour les immigrés. *Revue européenne des migrations internationales* 29 (2): 77–93. https://doi.org/10.4000/remi.6404.

Adam, Ilke, Marco Martiniello, and Andrea Rea. 2018. Regional Divergence in the Integration Policy in Belgium. One Country, Three Integration Programs, One Citizenship Law. In *Governing Diversity. Migrant Integration and Multiculturalism in North America and Europe,* ed. Andrea Rea, Emmanuelle Bribosia, Isabelle Rorive, and Djordje Sredanovic, 235–255. Brussels: Éditions de l'Université de Bruxelles.

Baglay, Sasha, and Delphine Nakache. 2014a. Immigration Federalism in Canada: Provincial and Territorial Nominee Programs (PTNPs). In *Immigration Regulation in Federal States*, ed. Sasha Baglay and Delphine Nakache, 95–116. Dordrecht: Springer Netherlands.

———, eds. 2014b. *Immigration Regulation in Federal States*. International Perspectives on Migration. Dordrecht: Springer Netherlands. https://doi.org/10.1007/978-94-017-8604-1.

Barker, Fiona. 2007. *Redefining the Nation: Sub-State Nationalism and the Political Challenges of Immigrant Integration*. Cambridge, MA: Harvard University.

———. 2010. Learning to Be a Majority: Negotiating Immigration, Integration and National Membership in Quebec. *Political Science* 62 (1): 11–36. https://doi.org/10.1177/0032318710370585.

———. 2015. *Nationalism, Identity and the Governance of Diversity*. London: Palgrave Macmillan UK. https://doi.org/10.1057/9781137339317.

Bélanger, Éric, Frédérick Bastien, and François Gélineau, eds. 2013. *Les Québécois aux urnes: Les partis, Les médias et les citoyens en campagne*. Paramètres. Montréal: Presses de l'Université de Montréal.

Bélanger, Éric, Richard Nadeau, Ailsa Henderson, and Eve Hepburn. 2018. *The National Question and Electoral Politics in Quebec and Scotland*. Democracy, Diversity, and Citizen Engagement Series 3. Montreal: McGill-Queen's University Press.

Beyens, Stefanie, Kris Deschouwer, Emilie van Haute, and Tom Verthé. 2017. Born Again, or Born Anew: Assessing the Newness of the Belgian New-Flemish Alliance (N-VA). *Party Politics* 23 (4): 389–399. https://doi.org/10.1177/1354068815601347.

Blais, André, ed. 2008. *To Keep or to Change First Past the Post? The Politics of Electoral Reform*. Oxford; New York: Oxford University Press.

Bouchard, Gérard. 2011. What Is Interculturalism. *McGill Law Journal* 56 (2): 435–470.

Caestecker, Frank, Bernadette Renauld, Nicolas Perrin, and Thierry Eggerickx. 2016. *Belg worden de geschiedenis van de Belgische nationaliteitsverwerving sinds 1830*. Mechelen: Wolters Kluwer.

Carens, Joseph H. 1995. Immigration, Political Community, and the Transformation of Identity: Quebec's Immigration Politics in Critical Perspective. In *Is Quebec Nationalism Just?: Perspectives from Anglophone Canada*, ed. Joseph H. Carens, 20–81. Montreal; Kingston: McGill-Queen's University Press.

Carlier, Jean-Yves, ed. 2010. *L'étranger face au droit*. Bibliothèque de la Faculté de droit de l'Université Catholique de Louvain 49. Brussels: Bruylant.

Chouinard, Tommy. 2018. C'est la "question de l'urne", dit Couillard. *La Presse*, September 11.

Clement, Jan, and Mieke Van De Putte. 2007. De bevoegdheidsverdeling inzake vreemdelingen en allochtonen. In *Burgerschap, inburgering, migratie*, ed. Frank Judo and Godfried Geudens, 27–46. Brussels: Larcier.

Daniel, Dominique. 2006. La Politique d'immigration du Québec. In *Politiques publiques: Le Québec comparé*, ed. Jean Crête, 43–69. Québec: Presses de l'Université Laval.

De Galembert, Claire, Olivier Rozenberg, and Cécile Vigour, eds. 2014. *Faire parler le parlement. Méthodes et enjeux de l'analyse des débats parlementaires pour les sciences sociales*. Droit et Société. Recherches et Travaux. Paris: LGDJ – Lextenso.

De Winter, Lieven. 2006. Multi-Level Party Competition and Coordination in Belgium. In *Devolution and Electoral Politics*, 76–95. Manchester: Manchester University Press.

De Winter, Lieven, Marc Swyngedouw, and Patrick Dumont. 2006. Party System(s) and Electoral Behaviour in Belgium: From Stability to Balkanisation. *West European Politics* 29 (5): 933–956. https://doi.org/10.1080/01402380600968836.

Deschouwer, Kris. 2009. The Rise and Fall of the Belgian Regionalist Parties. *Regional & Federal Studies* 19 (4–5): 559–577. https://doi.org/10.1080/13597560903310279.

———. 2012. *The Politics of Belgium*. 2nd ed. Comparative Government and Politics. Basingstoke: Palgrave Macmillan.

Dion, Mathieu. 2018. La CAQ et l'immigration: Huit questions à François Legault. *Radio-Canada*, mai 2018. https://ici.radio-canada.ca/nouvelle/1101318/caq-immigration-francois-legault-questions-mathieu-dion.

Erk, Jan. 2002. Le Québec entre la Flandre et la Wallonie: Une comparaison des nationalismes sous-étatiques belges et du nationalisme québécois. *Recherches sociographiques* 43 (3): 499. https://doi.org/10.7202/000609ar.

———. 2005. From Vlaams Blok to Vlaams Belang. The Belgian Far Right Renames Itself. *West European Politics* 28 (3): 493–502. https://doi.org/10.1080/01402380500085681.

———. 2014. FPTP Ain't All That Bad: Nationalist Parties, Immigrants, and Electoral Systems in Québec and Flanders. In *The Politics of Immigration in Multi-Level States*, ed. Eve Hepburn and Ricard Zapata-Barrero, 223–2406. London: Palgrave Macmillan UK.

Fournier, Bernard, and Min Reuchamps, eds. 2009. *Le Fédéralisme en Belgique et au Canada: comparaison sociopolitique*. 1st ed. Ouvertures sociologiques. Bruxelles: De Boeck.

Gagnon, Alain-G., and Jean-Denis Garon. 2019. Constitutional and Non-Constitutional Asymmetries in the Canada Federation: An Exploration into the Policy Fields of Immigration and Manpower Training. A Country Study on Constitutional Asymmetry in Canada. In *Constitutional Asymmetry in*

*Multinational Federalism*, ed. Patricia Popelier and Maja Sahadžić, 77–104. Cham: Springer International Publishing. https://doi.org/10.1007/978-3-030-11701-6_4.

Gagnon, Alain-G., and Raffaele Iacovino. 2007. *Federalism, Citizenship and Quebec*. Toronto: University of Toronto Press. https://doi.org/10.3138/9781442688094.

Gagnon, Alain-G., and Jean-Charles St-Louis, eds. 2016. *Les conditions du dialogue au Québec: laïcité, réciprocité, pluralisme*. Collection Débats. Montréal: Éditions Québec Amérique.

Gagnon, Alain-G., Micheline Milot, Leslie Seidle, and François Boucher. 2014. Rapport présenté au Ministère de l'immigration, de la diversité et de l'inclusion en vue d'élaborer un nouvel énoncé de politique. Montréal. http://www.midi.gouv.qc.ca/publications/fr/recherches-statistiques/ETU_AmenagDiversite_GagnonMilotSeidleBoucher.pdf.

Ganty, Sarah, and Pauline Delgrange. 2015. Heurs et malheurs des parcours d'accueil et d'intégration des étrangers en Belgique. *Revue du droit des étrangers* (185): 511–528.

Garnier, Adele. 2018. Resettled Refugees and Work in Canada and Quebec: Humanitarianism and the Challenge of Mainstream Socioeconomic Participation. In *Refugee Resettlement: Power, Politics, and Humanitarian Governance*, ed. Adele Garnier, Liliana Lyra Jubilut, and Kristin Bergtora Sandvik, 118–138. Studies in Forced Migration 38. New York: Berghahn Books.

Garon, Francis. 2015. Policy-Making for Immigration and Integration in Québec: Degenerative Politics or Business as Usual? *Policy Studies* 36 (5): 487–506. https://doi.org/10.1080/01442872.2015.1089984.

Gerring, John. 2017. Qualitative Methods. *Annual Review of Political Science* 20 (1): 15–36. https://doi.org/10.1146/annurev-polisci-092415-024158.

Goodman, Sara Wallace. 2010. Integration Requirements for Integration's Sake? Identifying, Categorising and Comparing Civic Integration Policies. *Journal of Ethnic and Migration Studies* 36 (5): 753–772. https://doi.org/10.1080/13691831003764300.

———. 2014. *Civic Integration and Membership Politics in Western Europe*. Cambridge: Cambridge University Press.

Guibernau, Montserrat. 1999. *Nations Without States: Political Communities in a Global Age*. Cambridge: Polity Press.

Gulasekaram, Pratheepan, and S. Karthick Ramakrishnan. 2015. *The New Immigration Federalism*. New York: Cambridge University Press.

Hawkins, Freda. 1988. *Canada and Immigration: Public Policy and Public Concern*. 2nd ed. Canadian Public Administration Series. Kingston: McGill-Queen's University Press.

Hepburn, Eve. 2009. Introduction: Re-Conceptualizing Sub-State Mobilization. *Regional & Federal Studies* 19 (4–5): 477–499. https://doi.org/10.1080/13597560903310204.

———. 2011. "Citizens of the Region": Party Conceptions of Regional Citizenship and Immigrant Integration. *European Journal of Political Research* 50 (4): 504–529. https://doi.org/10.1111/j.1475-6765.2010.01940.x.

Hepburn, Eve, and Ricard Zapata-Barrero, eds. 2014. *The Politics of Immigration in Multi-Level States*. London: Palgrave Macmillan UK. https://doi.org/10.1057/9781137358530.

Hobsbawm, Eric J. 1992. *Nations and Nationalism since 1780: Programme, Myth, Reality*. 2nd ed. Cambridge: Cambridge University Press.

Houle, France. 2014. Implementing Québec Intercultural Policy Through the Selection of Immigrants. In *Immigration Regulation in Federal States*, ed. Sasha Baglay and Delphine Nakache, 117–138. International Perspectives on Migration. Dordrecht: Springer Netherlands.

Iacovino, Raffaele. 2015. Contextualizing the Quebec Charter of Values: Belonging Without Citizenship in Quebec. *Canadian Ethnic Studies* 47 (1): 41–60.

Ignatieff, Michael. 1994. *Blood and Belonging: Journeys into the New Nationalism*. New York: Farrar, Straus, and Giroux.

Jacobs, Dirk. 2004. Alive and Kicking? Multiculturalism in Flanders. *JMS: International Journal on Multicultural Societies* 6 (2): 280–299.

Jeram, Sanjay, and Eleni Nicolaides. 2018, July 1–21. Intergovernmental Relations on Immigrant Integration in Canada: Insights from Quebec, Manitoba, and Ontario. *Regional & Federal Studies*. https://doi.org/10.1080/13597566.2018.1491841.

Jeram, Sanjay, Arno van der Zwet, and Verena Wisthaler. 2016. Friends or Foes? Migrants and Sub-State Nationalists in Europe. *Journal of Ethnic and Migration Studies* 42 (8): 1229–1241. https://doi.org/10.1080/1369183X.2015.1082286.

Jonghe, Delphine de, and Marie Doutrepont. 2012. Obtention de la nationalité et volonté d'intégration. Courrier hebdomadaire du CRISP 2152–2153 (27): 1. https://doi.org/10.3917/cris.2152.0005.

Joppke, Christian. 2004. The Retreat of Multiculturalism in the Liberal State: Theory and Policy. *The British Journal of Sociology* 55 (2): 237–257. https://doi.org/10.1111/j.1468-4446.2004.00017.x.

———. 2007. Beyond National Models: Civic Integration Policies for Immigrants in Western Europe. *West European Politics* 30 (1): 1–22. https://doi.org/10.1080/01402380601019613.

———. 2017. Civic Integration in Western Europe: Three Debates. *West European Politics* 40 (6): 1153–1176. https://doi.org/10.1080/01402382.2017.1303252.

Joppke, Christian, and F.L. Seidle, eds. 2012. *Immigrant Integration in Federal Countries.* Thematic Issues in Federalism 2. Montreal; Kingston: McGill-Queen's University Press.

Karmis, Dimitrios, and Alain-G. Gagnon. 1996. Fédéralisme et identités collectives au Canada et en Belgique: des itinéraires différents, une fragmentation similaire. *Canadian Journal of Political Science/Revue canadienne de science politique* 29 (3): 435–468.

Keating, Michael. 1996. *Nations Against the State: The New Politics of Nationalism in Quebec, Catalonia and Scotland: The New Politics of Nationalism in Quebec, Catalonia and Scotland.* Basingstoke; New York: Macmillan St Martin's Press.

———. 2001. *Plurinational Democracy: Stateless Nations in a Post-Sovereignty Era.* Oxford: Oxford University Press.

Kelle, Udo, Gerald Prein, and Katherine Bird. 1995. *Computer-Aided Qualitative Data Analysis: Theory, Methods and Practice.* London; Thousand Oaks, CA: Sage Publications.

Kelley, Ninette, and Michael J. Trebilcock. 2010. *The Making of the Mosaic: A History of Canadian Immigration Policy.* 2nd ed. Toronto: University of Toronto Press.

Kostakopoulou, Dora. 2010. The Anatomy of Civic Integration: The Anatomy of Civic Integration. *The Modern Law Review* 73 (6): 933–958. https://doi.org/10.1111/j.1468-2230.2010.00825.x.

Kostov, Chris. 2008. Canada-Quebec Immigration Agreements (1971–1991) and Their Impact on Federalism. *American Review of Canadian Studies* 38 (1): 91–103. https://doi.org/10.1080/02722010809481822.

Kymlicka, Will. 2001. Immigrant Integration and Minority Nationalism. In *Minority Nationalism and the Changing International Order*, ed. Michael Keating and John McGarry, 61–79. Oxford: Oxford University Press. https://doi.org/10.1093/0199242143.003.0004.

Labelle, Micheline. 2015. Politique d'immigration au Québec. In *L'Encyclopédie canadienne.* Toronto: Historica. https://www.thecanadianencyclopedia.ca/fr/article/politique-dimmigration-du-quebec.

Laxer, Emily, Rachael Dianne Carson, and Anna C. Korteweg. 2014. Articulating Minority Nationhood: Cultural and Political Dimensions in Québec's Reasonable Accommodation Debate. *Nations and Nationalism* 20 (1): 133–153. https://doi.org/10.1111/nana.12046.

Loobuyck, Patrick, and Dirk Jacobs. 2010. Nationalism, Multiculturalism and Integration Policy in Belgium and Flanders. *Canadian Journal for Social Research/Revue canadienne de recherche sociale* 3 (1): 29–40.

Lutz, Philipp. 2019, April. Reassessing the Gap-Hypothesis: Tough Talk and Weak Action in Migration Policy? *Party Politics.* https://doi.org/10.1177/1354068819840776.

Martiniello, Marco. 1995. Philosophies de l'intégration en Belgique. *Hommes et migrations* 1193 (1): 24–29. https://doi.org/10.3406/homig.1995.2569.

Martiniello, Marco, and Andrea Rea. 2004. *Affirmative Action: des discours, des politiques et des pratiques en débat.* Collection Carrefours 2. Louvain-la-Neuve: Academia-Bruylant.

May, Paul. 2016. Ideological Justifications for Restrictive Immigration Policies: An Analysis of Parliamentary Discourses on Immigration in France and Canada (2006–2013). *French Politics* 14 (3): 287–310. https://doi.org/10.1057/s41253-016-0004-7.

Montigny, Éric, and François Gélineau. 2019. Boussole électorale et configuration d'un système partisan: le cas du Québec. In *Démocratie(s), parlementarismes(s) et légitimité(s)/Democracy(ies), Parliamentarism(s) and Legitimacy(ies)*, ed. Philippe Poirier and Nadim Fahrat, 163–184. Brussels: Bruylant.

Newton, Lina. 2012. Policy Innovation or Vertical Integration? A View of Immigration Federalism from the States. *Law & Policy* 34 (2): 113–137.

Oakes, Leigh, and Jane Warren. 2009. *Language, Citizenship and Identity in Québec.* Basingstoke: Palgrave Macmillan.

Paquet, Mireille. 2016. *La fédéralisation de l'immigration au Canada.* Collection Politique mondiale. Montréal: Les Presses de l'Université de Montréal.

———. 2019. *Province-Building and the Federalization of Immigration in Canada.* Toronto; Buffalo; London: University of Toronto Press.

Pauwels, Teun. 2011. Explaining the Strange Decline of the Populist Radical Right Vlaams Belang in Belgium: The Impact of Permanent Opposition. *Acta Politica* 46 (1): 60–82. https://doi.org/10.1057/ap.2010.17.

Pilet, Jean-Benoit. 2005. The Adaptation of the Electoral System to the Ethno-Linguistic Evolution of Belgian Consociationalism. *Ethnopolitics* 4 (4): 397–411. https://doi.org/10.1080/17449050500348642.

Poirier, Johanne. 2009. Le partage des compétences et les relations intergouvernementales: la situation au Canada. In *Le Fédéralisme en Belgique et au Canada*, ed. Bernard Fournier and Min Reuchamps, 107–122. Bruxelles: De Boeck.

Pommée, Yanaël. 2017. Parcours d'intégration en communauté germanophone: de la construction d'un problème public à l'analyse d'une politique d'intégration. Master Thesis, Louvain-la-Neuve: UCLouvain, FOPES.

Proksch, Sven-Oliver, and Jonathan B. Slapin. 2015. *The Politics of Parliamentary Debate: Parties, Rebels, and Representation.* Cambridge: Cambridge University Press. https://doi.org/10.1017/CBO9781139680752.

Reichhold, Stephan. 2016. *L'accueil et l'intégration des nouveaux arrivants au Québec: particularités du cadre juridique et financier des mesures d'intégration, Public conference.* Toronto: The Glendon School of Public and International Affairs.

RepResent, Consortium EOS. 2019, June 4. Les flamands et les wallons ont voté pour des partis différents le 26 mai – mais leurs avis divergent moins sur les politiques publiques qu'ils souhaitent. *CEVIPOL* (blog). http://cevipol.ulb. ac.be/sites/default/files/20190605_note_for_the_media_flamands_et_wallons_ont_vote_différemment_br_v2_compl.pdf.

Rodriguez, Cristina. 2018. Enforcement, Integration, and the Future of Immigration Federalism. *Journal on Migration and Human Security* 5 (2): 509–540.

Rokkan, Stein. 2009. *Citizens, Elections, Parties: Approaches to the Comparative Study of the Processes of Development.* ECPR Press Classics. Colchester: ECPR Press.

Romainville, Céline. 2015. Dynamics of Belgian Plurinational Federalism: A Small State Under Pressure. *Boston College International and Comparative Law Review* 38 (2): 225–250.

Schertzer, Robert. 2015. Intergovernmental Relations in Canada's Immigration System: From Bilateralism Towards Multilateral Collaboration. *Canadian Journal of Political Science* 48 (2): 383–412. https://doi.org/10.1017/ S000842391500027X.

Schmidt, Vivien A. 2008. Discursive Institutionalism: The Explanatory Power of Ideas and Discourse. *Annual Review of Political Science* 11 (1): 303–326. https://doi.org/10.1146/annurev.polisci.11.060606.135342.

———. 2010. Taking Ideas and Discourse Seriously: Explaining Change Through Discursive Institutionalism as the Fourth "New Institutionalism". *European Political Science Review* 2 (1): 1–25. https://doi.org/10.1017/ S175577390999021X.

Simeon, Richard. 1990. Why Did the Meech Lake Accord Fail? In *Canada: The State of the Federation*, 15–40. Institute of Intergovernmental Relations: Kingston.

Spiro, Peter J. 2001. Fédéralisme et immigration: modèles et tendances. *Revue internationale des sciences sociales* 167 (1): 71. https://doi.org/10.3917/ riss.167.0071.

Strazzari, Davide. 2012. The Scope and the Legal Limits of the "Immigration Federalism": Some Comparative Remarks from the American, Belgian and the Italian Experiences. *European Journal of Legal Studies* 5 (2): 95–137.

Swenden, W. 2014. *Federalism and Regionalism in Western Europe: A Comparative and Thematic Analysis.* Basingstoke: Palgrave Macmillan.

Swenden, Wilfried, Marleen Brans, and Lieven De Winter. 2006. The Politics of Belgium: Institutions and Policy Under Bipolar and Centrifugal Federalism. *West European Politics* 29 (5): 863–873. https://doi. org/10.1080/01402380600968729.

Teney, Céline, and Dirk Jacobs. 2007. Le droit de vote des étrangers en Belgique: le cas de Bruxelles. *Migrations Société* 114 (6): 151–168. https://doi. org/10.3917/migra.114.0151.

Tessier, Kevin. 1995. Immigration and the Crisis in Federalism: A Comparison of the United States and Canada. *Indiana Journal of Global Legal Studies* 3: 211–244.

Tessier, Charles, and Éric Montigny. 2016. Untangling Myths and Facts: Who Supported the Québec Charter of Values? *French Politics* 14 (2): 272–285. https://doi.org/10.1057/fp.2016.1.

Tremblay, Arjun. 2019. *Diversity in Decline?: The Rise of the Political Right and the Fate of Multiculturalism*. Cham: Springer International Publishing. https://doi.org/10.1007/978-3-030-02299-0.

Varsanyi, Monica W., Paul G. Lewis, Doris Marie Provine, and Scott Decker. 2012. A Multilayered Jurisdictional Patchwork: Immigration Federalism in the United States. *Law & Policy* 34 (2): 138–158.

Vineberg, Robert. 1987. Federal-Provincial Relations in Canadian Immigration. *Canadian Public Administration/Administration publique du Canada* 30 (2): 299–317. https://doi.org/10.1111/j.1754-7121.1987.tb00085.x.

Vliegenthart, Rens. 2007. *Framing Immigration and Integration: Facts, Parliament, Media and Anti-Immigrant Party Support in the Netherlands*. Amsterdam: Vrije Universiteit Amsterdam. http://dare.ubvu.vu.nl/bitstream/1871/13082/5/8067.pdf.

Wodak, Ruth, and Teun A. van Dijk, eds. 2000. *Racism at the Top: Parliamentary Discourses on Ethnic Issues in Six European States*. The Investigation, Explanation and Countering of Xenophobia and Racism, v. 2. Klagenfurt: Drava Verlag.

Woehrling, José. 2000. Les droits et libertés dans la construction de la citoyenneté, au Canada et au Québec. In *Droits fondamentaux et citoyenneté*, ed. Michel Coutu, Pierre Bosset, Caroline Gendreau, and Daniel Villeneuve, 269–302. Montréal: Thémis.

Xhardez, Catherine. 2016, October. The Integration of New Immigrants in Brussels: An Institutional and Political Puzzle. *Brussels Studies*. https://doi.org/10.4000/brussels.1434.

———. 2017. *Intégrer pour exister? Nationalisme sous-étatique et intégration des immigrés en Flandre et au Québec*. Paris; Bruxelles: Sciences Po Paris & Université Saint-Louis Bruxelles.

Zapata-Barrero, Ricard, ed. 2009. *Immigration and Self-Government of Minority Nations*. Collection Diversitas, no. 3. Brussels; New York: P.I.E. Peter Lang.

## CHAPTER 10

# Relative Deprivation and Perceived Discrimination Among Quebec's English-Speaking Minority Communities: 'Second-Class Citizens' in a Multi-national Context?

*Pierre-Olivier Bonin*

## INTRODUCTION

English-speaking communities living in Quebec have historically constituted and remain to this day the largest linguistic minority of all Canadian provinces. In the 2016 census, the total number of Quebecers declaring English as their first language was estimated to be 1.103 million, an increase of 45,230 from 2011 (Statistics Canada 2017a).[1]

Anglo-Quebecers are in quite a unique situation as a linguistic minority. Although they may be seen as a linguistic minority, since the vast majority of Quebec's population speaks French as a first language, Anglo-Quebecers

---

[1] Stated differently, this represents an increase in the relative weight of the official language minority in Quebec, from 13.5% in 2011 to 13.7% in 2016.

---

P.-O. Bonin (✉)
University of Toronto, Toronto, ON, Canada
e-mail: po.rivestbonin@mail.utoronto.ca

© The Author(s) 2020
A.-G. Gagnon, A. Tremblay (eds.), *Federalism and National
Diversity in the 21st Century*, Federalism and Internal Conflicts,
https://doi.org/10.1007/978-3-030-38419-7_10

could also be seen as belonging to a linguistic majority, since the majority of Canadians speak English as a first language and since English remains the primary language of public life in Canada (Laponce 2006).[2] This multi-layered identity is further complicated if one takes municipalities into account. Data show that Quebec's English-speaking demography is heavily concentrated in the Greater Montreal area, with four out of five (79.4%) Anglo-Quebecers inhabiting that territory according to the 2016 census (Statistics Canada 2017b).[3] Furthermore, 'approximately half of Quebec's Anglophones […] comprise between 30 percent and 49.9 percent of the population of the municipality in which they live' (Corbeil et al. 2010, 15) and roughly one in five Anglophones live in municipalities in which they constitute the majority (ibid.). In other words, an Anglophone living in the province of Quebec may potentially hold a triple linguistic status: (1) that of a member of a linguistic minority group at the provincial level; (2) that of a member of a linguistic majority group at the federal level; (3) that of a member of a linguistic majority group at the municipal level (assuming of course that the municipality includes fewer Francophones as well as Allophones). A fourth layer could be added[4] when one recognises that English is the lingua franca at the international level and that Anglo-Quebecers can therefore also be seen to be members of a global 'majority'.[5]

Despite this multi-layered identity as well as evidence that native English fluency enhances economic mobility and symbolic capital (Bourdieu 1997), there seems to be a perception that Anglo-Quebecers are less than first-class citizens in Quebec, or are 'second-class citizens' of Quebec.[6] For

---

[2] Such a sociolinguistic context can be described as asymmetrical, a term that is also applicable to the institutional architecture of the Canadian federation, where different language regimes co-exist at the federal and provincial levels (Cardinal and Sonntag 2015; Cardinal and Normand 2011). For a detailed account of 'language regime', including its conceptual foundations and a portrait of the Canadian language regimes, see Cardinal and Sonntag (2015).

[3] Calculations made by the author using the Montreal 'census metropolitan area' and 'first official language spoken' variables.

[4] If we depart from purely quantitative considerations and delve into the more qualitative notions of power relations and status (e.g. Vandycke 1994).

[5] Indeed, despite the fact that English-as-a-first-language speakers constitute the third largest linguistic group in the world behind Mandarin and Spanish speakers, English remains the language spoken in the highest number of countries, with 65 countries across five continents (Leclerc 2017).

[6] A quick search in media archives reveals that this nomenclature dates back to the 1980s; in the Canadian Newsstream database, for example, the Montreal Gazette's publications are archived back to 1985 and testify to that observation.

example, in discussing the possibility of establishing an office of English language affairs (similar to the *Office québecois de la langue française*) in 2016, then-Quebec Premier Philippe Couillard declared that: 'For the moment, I don't see the necessity of doing this. They [English-speaking Quebecers] are first-class Quebecers and I want them to feel that way' (Boissinot 2016). And, when Kathleen Weil was named first minister responsible for relations with English-speaking Quebecers, Helena Burke, executive director of the Council for Anglophone Magdalen Islanders, welcomed the appointment as a means to remedy several issues, such as '[the] fact that [Anglophones] don't have access to a lot of services in English' (Page 2017). This sentiment was reaffirmed more recently during the English language leaders' debate of the 2018 provincial election when the debate's moderator asked the four candidates (Manon Massé, Jean-François Lisée, Philippe Couillard, and François Legault) what they would do to enhance the inclusivity of Anglo-Quebecers in the public sphere. She prefaced the question with the following declaration:

> Let's be clear: the English community recognises that French is the official language of Quebec, but despite the gestures of goodwill and the reassurances, many English-speaking Quebecers say they feel like second-class citizens here. (Quebec Votes 2018: English Debate)

There are also some preliminary indications that a perception of Quebec's English-speaking communities' 'second-class' status may be leading to some forms of collective action. For example, an article in the French language daily *La Presse* (2015) noted that 'discontent [was] on the rise among Anglo-Montrealers'[7] and cited an online petition titled 'It is time to close down the *Office Québécois de la langue française* (sic)'. When the newspaper article was first published, the petition had 6000 signatures; three months later, that number had reached 10,000 signatures; and, as of April 2016, it had reached 21,000 signatures.[8] The *La Presse* article also cites instances of activism by city councillor Ruth Kovac and by lawyer Harold Staviss urging private business owners to grant the English language more prominence on commercial signage.

---

[7] Author's translation.

[8] While it is difficult to verify the authenticity of the participants, the fact that several thousand individuals would take action to protest the existence of one of the core language policy instruments of the province can be taken as an indicator of dissatisfaction.

Are Anglo-Quebecers 'second-class citizens' in Canada's multi-national context? Does perception of one's 'second-class' status lead to remedial collective action? This chapter sets out to address these questions by drawing upon original data from an online survey conducted in 2017 that explores how Anglo-Quebecers perceive not only their own community's status, but the status of the province's Francophone linguistic majority. The chapter is divided into three sections. The first section of the chapter details the theoretical and conceptual underpinnings of this study, engaging relative deprivation theory and recent literature on perceived discrimination, and discussing their possible implications regarding collective action. The chapter's second section casts light on the operationalisation of the study's data. The chapter's third section presents the results of the study's hypothesis testing. In brief, the evidence presented in this chapter suggests that there exists a state of 'relative deprivation' and high levels of perceived discrimination among members of English-speaking minority communities in Quebec. Paradoxically, the relative deprivation indicators used here predict lower, not higher, likelihood of engagement in Anglo-Quebecer organisations; in addition, the study shows that those who perceive high levels of discrimination are slightly less likely to be engaged in organisational work or volunteerism. Consequently, the chapter concludes that the provincial government may need to take action for Anglo-Quebecers to feel fully included in Quebec society.

## RELATIVE DEPRIVATION, PERCEIVED DISCRIMINATION, AND COLLECTIVE ACTION

The notion of relative deprivation has its roots in social psychology, in the work of Samuel Stouffer and his *American Soldier* studies (Stouffer et al. 1949a, b; Stouffer 1962, cited in Pettigrew 2015). Stouffer used the concept to explain 'anomalies' observed such as: that 'the military police were more satisfied with their slow promotions than the air corpsmen were with their rapid promotions' and that 'African American soldiers in southern camps were more satisfied than those in northern camps despite the fact that the racist South of the 1940s remained tightly segregated by race' (Pettigrew 2015, 11). Relative deprivation offered a solution to such anomalies by suggesting that satisfaction with one's conditions should be construed as *relative* to the comparisons that are *immediately* available. Thus, in relation to the two cases mentioned above, 'the military police compared their promotions with other military police—not air corpsmen whom they rarely encountered' while 'black soldiers in the South compared their lot with black civilians in the South—not with black soldiers in the North who were out of view' (ibid). In brief, relative deprivation theory is based on the proposition that 'the negative affect associated with judgments of one's own status is not simply a function of one's objective status. Instead, [it varies] with the subjective assessment of one's status' (Bernstein and Crosby 1980). In other words, relative deprivation theorists contend that 'focusing on what individuals have or do not have can be misleading without understanding how they subjectively interpret the availability of resources' (Smith and Huo 2014, 232).

The most important subset of the literature on relative deprivation, as it specifically relates to the focus of this study, analyses its effect on participation in collective action and on political participation. Collective action studies using RD have found mixed support for the theory that RD increases likelihood of participation. For example, Leach et al. (2007), Pettigrew et al. (2008), and Walker and Mann (1987)) found support for their models while Gaskell and Smith (1984), Snyder and Tilly (1972), and Thompson (1989) did not.[9] A recent meta-analysis found, however, that using 'higher quality measures yield significantly stronger relationships' (Smith et al. 2012, 203), that it is too early to completely discard the theory, and that, on the contrary, it is still a valuable tool for the appraisal of a variety of phenomena, including collective action.

In light of the foregoing debate, a prudential approach advises a more limited research goal whereby RD is be expected to have but modest predictive power regarding participation in collective action. Consequently, the current case study does not purport to offer a comprehensive model of participation in collective action among Anglo-Quebecers. Rather, it offers to test a model of participation in organisational collective action, hereafter simply termed 'organisational activism', while incorporating and distinguishing between different dimensions of relative deprivation.[10]

---

[9] Others have concluded that the theory should be rejected altogether or that it has failed to meet any scientific consensus (e.g. Gurney and Tierney 1982; Brush 1996).

[10] A similar study has been conducted on nationalism among the francophone majority (Guimond and Dubé-Simard 1983), which constitutes further indication of the relevance of RD theory in the context of Canadian and Quebec politics.

## DATA, MEASUREMENT, AND OPERATIONALISATION

Data for this study were collected in 2017 using an online survey questionnaire distributed to participants and activists who were members of official language minority organisations and Facebook groups in the Canadian provinces of Quebec and Ontario.[11] The researcher first conducted several semi-structured interviews with employees of organisations and administrators of Facebook groups. He then asked the interviewees for their permission to send (through the organisations' Facebook page, email list, or any other appropriate means) an invitation to their respective organisation's membership and supporters to fill out the online survey questionnaire. All respondents were guaranteed anonymity and were invited to read a consent form prior to their participation in the study. A prize of 100 Canadian dollars was offered and distributed to one randomly selected respondent as an incentive to take part in the research project. The final English-speaking minority community sample comprises a total of 12 organisations and Facebook groups, whose members, followers, and supporters total 305 respondents.

Regarding the dependent variable, the questionnaire included a question that determined whether respondents were simply supporters or whether they were organisational activists. The question was labelled as follows: 'Are you currently working or volunteering for an Anglophone organization in Quebec [or Ontario] (choose "yes" if you do one, or both, of these)'. A total of 98 respondents out of 305 responded in the affirmative indicating that they were working or volunteering for an Anglophone organisation. This effectively created two subgroups for the sample and allowed for the conducting of predictive analyses of 'organisational activism', defined as a binary categorical variable.

Regarding independent variables, Gurney and Tierney (1982, 40) warn against using a 'one concept-one indicator' strategy; as is evident from the literature, the concept of RD is multidimensional. Therefore, this case study adopts a multi-indicator approach to the operationalisation of hypotheses and to the measurement of relative deprivation. Such an approach seems all the more appropriate since the idea of 'second-class citizens', which embodies the notion of relative deprivation here, allows for a multiplicity of interpretations.

---

[11] To be clear, the data pertaining to the Franco-Ontarian side of the study are neither used nor discussed in this article.

Two distinctions are relevant to the operationalisation of this study's hypotheses. One is a distinction between individual relative deprivation (hereafter 'Individual RD') and group relative deprivation (hereafter 'Group RD') that originates in the work of Runciman (1966). Guimond and Dubé-Simard (1983, 526), in the context of a study on Quebec nationalism, offer their understanding and elaboration of the distinction in discussing 'egotistic' and 'fraternal' relative deprivation (RD), which I have opted to rename, in the present study, due to their potentially negative connotations. The distinction is as follows:

> Egoistic RD is a type of personal discontent that occurs when an individual compares his or her own situation to that of others (in-group or out-group members), whereas fraternal RD is a more social discontent that occurs when an individual compares the situation of his or her group as a whole to that of an out-group.

Along similar lines, Olson and Hazlewood (1986, 2) define fraternal deprivation as 'the perception that one's reference group as a whole is deprived (usually relative to other groups)', whereas egoistic deprivation is understood to be 'the perception that one's own outcomes fall below a subjective standard (usually based on other individuals' outcomes)'. Reflecting these complexities, the hypotheses assessed in this chapter will thus include variables meant to capture both fraternal deprivation—hereafter 'group relative deprivation'—and egoistic—hereafter 'individual relative deprivation'.

A second distinction relevant to the operationalisation of the hypotheses rests on the evaluation of one's current condition against the past condition of the individual/group. As Buechler (2008, 1032) puts it,

> [...] strain emerges on the social–psychological level as people assess their current situation against reference groups or past or anticipated future situations. Whenever they find a benchmark that implies they could or should be better off, relative deprivation exists, and this psychological strain can trigger collective behavior.

Providing further justification for this distinction, Pettigrew (2015, 14) stresses that 'imagined alternatives, past experiences, and comparisons with similar others also strongly influence such feelings [of relative deprivation]' and Smith et al. (2012, 204) argue that political scientists have often 'focused on people's comparisons of their present situation with either their past, future, desired, or deserved selves'. Therefore, this study incorporates a *temporal* dimension of relative deprivation.

In light of these distinctions, this study uses a set of four variables will be used as indicators for the fraternal relative deprivation hypothesis (H1). Each of those variables measures a distinct dimension of a same binary outcome, that is, group relative deprivation. The first is an evaluation by respondents of their ingroup's current situation (the variable name will be 'InGrpCurrent' in the model below); the second, an evaluation of the outgroup's current situation ('OutGrpCurrent'); the third, an evaluation of the ingroup's past situation ('InGrpPast'); the fourth, an evaluation of the outgroup's past situation ('OutGrpPast'). Four standard control variables (age, gender, education, and living area) have also been added. Formally stated, the model can be expressed as follows:

**H1a** Group Relative Deprivation as a Predictor of Organisational Activism

$$\text{logit}\left(\text{PrOrgActivism}|\text{EngQc}\right) = \beta_0 + \beta_1 \text{InGrpCurrent} + \beta_2 \text{OutGrpCurrent} + \beta_3 \text{InGrpPast} + \beta_4 \text{OutGrpPast} + \left(\beta_7 \text{Age} + \beta_8 \text{Educ} + \beta_9 \text{Gender} + \beta_{10} \text{Area}\right)$$

This study uses two indicators for the individual dimension of relative deprivation.[12] The first indicator is an evaluation of the respondents' personal situation in recent years (whether it improved, remained unchanged, or deteriorated). The second indicator concerns the respondents' current state of happiness regarding their personal life in the province of Quebec. The same four standard control variables are added. Formally stated, the model can be expressed as follows:

**H1b** Individual Relative Deprivation as a Predictor of Organisational Activism

$$\text{logit}\left(\text{PrOrgActivism}|\text{EngQc}\right) = \beta_0 + \beta_1 \text{PersonalPast} + \beta_2 \text{PersonalHappiness} + \left(\beta_3 \text{Age} + \beta_4 \text{Educ} + \beta_5 \text{Gender} + \beta_6 \text{Area}\right)$$

---

[12] Unfortunately, the survey questionnaire only comprised two questions operationalisable as indictors for the egoistic relative deprivation hypothesis. This is likely to result in a weaker model, but the article will nonetheless present results.

A combination of both fraternal and egoistic relative deprivation is also possible, what the relative deprivation literature refers to as double relative deprivation. In applying this hypothesis, Foster and Matheson (1995) found that women who experienced double relative deprivation were more likely to engage into collective action. In light of this study's focus on collective action, it therefore seems appropriate to test the double relative deprivation hypothesis as another variant of the relative deprivation hypotheses. Formally stated, the model can be expressed as follows:

**H1c** Double Relative Deprivation as a Predictor of Organisational Activism

$$\text{logit}\left(\text{PrOrgActivism|EngQc}\right) = \beta_0 + \beta_1\text{GrpCurrent} + \beta_2\text{OutgroupCurrent}$$
$$+ \beta_3\text{GroupPast} + \beta_4\text{OutgroupPast} + \beta_7\text{PersonalPast} + \beta_8\text{PersonalHappiness}$$
$$+ \beta_9\text{Age} + \beta_{10}\text{Educ} + \beta_{11}\text{Gender} + \beta_{12}\text{Area}$$

To be absolutely clear, relative deprivation is not the only from of dissatisfaction that can lead to action; it can also be the result of perceived discrimination. Perceived discrimination has been hypothesised to trigger mobilisation by 'inciting ethnic minorities to take matters in their own hands and to speak up to provoke change' (Bilodeau 2017, 125). A host of empirical studies have been conducted in the United States on perceived discrimination within the country's Hispanic minority (e.g. Ono 2002; Michelson 2003; Schildkraut 2005; Kam et al. 2008). Antoine Bilodeau's (2017) study is one of the few studies of perceived discrimination in Canada and one of the few, broadly speaking, to draw a distinction between electoral and non-electoral political activities. His findings reveal that perceived discrimination among visible minorities has a double effect: it decreases the propensity of engaging in traditional political activities such as voting while simultaneously increasing propensity for engaging in alternative channels of political action. As this chapter examines Anglo-Quebecer organisational activism, which is a non-electoral type of political activity, it is thus hypothesised that *Anglo-Quebecers who perceive discrimination against their group are more likely to engage in organisational activism*. Formally stated, the model can be expressed as follows:

**H2** Perceived Discrimination as a Predictor of Organisational Activism

$$\mathrm{logit}\left(\mathrm{PrOrgActivism|EngQc}\right) = \beta_0 + \beta_1 \mathrm{PerceivedDiscr} + \beta_2 \mathrm{Age} + \beta_3 \mathrm{Educ}$$
$$+ \beta_4 \mathrm{Gender} + \beta_5 \mathrm{Area}$$

## Results and Findings

The following pages present the results and findings of this study's analysis, starting with an examination of descriptive statistics from the survey data. The descriptive statistics provide evidence suggesting that Anglo-Quebecers are in a state of group relative deprivation. Figure 10.1 shows that a large majority of 65% of Anglo-Quebecers judge that their ingroup's current living conditions are 'very poor' (29%) or 'below average' (36%). This is an indicator of RD as it relates to the implicit comparison with the other linguistic majority group (the 'average') at the present time.

Figure 10.2 shows the explicit outgroup comparison. Again, a large majority (72%) of Anglo-Quebecers judge that the current living conditions of the other linguistic group is either 'excellent' (24%) or 'above average' (48%). This is another indicator of RD, since it relates to the explicit comparison with the outgroup, that is, the linguistic majority group. A striking feature of the two bar charts presented so far is that they display almost perfectly symmetrically opposed patterns of frequency distributions.

Figure 10.3 shows the evaluation of respondents with regard to their ingroup's condition in recent years. Nearly two-thirds of respondents (64%) judge that their group's situation has 'deteriorated' (39%) or 'somewhat deteriorated' (25%) whereas slightly over a third of respondents

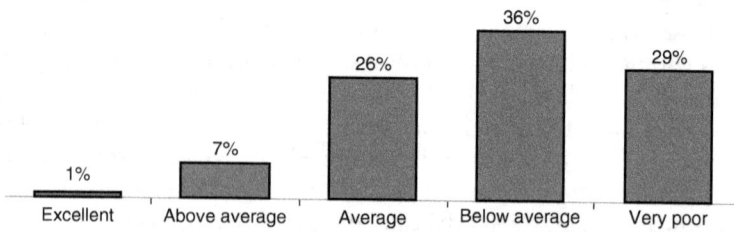

**Fig. 10.1** 'The current living conditions of Anglophones in the province of Quebec are ...'

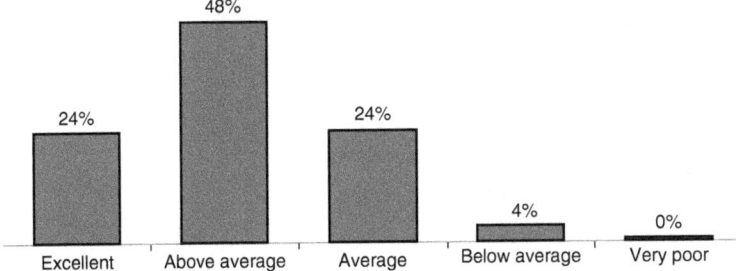

**Fig. 10.2** 'The current living conditions of Francophones in the province of Quebec are ...'

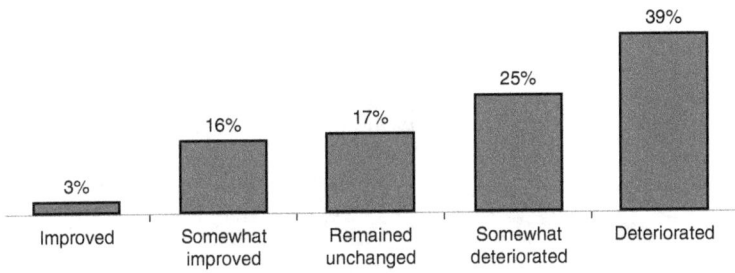

**Fig. 10.3** 'Would you say that, in the last years, the general situation of Anglophones in Quebec has...'

(36%) believe their group's situation has 'remained unchanged' (17%), that it has 'somewhat improved' (16%) or that it has 'improved' (3%).

Figure 10.4 presents the explicit outgroup comparison using the same temporal dimension. Three quarters of Anglo-Quebecers (75%) judge that the outgroup's situation has 'improved' or 'somewhat improved' in recent years, whereas about one-fifth (21%) believe that the outgroup's situation has 'remained unchanged' and only a handful think it has 'somewhat deteriorated' or 'deteriorated'. These findings stand in stark contrast to the evaluation that Anglo-Quebecers make regarding the evolution of their ingroup's situation in past years.

Figure 10.4 presents a nearly exact opposite pattern of frequency distribution to the one displayed in Fig. 10.3. In other words, when it comes to evaluating the ingroup's and the outgroup's condition (current and in the past) Anglo-Quebecer judge that their group is at a clear disadvantage in

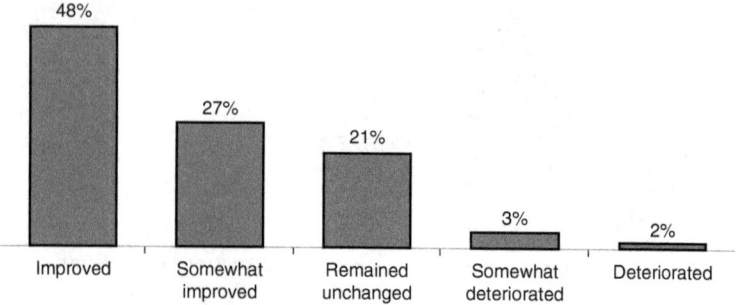

**Fig. 10.4** 'Would you say that, in the last years, the general situation of Francophones in Quebec has...'

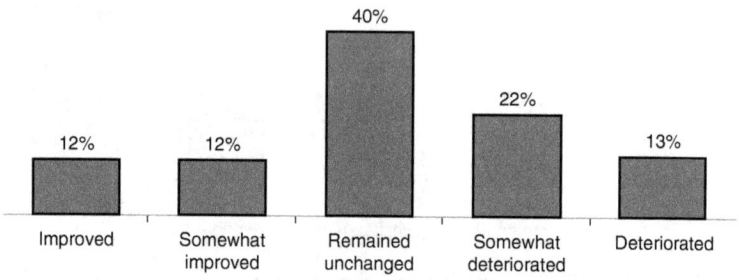

**Fig. 10.5** 'Would you say that, in the last years, your personal situation has ...'

contrast with the Francophone majority group. Taken together, all of the four indicators suggest the sampled respondents are in a state of group relative deprivation. This concurs with the expectations developed in the previous section.

As for indicators of individual relative deprivation, Fig. 10.5 shows that the largest proportion (40%) of respondents judges that their personal situation has remained stable in recent years. However, when one looks at Fig. 10.5's extremities, it is clear that there are more respondents who judge that their personal situation has deteriorated (36%) than those who believe it has improved (25%).

Figure 10.6 shows a far more even distribution of respondents when it comes to their self-reported current state of happiness. Approximately 39% of respondents declared being personally 'unhappy' or 'rather unhappy' with their life in the province of Quebec. Slightly more (44%)

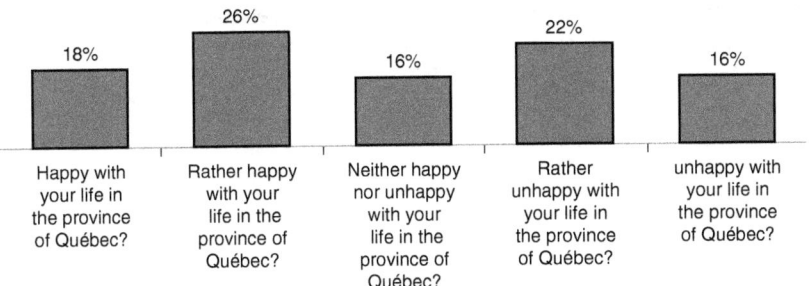

**Fig. 10.6** 'In general, would you say that you are personally [...] with your life in the province of Quebec?'

declared being personally 'happy' or 'rather happy' with their life in the province of Quebec. And about 16% declared being personally 'neither happy nor unhappy' with their life in the province of Quebec. Taken together, these indicators provide much weaker evidence supporting the notion the respondents as a whole are in a state of individual relative deprivation.

Table 10.1, provides the results from a logistic regression, the second step in this chapter's analysis (see Appendix A for operationalisation of dummy variables[13]). The first column presents results including only Group RD indicators, allowing to test hypothesis H1a; the second column presents results including only Individual RD indicators, allowing to test hypothesis H1b; the third column presents results including both group and individual RD indicators, allowing to test hypothesis H1c (i.e. the double deprivation hypothesis). All regressions include four standard sociodemographic control variables of age, gender, education, and region of residence.

Results from the logistic regression are displaying clear patterns that, for the most part, run counter to theoretical expectations. The first indicator of Group RD ('Ingroup Current') shows that, while holding other variables constant, the odds of being an organisational activist are 0.764 to 1 for respondents who judge that the ingroup's current living conditions are 'below average' or 'very poor' in reference to those judging that it is

---

[13] The rationale behind such an operationalisation stems naturally from theory. The notion of relative deprivation indeed implies a dichotomous state; either a group is in a state of relative deprivation or it is not, hence the relevance of a dummy variable.

**Table 10.1** Logistic regression: three relative deprivation models predicting organisational activism among Anglo-Quebecer respondents

|  | Group RD | Individual RD | Double RD |
|---|---|---|---|
|  | Odds ratio (95% C.I.) | Odds ratio (95% C.I.) | Odds ratio (95% C.I.) |
| *Group RD indicators (dummy variables)* | | | |
| Ingroup Current | 0.764** | | 0.890 |
|  | (0.630–0.926) | | (0.723–1.095) |
| Outgroup Current | 1.917*** | | 1.949*** |
|  | (1.562–2.353) | | (1.586–2.395) |
| Ingroup Past | 0.578*** | | 0.630*** |
|  | (0.479–0.698) | | (0.511–0.777) |
| Outgroup Past | 0.528*** | | 0.529*** |
|  | (0.430–0.649) | | (0.430–0.651) |
| *Individual RD indicators (dummy variables)* | | | |
| Personal Past | | 0.862 | 1.042 |
|  | | (0.718–1.044) | (0.839–1.296) |
| Personal current happiness | | 0.522*** | 0.651*** |
|  | | (0.433–0.629) | (0.524–0.808) |
| Age | 1.086** | 1.006 | 1.087** |
|  | (1.022–1.153) | (0.953–1.060) | (1.023–1.155) |
| Gender (Female) | 3.196*** | 2.672*** | 3.240*** |
|  | (2.575–3.967) | (2.196–3.251) | (2.608–4.025) |
| Education | 1.039 | 0.970 | 1.053 |
|  | (0.962–1.121) | (0.906–1.039) | (0.975–1.138) |
| Living area | | | |
|   Urban (ref. cat.) | (.) | (.) | (.) |
|   Suburban | 0.648*** | 0.723** | 0.679** |
|  | (0.520–0.807) | (0.591–0.884) | (0.543–0.848) |
|   Rural | 1.331** | 1.168 | 1.310* |
|  | (1.081–1.639) | (0.965–1.414) | (1.062–1.616) |
| Constant | 0.256*** | 0.371*** | 0.233*** |
|  | (0.152–0.431) | (0.246–0.558) | (0.138–0.394) |
| Pseudo-$R^2$ | 0.092 | 0.055 | 0.097 |

$*p < 0.05$, $**p < 0.01$, $***p < 0.001$

Note: Guidelines for the interpretation of the OLS $R^2$ may not be applicable to pseudo-$R^2$ (Smith and McKenna 2013). Use with caution 'average', 'above average', or 'excellent'.[14] This contradicts expectations. The effect, however, does not hold across models as it becomes statistically insignificant when adding Individual RD indicators to the regression (i.e. the double relative deprivation model, third column, hereafter 'Double RD').

The second GRD indicator ('Outgroup Current') measuring perceptions about the current outgroup's condition is in line with expectations. Respondents who judge that the francophone minority's current living conditions are 'above average' or 'excellent' are 1.917 times more likely to be activists than those who judge that it is 'average', 'below average', or 'very poor', ceteris paribus. The effect this time holds across both the GRD and the DRD models and remains statistically significant at the $p < 0.001$ level.

Results from the third GRD indicator ('Ingroup Past') run counter to expectations, since the odds of being an activist are, ceteris paribus, 0.578 to 1 for respondents who judge that their group's situation has 'deteriorated' or 'somewhat deteriorated' in relation to those who judge that it has 'remained unchanged', 'somewhat improved', or 'improved'. These results remain statistically significant at the $p < 0.001$ level when Individual RD indicators are added to the model, as seen in the third column.

The fourth GRD indicator ('Outgroup Past') yields similar results, holding other variables constant, with an odds ratio of 0.528 to 1 for respondents who judge that the outgroup's situation has 'improved' or 'somewhat improved' in comparison with respondents who judge that it has 'remained unchanged', 'somewhat deteriorated', or 'deteriorated'. Such results, again, contradict expectations.

All things considered, out of four GRD indicators, only one (Outgroup Current) corroborates the hypothesis that GRD fosters organisational activism. The three other indicators (Ingroup Current, Ingroup Past, and

---

[14] Traditionally, coefficients and odds ratios represented in regression tables are interpreted as indicating a change in $Y$ for each change of one unit in $X$. In the present case, the dependent variables ($X$) are all dummy variables operationalised as to distinguish between 'relatively deprived' (value of 1) or 'not relatively deprived' (value of 0) respondents. Hence the interpretation uses more expressive wording for the sake of clarity.

Outgroup Past) contradict theoretical expectations and one (Ingroup Current) loses statistical significance when adding Individual RD indicators to the model. It can thus be concluded that H1a is not supported; in fact, the evidence supports the opposite of theoretical expectations. In other words, the evidence shows that *the more a respondent is relatively deprived, the less likely they are to be an organisational activist* (except when it comes to the respondent's evaluation of the outgroup's current condition, wherein the more they are relatively deprived, the more likely they are to be an organisational activist).

As for the individual relative deprivation (IRD) model, the first indicator, 'Personal Past', yields statistically insignificant results across both the IRD and the DRD models (second and third column of results). That is, it does not seem to matter whether respondents judge that their personal situation has improved or deteriorated when it comes to predicting their likelihood of being an organisational activist.

The second indicator, 'Personal Current Happiness', however, is statistically significant across both the IRD and DRD models. Respondents who declare being personally 'rather unhappy' or simply 'unhappy' with their life in the province of Quebec are less likely to be activists than other respondents by a factor of 0.522. The effect holds across both the IRD and DRD models. Out of two indicators, only one here is statistically significant. And, once again, the evidence runs counter to theoretical expectations.

Taken together, only one of the two IRD indicators is statistically significant, and its effects contradict expectations. Therefore, the evidence does not support H1b; it partly supports the reverse hypothesis. In other words, the more respondents are in a state of individual relative deprivation, the less likely they are to be organisational activists.

As for H1c, the Double RD model yields about the same results as the Group RD and Individual RD models. A total of four out of six indicators have a statistically significant effect at the $p < 0.001$ level. Yet, once again, these effects are contrary to theoretical expectations, except for the Outgroup Current indicator. H1c can thus safely be rejected, since evidence supports, for the most part, the reverse hypothesis.

Lastly, at least two observations are worth noting regarding results from the control variables. First, holding other variables constant, female respondents are consistently more likely than their male counterparts (about 2.7 to 3.2 times) to be organisational activists. This is statistically significant at the $p < 0.001$ level. Second, holding other variables constant, respondents living in suburban areas are consistently less likely to be organisational activists than their peers living in an urban area, with an odds ratio ranging from (0.65 to 0.72) to 1, significant at the $p < 0.01$ level.

Below, the ideal types method (Long and Freese 2014) is used to both substantiate the meaning of results and to examine the possible interactions between indicators and dimensions of the relative deprivation constructs used in the regression models. Ideal types are defined as 'hypothetical observation[s] with substantively illustrative values' (Long and Freese 2014, location 7614).

Six ideal types have been conceptualised along the lines of the hypotheses formulated in this chapter. Recalling that the general guiding hypothesis was that the higher the state of relative deprivation, the higher the likelihood of organisational activism, it should thus be expected that adding indicators of relative deprivation would yield predictions of higher likelihoods of activism (hence the ordering of ideal types #1 to #6 are gradually adding RD indicators). An exception is made for the outlier indicator (Current Outgroup) discovered in the logistic regression results presented above; it has been isolated in a separate ideal type, since it was shown to be the only one having an effect in the expected direction. Holding the four sociodemographic control variables at their means, Table 10.2 shows predictions made with regard to each ideal type constructed.

Ranking predictions from highest to lowest, what follows is a portrait of how ideal types of relative deprivation can predict organisational activism. An Anglo-Quebecer would be the most likely to be an activist (Ideal Type #1), with a likelihood of 63.3% (58.1–68.5%) when they feel that: their linguistic minority group's condition is currently average or better than average while the francophone majority's condition is better than average; their own group's condition has remained unchanged or improved over the last years while the francophone majority's has remained unchanged or deteriorated; they are either indifferent or happy with regard to their life in the province of Quebec while their personal situation has remained unchanged or improved over the last years. Ideal Type #6 has the lowest likelihood of being an organisational activist (15.1%, with a confidence interval of 12.0–18.3%). The latter type of respondent

**Table 10.2**  Predicted probabilities by ideal types of respondents and indicators, control variables held at their means

| Ideal types | Group relative deprivation (GRD) | | | | Individual relative deprivation (IRD) | | Predicted probabilities (95% C.I.) |
|---|---|---|---|---|---|---|---|
| | Current ingroup | Current outgroup | Past ingroup | Past outgroup | Current happiness | Personal past | |
| 1. ¬GRD*, ¬IRD | X | ✓ | X | X | X | X | 0.633 (0.581–0.685) |
| 2. ¬GRD, ¬IRD | X | X | X | X | X | X | 0.470 (0.410–0.530) |
| 3. ¬GRD, IRD | X | X | X | X | ✓ | ✓ | 0.375 (0.289–0.461) |
| 4. GRD, ¬IRD | ✓ | ✓ | ✓ | ✓ | X | X | 0.339 (0.293–0.384) |
| 5. GRD, IRD | ✓ | ✓ | ✓ | ✓ | ✓ | ✓ | 0.258 (0.224–0.291) |
| 6. GRD*, IRD | ✓ | X | ✓ | ✓ | ✓ | ✓ | 0.151 (0.120–0.183) |

Notes: (1) checkmarks (✓) denote the presence of a relative deprivation indicator, whereas 'X' marks denote its absence. (2) '¬' denotes 'no state of'. (3) 'GRD*' denotes the GRD model modified accordingly with the evidence laid out in the logistic regression table; in Ideal Type #1, it includes in Ideal Type #1 the 'current outgroup' indicator whereas in Ideal Type #6, it excludes the 'current outgroup' indicator

would be characterised by a set of symmetrically reversed set of dispositions.[15]

Two additional features of the table are worth noting. First, the ranking of ideal types is displaying more or less of a linear effect. That is, the more RD indicators are added, the lower the predictions. It should be reiterated that such results go against theoretical expectations. Second, only the following pairs of predictions have overlapping confidence intervals: ideal types 2 and 3, and ideal types 3 and 4. The predictions are thus statistically significant and, most importantly, substantially significant, since they range from 63% to 15%, a difference of nearly 50%. Overall, the predictions

---

[15] For the sake of space, this ideal type will not be described. The reader can infer its description using the indicators configured in Table 10.5 and the survey response categories provided in the Appendix A.

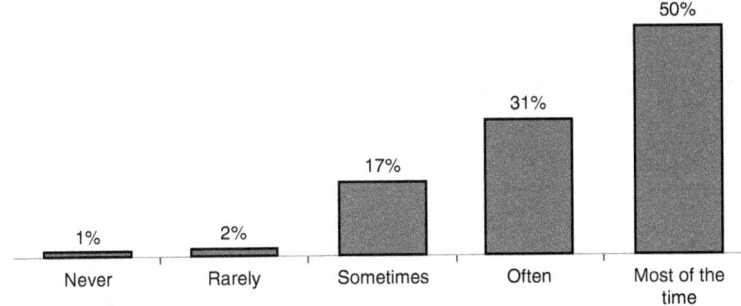

**Fig. 10.7** 'Do you think that the following groups [Anglophones in the province of Quebec] are facing discrimination in their respective province ...'

made using the ideal types method show a much clearer picture of the interactions between relative deprivation indicators.

Moving on to the next hypothesis, it should be reminded that expectations based on recent literature predict that *Anglo-Quebecers who perceive discrimination against their group are more likely to engage in organisational activism.* The underlying assumption here is that volunteering or working for Anglo-Quebecer organisations is a non-electoral type of political participation. Since Bilodeau (2017) found that visible minorities experiencing discrimination are more prone to engaging in the latter kind of activity, it seemed reasonable to conjecture that the same should apply to a linguistic minority.

Figure 10.7 provides some important initial descriptive statistics. Respondents from the Anglo-Quebecer sample leave no doubt that they believe their group is facing discrimination. Over half of respondents judge that it is the case 'most of the time'; about 31% say it happens 'often', and 17% 'sometimes'. Only about 3% of respondents declared that their group faces discrimination 'rarely' or 'never'.

To test whether there is any difference as to the likelihood of organisational activism according to levels of perceived discrimination, and given the skewness of the frequency distribution,[16] as shown in Fig. 10.7, the variable was recoded into three categories of answer representing three

---

[16] Too few observations in the 'never' and 'rarely' categories did not allow for the logistic regression to be computed; hence the need to regroup response categories.

**Table 10.3** Logistic regression: perceived discrimination predicting organisational activism among Anglo-Quebecer respondents

| Two levels of perceived discrimination | Odds ratio | 95% C.I. |
|---|---|---|
| *Discrimination levels* | | |
| Low (ref. category) | (.) | (.) |
| Moderate | 1.151 | (0.916–1.446) |
| High | 0.785* | (0.630–0.978) |
| *Control variables* | | |
| Age | 1.007 | (0.954–1.063) |
| Gender (Female) | 2.656*** | (2.185–3.228) |
| Education | 0.948 | (0.885–1.015) |
| LivArea= Urban area (ref. cat.) | (.) | (.) |
| LivArea= Suburban area | 0.685*** | (0.561–0.836) |
| LivArea= Rural area | 1.197 | (0.990–1.448) |
| Constant | 0.332*** | (0.214–0.515) |

$*p < 0.05$, $**p < 0.01$, $***p < 0.001$

Pseudo-$R^2$: 0.042

levels of perceived discrimination. Taking into account the distribution of respondents across the initial five categories of answer, the 'low' level category now includes all respondents (~20% of the sample) who chose either 'never', 'rarely', or 'sometimes'; the 'moderate' level includes respondents (31%) who answered 'often'; the 'high' level includes respondents (50% of the sample) who answered 'most of the time'. Table 10.3 shows results from the logistic regression for the perceived discrimination hypothesis.

Holding other variables at their means and using the low level of discrimination as a reference category, evidence shows that respondents who judge that their group experiences a high level of discrimination are significantly less likely to be organisational activists than respondents who perceive a low level of discrimination by a factor of 0.785, significant at the 0.05 level. To convey a better sense of the magnitude of the effect, Table 10.4 presents the marginal effects. Two different models regrouping the same variables into either two or three categories are shown.

Results displayed in the table above show that respondents who perceive that their group faces high levels of discrimination are between 7% to 10% less likely to be organisational activists than those who perceive low-moderate (see first column), low, or moderate (see second column) levels

**Table 10.4**   Marginal effect of perceived discrimination (control variables at their means)

| Two levels of perceived discrimination | Predicted probability (dichotomous) | 95% C.I. | Predicted probability (trichotomous) | 95% C.I. |
|---|---|---|---|---|
| Low-moderate | 0.372*** | 0.346–0.399 | | |
| High | 0.299*** | 0.274–0.323 | | |
| Low | | | 0.364*** | 0.321–0.408 |
| Moderate | | | 0.390*** | 0.357–0.424 |
| High | | | 0.295*** | 0.270–0.320 |

$*p < 0.05$, $**p < 0.01$, $***p < 0.001$

of discrimination for their group. This represents a small effect, but a nonetheless significant one, both statistically and substantively. It does not seem to make a difference whether the model operationalises perceived discrimination as a dichotomy or a trichotomy. Yet, the trichotomous model remains interesting, since it shows that the effect is not linear; those who perceive moderate levels of discrimination towards their group are more likely to be activists than those who perceive low levels of discrimination towards their group, although the confidence intervals overlap. With regards to the hypothesis, the evidence contradicts expectations. While it was conjectured that Anglo-Quebecers who judged that their group faces high levels of discrimination would be those most inclined to engage in organisational activities (i.e. a non-electoral type of political participation), results show that it is in fact the opposite case.

## DISCUSSION AND CONCLUSION

In undertaking the analysis of Anglo-Quebecer activism in light of relative deprivation theory and the notion of perceived discrimination, this case study has attempted to straddle the fence between theoretical advancement and idiographic research. Such an endeavour concurs with Noël's (2014) research stance, which stresses the importance of producing usable knowledge about one's own polity.

In the first decades of the development of relative deprivation theory, Guimond and Dubé-Simard (1983) found Group RD to be more important than Individual RD in explaining propensity to join protest movements. In light of the analysis conducted here, this finding can, to an extent, be replicated using the case of Anglo-Quebecer organisational activism. Indicators of group relative deprivation (what Guimond and Dubé-Simard termed 'fraternal' RD) performed better than indicators of individual relative deprivation (or 'egoistic' RD). Unexpectedly, however, the empirical evidence goes *against* traditional relative deprivation hypotheses based on the distinction between Individual and Group RD. In other words, the effect observed goes in the opposite direction to what was hypothesised; indicators used to measure relative deprivation across three different models showed that Anglo-Quebecer respondents were more likely to be activists when they were *not* in a state of relative deprivation.[17] Herein lies the first theoretical contribution of this chapter.

A second theoretical contribution consists of the findings about the relationship between perceived discrimination and organisational activism. Low levels of perceived discrimination were revealed to be better at predicting organisational activism than high levels.[18] While research has been done on the relationship between perceived discrimination and mobilisation among visible minorities in Quebec (Bilodeau 2017), this is the first

---

[17] An explanatory path to be further explored lies in the parameters of the research design. Indeed, the variable on the basis of which organisational activism was conceptualised here constitutes only a post hoc measurement of the transition between the demand-side and the supply-side of mobilisation. In plain language, this could mean that a state of relative deprivation might have led Anglo-Quebecer respondents to get involved in organisational activities *before* they could fill out the online survey questionnaire, and that, *from then on*, levels of relative deprivation may have decreased. The effect of relative deprivation might have been more salient if the analyst had collected data that captured the transitional period in the life of a politicised individual who makes the decision to take a step further in their engagement and get directly involved in organisational activism. A mechanism that might then decrease relative deprivation is that of self and group efficacy. Anglo-Quebecer organisational activists, for instance, may revise their opinions about the current state of their ingroup's condition after some time, to the extent that their direct political engagement is empowering them. This provides an interesting direction for future research.

[18] Closer inspection of the data revealed, however, that the effect is not linear. Hence the study conducted here highlights the need to take into account the multidimensionality of constructs. More specifically, (1) the logistic regression analysis conducted in this chapter and the models developed from the literature show the multidimensionality of abstract concepts such as 'relative deprivation', thus stressing the need to use multiple indicators in statistical hypothesis testing, and (2) the present application of Long and Freese's (2014) ideal types approach using predicted probabilities, such as in Table 10.5, shows that within-concept, single indicators, sometimes do not conform to assumptions of linearity implied in many dichotomous concepts of political science.

study to tackle the same issue by examining an official language minority in Quebec.[19]

This chapter provides a contribution as well with regard to empirical studies on Anglo-Quebecers. While the research design did not use a randomised sampling of the population—it would thus be premature to generalise to the whole population of the linguistic minority studied—it nonetheless provided additional evidence of the existence of a feeling of exclusion, if not alienation, among Quebec's Anglophone minority. The question remains open as to whether that sentiment is shared by a majority of the linguistic minority's population. The evidence provided in the pages above suggests that many Anglo-Quebecers may be concerned about the future of their communities and that many may even consider themselves to be 'second-class citizens'.

In the broader context of approaches for the management of diversity in multi-national, multicultural, and multiethnic democracies, such findings have important policy implications. If Quebec society is to foster policies tending towards the ideal of 'deep inclusion' rather than 'possible inclusion' or 'symbolic inclusion' (Karmis 2013), then proponents of interculturalism need to take linguistic diversity seriously. With the recent creation of the Secretariat for relations with English-speaking Quebecers, the Quebec government has taken a step towards greater recognition for the linguistic minority. But much remains to be done for all Anglophones to feel like full-fledged 'Québécois' and not 'second-class citizens' in a polity that prides itself on being the hub of the French fact in North America and, more specifically, in a context where relative deprivation does not necessarily lead to collective action and political engagement.

## Appendix A

The table below details how each variable in Table 10.5 has been operationalised as a dummy variable. In short, variables concerning the ingroup and the outgroup are scored with a value of '1' when respondents are located at the 'relatively deprived' end of the spectrum and with a value of '0' when they chose any of the three other categories of answer.

---

[19] Empirical indicators used, however, differ from those used by Bilodeau (2017).

**Table 10.5**    Operationalisation of the dummy variables for each model

| Dimensions | | Question label (dimension in italic) | Operationalisation of the dummy variables |
|---|---|---|---|
| Group relative deprivation | Ingroup RD | Ingroup Current (Q29_1): 'The current living conditions of *Anglophones in the province of Quebec* are …' | RD = 0 if 'Excellent', 'Above average' or 'Average' <br> RD = 1 if 'Below average' or 'Very poor' |
| | | Ingroup Past (Q33): 'Would you say that, in the last years, the general situation of *Anglophones in Quebec* has …' | RD = 0 if 'Improved', 'Somewhat improved' or 'Remained unchanged' <br> RD = 1 if 'Somewhat deteriorated' or 'Deteriorated' |
| | Outgroup RD | Outgroup Current (Q29_2): 'The current living conditions of *Francophones in the province of Quebec* are …' | RD = 0 if' or 'Average', 'Below average' or 'Very poor' <br> RD = 1 if 'Excellent' or 'Above average' |
| | | Outgroup Past (Q37): 'Would you say that, in the last years, the general situation of *Francophones in Quebec* has …' | RD = 0 if 'Remained unchanged', 'Somewhat deteriorated' or 'Deteriorated' <br> RD = 1 if 'Improved', 'Somewhat improved' |
| Individual RD | | Personal Past (Q34): 'Would you say that, in the last years, your personal situation has …' | RD = 0 if 'Improved', 'Somewhat improved' or 'Remained unchanged' <br> RD = 1 if 'somewhat deteriorated' or 'Deteriorated' |
| | | Personal current happiness (Q45): 'In general, would you say that you are personally …' | RD = 0 if 'Happy with your life in the province of Quebec', 'Rather happy with your life in the province of Quebec' or 'Neither happy nor unhappy with your life in the province of Quebec' <br> RD = 1 if 'Rather unhappy with your life in the province of Quebec' or 'Unhappy with your life in the province of Quebec' |

The double deprivation model simply includes all of the dimensions detailed in the table

## APPENDIX B: SURVEY QUESTIONS

| | |
|---|---|
| Group relative deprivation indicators | What is your opinion (or impression) regarding the following statements:<br>• The current living conditions of Anglophones in the province of Quebec are …<br>• The current living conditions of Francophones in the province of Quebec are …<br>Answers: excellent, above average, average, below average, very poor<br>Would you say that, in the last years, the general situation of Anglophones in Quebec has …<br>Answers: improved, somewhat improved, remained unchanged, somewhat deteriorated, deteriorated<br>Would you say that, in the last years, the general situation of Francophones in Quebec has …<br>Answers: improved, somewhat improved, remained unchanged, somewhat deteriorated, deteriorated |
| Individual relative deprivation indicators | Would you say that, in the last years, your personal situation has …<br>Answers: improved, somewhat improved, remained unchanged, somewhat deteriorated, deteriorated<br>In general, would you say that you are personally …<br>Answer: happy with your life in the province of Quebec, rather happy with your life in the province of Quebec, neither happy nor unhappy with your life in the province of Quebec, rather unhappy with your life in the province of Quebec, unhappy with your life in the province of Quebec |
| Perceived discrimination | Do you think that the following groups are facing discrimination in their respective province: Anglophones in the province of Quebec.<br>Answers: most of the time, often, sometimes, rarely, never |

## REFERENCES

Bernstein, Morty, and Faye Crosby. 1980. An Empirical Examination of Relative Deprivation Theory. *Journal of Experimental Social Psychology* 16: 442–456.

Bilodeau, Antoine. 2017. Mobilisation or Demobilisation? Perceived Discrimination and Political Engagement Among Visible Minorities in Quebec. *Political Science* 69 (2): 122–138.

Boissinot, Jacques. 2016. No Secretariat Of Anglophone Affairs: Couillard. *Montreal Gazette*, December 13. https://montrealgazette.com/news/quebec/no-secretariat-of-anglophone-affairs-couillard. Accessed July 24, 2019.

Bourdieu, P. 1997. *Language and Symbolic Power*. Cambridge, UK: Polity Press.

Brush, Stephen G. 1996. Dynamics of Theory Change in the Social Sciences. Relative Deprivation and Collective Violence. *Journal of Conflict Resolution* 40 (4): 523–545.

Buechler, Steven M. 2008. Social Strain, Structural Breakdown, Political Opportunity, and Collective Action. *Sociology Compass* 2 (3): 1031–1044.

Cardinal, Linda, and Martin Normand. 2011. Des accents distincts. Les régimes linguistiques ontarien et québécois. In *Les relations Quebec-Ontario. Un destin partagé?* ed. J.-F. Savard, A. Brassard, and L. Côté, 131–158. Quebec: Presses de l'Université du Quebec.

Cardinal, Linda, and Selma K. Sonntag. 2015. *State Traditions and Language Regimes*. Montreal and Kingston: McGill-Queen's University Press.

Corbeil, Jean-Pierre, Brigitte Chavez, and Daniel Peirera. 2010. *Portrait of Official-Language Minorities in Canada – Anglophones in Quebec*. Ottawa, ON: Statistics Canada.

Foster, Mindi D., and Kimberly Matheson. 1995. Double Relative Deprivation: Combining the Personal and Political. *Personality and Social Psychology Bulletin* 21 (11): 1167–1177.

Gaskell, George, and Patten Smith. 1984. Relative Deprivation in Black and White Youth: An Empirical Investigation. *British Journal of Social Psychology* 23: 121–131.

Guimond, Serge, and Lise Dubé-Simard. 1983. Relative Deprivation Theory and the Quebec Nationalist Movement: The Cognition-Emotion Distinction and the Personal-Group Deprivation Issue. *Journal of Personality and Social Psychology* 44 (3): 526–535.

Gurney, Joan, and Kathleen Tierney. 1982. Relative Deprivation and Social Movements: A Critical Look at Twenty Years of Theory and Research. *The Sociological Quarterly* 23: 33–47.

Kam, Cindy D., Elizabeth J. Zechmeister, and Jennifer R. Wilking. 2008. From the Gap to the Chasm. Gender and Participation among Non-Hispanic Whites and Mexican Americans. *Political Research Quarterly* 61 (2): 205–218.

Karmis, Dimitrios. 2013. Pluralism and National Identity(ies) in Contemporary Quebec: Conceptual Clarifications, Typology, and Discourse Analysis. In *Quebec: State and Society*, ed. Alain-G. Gagnon, 3rd ed., 69–96. Peterborough: Broadview Press.

Laponce, Jean. 2006. *Loi de Babel et autres régularités des rapports entre langue et politique*. Quebec: Presses de l'Université Laval.

Leach, Colin Wayne, Aarti Iyer, and Anne Pedersen. 2007. Angry Opposition to Government Redress: When the Structurally Advantaged Perceive Themselves as Relatively Deprived. *British Journal of Social Psychology* 46: 191–204.

Leclerc, Jacques. 2017. «L'inégalité des langues. (website). http://www.axl.cefan.ulaval.ca/Langues/1div_inegalite.htm. Accessed November 9, 2018.

Long, J. Scott, and Jeremy Freese. 2014. *Regression Models for Categorical Dependent Variables Using Stata*. Kindle ed.. College Station, TX: Stata Press.

Michelson, Melissa R. 2003. The Corrosive Effect of Acculturation: How Mexican Americans Lose Political Trust. *Social Science Quarterly* 84 (4): 918–933.

Noël, Alain. 2014. Studying Your Own Country: Social Scientific Knowledge for Our Times and Places. *Canadian Journal of Political Science* 47 (4): 647–666.

Olson, James M., and J. Douglas Hazlewood. 1986 [2014]. Relative Deprivation and Social Comparison: An Integrative Perspective. In *Relative Deprivation and Social Comparison*, ed. M. James, C. Peter Herman Olson, and Mark P. Zanna. New York: Psychology Press.

Ono, Hirmomi. 2002. Assimilation, Ethnic Competition, and Ethnic Identities of U.S.-Born Persons of Mexican Origin. *International Migration Review* 21 (2): 352–371.

Page, Julia. 2017. Kathleen Weil's Task Is to Mend Disconnect Between Government and Anglo Communities. CBC News. https://www.cbc.ca/news/canada/montreal/kathleen-weil-new-minister-english-relations-1.4349371. Accessed July 24, 2019.

Pettigrew, Thomas F. 2015. Samuel Stouffer and Relative Deprivation. *Social Psychology Quarterly* 78 (1): 7–24.

Pettigrew, Thomas F., Oliver Christ, Ulrich Wagner, Roel W. Meertens, Rolf van Dick, and Andreas Zick. 2008. Relative Deprivation and Intergroup Prejudice. *Journal of Social Issues* 64 (2): 385–401.

Quebec Votes 2018: English Debate. CBC News. https://www.youtube.com/watch?v=6AmiPzP0U0E. Accessed July 24, 2019.

Runciman, Walter G. 1966. *Relative Deprivation and Social Justice*. London: Routledge and Kegan Paul.

Schildkraut, Deborah J. 2005. The Rise and Fall of Political Engagement Among Latinos: The Role of Identity and Perceptions of Discrimination. *Political Behavior* 27 (3): 285–312.

Smith, Heather J., and Yuen J. Huo. 2014. Relative Deprivation: How Subjective Experiences of Inequality Influence Social Behavior and Health. *Policy Insights from the Behavioral and Brain Sciences* 1 (1): 231–238.

Smith, Thomas J., and Cornelius McKenna. 2013. A Comparison of Logistic Regression Pseudo $R^2$ Indices. *Multiple Linear Regression Viewpoints* 39 (2): 17–26.

Smith, Heather J., Thomas F. Pettigrew, Gina M. Pippin, and Silvana Bialosiewicz. 2012. Relative Deprivation: A Theoretical and Meta-Analytic Review. *Personality and Social Psychology Review* 16 (3): 203–232.

Snyder, David, and Charles Tilly. 1972. Hardship and Collective Violence in France, 1830 to 1960. *American Sociological Review* 37 (5): 520–532.

Statistics Canada. 2017a. English, French and Official Language Minorities in Canada (website). https://www12.statcan.gc.ca/census-recensement/2016/

as-sa/98-200-x/2016011/98-200-x2016011-eng.cfm. Accessed October 12, 2018.

———. 2017b. Montréal [Census Metropolitan Area], Quebec and Quebec [Province] (table). Census Profile. https://www12.statcan.gc.ca/census-recensement/2016/dp-pd/prof/details/page.cfm?Lang=E&Geo1=CMACA&Code1=462&Geo2=PR&Code2=24&Data=Count&SearchText=Montreal&SearchType=Begins&SearchPR=01&B1=Language&TABID=1. Accessed May 28, 2019.

Stouffer, Samuel A. 1962. *Social Research to Test Ideas: Selected Writings of Samuel A. Stouffer.* New York: Free Press.

Stouffer, Samuel A., Edward A. Suchman, Leland C. DeVinney, Shirley A. Starr, and Robin M. Williams. 1949a. *The American Soldier: Adjustment to Army Life. Vol. 1.* Princeton, NJ: Princeton University.

Stouffer, Samuel A., Arthur A. Lumsdaine, Marion Harper Lumsdaine, Robin M. Williams Jr., M. Brewster Smith, Irving L. Janis, Shirley Star, and Leonard S. Cottrell Jr. 1949b. *The American Soldier: Combat and Its Aftermath. Vol. II.* Princeton, NJ: Princeton University Press.

Thompson, J.L.P. 1989. Deprivation and Political Violence in Northern Ireland, 1922–1985: A Time Series Analysis. *Journal of Conflict Resolution* 33: 676–699.

Vandycke, Robert. 1994. Le statut de minorité en sociologie du droit. Avec quelques considérations sur le cas québécois. *Sociologie et sociétés* 26 (1): 87–97.

Walker, Lain, and Leon Mann. 1987. Unemployment, Relative Deprivation, and Social Protest. *Personality and Social Psychology Bulletin* 13 (2): 275–283.

## CHAPTER 11

# Internal Migration, Ethnic Federalism and Differentiated Citizenship in an African Federation: The Case of Ethiopia

*Yonatan T. Fessha and Beza Dessalegn*

## INTRODUCTION

Ethiopia is a federal polity that champions the recognition of ethnic diversity in a way that few other multiethnic and multinational federations do. The constitutional dispensation that it adopted more than two decades ago guarantees ethnic groups a wide range of self-rule rights, including in 'homelands' in which they form a majority. This has resulted in the establishment of a federation that is composed of ethnically delineated states and local government areas. However, over the last two decades, tensions have arisen between ethnic communities that are newly empowered and individuals that are not members of those communities.

Y. T. Fessha (✉)
University of the Western Cape, Cape Town, South Africa

B. Dessalegn
Hawassa University, Hawassa, Ethiopia

Postdoctoral Fellow, University of the Western Cape, Cape Town, South Africa

© The Author(s) 2020
A.-G. Gagnon, A. Tremblay (eds.), *Federalism and National Diversity in the 21st Century*, Federalism and Internal Conflicts,
https://doi.org/10.1007/978-3-030-38419-7_11

On the one hand, self-governing ethnic communities have limited or attempted to limit the right of individuals in order to protect their newly found demographic and political supremacy from those they consider as non-indigenes or internal migrants.[1] On the other hand, individuals who do not belong to the empowered ethnic communities are demanding respect for their constitutionally guaranteed citizenship rights, including the right to live and work in any part of the country and participate in the political decision-making process and institutions of the state in which they reside (FDRE Const Art. 39(3)). After all, those who happen to find themselves outside their 'designated ethnic territories' are still Ethiopians, whose fundamental rights and freedoms, according to the Constitution, must be respected irrespective of their place of residence. On a number of occasions, these tensions have led to disturbing developments including forced expulsions (which, at times, give the impression of being sponsored by state and local government authorities themselves).

This chapter analyses the tension between internal migration and the self-rule rights of ethnic communities in Ethiopia. The analysis proceeds as follows. First, it describes the plight of internal migrants. It then examines whether the distinction between indigenes and non-indigenes has a basis in the constitution and laws of the country. Subsequently the chapter explores whether this distinction is accompanied by laws and policies that engage in differentiated citizenship. This is followed by an examination of the efforts (if any) made by the House of Federation (HoF) to reconcile the potential impacts of differentiated citizenship—underscored by the legitimate fears of indigenous communities with the need to respect the fundamental rights of individuals. The chapter concludes by providing brief remarks on possible ways to resolve tensions between newly empowered ethnic communities and internal migrants. In brief, this chapter argues that, within the context of multiethnic (and multinational) federations, differentiated citizenship is necessary but insufficient to deal with the challenges of ethnic diversity. It must be complemented in such a way as to ensure that the protection and empowerment of ethnic communities does not unreasonably restrict the rights of individuals who do not belong to the empowered group.

---

[1] Internal migrants refer to individuals that do not belong to the groups that are 'indigenous' to the area they inhabit and are regarded as non-indigenes. These are individuals who have migrated to the state because of work, education or other related reasons. Indigenous communities are those ethnic communities that regard themselves or are regarded by law as communities that have historically inhabited the area and trace their 'ancestral roots' to the area in which they now reside.

## THE TENSION

It would be fair to expect that, in a country like Ethiopia, internal migration would not provoke the same reaction across the component units of the federation. The expectation might be that states that are home to an ethnic group that is numerically dominant would be less likely to be affected by migration and, hence, less worried about internal migration altering the dynamics of political dominance. By contrast, states where the population's ethno-cultural make-up is more likely to be influenced by internal migration might presumably be subject to more serious political worries. As the following paragraphs confirm, however, reality defies these expectations; the treatment of individuals who do not belong to the group that is empowered at subnational level is relatively similar across subnational units.

To wit, the case of the state of Benshangul Gumuz (hereafter the state of BG). Based on a 2007 population census, the so-called indigenous communities together account for 57.46% of the population of the state, while those that are not regarded as indigenes account for 42.54% of the population (FDRE Population Census Commission 2007). A significant section of the non-indigenes found themselves in what is today known as the state of BG as a result of state-sponsored (and at times forced) population transfers to the area, undertaken long before the introduction of federalism (Yntiso 2004). Yet land hungry migrants and farmers from other parts of the country have continued to settle in the state in search of a better life. This has been further facilitated by the construction of the Grand Ethiopian Renaissance Dam on the Nile River and the large-scale agricultural investments that have continued to attract a huge number of individuals from other parts of the country (Wuilbercq 2014). And, as is usually the case, those who come as migrant workers rarely return to their place of origin and tend to settle in the area permanently.

The continued and increasing internal migration to the state of BG, in particular from the states of Amhara and Oromia, has created serious anxiety among people that belong to the indigenous communities (Vaughan 2006, 17). Not only do they fear that their slim combined numerical majority will be reversed leading to the loss of their political dominance, but they are also wary of the economic burdens that such internal migration brings to the state (Vaughan 2006, 17; Kefale 2009, 172). Concerned with the increasing migration to the state and the resulting demographic changes, some have actively sought to limit the role of the 'others' within the state (Kefale 2009, 177).

Political parties that claim to represent indigenous communities in the state have been contesting elections on the promise that, once elected, they will ensure that the state is exclusively represented by members of the indigenous communities (Kefale 2009, 173). Some of the opposition parties in the state argue strongly that non-indigenous communities should leave the territory. They also reject the decision of the state to use Amharic, the federal working language, as the working language of the state government. For instance, Benshangul Peoples Liberation Movement (BPLM), an opposition party, campaigns for the introduction of Arabic as the official language of the state, whereas another opposition party, the Gumuz Peoples Liberation Movement (GPLM), campaigns for Gumuz to be the official language (Dessalegn 2016, 197–198). Although the ruling party of the state has not openly associated itself with such nativist positions, it has implemented a policy of preferential treatment that favour indigenes over other inhabitants in areas of employment and educational opportunities (Assefa 2014, 138).

In some cases, members of the ruling party have been complicit or have turned a blind eye to forced mass eviction of non-indigenes. Things came to a head in 2013 when the state government took the unprecedented step of evicting, *en masse*, non-indigenes (mainly ethnic Amhara) from one of the local districts (Yoseph 2013a). Reports indicate that not all non-indigenes were affected by the eviction; individuals that moved to the area as a result of the previous regime's resettlement policy were not affected. The eviction reportedly targeted those that moved to the area relatively recently, likely after the introduction of the federal arrangement in 1991. Apparently, the eviction has not discouraged migration to the state, as '[even] after the most controversial and publicized [sic] eviction that took place in 2013, 20 [trucks carrying] illegal migrants were sent back to where they came from and yet immediately after that another 50 [trucks] of illegal migrants entered the state' (quoted in Yoseph 2013b).

State authorities argued that the non-indigenes were evicted not because of their ethnic identity but because they undermined the ecological balance of the state by clearing forests for the purpose of settlement and establishing farmland (Yoseph 2013b). According to these authorities, only those migrants were sent back to their 'original places of residence' (Dessalegn 2016, 164). They furthermore insist that the state recognises the right of individuals to freedom of movement and the right to acquire land as long as it is done in accordance with the law regulating land administration and legal internal migrants are not affected (Dessalegn

2016, 164). By contrast, those evicted maintained that their eviction was based on indigeneity and that it was orchestrated by the district officials and police force with the excuse of protecting natural resources (Dessalegn 2016, 164). Even if one agrees with the state authorities that the actions of clearing forests could be in violation of a law, it is quite unclear how a citizen moving from one state to another can be regarded as an illegal immigrant who can be subjected to forced eviction.

The situation is similar in the Southern Nations Nationalities and Peoples Regional State (SNNPR). The state is home to no less than 56 ethnic groups that are divided into roughly 18 ethnicity-based local governments. Thirteen of these local governments were established for and named after a particular ethnic group, while the other five local governments are shared among the remaining ethnic groups. The SNNPR is also home to a sizeable population of non-indigenes. Reportedly, more than 600,000 individuals that belong to the Amhara and Oromo ethnic groups reside in the SNNPR. Like their counterparts in the state of BG, some of them were also subjected to forced eviction.

In 2012, many ethnic Amhara who moved to Guraferda, a local government area in the SNNPR, in search of farming plots were forcefully expelled and left to return to their kin state (i.e., the state of Amhara) (Negash 2012). Although the state government insisted that its decision to remove the settlers was motivated by environmental and conservation-related concerns for the area's forests, those that were subjected to forced expulsion insisted that the actions of the state government were ethnically motivated (Petition to the HoF, March 9, 2009). The actions of the state authorities have not, however, discouraged others from migrating to the state. In fact, due to the establishment of an industrial zone and other projects, individuals from other parts of the country have continued to migrate to the state looking for job opportunities (Woldemariam and Gebresenbet 2014).[2]

The situation in the SNNPR is compounded by the fact that the politics of indigeneity do not only prey on those that hail from outside the state but also affect those that regard the state as their homeland. As noted earlier, the state, home to numerous ethnic groups, is territorially organised into a number of local governments that are more or less ethnically defined. Members of ethnic communities that are given their own local

---

[2] The Hawassa City Industrial Park and the Omo-Kuraz Sugar Development Project have recently attracted thousands of migrant workers to the state.

government consider those that do not belong to their group as non-indigenes despite the fact that they hail from the same state (Fessha 2017). The latter, as a result, have been subjected to forced expulsions and displacements. The recent forced expulsions of individuals from the ethnically defined local government areas of Sidama, Wolayita and Gurage are an indication that what is at stake in the SNNPR is not only inter-state mobility but also intra-state mobility (Borkena 2018; Davidson 2018). It has been reported (Brook 2018a, b) that more than a dozen individuals were killed in the successive violence that broke out in Hawassa, Wolkite and Wolaita Sodo towns, the respective capitals of Sidama, Gurage and Wolayita local government areas (all located in the SNNPR). The targets of the violence were individuals who did not belong to local communities.

One might expect that the concerns that the so-called indigenous communities raise in the state of BG and to some extent in the SNNPR are not shared by those that regard themselves as the 'owners' of Oromia, the largest state in the federation. More than two-thirds of the populations of the state of Oromia belong to a single ethnic group, the Oromo. This may lead one to conclude that this is not a state that would feel threatened by internal migration and, as a result, one might expect less discrimination and eviction of communities on the basis of indigeneity. And yet, this is a state in which a series of evictions of individuals regarded as outsiders has taken place. This goes as far back as the early days of the federation, when individuals were subjected to human rights violation on the basis of indigeneity, in particular those that belong to the Amhara ethnic group (Abbink 2006, 389). More often than not, these violations have been reportedly accompanied by expulsions, often with the complicity of local authorities (Abbink 2011, 604). At the height of anti-government protests in Oromia, non-indigenous communities were repeatedly threatened with expulsions and, in some instances, forced to return to their 'place of origin' (Human Rights Council 2016).

The examples presented above defy the expectation that states that are overwhelmingly dominated by one particular ethnic group will feel less threatened by the presence and migration of individuals that do not belong to the group. Insofar as the treatment of internal migrants is concerned, states dominated by one particular ethnic group have proven to be just as unfriendly as states where ethnic minorities only maintain a slim majority and, as a result, face a real threat of numerical domination by internal migrants. Consequently, the politics of indigeneity are increasingly dominating the political wrangling that characterises the component units of the federation, irrespective of their demographic composition and ethnic balance, and this has commonly manifested itself in the form of evictions of those that are considered as 'outsiders'.

The forced displacement of communities gained momentum after the nation-wide anti-government protests that started to rock the country in 2015. It is also then that the country witnessed the expulsion of Tigrayans from parts of the state of Amhara as well as Wolayitas and Amharas from the state of Oromia (Lavers 2018). Forced expulsion of individuals on the basis of identity has become such a common occurrence that it was one of the key issues that Prime Minister Abiy Ahmed, during his swearing-in ceremony, pledged to address, declaring that his government would work with great resolve to guarantee the free and peaceful movement of citizens. Yet forced displacements have continued unabated even after the election of a new prime minister and the introduction of political reforms in April 2018. In fact, the situation has deteriorated so much that Ethiopia has become the country with the highest number of internally displaced people (UNICEF 2019). By June 2018, close to a million people were displaced as a result of the Gedeo-Guji conflict in the state of Oromia (Obulutsa 2018). At the centre of these expulsions and human rights violations is the distinction made between individuals on the basis of indigeneity; the following section examines whether this widely prevalent distinction has its basis in law or practice.

## The Basis for the Politics of Indigeneity: Law and Practice

Ethnicity is the principal, if not the sole, basis for the political and administrative organisation of the federation. This was made clear by the transitional government that was set up after the fall of the military government in 1991 and that adopted Proclamation 7/1992, creating 14 regions (Art 3(1)). Although the proclamation gave the regions a numerical designation (Region 1 to Region 14), it clearly indicated for which ethnic group a particular region was created (Proclamation 7/1992 Art 3(1)).[3] In circumstances where the proclamation recognised a region as a home to more than one ethnic group, it even indicated which ethnic group(s)

---

[3] The only exception was region 14 (the federal capital of Addis Ababa), which was not associated with a particular ethnic group—though the Oromo, the largest ethnic group in the country, are given special rights over the capital.

enjoy(s) political supremacy (Proclamation 7/1992 Art 3(2) (a)). This is despite the evident ethnic heterogeneity that characterises all regions. It is probable that this marked the beginning of the division of the population of the component units of the federation into owners and guests.

In what can be described as a continuation, the federal constitution that was adopted in 1995 maintained the ethnic framework of the federation even if it reduced the number of subnational units from 14 to 9. The decision in the constitution to name at least six of the nine states after the name of a particular ethnic group, thereby associating each of these states with a particular group, is one important indication of the intentions of the constitution's authors to continue to legitimise the dichotomy of owners and guests. The two exceptions are the SNNPR and Gambella. Yet the local governments that constitute these two states are, by and large, named after particular ethnic groups.

The dichotomisation is further codified by some of the state constitutions that have explicitly entrenched the same distinction. For instance, two states (Benshangul Gumuz and Gambella) have used their respective constitutions to explicitly identify particular ethnic groups and recognise them as indigenous to the area, thereby classifying the remaining residents as non-indigenes (Benshangul Gumuz Constitution Art 2; Gambella Constitution Art 46)). The states whose constitutions do not explicitly categorise their residents into indigenous and non-indigenous, like the states of Amhara, Tigray, Somali, Afar, Harari and Oromia, nevertheless recognise the dichotomy. This is evidenced by the designations of the states and by the fact that the respective constitutions of these states vest sovereignty in the dominant (indigenous) ethnic group and not in the people of the states (Van der Beken 2012, 246–247). The constitutions of the states of Oromia, Afar, Somali, Harari and Tigray vest the power of sovereignty solely in the dominant (otherwise indigenous) ethnic group.[4] It must be noted that the constitution solely empowers groups that are considered indigenous even when those regarded as outsiders (non-indigenes) have demographic superiority and territorial concentration. The end result is a federation that has separated its citizens into indigenous and non-indigenous, guests and owners (Fessha 2018), natives and non-natives.

---

[4] By contrast, the constitution of the state of Amhara vests sovereignty in the people of the Amhara state rather than the dominant ethnic group, namely the Amhara.

## Differentiated Citizenship?

Distinct from national citizenship, subnational citizenship is understood to refer to the status of membership to a political community, an ethnonational group or a self-governing community. It is distinguished from nationality, which signifies an individual's relationship (internal and external) with a sovereign state. Benefits from subnational citizenship strictly depend on membership to a designated group (Bauböck 2006, 16–17). Depending on the interest they seek to protect, a federation might justify the introduction of differentiated citizenship based on different reasons. Generally speaking, however, the three main aims of subnational citizenship in multiethnic federations are protection of subnational identities, allocation of local natural resources and access to their utilisation on a preferential basis and putting restrictions on the internal migration of citizens (Sadiq 2009, 11–12).

One federation in Africa that has adopted differentiated citizenship, albeit implicitly, is Nigeria, where there is no formal subnational citizenship but states are allowed to favour their members over others (Ejobowah 2013). In Nigeria, the constitutionally entrenched 'federal character principle' requires that the president appoint at least one minister from each state—each which must be an indigene of the state (Bello 2012). Although the constitution does not explicitly mandate the use of the principle of indigeneity in the organisation and functioning of state and local governments, two sets of citizenship are at least evident in today's Nigeria as a result of the application of the indigeneity principle at the local level (Fessha 2018, 61). While the constitution and nationality laws determine citizenship at the national level, subnational citizenship is determined on the basis of an individual's ability to trace membership to a local government area through one's ancestors. Indigeneity, in other words, is the basis for subnational citizenship. Local governments regularly issue 'certificates of indigeneity', which serve as legitimate proof of membership to a local government area (Fourchard 2015). These certificates are highly sought after and valued as the status of indigeneity comes with a range of benefits. For instance, it leads to exclusive access or priority for members of a particular group when it comes to employment and educational opportunities (Suberu 2010, 459). Non-indigenes are refused employment in civil services and are charged higher fees at state-owned universities (Fessha 2018, 61). In most circumstances, non-indigenes, despite being able to vote, are also not entitled to run for or hold elected office (Fessha 2018, 61; Suberu 2010, 465–466).

One African country that has explicitly recognised differentiated citizenship is the Union of Tanzania, comprising mainland Tanzania and Zanzibar. In the autonomous territory of Zanzibar, 'special rights' are accorded to subnational citizens known as 'Zanzibari'. The constitution of Tanzania, when conferring rights, distinguishes between, everyone, citizens and Zanzibari. The Zanzibari are given preferential rights with respect to the right to vote, the right to political participation, the right to work and appointment to important public offices in the territory of Zanzibar (Suksi 2011, 210–212). The right to subnational citizenship is determined based on a separate law known as the Zanzibari Act (Suksi 2011, 211). This law also provides the basis by which newcomers can become Zanzibari through naturalisation. The two most important requirements for becoming Zanzibari are that the applicant must have resided in Zanzibar for a consecutive period of 15 years with the intention of continuing to reside and must demonstrate adequate ability to read and to write Kiswahili (Suksi 2011, 211–212). Furthermore, with the view to combat or discourage internal migration from mainland Tanzania, the Land Tenure Act has attached one's prospective access to land to being a Zanzibari (Suksi 2011, 213).

In the case of Ethiopia, there may not be explicit laws that directly forbid individuals who do not belong to a locally empowered group from permanently settling, buying land or holding local government jobs. At first glance, the constitutions and laws of the states do not appear to engage in differentiated treatment. There is, however, enough evidence to indicate that the states engage in practices that favour their members over others in many areas of public life. This is the case, for example, in terms of holding public office and political representation. There are also differentiated treatments in terms of securing local government employment, education scholarships and land.

The electoral law, for example, does not seem to discourage the free movement of citizens. The residency requirement with respect the right to vote is not particularly stringent. Any person who has been residing within an electoral constituency for at least six months has the right to vote in general or local elections (Proclamation 532/2007 Art 33(1)(c)). One may be tempted to argue that this less stringent requirement allows those that migrate from other parts of the country to easily influence the political dynamics of ethnically defined states and local administrations in their favour and to do so within a very short period of time. Undoubtedly, this would pose a threat to the political empowerment of indigenous communities. It is this kind of concern that perhaps explains the decision of some political parties in the state of BG to call for the limitations on the right of non-indigenes to stand for political office (Dessalegn 2016, 197–198).

There are a number of factors that are used to limit the right of non-indigenes to hold public office. For one, there is the strict language proficiency requirement that the electoral law requires in order to stand for public office. A candidate must be competent enough to converse in the working language of the state in order to stand for political offices (Soboka 2008, 94). In the states that have picked the language of the dominant ethnic group as the working language of the state government, this means that many non-indigenes are excluded from contesting political office (Dessalegn 2018, 9). Second, electoral districts are drawn in some of the states in a manner that divides non-indigenous communities into several constituencies (Dessalegn 2018, 11–16). In a country that uses the first-past-the-post electoral system, this means that non-indigenes are not properly represented. Third and, more importantly, is the political practice of the ruling party fielding candidates that belong only to indigenous groups, even in areas where non-indigenes are found in huge numbers. This has resulted in a situation where individuals that belong to indigenous communities continue to dominate the political process even when they are not numerically dominant (see Kefale 2009, 176).

Traces of differentiated treatment can also be noticed in the areas of employment in the states that use the language of the dominant ethnic group as the language in which government affairs are conducted. The constitution allows each state to determine its own language policy. This has largely resulted in monolingualism where the language of the numerically dominant ethnic group is used as the language of state government (Fessha 2009). This is particularly the case in the relatively more ethnically homogenous states of Amhara, Tigray, Oromia, Somali and Afar. The relatively more ethnically diverse states of Gambella, Benshangul Gumuz and the SNNPR are also multilingual as they have adopted Amharic as the language of work. It is only the state of Harari that has adopted two languages as working languages of the state.

State governments require employees to be competent in the working language of the state. There are states like Tigray whose constitution provides that jobs which by their nature do not require language proficiency can be taken up by those who are not proficient in the working language of the state (Tigray Constitution Art 33). That situation, however, is the exception rather than the rule. In almost all other states, strict language proficiency requirements are in place to determine employment in the state civil service. Even in states like the SNNPR that adopted the federal working language as the working language of the state, a local language proficiency requirement is in place if one wants to work in local government offices (SNNPR Constitution Article 33).

The mandatory requirement of language proficiency on its own, however, would not normally be considered as a factor that entrenches differentiated citizenship as long the state governments allow the employment of individuals that are proficient in the language of the state government irrespective of the ethnic group they belong to. The problem is that reports indicate that language policy has been used by state governments to unfairly marginalise non-indigenes from working in the offices of state governments even in circumstances when they are clearly conversant in the working language of the state (Assefa 2014, 138). This denies many who do not belong to the locally empowered group the opportunity to be an equal part of the local community without undermining the community's rights. The practice of the language policy of state governments, as it is now, ends up facilitating differentiated citizenship.

Another area where traces of differentiated citizenship can be found is access to and utilisation of land. In an agrarian society like Ethiopia, the value of access to land cannot be overstated. In fact, the lack of access to adequate farming plots is one of the major driving forces behind internal migration (Van der Beken 2012, 252; Vaughan 2006, 11). For instance, the hugely uninhabited and fertile soil of the BG region is a major reason why the area attracts rural migrants from the states of Amhara and Oromia. The constitution vests the right of ownership of land with the nations, nationalities and peoples of Ethiopia (i.e., ethnic groups) (FDRE Const Art 40(3)). Precisely because of that, some argue that an individual has to be a member of an ethnic group to access and use land (Behailu 2015, 30; Ambaye 2012). According to this understanding, access to land is not a right extended to all as citizens but only to individuals who can trace membership to the ethnic group that inhabit the area; this may not, however, be a definitive interpretation of the position of the constitution on land rights.

The land policy of the Ethiopian federation is largely based on the model of state ownership that gives citizens equal land rights. The Rural Lands Administration and Use Proclamation 456/2005 authorises free access to rural lands for all residents who intend to engage in farming activities and makes no mention of ethnicity (Art 5). Individuals who are not indigenous to the area have equal rights to land as those that are indigenous. The problem, however, is that ethnic federalism is often interpreted to suggest the prioritisation of 'the land rights of "indigenous" inhabitants and that "ethnic outsiders have a weaker claim to land than indigenous inhabitants"' (Lavers 2018, 469). Studies have confirmed that the territorial rationale of ethnic federalism, which seems to suggest that access to land requires membership to an ethnic group that is indigenous to the area, underlies the practice of forced expulsion of non-indigenes from their framing plots—at times sponsored by local authorities (Ambaye 2015; Lavers 2018). As noted by Lavers (2018, 481), 'the territorial implications of ethnic federalism provided a rationale for the displacement of an ethnic minority in response to growing resource shortages' and 'state agencies promoted the eviction of non-indigenous minorities, facilitating their return to their "home" region' (481). In short, the federal dispensation has given communities and authorities the basis to claim that citizens do not have equal access right to land, especially in circumstances where they live outside of their ethnic homelands.

## Balancing Differentiated Citizenship with the Right of the Individual

It is possible that differentiated citizenship serves to quell the anxiety of native communities becoming outsiders in an area they consider their homeland. It might also allow communities to protect their interests by making it possible for them to exercise control over resources and have a greater say in matters that affect them. Yet, as much as it can be a 'source of unity and stability in a multinational democracy' (Ejobowah 2013, 731; Gagnon and Tully 2001), a differentiated citizenship regime also has the tendency to solidify and institutionalise differences. Under such circumstances, the relationship between indigenes and non-indigenes increasingly becomes competitive and, in worst-case scenarios, may turn violent (Ejobowah 2013, 733). More specifically, there is a risk that aspects of differentiated citizenship may amount to unreasonable restrictions on individual rights. Any restriction influenced by a law based on differentiated citizenship must, therefore, find a decent balance between the right of indigenous communities to self-government and the right of individuals, including non-indigenes, to enjoy reasonable mobility rights with sufficient guarantees that they, as citizens, have the right to make a living in any part of their country. Maintaining that balance constitutes a major challenge.

In this regard, the House of Federation (HoF), the body that is tasked with the duty of interpreting the Constitution and resolving constitutional disputes, could play a role in identifying parameters within which state governments can engage in legitimate differentiated citizenship.[5] However, it is very difficult to claim that the HoF has made use of the opportunities that presented themselves to deal with the tension between individual rights and the right to self-rule. One such opportunity had to do with the state of BG. The case involved a claim by a group of non-indigenes that an electoral law that made proficiency in the language of the state a condition for standing as a candidate for public office violated their constitutional right to be elected (Decision of the HoF 2008, 15–34). At the centre of the case is the tension between an individual right to stand as a candidate and the right of ethnic communities to self-rule.

In its decision, the HoF declared that the constitution mandates the equal enforcement of both individual and group rights and that both rights can be implemented in a mutually inclusive way. According to the House of Federation, there is no need for a trade-off (Decision of the HoF 2008, 25–34). Yet, in determining whether language proficiency is a legitimate restriction on the right to be elected, the HoF did not deal with the tension between individual rights and the rights of communities to self-determination. It resolved the matter based on pragmatic or functional grounds and validated the law that requires proficiency in the working language of the state as a condition to stand for election. It argued that effective representation of the electorate requires the candidate to be proficient in the language of the state parliament. The decision of the HoF to solve the case on pragmatic grounds means that the decision contributes little to the jurisprudence on differentiated citizenship and, more specifically, on how the two sets of rights can be reconciled.[6] But it has the effect

[5] It must be noted that the Ethiopian constitution excludes courts from interpreting the constitution and adjudicating constitutional disputes. That power is given to the House of Federation. Of course, courts should have been utilised as legitimate checks against subnational authorities that orchestrated or played a role in mass evictions and unlawful restrictions on freedom of movement. However, the record of Ethiopian courts in the enforcement of fundamental rights and freedoms is not encouraging. They have done little or nothing in protecting victims of forced expulsion, whose properties have been illegally confiscated, looted or destroyed (The World Bank 2004).

[6] The Council of Constitutional Inquiry (CCI), which advises the HoF on constitutional interpretation issues, suggested by a majority vote that the language proficiency requirement be scrapped in the Benishangul Gumuz case, arguing that taking language as a requirement to stand for political candidature violates Article 38 of the FDRE constitution. However, the

of denying representation to the millions of ethnic migrants who reside in the states that use the language of the dominant ethnic group as the working language of the state government and who often are not proficient in the working language of those states.[7]

## Conclusion: Towards an Equilibrium

The Ethiopian constitution empowers communities that were marginalised in the past. In doing so, however, it has relegated individuals that do not belong to the newly empowered groups to second class citizens. The federation is struggling to keep the promises of equal citizenship while pursuing the legitimate constitutional commitment to empower communities that were marginalised in the past. How can a federation achieve this delicate balance?

As argued elsewhere, perhaps one way is to extend differentiated citizenship that is mediated by reasonable requirements of residency and language proficiency, where relevant. This allows the federated states to continue favouring their members over others. But newcomers can also acquire subnational citizenship and benefit from the preferential treatments as long as they meet reasonable requirements. More importantly, individuals cannot be denied subnational citizenship because of their ethnic group.

At the same time, the federation and the states must be allowed to incorporate rules that guarantee special interests of indigenous communities. The latter could be achieved in a number of ways that slightly deviate from the norm of equal treatment. It might entail the provision of benefits that may not be available to all residents of a state. It can be done by way of reserving some of the appointments in the most important decision-making bodies of state and local governments to members of the indigenous communities. The scheme could also include reserving seats for

---

minority position in the CCI opined that the language proficiency requirement should be seen in light of the whole federal architecture and in particular with the rights of indigenous groups whose access to political power, the use of their language and associated cultural rights had already long been curtailed (Advisory Opinion of the CCI 2008, 14–33).

[7] The HOF was given another opportunity to deal with a similar situation when victims of another group of non-indigenes complained about the violation of their freedom of movement, freedom to choose residence and freedom to pursue a livelihood of their choice (Petition to the HoF March 9, 2009). However, The HoF did not give a formal response to the petition.

members of the indigenous communities in the relevant deliberative body. It might also include giving veto power to the representatives of the indigenous communities on matters that affect their communities.

These deviations from a policy of pure equal citizenship can be justified on two grounds. Some of the measures mentioned above can be justified by the principle of substantive equality. According to this view, true equality cannot be attained by treating everybody equally. In some cases, a constitutional commitment to the achievement of true equality requires extending preferential treatment to members of indigenous communities. It requires that the state favour members of such communities over others. This is particularly true when the community has been historically oppressed and alienated. According to this view, the decision of a state to reserve university education admissions and scholarships for members of indigenous communities that were disadvantaged in the past would not be problematic. Extending preferential treatment to groups that have been marginalised in the past does not constitute a breach of equal citizenship. It, in fact, represents a means of achieving a truly equal society. It is now well established that extending equal treatment in a context of a history of discrimination and marginalisation would only be perpetuating the same trend of unequal relationship. However, the extension of preferential treatment on the basis of substantive equality cannot justify extending indefinite preferential treatment. Such measures must be circumscribed and transitory. Otherwise, extending preferential treatment may not advance the causes of justice or equal citizenship.

The extension of special measures to indigenous groups on a permanent basis can only be tolerated if the measures can be justified based on the self-governing rights of the member states of the federation. According to this argument, the provision of special measures is permissible as long as the measures are necessary for the communities to maintain their distinctiveness and exercise control over matters that are relevant to them. These measures may not be transitory but they must be limited in nature and scope. It is not every preferential treatment that can be justified on the basis of self-rule. The reservation of university admission to indigenes on a permanent basis would not be justified by the self-governing rights of a community. The power to veto decisions that affects the cultural, political and economic interest of the community could probably be justified. In short, permanent measures that deviate from the norm of equal treatment should be acceptable only if they are aimed at recognising and giving effect to the distinctive status of the communities and the right to manage their own affairs within a federal state.

## References

Abbink, Jon. 2006. Ethnicity and Conflict Generation in Ethiopia: Some Problems and Prospects of Ethno-Regional Federalism in Ethiopia. *Journal of Contemporary African Studies* 24 (3): 408–441.

———. 2011. Ethnic Based Federalism and Ethnicity in Ethiopia: Reassessing the Experiment after 20 Years. *Journal of Eastern African Studies* 5 (4): 596–618.

Advisory Opinion of the CCI on the Benshangul Gumuz Election Case. 2008. The House of the Federation of the Federal Democratic Republic of Ethiopia. *Journal of Constitutional Decisions* 1: 18–21.

Ambaye, Daniel W. 2012. Ethiopia Yemanat (Whose Land Is the Land [Ethiopia] (Newspaper Article). *Reporter Amharic*, March 28.

———. 2015. *Land Rights and Expropriation in Ethiopia*. Heidelberg; New York; Dordrecht; London: Springer.

Assefa, Getachew. 2014. *Constitutional Protection of Human and Minority Rights in Ethiopia: Myth v. Reality*. PhD Thesis, University of Melbourne.

Bauböck, Rainer. 2006. Citizenship and Migration: Concepts and Controversies. In *Migration and Citizenship: Legal Status, Rights and Political Participation*, ed. Rainer Bauböck, 15–31. Amsterdam: Amsterdam University Press.

Behailu, Daniel. 2015. *Transfer of Land Rights in Ethiopia: Towards a Sustainable Policy Framework*. The Hague: Eleven International Publishing.

Bello, M.L. 2012. Federal Character as a Recipe for National Integration: The Nigerian Paradox. *International Journal of Political and Good Governance* 3 (30): 1–17.

Benshangul Gumuz Region Constitution. Proclamation No 31 2002, The Revised Constitution of the Benishangul Gumuz Regional State, Lisane Hig Gazeta of the Benishangul Gumuz Regional State.

Borkena. 2018. Ethiopia Admits 15 Killed in Hawassa Violence. https://borkena.com/2018/06/17/ethiopia-admits-at-15-killed-in-hawassa-violence/.

Brook Abdu, The Reporter. 2018a, June 23. Sidama Zone Detains 226 in Relation to Deadly Conflict. https://www.thereporterethiopia.com/article/sidama-zone-detains-226-relation-deadly-conflict. Accessed July 11, 2019.

———. 2018b, July 5. Sidama Zone Head, Hawassa Mayor Resign. https://www.thereporterethiopia.com/article/sidama-zone-head-hawassa-mayor-resign. Accessed July 1, 2019.

Davidson, William. 2018. Ethiopia Observer, Deadly Violence Hits Hawassa as Protesters Call for Sidama State. https://www.ethiopiaobserver.com/2018/06/14/deadly-violence-hits-hawassa-as-protesters-call-for-sidama-state/.

Decision of the HoF on the Benshangul Gumuz Election Case. 2008. The House of the Federation of the Federal Democratic Republic of Ethiopia. *Journal of Constitutional Decisions* 1: 14–33.

Dessalegn, Beza. 2016. *Ethnic Federalism and the Right to Political Participation of Regional Minorities in Ethiopia*. PhD Thesis, Addis Ababa University.

———. 2018. Challenges of Ethnic Representation in Ethiopia and the Need for Reform. *Mizan Law Review* 12 (1): 1–28.

Ejobowah, John Boye. 2013. Ethnic Conflict and Cooperation: Assessing Citizenship in Nigerian Federalism. *Publius: The Journal of Federalism* 43 (4): 728–747.

FDRE Constitution. Proclamation No. 1/1995, Proclamation of the Constitution of the Federal Democratic Republic of Ethiopia, Federal Negarit Gazeta, 1st Year No.1, Addis Ababa-21st August, 1995.

FDRE Population Census Commission. 2007. Statistical Report of the 2007 Population and Housing Census. *Central Statistical Authority*.

Fessha, Yonatan Tesfaye. 2009. A Tale of Two Federations: Comparing Language Rights Regimes in South Africa and Ethiopia. In *Issues of Federalism in Ethiopia: Towards an Inventory*, ed. Tsegaye Regassa, 115–160. Ethiopian Constitutional Law Series (2). Addis Ababa: Addis Ababa University Press.

———. 2017. The Original Sin of Ethiopian Federalism. *Ethnopolitics* 16 (3): 232–245.

———. 2018. Empowerment and Exclusion: The Story of Two African Federations. In *Revisiting Unity and Diversity in Federal Countries: Changing Concepts, Reform Proposals and New Institutional Realities*, ed. Alain-G. Gagnon and Michael Burgess, 57–78. Leiden; Boston: Brill Nijhoff.

Fourchard, Laurent. 2015. Bureaucrats and Indigenes: Producing and Bypassing Certificates of Origin in Nigeria. *Africa* 85 (1): 37–58.

Gagnon, Alain-G, and James Tully, eds. 2001. *Multinational Democracies*. Cambridge: Cambridge University Press.

Gambella Constitution. Proclamation No. 27/2002, The Revised Constitution of the Gambella National Regional State, Negarit Gazeta of the Gembella Peoples' National Regional State.

Human Rights Council. 2016. Stop Immediately the Extra-Judicial Killings, Illegal Detentions, Beatings, Intimidation and Harassment Committed by Government Security Forces!!. 140th Special Report, Addis Ababa.

Kefale, Asnake. 2009. *Federalism and Ethnic Conflict in Ethiopia: A Comparative Study of the Somali and Benishangul-Gumuz States*. PhD Thesis, University of Leiden.

Lavers, Tom. 2018. Responding to Land Based Conflict in Ethiopia: The Land Rights of Ethnic Minorities Under Federalism. *African Affairs* 117 (468): 462–484.

Negash, Assefa. 2012. *Why Have the Amharas Once Again Become Victims of Ethnic Cleansing by TPLF?* http://tassew.files.wordpress.com/2012/04/amaras_ethnic_cleansing_by_tplf_dr_assefa_negash.pdf.

Obulutsa, George. 2018, July 4. *Reuters.* Violence in Southern Ethiopia Forces More Than 800,000 to Flee. https://www.reuters.com/article/us-ethiopia-violence/violence-in-southern-ethiopia-forces-more-than-800000-to-flee-idUSKBN1JU14W.

Petition to the HoF by the Victims of Expulsion in Guraferda District Dated (Yekati 30, 2001 E.C.), on File with the Secretariat of the HoF, Addis Ababa.

Proclamation 456/2005, Federal Democratic Republic of Ethiopia Land Use and Administration Proclamation, 11th Year, No 44, Addis Ababa, 15th July, 2005.

Proclamation No 532/2007, The Amended Electoral Law of Ethiopia Proclamation, Federal Negarit Gazeta, 13th Year, No. 53, Addis Ababa, 25th June 2007.

Proclamation No 7/1992, A Proclamation to Provide for the Establishment of National/Regional Self-governments, Negarit Gazeta 51st Year No 2, Addis Ababa, 14th January 1992.

Sadiq, Kamal. 2009. When Being "Native" Is Not Enough: Citizens as Foreigners in Malaysia. *Asian Perspective* 33 (1): 5–32.

Soboka, Takele. 2008. The Interplay of Equality Clause and Affirmative Action Measures under the Ethiopian Constitution: The Benishangul Gumuz Case and Beyond. In *The Constitutional Protection of Human Rights in Ethiopia: Challenges and Prospects*, ed. Girmachew Alemu and Sisay Alemahu. Ethiopian Human Rights Law Series, Vol. 2. Addis Ababa: Addis Ababa University Press.

Suberu, Rotimi. 2010. The Nigerian Federal System: Performance, Problems and Prospects. *Journal of Contemporary African Studies* 28 (4): 459–477.

Suksi, Markku. 2011. *Sub-State Governance Through Territorial Autonomy: A Comparative Study in Constitutional Law of Powers, Procedures and Institutions.* Berlin; Heidelberg: Springer-Verlag.

The World Bank. 2004. Ethiopia: Legal and Judicial Sector Assessment The World Bank.

Tigray Region Constitution. Proclamation No 45/ 2001, A Proclamation issued to approve the Revised Constitution of Tigray Regional State, Negarit Gazette of the Tigray Regional State.

UNICEF. 2019. Ethiopia: Humanitarian Situation Report. https://reliefweb.int/sites/reliefweb.int/files/resources/UNICEF%20Ethiopia%20Humanitarian%20Situation%20Report%20-%20July%202018.pdf.

Van der Beken, Christophe. 2012. *Unity in Diversity-Federalism as a Mechanism to Accommodate Ethnic Diversity: The Case of Ethiopia.* Berlin: Lit Verlag.

Vaughan, Sarah. 2006. Conflict & Conflict Management in & Around Benishangul-Gumuz National Regional State. *Report Produced Under the Ministry of Federal Affairs (MoFA) Institutional Support Project (ISP).*

Woldemariam, Tewolde, and Fana Gebresenbet. 2014. Socio-political and Conflict Implications of Sugar Development in Salamago Wereda, Ethiopia. In *A Delicate Balance: Land Use, Minority Rights and Social Stability in the Horn of Africa*, ed. Mulugeta Gebrehiwot Berhe, 117–143. Addis Ababa: Institute for Peace and Security Studies, Addis Ababa University.

Wuilbercq, Emeline. 2014, July 14. *The Guardian*. Ethiopia's Nile Dam Project Signals Its Intention to Become an African Power. https://www.theguardian.com/global-development/2014/jul/14/ethiopia-grand-renaissance-dam-egypt.

Yntiso, Gebre. 2004. Resettlement Risks and Inter-Ethnic Conflict in Metekel, Ethiopia. *Ethiopian Journal of the Social Sciences and Humanities* 2 (1): 45–67.

Yoseph, Nafekot. 2013a. *Ye Benshangul Tefenakayoch Temesewach Honu* (Evictees of Benshangul Have Become Aid Recipients). http://www.addisadmassnews.com/index.php?option=com.

———. 2013b. *LeAmetate Nurowachewene beBenshangul Yaderegu Zegoche Tebareru* (Citizens That Have Been Residing in Benshangul for Years Were Evicted). http://www.addisadmassnews.com/index.php?option=com.

## CHAPTER 12

# Ensuring a Future for Indigenous Languages in Canada: Can 'Consequentialist' Multinational Federalism Provide an Answer?

*Emmanuelle Richez and Tejas Pandya*

## INTRODUCTION

Census data on the status of Indigenous languages in Canada illustrates the precarious position in which Indigenous language minorities continue to find themselves. Overall, the 2016 Census of Population (Statistics Canada 2017), which provides the most up-to-date data on the state of Indigenous languages in Canada, shows that more than 70 Indigenous languages (divided across 12 language families) are spoken in the country. The Canadian census also brings to light trends that may be concerning for the future of Indigenous languages and language minorities. We have highlighted some of these trends below:

---

The authors of this manuscript are non-Indigenous and write from a settler's perspective. As allies of Indigenous Peoples, they seek to identify ways Canadian federalism can be adapted to increase the vitality of Indigenous languages.

---

E. Richez (✉) • T. Pandya
University of Windsor, Windsor, ON, Canada
e-mail: emmanuelle.richez@uwindsor.ca; pandy117@uwindsor.ca

© The Author(s) 2020
A.-G. Gagnon, A. Tremblay (eds.), *Federalism and National Diversity in the 21st Century*, Federalism and Internal Conflicts,
https://doi.org/10.1007/978-3-030-38419-7_12

- The census shows that, on the one hand, 'the number of people in the Aboriginal population who could speak an Aboriginal language increased by 3.1%' due to the fast-growing Indigenous population. On the other hand, the census also shows that the number of Indigenous Peoples who 'reported being able to conduct a conversation in an Indigenous language dropped to 15.6% down from 21.4% in 2006'.

- The census shows that more individuals speak Indigenous languages as a second language rather than as their mother tongue. In 2016, 12.5% of the Indigenous population, which is to say 208,720 people, reported an Indigenous language as their mother tongue 'either as a single response or in combination with another language'. Yet the census also shows that the total number of Indigenous Peoples who were able to speak an Indigenous language was 260,500, which suggests that more people speak Indigenous languages as a second language rather than as a mother tongue. To be sure, individuals learning Indigenous languages as a second language are important to Indigenous language preservation and revitalisation. But it is also a double-edged sword as the census clearly acknowledges that: '[l]earning an Aboriginal language at home in childhood as a primary language is a crucial element of long-term viability of Aboriginal languages'.

- There is evidence of a significant difference in fluency across age cohorts. Elders were more likely to be able to speak an Indigenous language compared to those from a younger demographic. The census shows that '35.6% of First Nations seniors could speak an Aboriginal language, compared with 24.5% in the 25-to-64 age group, 16.5% in the 15-to-24 age group, and 15.8% in the 0-to-14 age group'.

- The situation of the Métis is arguably the direst.[1] According to the census, '1.7% of the Métis population reported being able to conduct a conversation in an Aboriginal language' (Statistics Canada 2017). Moreover, 'a higher percentage of Métis seniors reported an Aboriginal mother tongue and the ability to speak an Aboriginal language, compared with their younger counterparts' (Statistics Canada 2017). Even so, Métis seniors, 65 years of age or more, were themselves only 3.4% likely to have an Indigenous mother tongue and only 4% were able to conduct a conversation in an Indigenous language.

---

[1] Section 35(2) of the Constitution Act, 1982 identifies three categories of 'aboriginal peoples': Indian, Inuit and Métis.

In light of these trends, this chapter asks two questions: what is the Canadian federation doing to protect, to preserve or to revitalise Indigenous languages? And, within the context of this volume's central themes, can 'consequentialist' multinational federalism help to ensure a future for Indigenous languages in Canada?

In theory, a federal state such as Canada should be better equipped to preserve, protect, revitalise as well as accommodate minority languages and language minorities than a unitary state, where minority languages often lack recognition or are outright mistreated (Cardinal 2008, 26). However, a federation's success in alleviating the linguistic insecurities of minorities is also likely to be contingent on whether or not the federation also embraces its *multinational* character and thus sets out to recognise and empower its constitutive national groups (Gagnon 2000). If that step is taken, the fate of language minorities may then further depend on whether a federation embraces 'symbolic' multinationalism or 'consequentialist' multinationalism. According to Jean-François Caron and Guy Laforest (2009) 'symbolic' multinationalism entails a soft recognition of intra-state diversity that 'limits the recognition of multinationalism to purely symbolic elements, such as the constitutional or parliamentary affirmation of the multinational character of a state' (41). They argue that, on the other hand, 'consequentialist' multinationalism is fundamentally rooted in recognising the national diversity that exists within a state and the right of different national groups to pursue self-determination (ibid.). In practice, 'consequentialist' multinationalism can be implemented through the 'devolution of powers or the establishment of a federal structure [which] enables federal entities composed of minority nations to benefit from a differential treatment, usually through asymmetrical policies' (Caron and Laforest 2009, 42). As such, Caron and Laforest contend that 'consequentialist' multinationalism, with its underlying promise of national recognition and national empowerment, is the model for managing the diversity that Canada should strive for but that it has thus far failed to reach.

In brief, this chapter employs the concept of 'consequentialist' multinational federalism as a means to assess the current state of federal, provincial and territorial measures to protect Indigenous languages in Canada. In arriving at its assessment, this chapter first explores past practices aimed at assimilating Indigenous Peoples and recent calls for action in Indigenous language matters, and, in so doing, provides the contextual backdrop for this chapter's discussion. Second, the chapter provides a summary of the breadth and limitations of existing Indigenous language rights protections at the federal, provincial and territorial, and treaty levels. Third, and following from the previous point, the chapter offers preliminary insight into what 'symbolic', and more importantly, 'consequentialist' multinational solutions might look like in response to calls for action in Indigenous language matters and in redressing the limitations of existing federal, territorial and provincial Indigenous language rights protections. This chapter concludes that 'consequentialist' multinational solutions to protecting and preserving Indigenous languages would entail, as preconditions, strengthening Indigenous sovereignty through treaties and enshrining nation-to-nation negotiation but that, for a number of reasons, these solutions might be difficult to achieve.

## HISTORICAL AND CURRENT CONTEXT

### *Past Practices of Assimilation*

During the negotiations that led to Confederation in 1867, First Nations were not consulted and the relationship between settlers and First Nations was determined unilaterally (Royal Commission on Aboriginal Peoples Volume 1, 1996a, 165). As Malcolm Montgomery documents: 'The first prime minister, Sir John A. Macdonald [...] informed Parliament that it would be Canada's goal "to do away with the tribal system and assimilate the Indian people in all respects with the inhabitants of the Dominion"' (qtd. in Royal Commission on Aboriginal Peoples Volume 1, 1996a, 165). Tragically, the government set out to realise this goal starting in the 1870s through the implementation of the residential school system, during which roughly 150,000 Indigenous children were forcibly removed from their families to have their language and culture stripped away for the purposes of linguistic, cultural and religious assimilation (Indigenous and Northern Affairs Canada 2019). Although most residential schools closed during the mid-1970s, the last federally run school closed only in 1996 (Indigenous and Northern Affairs Canada 2019).

In addition to the emotional, physical and sexual abuse that students suffered, they were also discouraged and often outright prohibited from speaking their own languages (Truth and Reconciliation Commission of Canada 2015, 4), leading to what can best be described as a 'cultural genocide' (Truth and Reconciliation Commission of Canada 2015, 1). The consequences of the residential school system and of colonialism in general have persisted into the present. Linguist Michael Krauss estimates that 300 Indigenous languages were spoken fluently in Canada and the

US in the fifteenth century (Galley 2016, 1); roughly 70 Indigenous languages are now spoken in Canada (Statistics Canada 2017),[2] many of which are now endangered (Galley 2016, 1).

Stephen Harper's Conservative government developed a formalised compensation package for victims of the residential school system in 2007. More specifically, 1.9 billion dollars was to be given to those who were forced to attend residential schools, and as of September 30, 2013, 1.6 billion of this sum had been paid out (CBC News 2016). And, on June 11, 2008, Prime Minister Harper publicly apologised on behalf of all Canadians and the Government of Canada for sending Indigenous children to residential schools. He stated in his speech that '[t]he government now recogni[s]es that the consequences of the Indian Residential Schools policy were profoundly negative and that this policy has had a lasting and damaging impact on Aboriginal culture, heritage and language [...] We are sorry' (Indigenous and Northern Affairs Canada 2008).

Other apologies for the residential school system include those of numerous church officials, including an informal apology from Pope Benedict XVI, and a formal apology from Prime Minister Justin Trudeau. In the 1990s, many churches involved in the injustice of residential schools apologised. These churches include the Anglican Church of Canada, the Presbyterian Church and the United Church of Canada (CBC News 2016). In 2009, Pope Benedict XVI voiced his 'sorrow' for the 'deplorable' treatment that Indigenous children had to endure due to the Church's involvement in residential schools.[3] On November 24, 2017, Prime Minister Trudeau apologised to residential school survivors in Newfoundland and Labrador (Justin Trudeau 2017). Also in 2017, during a visit to the Vatican, Trudeau asked Pope Francis if he would apologise for the Catholic Church's role in administering residential schools. However, in March 2018, Pope Francis decided that he would not apologise for the Church's role in residential schools.

---

[2] Sources differ on how many Indigenous languages there are as it depends on how the languages are categorised.

[3] Phil Fontaine, the Assembly of First Nations Leader at the time, was disappointed that the Pope did not give an official apology, but hoped that the Pope's words would be enough '[to] 'close the book' on the issue of apologies for residential school survivors' (CBC News 2016). However, Fontaine later stated that his words had been taken out of context and that '[he] would never say anything to diminish what happened nine years ago, but I also call on the Catholic Church, and the Canadian Conference of Catholic Bishops, to honour its commitment to reconciliation and healing' (CBC 2018).

## Calls for Action

Despite these apologies and the financial settlement granted to residential schools survivors, the problem of Indigenous cultural genocide and its impact on Indigenous languages has yet to be adequately redressed. In fact, national and international reports have called and continue to call for better protection of Indigenous languages in Canada.

### Royal Commission on Aboriginal Peoples

The final report rendered in 1996 by the Royal Commission on Aboriginal Peoples (established in 1991, hereinafter 'RCAP') is perhaps the most crucial call for action in protecting Indigenous languages in Canada. The purpose of the RCAP was to identify points of contention between Indigenous Peoples, the Canadian government, and Canadian society, and then offer potential solutions to try to ease tensions (Library and Archives Canada 2019). The leadership of the RCAP consisted for the most part of Indigenous scholars and can therefore be viewed as representative of an Indigenous voice.

In the end, the RCAP provided 440 recommendations that called for major changes to the relationship between Indigenous Peoples and non-Indigenous Peoples as well as the government (Troian 2016). Regarding language rights for Indigenous Peoples, the RCAP stressed the importance of language preservation efforts in order to maintain Indigenous culture (RCAP Volume 1, 1996a, 6). Most importantly, the RCAP implored that:

> Federal, provincial and territorial governments recognise promptly that determining Aboriginal language status and use is a core power in Aboriginal self-government, and that these governments affirm and support Aboriginal nations and their communities in using and promoting their languages and declaring them official languages within their nations, territories and communities where they choose to do so. (RCAP Volume 5, 1996b, 222)

Indigenous Peoples have thus noted that, through the RCAP, any long-term solution to the preservation of Indigenous languages would be linked to self-government.

### Truth and Reconciliation Commission

Another major call to action came in 2015 with the release of the final report of the Truth and Reconciliation Commission of Canada (hereinafter 'TRC') which addressed the issue of language and culture within Indigenous communities. The TRC was created from the Indian Residential Schools Settlement; it created a forum for residential school survivors to tell their stories and set out to compile this knowledge and all other knowledge on residential schools in order to document the whole truth and to lay the groundwork for reconciliation (TRC 2015, Preface).

Of the 94 points outlined in the 'Calls to Action' section in the TRC's final report, four are particularly important within the context of this discussion. Point 13 of the report calls upon the federal government to acknowledge Indigenous language rights (TRC 2015, 321). Point 14 of the final report calls upon the federal government to 'enact an Aboriginal Languages Act' (TRC 2015, 321); this point incorporates numerous principles such as that of Indigenous language rights being reinforced by treaties and that of the federal government having a responsibility to revitalise and to preserve Indigenous languages (TRC 2015, 321). Point 15 calls upon the federal government to appoint an 'Aboriginal Languages Commissioner' (TRC 2015, 321). Lastly, point 16 requests that postsecondary institutions create programmes that teach Indigenous languages (TRC 2015, 322).

*Senate Bill*
A series of calls to action have come from the Canadian Senate and, more specifically, from Liberal Senator Serge Joyal who, since 2009, has lobbied for greater linguistic rights for the Indigenous Peoples in Canada. Senator Joyal's first call to action came in 2009 when he introduced Bill S-237, titled *An Act for the advancement of the aboriginal languages of Canada and to recognise and respect aboriginal language rights*; while the Bill reached a second reading, it was stopped in its tracks due to the prorogation of the Canadian Parliament in December, 2009. Six years later, in 2015, Senator Joyal introduced Bill S-229, an identical piece of legislation to Bill S-237 which met the same fate as the first initiative. Undeterred by past legislative inaction and following the electoral victory of the Trudeau Liberals in October 2015, Senator Joyal introduced a third iteration of Bill S-237: Bill S-212. This third iteration specifically stated that 'the Government of Canada is committed to preserving, revitali[s]ing, and promoting aboriginal languages in Canada by protecting them and using them where appropriate' (Bill S-212, 2015). It also stated that the designated Minister 'shall take the measures the Minister considers appropriate to implement' (Bill S-212, 2015), such as supporting Aboriginal

governments to 'give official status to aboriginal languages for the purposes of conducting local governance activities', supporting the use of 'aboriginal languages as the language of instruction in all schools that are operated on reserves', supporting Aboriginal language teachers and supporting programmes that help Aboriginal persons to learn their languages (Bill S-212, 2015).

Bill S-212 had its second reading in May, 2016, at which point Senator Joyal pointed out that in *Haida Nation v. British Columbia* (2004), the Supreme Court of Canada had concluded that Indigenous Peoples 'were never conquered' (Debates of the Senate 2016). For him, this meant that Indigenous Peoples still possessed their rights, including, among others, their cultural and linguistic rights (Debates of the Senate 2016). Furthermore, Joyal informed Parliament that 'Aboriginal language rights are reinforced by treaties' and that in 1982, treaty rights were 'entrenched' in section 35 of the Constitution Act (Debates of the Senate 2016). Lastly, Joyal brought up the point that the United Nations Declaration on the Rights of Indigenous Peoples (2007; hereinafter 'UNDRIP')—to which Canada is a signatory—supports language rights. While Bill S-212 was eventually referred to committee in December, 2016, work on it has since stalled.[4]

### The Trudeau Government's Engagement

Following his 2015 electoral victory, Prime Minister Justin Trudeau has insisted that '[n]o relationship is more important to [him] and to Canada than the one with Indigenous Peoples' (Laforest and Dubois 2017). In 2016, he delivered a speech to the Assembly of First Nations Special Chiefs Assembly during which he pledged to implement all 94 points in the 'Calls to Action' section of the TRC's final report (Trudeau 2016). He also declared his 'unqualified support' (Trudeau 2016) for the UNDRIP.

With the aim of eventually introducing legislation designed to preserve, to protect and to revitalise Indigenous languages, the Trudeau government engaged with Indigenous Peoples across Canada in 2017–2018 to get their perspective on what should and should not be included in the law. Several participants emphasised the critical condition of their languages as well as the need for legislation that acknowledged differences between language groups and accommodated their needs accordingly. Participants also stressed the importance of Indigenous involvement in

---

[4] No further action on the bill has been taken as of January 2020 (time of writing).

decision-making processes and in control over programmes. While the Trudeau government has claimed that 'support for legislation was high' (Canadian Heritage 2018), the Assembly of First Nations has expressed the view that talks with the government were rushed, superficial and lacking in transparency (Assembly of First Nations 2018, 2). Despite this difference in perspectives, the Trudeau government followed through on in its engagement with Indigenous Peoples and introduced Bill C-91—*An Act Respecting Indigenous Languages* which received royal assent in June, 2019; this legislation is discussed in greater detail further on in this chapter.

## EXISTING FEDERAL PROTECTIONS

### *Institutional and Procedural Accommodations*

The federal government has put together a mixed bag of institutional protections for Indigenous languages; some of these fail to match the protections offered to other languages in Canada while others seem promising. For instance, since 2009, the Government of Canada has celebrated 'Linguistic Duality Day' on the second Thursday of September, emphasising contributions of the French and English languages to the federal apparatus and to Canadian culture more generally (Council of the Network of Official Languages Champion 2018). Yet while June 21 is designated as National Indigenous Peoples Day in Canada and is meant to celebrate Indigenous Peoples' culture and heritage (Canadian Heritage 2019a), there is to date no event that specifically celebrates Indigenous languages.

Additionally Indigenous Languages do not receive the same institutional treatment as French and English do via the *Official Languages Act*. This piece of legislation provides 'that English and French are the official languages of Canada and have equality of status and equal rights and privileges as to their use in all institutions of the Parliament and government of Canada' (Official Languages Act 1988: Preamble). Notably, it guarantees that official languages may be used by everyone in debates and other proceedings of Parliament and will be afforded simultaneous interpretation from one language to another (Official Languages Act 1988: ss 4(1)-4(2)). It also states that all acts, official reports of debates and other proceedings of Parliament must be published in both French and English (Official Languages Act 1988: ss 4(1)-4(3)).

To be sure, since 2018, Members of Parliament (MPs) have been given the right to speak Indigenous languages in the House of Commons, including parliamentary committees (House of Commons 2018, 25). Simultaneous interpretation in French and English is given for speeches in Indigenous languages as long as the speaker gives a two-day notice (House of Commons 2018, 25). The Senate of Canada has made similar procedural arrangements, but only for Inuktitut. This arrangement stemmed from a 2008 Senate Committee report which recommended that Senators have the ability to speak Inuktitut as a 'pilot project' with the end goal being that 'other Indigenous languages' be accommodated in the Senate chamber (House of Commons 2018, 10). While Inuktitut has been used in the Senate since interpreting services have been made available (House of Commons 2018, 10), this end goal has not yet been reached. Moreover, no procedure has been put in place to ensure automatic translation of laws and official reports of debates and other proceedings of Parliament are translated in Indigenous languages.

Over the years, the federal government has increased its number of programmes that aid Indigenous Peoples in using their languages in public institutions. For example, the Indigenous Courtwork Program serves to aid Indigenous Peoples in the criminal justice system by ensuring that they receive just and 'culturally relevant treatment' (Department of Justice 2017). This has meant, inter alia, assisting Indigenous Peoples in overcoming language barriers, so that they may better understand the charges levied against them and may better defend themselves (Department of Justice 2017). Provincial and territorial governments are eligible to receive federal funding for the programme, and all Indigenous individuals that are 'in conflict with the law' are eligible to receive services from the programme (Department of Justice 2017). The programme operates in all provinces and territories except for Prince Edward Island, Newfoundland and Labrador, and New Brunswick (Department of Justice 2017).

### Federal Funding of Education

The federal government provides funding for primary and secondary First Nations students who reside on reserves. It also provides funding for First Nations post-secondary educational attainment and does likewise for eligible Inuit students (Indigenous Services Canada 2019a). From 2016 to 2017, the federal government invested 1.94 billion dollars into First Nations primary and secondary education, with 275 million going towards language and culture (Indigenous Services Canada 2019b). The federal government also provides funding to First Nations and Inuit Peoples for cultural education centres. Cultural education centres develop cultural programming to ensure the preservation, protection and revitalisation of Indigenous language and culture (Indigenous Services Canada 2019c). Roughly 100 First Nations centres and 8–10 Inuit centres are funded per year (Indigenous Services Canada 2019c). Additionally, the government has implemented the Child First Initiative, which guarantees Inuit children's access to healthcare, education and social programmes, regardless of where one resides (Indigenous Services Canada 2019d).[5] In regard to education, this includes elements such as tutoring, transportation and assistive technologies (Indigenous Services Canada 2019d). Despite these programmes and funding efforts, First Nations children who live on reserves receive at least 30% less in education funding than those children receiving instruction under provincial jurisdiction (Porter 2016).

For the Métis, the federal government enacted the *Canada-Métis Nation Accord* in April 2017. Part of the Accord mentions education stating that 'the Parties will explore the need for and approaches to establishing linkages and cultural supports for Métis Nation students (K to 12) to improve their educational outcomes' (Canada-Métis Nations Accord, 'Education'). In terms of actual action, the federal government invested 10 million dollars in the 2018 budget to support existing Métis Nation endowments for post-secondary education (Indigenous Services Canada 2018). The Accord only discusses potential language protections under the general ambit of 'Language and Culture', which is listed as one of 12 'Future Priorities'.

On February 27, 2012, Parliament unanimously passed the 'Shannen's Dream'[6] motion which declared that 'all First Nations children have an equal right to high-quality, culturally-relevant education' (House of Commons 2012). Among other things, it stressed the government's commitment to financially support First Nations education and to ensure that the quality of the First Nations education system is at the very least on par with the provincial education system (House of Commons 2012).

Subsequently, the Harper government attempted to pass Bill C-33—*the First Nations Control of First Nations Education Act*. The purpose of this bill was to enable First Nations to administer schools on reserves (Bill C-33: s 3). It proposed giving 1.9 billion dollars in federal funding towards First Nations education, with various sections highlighting the use and

---

[5] Upon condition of their request being accepted.

[6] Shannen was an Attawapiskat First Nation youth who petitioned the federal government to improve its funding for First Nations education. Shannen passed away at 15 before her dream was realised.

importance of First Nations language in education (The Canadian Press 2014). For example, section 21 (2) of Bill C-33 states that a First Nations language may be used in school as a language of instruction, in addition to English or French (Bill C-33). And, section 21 (3) notes that First Nations Councils may decide to offer a First Nations language or culture course for students (Bill C-33).

While the bill received enthusiastic support from Shawn Atleo, the First Nations National Chief at the time, it only received cautious approval from the Chiefs of the Assembly of First Nations (The Canadian Press 2014). This cautious approval soon eroded; the Chiefs of the Assembly of First Nations argued that they had not been involved in the drafting of Bill C-33, that funding provided in the bill was insufficient, and that, despite the bill's title, the government would still maintain great control over Indigenous education since the Assembly of First Nations could not negotiate with the government on behalf of First Nations (Holloway 2014). After a second reading in Parliament, the bill was put on indefinite hold.

### Language Revitalisation Programmes

The Government of Canada has been more successful with programmes intended to support the revitalisation of Indigenous languages, such as The Aboriginal Peoples Program. This programme has two main components that deal with Indigenous languages: 1. The Aboriginal Languages Initiative and 2. Northern Aboriginal Broadcasting. The Aboriginal Languages Initiative is a programme that 'supports the preservation and revitalisation of Indigenous languages through community based projects' (Canadian Heritage 2019b). Examples of eligible community-based projects include having language camps, documenting or recording endangered Indigenous languages and developing programmes to train Indigenous language teachers (Canadian Heritage 2019b). The Northern Aboriginal Broadcasting component 'supports the production and distribution of Indigenous audio and visual content' (Canadian Heritage 2019c). Overall, Northern Aboriginal Broadcasting seeks to protect and to revitalise Indigenous languages by ensuring that people are able to hear and listen to Indigenous languages; in order to be eligible for funding, organisations must ensure that they provide broadcasting to the Canadian North (north of the 55th parallel) (Canadian Heritage 2019c).

The Trudeau government's newly adopted Bill C-91—*An Act Respecting Indigenous Languages*—builds on language revitalisation programmes. It 'establishes an Office of the Commissioner of Indigenous

Languages that will be responsible for conducting research on the use and vitality of Indigenous languages, funding language revitalisation and promotion programs and managing complaints made under the Act' (Richez et al. 2019, 1). Bill C-91 does not, however, acknowledge new and enforceable language rights for Indigenous communities, and it does not recognize the same official language status to Indigenous languages that has been afforded to French and English in Canada. Perhaps more importantly, the bill fails to recognise Indigenous Peoples' true decision-making powers over the revitalisation and promotion of their own languages.

## PROVINCIAL AND TERRITORIAL PROTECTIONS

### *Official Language Recognition*

Protections for Indigenous languages in Canadian provinces and territories vary greatly. As one can see in Table 12.1, the three territories—the Yukon, the Northwest Territories and Nunavut—have instituted some important protections for Indigenous languages, whereas most provinces have instituted few protections. Following the example of the federal government, the territories have passed legislation that recognises French and English as official languages. However, two territorial jurisdictions have gone a step further and have provided official recognition to some Indigenous languages: the Northwest Territories' *Official Languages Act* (1988: s 6) recognises Chipewyan, Cree, Gwich'in, Inuinnaqtun, Inuktitut, Inuvialuktun, North Slavey, South Slavey and Tåîchô as official languages while Nunavut's *Official Languages Act* (2008. s 4(1)) does the same for the 'Inuit language'. In both territorial jurisdictions, individuals have the right to use official Indigenous languages 'in the debates and other proceedings of the Legislative Assembly' (*Official Languages Act* 1988, s 6; *Official Languages Act* 2008, s 4). In the Yukon, '[e]veryone has the right to use [...] a Yukon aboriginal language in any debates and other proceedings of the Legislative Assembly' (*Languages Act* 2002, s 3(1)), however, and by contrast to the two other territorial jurisdiction, these languages have not been acknowledged as having official status.

Protections that help Indigenous Peoples use their languages in the public sphere, such as those related to governmental services, court proceedings and healthcare delivery, are almost all available in all the territories, and are available in a few of the provinces. Nunavut's *Official Languages Act* (2008) declares that members of the public have the right to communicate in and to receive services in the 'Inuit Language'. As for

**Table 12.1**  Provincial and territorial protections for Indigenous languages

| | Government services | Legislative assembly | Courts | Health | Instruction | Complaints | Revitalisation |
|---|---|---|---|---|---|---|---|
| Yukon | • | • | • | • | • | • | • |
| Northwest Territories | • | • | • | • | • | • | • |
| Nunavut | | • | | | • | • | • |
| British Columbia | | | | | • | | |
| Alberta | | | • | | • | | |
| Saskatchewan | | | | | • | | |
| Manitoba | | | | • | • | | • |
| Ontario | | | | • | • | | • |
| Quebec | | | | | • | | |
| New Brunswick | | | | | • | | |
| Nova Scotia | | | | | | | • |
| Prince Edward Island | | | | | | | |
| Newfoundland and Labrador | | | | • | • | | |

The data collected for Table 1 comes from provincial and territorial legislation and policy documents. Provincial and territorial governments were also consulted through access to information requests. All provinces and territories responded to the requests with the exception of Prince Edward Island. Notably though, the governments of Alberta and Quebec stated in their response that they would not be able to send the authors the information requested. The key sources used for the territories were the Yukon's *Languages Act*, the Northwest Territories *Official Languages Act* and Nunavut's *Official Languages Act*. For British Columbia the 2019 budget was used. For Alberta the Indigenous Languages in Education Grant programme was used. For Saskatchewan the Inspiring Success: First Nations and Métis PreK-12 Education Policy Framework was used. For Manitoba the K-12 Aboriginal Languages and Cultures: Manitoba Curriculum Framework of Outcomes was used. For Ontario the First Nation, Métis and Inuit Education Policy Framework was used. For Quebec the *Education Act for Cree, Inuit and Nasakpi Native Persons* was used. For New Brunswick a letter sent from the Minister of Aboriginal Affairs to the authors was used. This letter outlined what the province is doing to promote Indigenous languages, and in particular expressed the promotion of Mi'kmaq and Wolastoqey/Maliseet through education courses in the province. For Nova Scotia the *Education Act* was used. Lastly, for Newfoundland and Labrador a letter sent from the Deputy Minister of Indigenous Affairs was used. This letter outlined what the province is doing to support Indigenous languages in education, and also detailed what the province is doing for Indigenous language translation in healthcare. This list of sources is not comprehensive. A full list of sources is available upon request the Northwest Territories *Official Languages Act* (1988: s 9(2)), it states that official Indigenous languages 'may be used by any person in any court established by the Legislature'. All the territories and a few provinces offer legal guarantees for health service delivery in Indigenous languages. For example, Nunavut's *Inuit Language Protection Act* (2008: s(2)(a)(ii)) stipulates that '[a]n organisation shall communicate with the public in the Inuit Language when delivering [...] health, medical, and pharmaceutical services'. Furthermore, individuals living in the Canadian North can file complaints with territorial administrations if their linguistic rights are not enforced. For example, the Northwest Territories' *Official Languages Act* (1988) outlines the duty of the Languages Commissioner to investigate 'reasonable complaint[s]' that government has not recognised the status of an official language and/or has failed to comply with either legislation pertaining to official languages or to the spirit of the legislation.

### Language Revitalisation Programmes

Language revitalisation programmes are present in both territories and provinces. For example, Section 24(2)(f) of the *Inuit Language Protection Act* (2008) supports language revitalisation in Nunavut by tasking the Minister of Languages with identifying 'technologies for Inuit Language media distribution or access [...] that have the greatest potential to promote the use or revitalisation of the Inuit Language, including print, film, television, radio, digital audio or video, [and] interactive or any other media'. And, at the provincial level, Quebec's *Education Act for Cree, Inuit, and Naskapi Persons* (1988) states that the school board is able 'to develop courses, textbooks and teaching materials designed to preserve and transmit the language and culture of the Cree' (*Education Act for Cree, Inuit, and Naskapi Persons* 1988, s 575 (h)) and establishes similar provisions for the Inuit people (*Education Act for Cree, Inuit, and Naskapi Persons* 1988, s 663 (2)).

## TREATY LEVEL PROTECTIONS

The treaty-making process between the Crown and Indigenous communities started prior to Confederation (Crown-Indigenous Relations and Northern Affairs Canada 2018). Treaties are, in general, a way for Indigenous communities to 'delegate certain responsibilities to the Crown in return for the government's assistance' (Ladner 2003, 176).

Historical treaties are vague when it comes to guaranteeing linguistic rights, especially with respect to education for Indigenous students (Leitch 2006, 108). However, since 1975, the federal and provincial Crown have signed modern treaties, also known as comprehensive land claims agreements (Council of the Network of Official Languages Champion 2018). Modern treaties are characterised by a more expansive recognition of land titles and resource management powers for Indigenous Peoples than historical treaties (Council of the Network of Official Languages Champion 2018). Perhaps more importantly, modern treaties are a way of implementing self-government for Indigenous Peoples in Canada, which is seen as an inherent right (Ladner 2003, 175), and as Chris Alcantara (2007) notes, they can potentially vest Indigenous Peoples with greater control over their culture (353), especially concerning language matters.

Figure 12.1 depicts the percentage of modern treaties by category of Indigenous language protections.[7] As one can see, there is wide variation in the language categories that are present in modern treaties.

Figure 12.1 reveals that roughly three quarters of modern treaties provide protections in the areas of language preservation, education and governmental communication. For example, falling under the category of language preservation, the *Champagne and Aishihik First Nation Final Agreement* (1993: s 13.1.1.2) states that an objective of the Agreement is 'to promote the recording and preservation of traditional languages, beliefs, oral histories including legends, and cultural knowledge of Yukon Indian People for the benefit of future generations'. An example of a protection in education is the *Northeastern Quebec Agreement* (1978: s 11.19), which states that 'the teaching languages for the Naskapis of Québec attending the Naskapi school shall be Naskapi'. Notably, it is an 'objective' of the treaty to have French used as a teaching language as well

---

[7] As of 2018, 26 modern treaties have been signed and more than 70 are currently under negotiation (Land Claims Agreements Coalition 2019) and, as Abele and Prince (2009, 576) contend, this is leading, slowly but surely, to the development of a third level of government in Canada. Within this emerging context, The *Government of Canada's Approach to Implementation of the Inherent Right and the Negotiation of Aboriginal Self-Government* has underscored the importance of including linguistic rights in modern treaties (Crown-Indigenous Relations and Northern Affairs Canada 2010). However, only a few of the comprehensive land claim agreements that have been finalised have also included protections of linguistic rights (Leitch 2006, 115). This is because an interim comprehensive claims policy, *Renewing the Comprehensive Land Claims Policy: Towards a Framework for Addressing Section 35 Rights* (Aboriginal and Northern Affairs Canada 2014) does not mandate that language protections be included (Richez et al. 2019, 3).

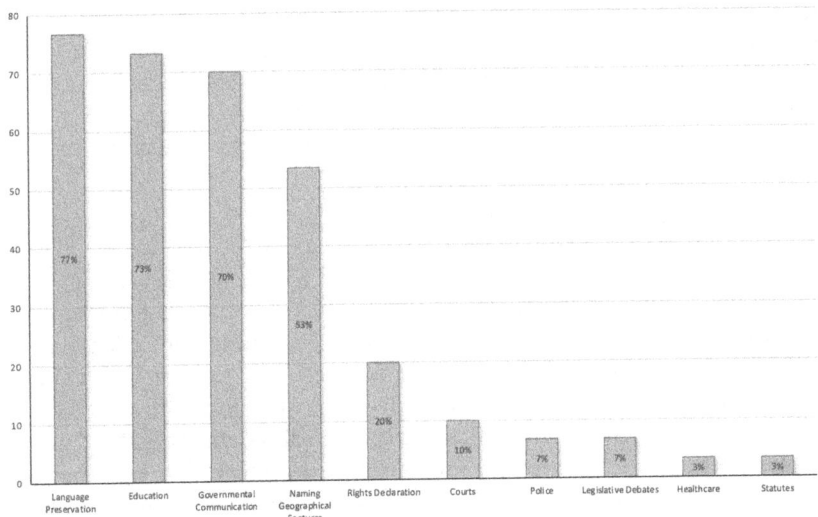

**Fig. 12.1**  Percentage of modern treaties by category of language protections. (All 30 Modern Treaties were analysed. The list of the Treaties was found on the 'Crown-Indigenous Relations and Northern Affairs Canada' website. https://www.rcaanc-cirnac.gc.ca/eng/1100100030580/1542728997938)

so that students may have the opportunity to pursue higher education in Quebec (*Northeastern Quebec Agreement* 1978: s 11.19). While the same is also implied with English, the salient point is that the dominant language in the Naskapi school is Naskapi. An example of protection regarding governmental communication is found in the *James Bay and Northern Quebec Agreement* (1975: s 13.8, 10.0.1, 10.0.12) which ensures that individuals in certain areas of Quebec have services in Inuttituut from the Regional Government, and in Cree from public corporations representing Cree communities.

Figure 12.1 also shows that approximately half of the treaties contain information on the naming of geographical features. An example of this category is the *Vuntut Gwitchin First Nation Final Agreement* which states that the Vuntut Gwitchin First Nation must be consulted when park features within their territory are named or renamed (1993: s 8.6). However, when it comes to the other categories of language protection, little has been done: only one in five modern treaties makes rights declarations pertaining to language[8]; one in ten treaties provides guarantees for the use of Indigenous languages in court proceedings, police services delivery and in legislative debates[9]; and only one treaty includes protections for Indigenous languages in the delivery of healthcare services or warrants the publication of statutes in an Indigenous language.[10]

## CAN 'CONSEQUENTIALIST' MULTINATIONAL FEDERALISM PROVIDE AN ANSWER?

This chapter has shown that federal, provincial and territorial governments in Canada have instituted measures to protect Indigenous languages, albeit in different ways and to varying degrees. It is, however, difficult to be confident in their capacity to provide for the long-term vitality of Indigenous languages. Given that multinational federalism is fundamentally based on the recognition, protection and preservation of intra-state diversity, can it provide a path forward for the long-term survival of Indigenous languages? What then (borrowing Caron and Laforest's framework) might 'symbolic' and 'consequentialist' solutions for the preservation, protection and revitalisation of Indigenous languages in Canada look like?

Possible 'symbolic' solutions might entail public celebrations of Indigenous languages (similar to the annual celebration of Linguistic Duality Day) as well as facilitating the use and simultaneous interpretation (to French and English) of Indigenous languages in legislative debates (i.e., parliamentary committee hearings, House of Commons debates and proceedings of the Senate of Canada). Although practical concerns do exist when it comes to this type of 'symbolic' solution, such as the possible

---

[8] For example, the Nisga'a Treaty specifies that 'Nisga'a citizens have the right to practice the Nisga'a culture, and to use the Nisga'a language, in a manner consistent with t[he] Agreement' (chapter 2 s 7).

[9] An example in the category of police services delivery is found in the *James Bay Agreement* (1975, s 19.1.9), which states that the training for police candidates at the Quebec Police Institute 'shall be conducted in both French and English, and in the Cree language where appropriate'. Additionally, books and other appropriate training material for police candidates at the Institute should be provided in Cree 'when possible' (*James Bay Agreement* 1975, s 19.1.9).

[10] The *Labrador Inuit Land Claim Agreement* (2005) is the only treaty to include protections for Indigenous languages in the delivery of healthcare services. It states that the Nunatsiavut government may make laws that ensure translation and interpretation in Inuktitut for medical purposes (Labrador Inuit Land Claim Agreement 2005: s 17.13.1 (j)).

lack of qualified interpreters (House of Commons 2018, 10), the use and simultaneous interpretation of Indigenous languages would, at the bare minimum, ensure that these languages are recognised in the day-to-day proceedings of the locus of federal power in Canada and provide a daily reminder of Canadian diversity and the truly plurinational character of Canada. Taking this 'symbolic' solution a step further, the federal government could also take inspiration from the European Parliament which translates its laws into 24 different languages (News European Parliament n.d.). In the Canadian context, laws could be translated into Cree, Inuktitut, Ojibway, Oji-Cree, Montagnais, Mi'kmaq, Atikamekw, Blackfoot—the eight Indigenous languages that pass the 5000 speaker threshold (Statistics Canada 2017).

One hybrid solution—encompassing both 'symbolic' and 'consequentialist' multinationalisms—could entail acknowledging Indigenous languages as having official language status at the provincial and federal levels. The precursor of such a project is already in motion at the federal level. On the heels of the TRC's call to enact legislation that would enforce Indigenous Peoples' internationally recognised rights under UNDRIP, the Government of Canada adopted Bill C-91—*An Act Respecting Indigenous Languages* (2019). While this legislation is limited, as we have noted above, it may represent a 'symbolic' step towards a more 'consequentialist' solution that would parallel the adoption of the *Official Languages Act* in 1969, a law that not only recognised French and English as official languages but was also a necessary step towards the recognition of French Canadians as one of the country's founding nations (Kymlicka 2007, 12). A more 'consequentialist' legislation would have to embrace a 'reconciliatory' approach to federalism, meaning that it not only 'encourages dialogue, collaboration and partnership' between Indigenous communities and the federal government in linguistic matters but that it also 'recognises the sovereignty of [...] Indigenous partners' (Laforest and Dubois 2017).

Treaty scope expansion may open up the doors for truly 'consequentialist' solutions to the preservation, protection and revitalisation of Indigenous languages in that it reifies the framework of nation-to-nation relationships and in that it is also considered the only way to achieve decolonisation and self-government (Ladner 2003, 167) and thus to create a third order of government in Canada. Given that linguistic expertise and knowledge is highly localised and based primarily in Indigenous communities (see Dementi-Leonard and Gilmore 1999; Hermes et al. 2012;

Liddicoat and Baldauf 2008; Reyhner 1999), the empowerment of Indigenous self-government would seem to provide a critical means to ensure the long-term survival of Indigenous languages.

In sum, treaty scope expansion and treaty negotiation that emphasises a nation-to-nation relationship between Indigenous Peoples and the Crown would seem to provide a more direct path to 'consequentialist' multinationalism, to Indigenous self-government and to the preservation of languages that 'encode distinct ways of understanding and relating to life and to the world' (Neigh 2015). However, for a few important reasons, this 'consequentialist' solution may not be easy to achieve and, if realised, may not be easy to sustain. For one, treaty negotiations have been marked by clear power imbalances, which is to say that the Crown has had the upper-hand vis-à-vis Indigenous groups (Alcantara 2007, 353). Additionally, treaty negotiations are often lengthy, in some cases taking more than 35 years (Alcantara 2007, 356). Furthermore, treaties only cover local rights as opposed to pan-Canadian rights, potentially creating inequalities between Indigenous communities. Perhaps most importantly, and as history has shown, treaty rights have often been limited by the federal government (Orkin 2003, 446).

## REFERENCES

Abele, Frances, and Michael Prince. 2009. Four Pathways to Aboriginal Self-Government in Canada. *American Review of Canadian Studies* 36 (4): 568–595.

Aboriginal Affairs and Northern Affairs Canada. 2014. *Renewing the Comprehensive Land Claims Policy: Towards a Framework for Addressing Section 35 Aboriginal Rights.*

Alcantara, Christopher. 2007. To Treaty or Not to Treaty? Aboriginal Peoples and Comprehensive Land Claims Negotiations in Canada. *The Journal of Federalism* 38 (Publius): 343–369.

Assembly of First Nations. 2018. Canada's Proposed Recognition and Implementation of Indigenous Rights Framework: Issues Summary. *AFN Policy Forum: Affirming First Nations Rights, Title and Jurisdiction* (September 11–12). https://www.afn.ca/wp-content/uploads/2018/08/Issues-Summary-ENG.pdf.

Bill C-33. An Act to Establish a Framework to Enable First Nations Control of Elementary and Secondary Education and to Provide for Related Funding and to Make Related Amendments to the Indian Act and Consequential Amendments to Other Acts. 2nd Session, 41st Parliament (First Reading 10 April, 2014).

Bill C-91. An Act Respecting Indigenous Languages. 1st Session, 42nd Parliament (First Reading 5 February, 2019).

———. An Act Respecting Indigenous Languages. 1st Session, 42nd Parliament (Third Reading 9 May, 2019).

Bill S-212. An Act for the Advancement of the Aboriginal Languages of Canada and to Recognize and Respect Aboriginal Language Rights. 1st Session, 42nd Parliament (First Reading 9 December, 2015).

Bill S-22. An Act for the Advancement of the Aboriginal Languages of Canada and to Recognize and Respect Aboriginal Language Rights. 2nd Session, 41st Parliament (First Reading 9 June, 2015).

Bill S-237. An Act for the Advancement of the Aboriginal Languages of Canada and to Recognize and Respect Aboriginal Language Rights. 2nd Session, 40th Parliament (First Reading 28 May, 2009).

Canada, Parliament, Debates of the Senate, 42nd Parliament, 1st Session, Vol 150 (17 May, 2016) (Hon Nicole Eaton).

Canada-Métis Nations Accord. 2017. The Government of Canada and The Métis Nation, April 13.

Canadian Heritage. 2018. 2017–2018 Early Engagement Sessions: Indigenous Languages Legislation. Canadian Heritage, May 14. https://www.canada.ca/en/canadian-heritage/campaigns/indigenous-languages-legislation/engagement-sessions.html.

———. 2019a. National Indigenous Peoples Day. Canadian Heritage, June 7. https://www.canada.ca/en/canadian-heritage/campaigns/indigenous-peoples-day.html.

———. 2019b. Aboriginal Languages Initiative – Aboriginal Peoples' Program. Canadian Heritage, May 9. https://www.canada.ca/en/canadian-heritage/services/funding/aboriginal-peoples/northern-broadcasting.html.

———. 2019c. Northern Aboriginal Broadcasting – Aboriginal Peoples' Program. 2019. Canadian Heritage, May 9. https://www.canada.ca/en/canadian-heritage/services/funding/aboriginal-peoples/northern-broadcasting.html.

Cardinal, Linda. 2008. Introduction. In Le fédéralisme asymétrique et les minorités linguistiques et nationales, ed. Linda Cardinal, 7–30. Sudbury: Prise de parole.

Caron, Jean-François, and Guy Laforest. 2009. Canada and Multinational Federalism: From the Spirit of 1982 to Stephen Harper's Open Federalism. Nationalism and Ethnic Politics 15 (1): 27–55.

CBC News. 2016. A History of Residential Schools in Canada. May 16. https://www.cbc.ca/news/canada/a-history-of-residential-schools-in-canada-1.702280.

———. 2018. First Nations Leader Says Catholic Bishops Misused His Words in Letter About Papal Apology. April 17. https://www.cbc.ca/news/indigenous/phil-fontaine-bishops-conference-letter-pope-apology-1.4624122.

*Champagne and Aishihik First Nation Final Agreement.* 1922. The Government of Canada, The Champagne and Aishihik First Nations, and the Government of the Yukon, June 19.

Constitution Act, 1867. 30 & 31 Victoria, c. 3 (U.K.).

Council of the Network of Official Languages Champion. 2018. Linguistic Duality Day. *Council of the Network of Official Languages Champion*, September 12. https://osez-dare.aadnc-aandc.gc.ca/eng/1390851431175/13 90851450740.

Crown-Indigenous Relations and Northern Affairs Canada. 2010. The Government of Canada's Approach to Implementation of the Inherent Right and the Negotiation of Aboriginal Self-Government. *Crown-Indigenous Relations and Northern Affairs Canada*, September 15. https://www.rcaanc-cirnac.gc.ca/eng/1100100031843/1539869205136.

———. 2018. Treaties and Agreements. *Crown-Indigenous Relations and Northern Affairs Canada*, September 11. https://www.rcaanc-cirnac.gc.ca/eng/1100100028574/1529354437231.

Dementi-Leonard, Beth, and Perry Gilmore. 1999. Language Revitalization and Identity in Social Context: A Community-Based Athabaskan Language Preservation Project in Western Interior Alaska. *Anthropology & Education Quarterly* 30 (1): 37–55.

Department of Justice. 2017. Indigenous Courtwork Program. *Department of Justice*, June 22. https://www.justice.gc.ca/eng/fund-fina/gov-gouv/acp-apc/index.html.

Gagnon, Alain-G. 2000. Canada: Unity and Diversity. *Parliamentary Affairs* 53 (1): 12–26.

Galley, Valerie. 2016. Revitalizing Indigenous Languages Is Key to Reconciliation. *Policy Options (Online)* 06: 1–5. https://search-proquest-com.ledproxy2.uwindsor.ca/docview/1799185035?accountid=14789.

*Haida Nation v British Columbia*, 2004 SCC 73 at para 25, [2004] SCR 73.

Harper, Stephen. 2008. Prime Minister Harper Offers Full Apology on Behalf of Canadians for the Indian Residential Schools System. Speech. *Indigenous and Northern Affairs Canada*, June 11.

Hermes, Mary, Megan Bang, and Ananda Marin. 2012. Designing Indigenous Language Revitalization. *Harvard Educational Review* 82 (3): 381–402.

Holloway, Gloria. 2014. Conservatives Put First Nations Education Bill 'on Hold' After Atleo Quits. *The Globe and Mail*, May 5. https://www.theglobeandmail.com/news/politics/conservatives-put-first-nations-education-bill-on-hold-after-atleo-quits/article18460523/.

House of Commons. 2012. *Journals*, 1st Session, 41st Parliament, No. 84 (27 February).

———. 2018. Standing Committee on Procedure and House Affairs, *The Use of Indigenous Languages in Proceedings of the House of Commons and Committees* (June) (Chair: Larry Bagnell).

Indigenous and Northern Affairs Canada. 2019. Indian Residential Schools. *Indigenous and Northern Affairs Canada*, February 21. https://www.aadnc-aandc.gc.ca/eng/1100100015576/1100100015577.

Indigenous Services Canada. 2019a. Education. *Indigenous Services Canada*, April 1. https://www.sac-isc.gc.ca/eng/1100100033601/1521124611239.

———. 2019b. Kindergarten to Grade 12 Education. *Indigenous Services Canada*, April 1. https://www.sac-isc.gc.ca/eng/1100100033676/1531314895090.

———. 2019c. First Nations and Inuit Cultural Education Centres Program. *Indigenous Services Canada*, February 27. https://www.sac-isc.gc.ca/eng/1100100033700/1531398486038.

———. 2019d. Supporting Inuit Children. *Indigenous Services Canada*, March 11. https://www.canada.ca/en/indigenous-services-canada/services/first-nations-inuit-health/supporting-inuit-children.html?_ga=2.226753115.777786335.1537195149-1862361667.1520859166.

———. 2018. The Government of Canada Proudly Supports the Métis Nation Education Conference. *Indigenous Services Canada*, March 21. https://www.canada.ca/en/indigenous-services-canada/news/2018/03/the-government-of-canada-proudly-supports-the-metis-nation-education-conference.html.

*James Bay and Northern Quebec Agreement*. The Government of Quebec, the James Bay Energy Corporation, the James Bay Development Corporation, Hydro-Québec, the Grand Council of the Crees of Quebec, the Northern Quebec Inuit Association, and the Government of Canada, 11 November, 1975.

Kymlicka, Will. 2007. Ethnocultural Diversity in a Liberal State: Making Sense of the Canadian Model(s). In *Belonging? Diversity, Recognition and Shared Citizenship in Canada*, ed. Keith Banting, Thomas Courchene, and Leslie Seidle, 39–86. Montreal: Institute for Research on Public Policy.

Ladner, Kiera. 2003. Treaty Federalism: An Indigenous Vision of Canadian Federalism. In *New Trends in Canadian Federalism*, ed. François Rocher and Myriam Smith, 2nd ed., 167–194. Peterborough: Broadview Press.

Laforest, Guy, and Janique Dubois. 2017. Justin Trudeau and 'Reconciliatory Federalism'. *Policy Options*, June 19. https://policyoptions.irpp.org/magazines/june-2017/justin-trudeau-and-reconciliatory-federalism.

Land Claims Agreements Coalition. What Is a Modern Treaty? 2017. *Land Claims Agreements Coalition*. http://landclaimscoalition.ca/modern-treaty/.

Leitch, David. 2006. Canada's Native Languages: The Right to First Nations to Educate Their Children in Their Own Languages. *Constitutional Forum* 15 (3): 107–120.

Library and Archives Canada. 2019. Royal Commission on Aboriginal Peoples. *Library and Archives Canada*, May 6. https://www.bac-lac.gc.ca/eng/discover/aboriginal-heritage/royal-commission-aboriginal-peoples/Pages/introduction.aspx.

Liddicoat, Anthony J. and Richard B. Baldauf Jr. 2008. Language Planning in Local Context: Agents, Context, and Interactions. In *Language Planning and Policy: Language Planning in Local Contexts*, eds. Anthony J. Liddicoat and Richard B. Baldauf Jr., 3–17. Clevedon: Multilingual Matters.

Neigh, Scott. 2015. Grassroots Revitalization of Indigenous Languages and Traditional Knowledge (Podcast). *Rabble.ca*. http://rabble.ca/podcasts/shows/talking-radical-radio/2015/09/grassroots-revitalization-indigenous-languages-and-trad.

News: European Parliament. Which Languages Are in Used in the Parliament? n.d. *News: European Parliament*. http://www.europarl.europa.eu/news/en/faq/21/which-languages-are-in-use-in-the-parliament.

*Nisga'a Final Agreement*. Nisga'a, the Government of Canada, and the Government of British Columbia, 27 May 1998.

*Northeastern Quebec Agreement*. The Naskapi Band of Schefferville, the Government of Quebec, the James Bay Energy Corporation, the James Bay Development Corporation, Hydro-Québec, the Grand Council of the Crees of Quebec, the Northern Quebec Inuit Association, and the Government of Canada, 31 January, 1978.

Official Languages Act, RSC 1985 c 31.

Orkin, J. Andrew. 2003. When the Law Breaks Down: Aboriginal Peoples in Canada and Governmental Defiance of the Rule of Law. *Osgoode Hall Law Journal* 41 (2–3): 445–463.

Porter, Jody. 2016. First Nations Students Get 30 Per Cent Less Funding Than Other Children, Economist Says. *CBC News*, March 14. https://www.cbc.ca/news/canada/thunder-bay/first-nations-education-funding-gap-1.3487822.

Reyhner, Jon. 1999. Introduction: Some Basics of Indigenous Language Revitalization. In *Revitalizing Indigenous Languages*, ed. Jon Reyhner, Gina Cantoni, Robert N. St. Clair, and Evangeline Parsons Yazzie, v–xx. Flagstaff, AZ: Northern Arizona University.

Richez, Emmanuelle, Rebecca Major, and Tejas Pandya. 2019. House of Commons Standing Committee on Canadian Heritage Regarding Bill C-91. *Revitalizing and Promoting Indigenous Languages through Recognition, Self-Government, and Effective Consultations*. Ottawa: House of Commons Committee on Canadian Heritage.

Royal Commission on Aboriginal Peoples. 1996a. *Looking Forward Looking Back*. Vol. 1. Communication Group: Ottawa.

———. 1996b. *Renewal: A Twenty-Year Commitment*. Vol. 5. Communication Group: Ottawa.

Statistics Canada. 2017. The Aboriginal Languages of First Nations People, Métis and Inuit. *Census in Brief*, October 25. https://www12.statcan.gc.ca/census-recensement/2016/as-sa/98-200-x/2016022/98-200-x2016022-eng.cfm.

The Canadian Press. 2014. How the First Nations Education Act Fell Apart in Matter of Months. *CBC News*, May 11. https://www.cbc.ca/news/politics/how-the-first-nations-education-act-fell-apart-in-matter-of-months-1.2639378.

Troian, Martha. 2016. 20 Years Since Royal Commission on Aboriginal Peoples, Still Waiting for Change. *CBC News*, March 3. https://www.cbc.ca/news/indigenous/20-year-anniversary-of-rcap-report-1.3469759.

Trudeau, Justin. 2016. Prime Minister Justin Trudeau's Speech to the Assembly of First Nations Special Chiefs Assembly. *Justin Trudeau, Prime Minister of Canada*. Speech, December 6. https://pm.gc.ca/eng/news/2016/12/06/prime-minister-justin-trudeaus-speech-assembly-first-nations-special-chiefs-assembly.

———. 2017. Remarks by Prime Minister Justin Trudeau to Apologize on Behalf of the Government of Canada to Former Students of the Newfoundland and Labrador Residential Schools. Justin Trudeau, Prime Minister of Canada. Speech, November 24. https://pm.gc.ca/eng/news/2017/11/24/remarks-prime-minister-justin-trudeau-apologize-behalf-government-canada-former.

Truth and Reconciliation Commission of Canada. 2015. *Honouring the Truth, Reconciling for the Future: Summary of the Final Report of the Truth and Reconciliation Commission of Canada*. Ottawa: Truth and Reconciliation Commission of Canada.

*United Nations Declaration on the Rights of Indigenous Peoples.* 2007. GA Res. 61/295, UN GAOR, 107th Sess., Supp. 49, UN. Doc. A/61/49.

*Vuntut Gwitchin First Nation Final Agreement.* 1993. The Government of Canada, The Vuntut Gwitchin First Nation and the Government of the Yukon, 29 May.

# PART IV

# Conclusion

CHAPTER 13

# Roadblocks and Roadmaps to Multinational Federalism

*Alain-G. Gagnon and Arjun Tremblay*

## INTRODUCTION

This conclusion sets out to highlight the main challenges and roadblocks to as well as the roadmaps and potential opportunities for fully realizing the federal promise in deeply diverse multinational states in the twenty-first century. Before doing so, however, this conclusion shows how the various chapters provide us with a set of indicators of a transition to a *substantive* multinational federalism, above and beyond the procedural features associated with asymmetrical institutional arrangements. The conclusion then highlights a series of major roadblocks to the institutionalization of multinational federalism and to its substantive deepening, ranging from the absence of a multinational self-consciousness to multinationalism's blind-

A.-G. Gagnon (✉)
Department of Political Science, Université du Québec à Montréal, Montréal, QC, Canada
e-mail: gagnon.alain@uqam.ca

A. Tremblay
Department of Politics and International Studies, University of Regina, Regina, SK, Canada
e-mail: Arjun.tremblay@uregina.ca

© The Author(s) 2020
A.-G. Gagnon, A. Tremblay (eds.), *Federalism and National Diversity in the 21st Century*, Federalism and Internal Conflicts,
https://doi.org/10.1007/978-3-030-38419-7_13

317

spot concerning other forms of diversity. Finally, the conclusion also introduces preliminary roadmaps for realizing the promise of multinational federalism in deeply diverse settings. In brief, we conclude that there is no single institutional path to overcoming the challenges to achieving a true multinational federalism in the twenty-first century. Instead, the way forward likely depends on the mutual good will of majority and minority political actors, on decision making guided by three principles (moderation, dignity and hospitality) and on receptiveness to the design and implementation of other emancipatory institutional initiatives.

## Substantive Multinational Federalism: Indicators of a Successful Transition

How do we know that a polity has become a multinational federation? In the past, the study of multinational federalism has employed a procedural perspective to answer this question. That is to say scholars have tended to focus on the presence of certain key mechanisms and institutions as indications that a deeply diverse federation has recognized and accommodated territorially concentrated national and ethnic minorities and therefore that it has, in fact, become a multinational federation. Many scholars (e.g. Kymlicka 2004; Tillin 2007; Zuber 2011; Gagnon and Burgess 2018; Fessha and Bezabih 2019) agree that the key mechanisms/institutions indicative of a multinational federation are asymmetrical arrangements 'that grant different competencies and group-specific rights' (Stepan 2005: 257); Jean-François Caron and Guy Laforest (2009: 49) have gone so far as to argue that asymmetrical arrangements are indicative of a shift towards 'consequentialist multinationalism'. However, as the study of the quality of democracy and the study of good governance have shown us,[1] there is a clear distinction between the adoption of mechanisms/institutions, on the one hand, and their ability to produce beneficial outputs, on the other. There is also no guarantee that the adoption and persistence of formal institutions over time is in any way an accurate reflection of the 'quality' of informal institutions, which is amply clear when we contrast the survival of formal democratic institutions with the ongoing weakening of democratic norms across liberal polities. Consequently, procedural analysis should always be complemented with a series of substantive

---

[1] See Diamond and Morlino (2005) in relation to the limitations of procedural democracy and Rothstein and Teorell (2008) and Aucoin et al. (2011) on the distinction between government and good governance.

considerations. This is, in fact, what several chapters in this volume accomplish by identifying a set of indicators of a successful transition to a substantive multinational federalism above and beyond the enshrinement of asymmetry.

A key indicator of a successful transition to substantive multinational federalism is the existence of various 'practices' of multinational federalism. This indicator comes to light in James Kennedy's cross-case comparison of four multinational polities (interwar Czechoslovakia, post-Quiet Revolution Canada, post-Franco Spain and post-devolution United Kingdom). As we have seen, in comparing these polities, Kennedy draws a distinction between the institutions of liberal democracy, the institutions of federalism (which include asymmetrical arrangements), and the practices of federalism. He concludes both that 'the institutions of federalism are not a guarantee of the practices of federalism' –thus reaffirming the distinction between procedural and substantive understandings of federalism– and that the practices of federalism are absolutely necessary 'to safeguard territorial accommodation and to effectively reconcile unity and diversity'. He goes on to argue that these practices must be based on 'civility', that they 'must be grounded in the tolerance of territorial diversity, most especially when territories are understood in national or ethnic term', and that they must be rooted in shared norms that are immune to the vagaries of political competition. Based on Kennedy's analysis, one could therefore argue that a successful transition to substantive multinational federalism should provide evidence of these practices in public discourse and in state public policies and, at that, from one government to the next.

A successful transition to substantive multinational federalism could also mean that central governments employ the guiding principle of territorial *partiality*. This indicator can be inferred from the main arguments developed by John Kincaid in his chapter on the 'Origins and Consequences of American Multicultural Federalism', wherein he describes an alternative model of non-territorial accommodation in a deeply diverse polity. To be clear, Kincaid's description of 'multicultural federalism' differs significantly from Reeta Chowdhari Tremblay's (2005) understanding of 'multicultural federalism'. Whereas the latter is a model for managing diversity that combines regional accommodation with the empowerment of local ethnic representation, the former describes a political system that embraces 'territorial neutrality' and that '[accommodates] diverse cultural preferences by minimizing federal interference with the political and cultural affairs of the constituent states but allowing market and political forces to mitigate cultural establishments'. By contrast to Kincaid's conception of 'multicultural federalism', multinational federalism cannot, by definition, be 'territorially neutral' when it comes to the preservation and protection of territorially concentrated cultural pluralism. Therefore, another indicator of a successful transition to substantive multinational federalism could be declarations and the design of public policy by the central government signalling an active and ongoing engagement in protecting and preserving the distinct languages, identities, cultures and traditions of the polity's constituent nations and territorially concentrated ethnic groups.

Central governments can help to protect and preserve these distinct languages, cultures, identities and traditions in two important ways: (a) through the implementation of electoral reform and (b) by facilitating an equitable distribution of economic resources across the polity's constituent nations and/or territorially concentrated ethnic groups. These indicators of a successful transition to substantive multinational federalism, above and beyond the institutionalization of asymmetry, are suggested by Christoph Niessen et al.'s qualitative comparative analysis of 'successful' and 'failed' dyadic federations. As a reminder, their study shows that the success of dyadic federations depends *inter alia* on certain institutional features—proportional electoral systems and national party systems—and on a relatively equal economic distribution across the polity. Their findings suggest that first-past-the-post electoral systems may not be an ideal procedural feature of a multinational federation and that shifts towards proportional electoral systems in a deeply diverse polity could be seen as a move favouring the establishment of substantive multinational federalism. These findings would also seem to imply that, in deeply diverse federal settings, the creation and continuity of forms of fiscal federalism—such as Canada's Equalization Program and Territorial Financing Formula—that redistribute centrally collected taxation revenue to the federation's constitutive units to ensure the fair, equitable and comparable delivery of public services across the polity could also be seen as evidence of substantive multinational federalism at work.

Another key indicator of a successful transition to a substantive multinational federalism is evidence that the central and sub-national governments have adopted a pluralist understanding of multinational federalism. This indicator is suggested by Emmanuelle Richez and Tejas Pandya's analysis of Indigenous languages in Canada which, the authors argue, have not been afforded the same protections as the French language and, consequently, are now at great risk of disappearing. In turn, they argue that a possible 'consequentialist' multinational solution to revitalizing Indigenous languages in Canada would entail *inter alia* 'treaty scope expansion and treaty negotiation that emphasizes a nation-to-nation relationship between Indigenous peoples and the Crown'. Their chapter shows that not all constitutive nations of a multinational federation have received the same full and equitable recognition. This suggests that the 'dyadic' nature of certain polities—meaning simply that they comprise two communities that dominate the political arena and that are represented in national level institutions—can obfuscate their actual complex multinational character and it means that truly substantive multinational federalism requires the empowerment of *all* minority nations.

A final indicator of a successful transition to substantive multinational federalism can be drawn from Yonatan T. Fessha and Beza Dessalegn's analysis of the enshrinement of group-differentiated rights in Ethiopia which, they contend, should not come at the expense of the protection of equal citizenship. Their argument implies there are limits to the 'tolerance of territorial diversity' and that practices of substantive multinational federalism cannot be disassociated from the robust protection of individual rights both without and within the territories of minority nations and large ethnic groups.

In brief, this volume's chapters advance a definition of multinational federalism as both a procedural and a substantive outcome or 'destination'. A multinational federation must, in addition to enshrining an asymmetrical division of powers that empowers territorially concentrated national and ethnic minorities, also actively pursue: the equitable redistribution of economic resources across constituent units, the full recognition empowerment of all of the polity's constitutive historical nations, and the preservation and protection of minority cultures and languages, all within the context of the protection of individual democratic rights and ongoing civil dialogue between the federation's partners.

## ROADBLOCKS TO PROCEDURAL AND SUBSTANTIVE MULTINATIONAL FEDERALISM

Several of this volume's chapters also help to identify obstacles or roadblocks both to the realization of procedural multinational federalism and to its deepening in the form of substantive multinational federalism. Perhaps the most obvious roadblocks to procedural as well as to substantive multinational federalism come to light in John Kincaid's explanation as to why 'the United States has never aimed to be multinational or pluri-national in the contemporary sense of those terms'. Of the explanatory factors that Kincaid develops, two stand out as most likely to bring any discussion of a transition to multinational federalism in a deeply diverse polity to a screeching halt: (1) The absence of (what could be called) a multinational self-consciousness; meaning that minority groups fail to see themselves as nations distinct from a majority nation in regards to lan-guage, identity, religion, tradition, custom or culture; and (2) the absence of a territorially concentrated culturally distinct jurisdiction, which would mean that central governments would have no real incentive to recognize minorities and to adopt asymmetrical institutional arrangements given that there is no significant overlap between national identity and territory.

A 'stop-dead' impediment to a transition to substantive multinational federalism, where some form of asymmetry already exists, would seem to be the sequence in which the decentralization of political autonomy, the processes of state- and nation-building, and democratisation has taken place. The sequence of these three factors is addressed by Susan J. Henders in her analysis of the nested decentralization process involving China and the Hong Kong Special Administrative Region. According to Henders, the fact that decentralization has preceded these two other processes in China-Hong Kong has exacerbated exclusionary and non-substantive notions of belonging and citizenship, thus preventing the deepening of self-government in Hong Kong and, in actuality, contributing to its pre-cipitous decline.

National governments in multinational states with existing autonomy arrangements can also play a role in preventing a shift to and the deepen-ing of multinational federalism and, in some cases, they can also do signifi-cant damage in facilitating the retrenchment of autonomy arrangements. As it has been noted by various scholars, national governments—in uni-tary states as well as in federal states—tend to adopt a centralizing or 'uni-tarist' approach to decision making and to the distribution of powers and competencies (see Requejo 2004; Bohman 2007). Logically, this approach should present significant challenges to the realization, deepening and persistence of multinational federalism, a model for managing diversity that requires the decentralization of authority by central governments to territorially concentrated minority nations and ethnic groups and (as noted above) that also requires central governments to adhere to the prin-ciple of territorial *partiality* in their conduct. These challenges are very well likely to be amplified when right-wing populist political parties accede to power; this is due both to the logical inconsistency between ideological positions of right-wing political parties and the politics of diversity (Tremblay 2019) and in light of the inclination of right-wing populist parties towards embracing mono-national political projects and political discourse (see Betz 2002; Gagnon and Tremblay 2019).

Supporting evidence for these claims can be found in Lucía Payero-López's assessment of the Spanish state's response to the declaration of Catalan independence in 2017. More specifically, her chapter shows that in Spain, a unitary state with some federal features, the central government, then under the leadership of Mariano Rajoy and the conservative right-wing *Partido Popular*, never really considered the legitimacy of Catalan demands for self-government. Furthermore, it was the Rajoy government that effectively bypassed Section 189 and misapplied Article 155 of the Spanish constitution, thus bringing into question Spain's federalizing prospects and the continuing legitimacy of the Statute of Autonomies and of Spanish democracy itself.

The 'ambiguous' institutional design of autonomy arrangements themselves may also play a role in sealing their fate and in stunting the prospects of multinational federalism. This is the crux of the argument that Jean-François Dupré develops in his chapter on the dual processes of national integration and authoritarianization ongoing in Hong Kong. He attributes these processes largely to Beijing's reinterpretation of formal and informal institutions: the Hong Kong Basic Law, the 'One Country, Two Systems' principle, Functional Constituencies and indirect voting mechanisms. In so doing, he employs James Mahoney and Kathleen Ann Thelen's four-point typology of subtle and gradual forms of institutional change, focusing specifically on institutional 'conversion'. This type of subtle and gradual institutional change occurs only when institutions have a high degree of ambiguity and are thus open to interpretation and when the political systems offer defenders of the status quo 'weak veto possibilities' (Mahoney and Thelen 2010: 18–19).

To be absolutely clear: an unambiguous institutional design may be just as bad, if not worse, for the near and longer-term prospects of autonomy arrangements. This should become apparent when we take a deeper look at Mahoney and Thelen's (2010) theory of subtle institutional change. Their theory combines two variables: (1) whether or not defenders of the institutional status quo control critical veto points or, in their words, whether or not defenders of the status quo have 'strong' or 'weak' 'veto possibilities' (18); and (2) the design of 'targeted' institutions themselves and, more particularly, the degree to which they 'afford actors opportunities for exercising discretion in interpretation or enforcement' (ibid.). In combining these two variables, Mahoney and Thelen contend that four possible outcomes can occur when institutions are 'targeted': 'displacement', 'layering', 'drift' and 'conversion'. According to their typology, 'displacement' entails a radical rupture of the institutional status quo while 'layering' leaves existing institutions intact but combines them with others, 'conversion' entails the active redeployment of institutions to serve purposes other than those they were originally designed to accomplish and 'drift' occurs when an institutions stray away from their original mission (without entailing their active redeployment). Each of these institutional outcomes results from a combination of the two aforementioned variables. These combinations and their resulting institutional outcomes are listed in Table 13.1.

Extending Mahoney and Thelen's theory to the present discussion has three major implications. The first major implication is that in a multinational federal or quasi-federal multinational setting, minority nations and territorially concentrated ethnic groups are likely to hold weaker veto possibilities, meaning that the fate of autonomy arrangements should rest mainly in the hands of central and national governments. The second major implication is that, if we hold the weak veto possibilities of minority nations and territorially concentrated ethnic groups constant, then the degree of institutional ambiguity becomes the critical factor in determining institutional outcomes. And, following from the previous point, the third major implication is that national governments may be tempted to 'displace' autonomy arrangements if they are relatively unambiguous (i.e. have a low level of discretion in interpretation/enforcement) and if push comes to shove. In other words, a non-malleable autonomy arrangement

**Table 13.1**  Institutional outcomes

|  | Low level of discretion in interpretation/enforcement | High level of discretion in interpretation/enforcement |
|---|---|---|
| Strong veto possibilities | Layering | Drift |
| Weak veto possibilities | Displacement | Conversion |

Source: Mahoney and Thelen (2010: 19)

may, under the wrong circumstances, actually open the door for the return to symmetrical federalism or to a unitary state structure.

Perhaps the biggest roadblock to the full realization of substantive multinational federalism is brought to light in each of the five chapters of the third section of this volume. More specifically, these chapters highlight the ineffectiveness or inability of federal multinational polities to fully recognize and to accommodate collective identities *other* than those of territorially concentrated ethnic groups and minority nations. As noted in the previous section, Richez and Pandya discuss this lacuna within the context of their analysis of the decline of Indigenous languages in Canada.

However, the failure of multinational federations to recognize collective identities does not stop there; other groups fall within multinational federalism's blind-spot, particularly when one looks at the way in which diversity is being managed within minority nations and in territorially concentrated ethnic groups. For one, multinational federations have not been successful in protecting and preserving diversity borne out of internal and international migration. In fact, as both Isabelle Côté and Mira Raatikainen (in regard to three Asian multinational polities) and Fessha and Dessalegn (in relation to the Ethiopian federation) show, internal migrants have been met with strong resistance from within sub-national minority communities and, at least in India and Malaysia, the decentralization of authority to sub-national governments has, by all appearances, amplified the tensions between host societies and migrants. And, as Catherine Xhardez shows in her comparison between patterns of immigration federalism in Belgium and Canada, a greater decentralization of authority to Flanders in matters of immigration has actually coincided with an anti-multicultural civic integrationist turn within the Flemish minority nation. Finally, as Pierre-Olivier Bonin illustrates in his chapter, the blind-spot can also extends to groups, such as Anglo-Quebecers, who are mainly viewed as members of a majority group while their actual minority status in Quebec and their 'perceived discrimination' is overlooked. In brief, these five chapters appear to confirm Dimitrios Karmis' concern (2008) that 'multinationalism' may be both conceptually and institutionally constraining in that it cannot provide forms of minority recognition and accommodation to fully enfranchise non-territorially concentrated collective identities.

## ARE THERE ROADMAPS TO MULTINATIONAL FEDERALISM?

Based on the foregoing analysis, the final pages of this volume provide preliminary roadmaps to the development of a sustainable and deeply democratic multinational federalism in the twenty-first century. First and foremost, it seems absolutely clear that the way forward means that democratisation must precede decentralization and the recognition of territorially concentrated minorities. While the enshrinement of a robust framework of liberal individual rights alongside the recognition of territorially concentrated minorities is necessary for substantive multinational federalism to emerge, it is equally important that this process occur within a pre-existing context of free and fair elections and other democratic institutions. When the decentralization process takes place first, as it has in China and Hong Kong, there are no existing mechanisms to ensure that governments are held accountable for fulfilling promises of an asymmetrical division of power or for expanding multinational federal institutions. Consequently, democracy is an essential first step in the realization of multinational federalism in both its procedural and substantive manifestations. Conversely, the ongoing process of 'de-democratization' which was precipitated by the 2008 global financial crisis (see Alonso and Lombardo 2018; Antonio 2019) does not bode well for the future of multinational federalism in deeply diverse multinational polities.

A revitalization of 'federal trust' may be needed to prevent the retrenchment of multinational federalism. There is no clear solution to the institutional design of autonomy arrangements and asymmetrical arrangements; an 'ambiguous' institutional can be redeployed by national governments and 'unitarist' political elites to serve centralizing objectives yet a fundamentally 'unambiguous' institutional design also could leave these actors with no other choice or incentive but to turn their backs completely on multinational federalism if forced to make a binary choice. Where institutional ambiguity does exist, Jan Erk and Alain-G. Gagnon (2000) argue that the persistence and expansion of multinational federalism is then likely to depend on 'federal trust', which they define as; '[the] confidence that is assumed to exist between the parties of a federal partnership—in other words, reliance on the integrity of one another and an overall commitment to the maintenance of the partnership' (94). This suggests that the fate of multinational federalism may depend on the goodwill of partners in the federation, something that seems to be in increasingly short supply in many multinational democracies.[2]

Arriving at a substantive and pluralist multinational federalism may ultimately depend on whether or not governments embrace the principles of moderation, dignity and hospitality. One of the key challenges facing multinational polities is their ability to recognize and to accommodate territorially concentrated diversity as well as other collective identities. One way that governments in these deeply diverse polities can overcome this challenge is by embracing the principles of moderation, dignity and hospitality. This perspective combines considerations on the future of minority nations in an 'age of uncertainty' (Gagnon 2014) with considerations of cultural, religious and linguistic accommodation of polyethnic minorities (i.e. minorities borne out migration) in the 'age of migration' (Castles et al. 2013). In brief, its aim is to 'enlarge contexts of choice and acts as a means to stop the atomizing effects of procedural liberalism' (Gagnon 2014: 99). It requires: 'moderation' in the form of restraint from both majority nations and minority nations in the pursuit of cultural and linguistic protections; 'dignity' in the form of mutual respect between partners in the federation for the pursuit of self-determination and self-government; and 'hospitality' which means not only recognizing intra-national minorities but also empowering them to mobilize on collective lines.

Embracing these principles would require coupling multinational federal institutions with the implementation of interculturalism at the subnational level. Interculturalism is a model for managing diversity that has been promoted by academics and policy makers in Quebec over the last four decades. It accepts that democratic societies are composed of a multitude of collective identities, promotes active citizenship and understands that national identities are always evolving. Interculturalism also invites members of various communities to display their differences publicly, and, in so doing, to encourage the further democratic deepening of decision making. In brief, interculturalism and multinational federalism are compatible and complementary; interculturalism can help to fulfil the principle of hospitality within minority nations and territorially concentrated ethnic

---

[2] In Canada, for example, the emergence of a Western Canadian separatist movement (the so-called WEXIT movement) in Alberta, Saskatchewan and Manitoba in the wake of the 2019 federal elections would seem to be evidence of a growing distrust between Western Canada and the federal government as well as with other regions and provinces.

groups in regard to both internal and international migration while multinational federalism can help deeply diverse societies to enshrine the principles of moderation and dignity between majority nations and minority nations and territorially concentrated ethnic groups.

Multinational federalists must also be open and attentive to the creation of non-multinational emancipatory institutional arrangements. One of the major lacuna in multinational polities is their failure to fully recognize Indigenous Peoples. While multinationalism may provide a 'consequentialist' remedy to this lacuna, as it has been argued in this volume, other institutional solutions, such as Indigenous multilevel governance, may better reflect the unique desire and ambitions of Indigenous Peoples. By contrast to multinational federalism, which is a political and institutional project that entails top-down devolution of competencies, Indigenous multilevel governance is bottom-up political project through which Indigenous communities '[define] for themselves what self-government looks like and [use] whatever tools at hand to give expression to their vision of self-determination' (Dubois and Saunders 2013: 205–206). In sum, proponents of multinational federalism must accept the challenge of imagining a truly pluralist federalism and therefore must also be receptive to the creation of a complex institutional architecture.

## REFERENCES

Alonso, Alba, and Emanuela Lombardo. 2018. Gender Equality and De-Democratization Processes: The Case of Spain. *Politics and Governance* 6 (3): 78.

Antonio, Robert J. 2019. Reactionary Tribalism Redux: Right-Wing Populism and De-Democratization. *The Sociological Quarterly* 60 (2): 201–209.

Aucoin, Peter, Mark D. Jarvis, and Lori Turnbull. 2011. *Democratizing the Constitution: Reforming Responsible Government.* Toronto: Edmond Montgomery.

Betz, Hans Georg. 2002. Contre la mondialisation: xénophobie, politiques identitaires et populisme d'exclusion en Europe occidentale'. *Politique et Sociétés* 21 (2): 9–28.

Bohman, James. 2007. *Democracy Across Borders: From Demos to Demoi.* Cambridge, MA: MIT Press.

Caron, Jean-François, and Guy Laforest. 2009. Canada and Multinational Federalism: From the Spirit of 1982 to Stephen Harper's Open Federalism. *Nationalism and Ethnic Politics* 15 (1): 27–55.

Castles, Stephen, Mark J. Miller, and Hein de Haas. 2013. *The Age of Migration.* 5th ed. London: Palgrave Macmillan.

Diamond, Larry J., and Leonardo Morlino. 2005. *Assessing the Quality of Democracy.* Baltimore, MD: Johns Hopkins University Press.

Dubois, Janique, and Kelly Saunders. 2013. "Just Do It!": Carving Out a Space for the Métis in Canadian Federalism. *Canadian Journal of Political Science* 46 (1): 187–214.

Erk, Jan, and Alain-G. Gagnon. 2000. Constitutional Ambiguity and Federal Trust: Codification of Federalism in Canada, Spain and Belgium. *Regional and Federal Studies* 10: 92–111.

Fessha, Yonatan T., and Biniyam N. Bezabih. 2019. Federation Among Unequals. A Country Study of Constitutional Asymmetry in Ethiopia. In *Multinational Federalism: Managing Multinationalism in Multi-tiered Systems,* ed. Patricia Popelier and Maja Sahadžić, 137–162. Cham, Switzerland: Springer International Publishing; Palgrave Macmillan.

Gagnon, Alain-G. 2014. *Minority Nations in the Age of Uncertainty: New Paths to National Emancipation and Empowerment.* Toronto: University of Toronto Press.

Gagnon, Alain-G., and Michael Burgess, eds. 2018. *Revisiting Unity and Diversity in Federal Countries: Changing Concepts, Reform Proposals and New Institutional Realities.* Leiden: Brill Nijhoff.

Gagnon, Alain-G., and Arjun Tremblay. 2019. Federalism and Diversity: A New Research Agenda. In *A Research Agenda for Federalism Studies,* ed. John Kincaid, 129–139. Cheltenham: Edward Elgar.

Karmis, Dimitrios. 2008. Pluralism and National Identity(ies) in Contemporary Québec: Conceptual Clarifications, Typology, and Discourse Analysis. In *Québec: State and Society,* ed. Alain-G. Gagnon, 3rd ed., 69–96. Toronto; Buffalo: University of Toronto Press.

Kymlicka, Will. 2004. *Politics in the Vernacular Nationalism, Multiculturalism and Citizenship.* Oxford: Oxford University Press.

Mahoney, James, and Kathleen Ann Thelen. 2010. *Explaining Institutional Change: Ambiguity, Agency, and Power.* Cambridge: Cambridge University Press.

Requejo, Ferran. 2004. Value Pluralism and Multinational Federalism. *Australian Journal of Political Theory* 50 (1): 23–40.

Rothstein, Bo, and Jan Teorell. 2008. What Is Quality of Government? A Theory of Impartial Government Institutions. *Governance: An International Journal of Policy, Administration and Institutions* 21 (2): 165–190.

Stepan, Alfred. 2005. Federalism and Democracy: Beyond the U.S. Model. In *Theories of Federalism: A Reader,* ed. Dimitrios Karmis and Wayne J. Norman, 255–268. New York: Palgrave Macmillan US.

Tillin, Louise. 2007. United in Diversity? Asymmetry in Indian Federalism. *Publius* 37 (1): 45.

Tremblay, Reeta Chowdhari. 2005. Afghanistan: Multicultural Federalism as a Means to Achieve Democracy, Representation and Stability. In *From Power Sharing to Democracy: Post-Conflict Institutions in Ethnically Divided Societies*, ed. Sid Noel, 198–214. Montréal; Kingston: McGill-Queen's University Press.

Tremblay, Arjun. 2019. *Diversity in Decline? The Rise of the Political Right and the Fate of Multiculturalism*. Cham, Switzerland: Springer International Publishing; Palgrave Macmillan.

Zuber, Christina Isabel. 2011. Understanding the Multinational Game: Toward a Theory of Asymmetrical Federalism. *Comparative Political Studies* 44 (5): 546–571.

# Index[1]

---

[1] Note: Page numbers followed by 'n' refer to notes.

© The Author(s) 2020
A.-G. Gagnon, A. Tremblay (eds.), *Federalism and National Diversity in the 21st Century*, Federalism and Internal Conflicts, https://doi.org/10.1007/978-3-030-38419-7

CPSIA information can be obtained
at www.ICGtesting.com
Printed in the USA
LVHW080313280321
682719LV00016B/863

9 783030 384210